How Ottawa Spends 2001-2002

Power in Transition

Edited by
Leslie A. Pal

OXFORD
UNIVERSITY PRESS

OXFORD
UNIVERSITY PRESS

70 Wynford Drive, Don Mills, Ontario M3C 1J9
www.oupcan.com

Oxford University Press is a department of the University of Oxford.
It furthers the University's objective of excellence in research, scholarship,
and education by publsihing worldwide in

Oxford New York

Athens Auckland Bangkok Bogotá Buenos Aires Cape Town
Chennai Dar es Salaam Delhi Florence Hong Kong Istanbul Karachi
Kolkata Kuala Lumpur Madrid Melbourne Mexico City Mumbai Nairobi
Paris São Paulo Shanghai Singapore Taipei Tokyo Toronto Warsaw

with associated companies in Berlin Ibadan

Oxford is a trade mark of Oxford University Press
in the UK and in certain other countries

Published in Canada
by Oxford University Press

Copyright © Oxford University Press Canada 2001

The moral rights of the author have been asserted

Database right Oxford University Press (maker)

First published 2001

All rights reserved. No part of this publication may be reproduced,
stored in a retrieval system, or transmitted, in any form or by any means,
without the prior permission in writing of Oxford University Press,
or as expressly permitted by law, or under terms agreed with the appropriate
reprographics rights organization. Enquiries concerning reproduction
outside the scope of the above should be sent to the Rights Department,
Oxford University Press, at the address above.

You must not circulate this book in any other binding or cover
and you must mpose this same condition on any acquirer.

Canadian Cataloguing in Publication Data

The National Library of Canada has catalogued this publication as follows:
Main entry under title:
How Ottawa spends
1983
Prepared at the School of Public Administration, Carleton University.
Continues: How Ottawa spends your tax dollars.
Includes bibliographical references.
ISSN 0822-6482
ISBN 0-19-541669-4 (2001-2002)

1. Canada – Appropriation and expenditures – Periodicals. I. Carleton University.
School of Public Administration

HJ7663.S6   354.710072'2   C84-030303-3

1 2 3 4 - 04 03 02 01

This book is printed on permanent (acid-free) paper ∞
Printed in Canada

CONTENTS

	Preface	v
1	How Ottawa Spends 2001-2: Power in Transition *Leslie A. Pal*	1
2	Priming the Electoral Pump: Framing Budgets for a Renewed Mandate *Geoffrey E. Hale*	29
3	How Ottawa Plans: The Evolution of Strategic Planning *Evert A. Lindquist*	61
4	Managing in the New Public Service: Some Implications for How We Are Governed *Anne Perkins and Robert P. Shepherd*	95
5	Aiming for the Middle: Challenges to Federal Income Policy *Gerard W. Boychuk*	123
6	From Charity to Clarity: Reinventing Federal Government-Voluntary Sector Relationships *Susan D. Phillips*	145
7	Citizenship by Instalments: Federal Policies for Canadians with Disabilities *Michael J. Prince*	177

8	The Case of the Disappearing Targets: The Liberals and Gender Equality *Sandra Burt and Sonya Lynn Hardman*	201
9	New Economy/Old Economy? Transforming Natural Resources Canada *G. Bruce Doern and Monica Gattinger*	223
10	Regional Development Policy: A Nexus of Policy and Politics *Rodney Haddow*	247
11	A Delicate Dance: The Courts and the Chrétien Government *Rainer Knopff*	277

Appendix A: Political Facts and Trends	305
Appendix B: Fiscal Facts and Trends	313
Abstracts/Résumés	331
Contributors	343

PREFACE

This is the fourth edition of *How Ottawa Spends* that I have been privileged to edit, and regrettably it will be my last. It has been a fascinating time in which to try to chronicle key Canadian public policy developments, and I think that the stable of authors we assembled over the past four issues did a remarkable job of illuminating both the larger themes that have dominated important policy areas and the details of organizational change and policy development. The first edition of *How Ottawa Spends* that I edited had a unique and—for this series—unprecedented theme. For the first time in a generation, after a continuous string of deficits, the federal government in 1998 was projecting a balanced budget. This was about more than money, of course, since a budget is both a summation and a projection of key policy decisions and choices made by a government. The Liberals were able to project a balance in 1998 because they had determinedly cut expenditures (especially transfers to the provinces) and raised taxes, starting in 1995. They succeeded beyond their wildest dreams, since those dreams had called only for a reduced deficit, not balance, and certainly not surplus.

The story of the last two years and the two previous editions of *How Ottawa Spends* was the story of the policy changes the Liberals had to embrace in order to achieve their budgetary targets. As surpluses continued to grow, Finance Minister Paul Martin could simultaneously promise reduced taxes, increased expenditures (especially on health care), and continued payments against the national debt. Last year's edition focussed on how the Liberals were building the foundations for re-election, particularly through the tax cuts in the February 2000 election. The book also argued, however, that the party seemed to be running out of ideas and energy, and simply recycling elements of its 1993 platform. The election campaign came sooner than most anticipated, and featured a remarkably reinvigorated and united Liberal party led by Jean Chrétien hammering away at a new but ultimately unsuccessful rival in the form the Canadian Alliance party, led by Stockwell Day. And so this year's edition is focussed on the theme of transition—most fundamentally the transition of power from one government to another, even if it remains Liberal. We examine the October 2000 economic statement and the January 2001

Speech from the Throne, as well as developments in key policy areas, to show how the Liberals are handling their responsibilities after re-election. Continued opposition criticism of the Prime Minister over alleged improprieties surrounding a golf course and hotel in his riding have, as of April 2001, derailed serious policy discussion in the House of Commons in favour of personal attacks, and have once again raised concerns that the government seems rudderless. But the essays in this volume go deeper and explore both the failures and the successes of the federal Liberals as they move into their third consecutive term in government.

As always, the authors laboured under stringent deadlines, and I would like to thank them for their professionalism and their commitment. Virtually all of them had their manuscripts in on time (and some even a little early!), and they responded quickly and thoroughly to all of our editorial queries and pestering. I would also like to thank the outstanding editorial team that once again defied the odds and got a fine volume out in record time. Rachel Laforest served once again as the project's research assistant, and was responsible for compiling both Fiscal Facts and Trends and Political Facts and Trends, which appear as appendices at the end of the book. Michele Morrison served as production assistant, meaning that she had to master the intricacies of desktop publishing (with some kind help from Jackie Carberry) and somehow miraculously turn raw manuscripts into a polished book. She also carried most of the burden of logistics and organization for the project, keeping the entire team on track. Martha Clark, the School Administrator, ensured that the project had sufficient resources in the right quantities and at the right time to make everything run smoothly. Despite considerable demands on her own time, she cheerfully pitched in on evenings and weekends to see the book through to completion. Oxford University Press was once again an exemplary partner in our enterprise, I would like to thank Phyllis Wilson and am particularly grateful to Laura Macleod for her strong support of the series. Douglas Campbell's superb copy-editing talents were once again at our disposal, and his deft touch can be felt in the thousands of small details that make a manuscript of this size and complexity not only readable, but pleasurably so. The chapter abstracts were translated into French by Sinclair Robinson and Nandini Sarma.

It is also my pleasure to thank the School of Public Policy and Administration at Carleton University for its institutional support, and to acknowledge the strong support of individual colleagues and students. Always one of the premier schools in the country and one of the best in the world, the School recently changed its name from the School of Public Administration to include public policy in its title. This is a shift that marks a gradual evolution in the School's focus, an evolution that in part has been reflected in the character of *How Ottawa Spends*, with its strong and growing policy focus.

Leslie A. Pal
Ottawa
April 2001

The opinions expressed by the contributors to this volume are the personal views of the authors of individual chapters and do not necessarily reflect the view of the Editor or the School of Public Policy and Administration at Carleton University.

1

How Ottawa Spends 2001-02: Power in Transition

LESLIE A. PAL

Last year's edition of *How Ottawa Spends* ended with portents of the challenges the Liberals would have to face in the coming year. The February 2000 budget had forecast yet more mountainous surpluses, which Finance Minister Paul Martin had pumped into social spending and some surprise tax cuts. Yet, apart from the tax cuts, the budget's main themes repeated those of previous years. The Liberals then came through a mandatory leadership convention in March that was as adulatory of Jean Chrétien as could be hoped, but still revealed discord between Martin supporters and the Prime Minister over his leadership. Chrétien seemed in control of events, but was regularly criticized in the press as being over the hill, yesterday's man, without vision or real purpose aside from simply retaining the privileges of power. It did not help that the Canadian Alliance was finally launched in the summer with its new, telegenic leader, Stockwell Day. The Alliance decided to play up the contrasts between the two men almost immediately after Day won the leadership over his main rival, Preston Manning: it would try to show Day as athletic, crisp, and fresh, and portray Chrétien as stale and doddering. The strategy seemed at first to work, and through the summer and even into September the Liberals glumly assumed that they would have to wait until the spring to call an election. Even more glumly, some assumed that Jean Chrétien would lead them in that fight; others hoped that Paul Martin would take over the reins of both the party and the government.

As readers know, Jean Chrétien suddenly decided—much to the horror of some of his closest advisors and a sizable chunk of his backbench—that he would not wait until the spring but instead call a snap election for 27 November. With the benefit of hindsight, it was a masterstroke. The Liberals were returned for a virtually unprecedented third term with a strengthened majority in the House of Commons. They stopped the Canadian Alliance cold at the Manitoba-Ontario border (the Alliance picked up only two seats in Ontario, when the key rationale of the change of party name and policy from Reform had been to breach that province), raised their proportion of the vote and of seats in Quebec (and thereby punctured the Bloc Québécois and the separatist cause—Quebec premier Bouchard announced his resignation in January 2001), and even managed to steal some seats from both the New Democratic Party and the Progressive Conservatives (cadaverous though these parties are, they did barely manage to hang on to official party status).

It must be remembered, though, that at the time when, having moved his pieces into position, he finally called the election on 17 October 2000, the strategy of going sooner rather than later seemed risky indeed. While polls continued to show high levels of support for the Liberals, the Canadian Alliance had been attracting favourable attention, and Stockwell Day, freshly victorious from a by-election in British Columbia, had entered the House of Commons as the Leader of the Official Opposition. His first moves were slightly maladroit, but it seemed that he was a formidable campaigner, and that the party had an attractive and attention-grabbing policy alternative of deep tax cuts that would lead eventually to a flat tax. Moreover, the Liberals had continued to face criticism on health care cuts, the job grants scandal at Human Resources Development Canada (HRDC), and divisions between Martin and Chrétien—criticism that could hobble an effective campaign. When Chrétien made his decision, the chattering class quickly concluded that the best the Liberals could hope for was a minority government or a razor-thin majority. Virtually everyone—except Jean Chrétien—assumed it would be a close fight.

It is a testament to the political instincts and skill of a man who delights in being underestimated that he was right and everyone else was wrong. Not only was he right, but his vindication was a crushing one—the Canadian Alliance made some gains, but far short of what it had expected after all its efforts in redesigning the party and taking the risk of selecting a new, untried leader. The Bloc Québécois, which ran a strong and confident campaign, held its own in votes cast (it had only 8001 fewer votes in 2000 than in 1997), but nonetheless went from 44 seats to 38. This was largely due to the collapse in the Conservative vote in Quebec, which switched to the Liberals and gave them an increase of 10 seats in that province. Any grumblings within the Prime Minister's own ranks about his leadership were silenced, and he emerged from the campaign firmly in control of his party, the House of Commons, the country, and perhaps even of history's judgment on his political acumen and campaigning skills.

The Liberals are therefore set for at least another four years of governing Canada. As our sub-title indicates, this will be a time of 'power in transition' in several senses. First, it is highly likely (though the man defies prediction) that Chrétien will finally leave the political scene and make way for either Paul Martin or a personal protégé such as Brian Tobin (Minister of Industry, and former premier of Newfoundland and Labrador). Second, if Chrétien's departure occurs close to the end of his term, this will leave time for him to establish the policy legacy he apparently wants so badly to bequeath to the country. The early signs of that legacy were evident in the January 2001 Speech from the Throne, discussed below. The third transition is more subtle, but just as important. Despite their successes, the Liberals seemed to run out of policy steam in their second mandate in 1997-2000. Their campaign platform was thin—there was little beyond the ritualistic pouring of more money into health care and nebulous promises to make Canada a 'smart country'. The Liberals have been remarkably successful in government—indeed, one of the most successful democratic political parties in the world—but by October 2000 they seemed bereft of fresh ideas. This next term in office will therefore be crucial in deciding where the government wants to lead the country, how it can articulate a new vision with a new leader without repudiating the legacies of the last ones, and how it can once again outflank its rivals across the political spectrum. In a sense this will be the most interesting transition of all—the transition from twentieth- to twenty-first-century Liberalism. There are many ingredients to the party's success, but a key one is adaptability. In the face of threats from the left, it absorbs and steals left-wing ideas. In the face of threats from the right, it shifts to absorb conservative policies. Over the past decade it has managed to be all things to all people, blending the rhetoric of the left (sharing) with the rhetoric of the right (efficiency and tax cuts). The next four years see it poised for yet another re-invention.

POWER IN TRANSITION:
THE ELECTION CAMPAIGN AND AFTERMATH

Election campaigns start at least one year before the writ is actually dropped. The November 2000 campaign could be said to have begun even earlier—in September 1998—with the decision by the Reform party of Canada to launch a 'unite the right' movement that would bring together Reform with the Progressive Conservatives, end vote-splitting, and turn the resulting party into a viable alternative to the Liberals. The Progressive Conservatives under Joe Clark refused to be wooed, and so the Reform party decided that its next best alternative was to re-invent itself as a new party and have a leadership convention to grab attention and headlines. The new party was launched at a convention in January 2000 (though it had to be ratified through a referendum of Reform party members in March 2000), with a leadership convention to follow in June. It was already clear at this stage that the Canadian Alliance would distinguish itself from the Liberals on the basis of a strong tax-cutting platform. Alliance would argue that while the Liberals had indeed balanced the budget (as Reform had demanded years earlier), they had continued to keep taxes high so that they could spend on pet programs. Sensing the shift in the political winds, Paul Martin included one big surprise in his 28 February 2000 budget—the announcement of $20 billion in major tax reductions over four years.[1] This was combined with the by now ritualistic 're-investment' in health care and new spending in a range of boutique programs to support the new economy and innovation.

The Liberals had their own four-day party convention starting on 16 March 2000, gathering over 2,000 sweaty delegates in a Vancouver arena to mull over policy resolutions. But everyone knew that the real issue was whether Jean Chrétien would run again or not. The question became even more pointed than it might normally have been when stories surfaced that Martin supporters had met secretly with several MPs at a Toronto airport hotel to plan a leadership coup. The news broke during the convention, and Martin at first tried to avoid reporters, then gave only tepid indications of support for the Prime Minister. One Chrétien loyalist commented, 'These guys haven't stopped.... It's foolish to say it's over. They are trying to destabilize the prime minister. It's almost like a coup d'état.'[2] The leader received more bad news during the convention: a poll showed that 45 per cent of Canadians would prefer Paul Martin to Jean Chrétien as leader.[3] While Chrétien's early speeches to the convention received polite applause—as well as some puzzled looks as he recounted political experiences in the 1960s that easily predated much of his audience—Martin was crushed by enthusiastic crowds wherever he went.

But this was a party convention, not a leadership review. There was no mechanism to force a review, and as for the calls from some federal MPs and Quebec provincial Liberal MNAs for Chrétien's resignation, he could simply ignore them, as he could ignore newspaper reports that fundraising for the party was flat, in large part because of his lack of personal appeal. Paul Martin, on the other hand, could be counted on to draw large ecstatic crowds of supporters ready to write cheques for the Liberal Party of Canada. In one sense, however, Chrétien did respond to the pressure—he tirelessly reiterated his intention to lead the party into the next election campaign, sometime in the next two years. Perhaps more importantly, though only a few commentators picked it up at the time, he gave a precise preview of his election campaign platform and messages. As he put it in his closing speech to the convention, 'There will be no doubt in the mind of anybody that I will be there in the next election.'[4] In an almost perfect echo of the highly charged and polarizing strategy he would adopt in just over six months, Chrétien painted the Canadian Alliance as enemies of medicare, regional equalization, the Charter of Rights and Freedoms, and a fair tax system. He referred to the Liberals as the party of 'shared opportunity'—the exact title of what would become the Liberals' third 'Red Book' policy platform. Attacking the Alliance as a coalition of extremists and fundamentalists, Chrétien clearly was enjoying himself: 'The Canadian Alternative that brings together the charisma of Preston Manning, the compassion of Deborah Grey, the broad-mindedness of Stockwell Day, and the common touch of Conrad Black."[5] This was more than empty sloganeering—members of the Reform party were famous for awkward stream-of-consciousness comments on homosexuals, marriage, law and order, abortion, Aboriginal rights, and even that most sacred of Canadian cows, universal health care. Chrétien was evidently coming to the belief that the new party would become a vehicle for kooks and crazies and that it would undermine the achievements of all the Liberal governments he had served since Lester B. Pearson's in the 1960s. Counter-intuitively, for a man widely thought to be a pragmatic manager without much vision, Chrétien was inching toward a campaign of values. The campaign would be a battle between the best of the Canadian values of sharing and tolerance—as of course expressed by the Liberals—and what he was later to refer to as the 'dark side of human nature'—the cold heart of the Alliance, however much it might deny the characterization.

Despite the rough patch during the convention, senior Liberals, including Paul Martin, closed ranks to support the leader and deny any rumours of internecine warfare. But rumours persisted through the summer, especially as the Liberals' polling numbers softened in the face of almost continuous coverage of the Canadian Alliance, its leadership campaign in June and July, and then Stockwell Day's successful run in a by-election for the seat of Okanagan-Coquihalla in British Columbia. In fact, the Alliance had been almost continuously in the news since March 25, when over 65 per cent of Reform members approved the creation of a new party. That led to a leadership convention in June, at which Stockwell Day, the former Treasury Minister in the government of Alberta, pulled off a surprise first-place finish among a field of four candidates (the other three were Preston Manning, Tom Long, and Keith Martin). A run-off was held on 8 July, in which Day defeated Preston Manning with a decisive 63 per cent of the ballots. It was a surprise, because Day, while well known in Alberta, had no profile outside that province. Moreover, Preston Manning had virtually created the Reform party and had been the architect of its dissolution in favour of the Canadian Alliance. To lose the party and the movement he created was disappointing, but he pledged his support to the new leader, and Day began to make plans to find a seat in time to enter Parliament when it re-convened in September. He also faced the challenges of dealing with a party caucus that had largely supported Manning, and developing a new team to run the party's day-to-day operations.[6] But there was no doubt that he had strong initial appeal: youthful in appearance, athletic, experienced in government at the provincial level, allegedly bilingual (this turned out to be a stretch), with a colourful set of life experiences that included being an auctioneer and a manual labourer, Day was apparently telegenic and personable. He naturally attracted attention, but also did his best to craft photo-opportunities and stage events to show off his youthfulness and energy.

On 19 September, by-elections were held at both ends of the country—Stockwell Day running in Okanagan-Coquihalla (British Columbia) and Joe Clark, who, after nineteen months as leader of the Progressive Conservatives, had finally decided to run for a seat and enter the House of Commons, in Kings-Hants (Nova Scotia). The two men both won their races, and prepared to enter the House less than a week later. It had been a summer of almost non-stop politics, and spirits were high among the two main opposition parties in that they would now have new leaders in the House to square off against a lacklustre prime minister, some of whose own party members had been calling on him to resign. Adding more oxygen to these flames was the growing sense that an election would possibly be called in the fall rather that the spring. Senior Liberals were cited as saying that the Prime Minister had all but made up his mind by the end of August that it would be better to risk the wrath of the electorate by going back to them early after only three and a half years than to give Stockwell Day a chance to hone his skills and organize his party for a campaign in the spring.[7] Party polling showed that the 40 per cent lead the Liberals had enjoyed over the Reform/Alliance had dropped by half—a good performance by Day and a strong organization could severely threaten the government. At a Liberal caucus retreat in Winnipeg at the end of August, several MPs voiced doubts about going that soon.[8] Referring derisively to those unnamed Liberal members who feared an election against the Alliance as 'nervous Nellies', Chrétien gave a rousing speech to his troops and a biting attack on Day to the press. True to the line he had developed earlier in March, Chrétien referred to the 'unholy Alliance' that would would reject the values of the vast majority of Canadians while appealing to 'Quebec separatists and radical decentralists, the rich, the gun lobby and social conservatives who would deny the rights of women and homosexuals.'[9] Again, as he had in March, Chrétien explicitly disagreed with the suggestion that the election was about change, and therefore that the key Liberal response to the Alliance should be in terms of new policies. Instead, he again highlighted the differences in values—the differences between 'Canadian values' and 'theirs'.

Chrétien may still have been undecided about whether to go in the fall or in the spring, but he began to take a series of measures to shore up any potential weak spots the Liberals might expose in a campaign. Given the Liberals' fiscal record, there were not many. One was health care, with continued complaints about lengthening waiting lists and inadequate services—all due, it was claimed, to federal cuts. On 11 September, the first ministers agreed to pump $23.4 billion more federal monies into health and early childhood development. This was in addition to four earlier infusions of cash that had been made since the original cuts had been announced in the 1995 budget; the Liberals could feel secure on this front. Another weakness was Atlantic Canada, where the Liberals had lost 20 seats in the 1997 election. If they were to go into an election in the fall, with strong competition from the Alliance and the Progressive Conservatives, a few new seats in Atlantic Canada could mean the difference between a majority and a minority government. The Liberals had already begun mending fences in June, when they announced a $700 million Atlantic investment fund to pump money into universities, colleges, research labs, and high-tech firms. Chrétien's next step was to lure Brian Tobin, the recently elected premier of Newfoundland and Labrador (who had promised to serve out his term), back into the cabinet on 16 October. Popular in Atlantic Canada, Tobin would be a formidable campaigner in the region. Another weakness was the lack of any real rationale for an early election. Despite Chrétien's over-heated rhetoric, there was no 'clash of civilizations' that suddenly required going to the polls at least six if not 18 months early. Stockwell Day took care of this problem for him, by foolishly challenging him in the House on 25 September to call a fall election. Barely concealing a grin, the Prime Minister shrugged and admitted to the press that he might have to call a fall election, since the opposition parties were calling for one. A final danger was the impending report by the Auditor-General on the HRDC grants scandal.

The report was due in October, and given the firestorm the issue had created earlier in the year, it could be anticipated to draw much attention. The report, which was issued on 17 October, cited breaches of authority, improper payment practices, and limited monitoring of recipient projects' finances and activities.[10] It could be anticipated that the Auditor-General's oral briefing to the Public Accounts Committee on 19 October would draw tremendous media attention. Unfortunately the meeting could not be held, since all nine Liberal members of the committee were somehow unable to find the room. Miraculously, the Auditor-General, all of the press, and members of the opposition parties had no such difficulty.

Predictably, there was an outcry, but Liberal agenda-management was at its peak. On 18 October, the day *before* the Auditor-General was to appear before the Committee, Paul Martin rose in the House to read an 'economic statement' that was in fact a mini-budget. It was a carefully crafted election document, designed to highlight and reinforce Liberal strengths and target the opposition. The key to the mini-budget was the Liberals' fear that the Alliance's talk of deeper tax cuts—to the extent of promising a flat tax of 17 per cent—might prove attractive and would be the 'wedge' issue that would define clear policy differences between the two parties. Paul Martin had already taken a page from the Alliance book on tax cuts with the ones he had announced previously in the February budget. The mini-budget essentially accelerated those cuts, wiping out any substantive difference between the parties.[11] In February Martin had offered cuts that would total $58 billion over five years. The mini-budget introduced measures that would boost the cuts to $93 billion, and that accelerated their implementation by reducing rates and adjusting tax brackets as of 1 January 2001. The middle and upper personal income tax rates, for example, would go from 24 per cent to 22 per cent (for income between $30,754 and $61,609), and from 29 per cent to 26 per cent (for income between $61,609 and $100,000). These were joined by other measures, such as the elimination of the surtax on taxable incomes over $85,000, a one-time rebate of $125 ($250 per family) for home heating fuel costs, and increases in the disability tax credit and in the National Child Benefit. In addition, Martin offered a bouquet of business tax breaks such as a 1 percentage point cut in the corporate tax rate and an immediate reduction in the capital gains tax. Despite these major tax cuts, Martin was also able to say that the government would pay down at least $10 billion on the national debt that year, on top of the $12 billion it had paid down the previous fiscal year. And in fine partisan fashion, Martin ended his statement with a shot at the Alliance flat tax idea—something he said that the Liberals would never introduce, because it gave disproportionate relief to the rich, unlike Liberal tax cuts, which favour the less advantaged. Not surprisingly, the election was called four days later, on 22 October, for Monday, 27 November.

Despite Chrétien's careful manoeuvres in the previous weeks, the election call was still a gamble. The election was widely understood to be unnecessary, and many speculated that its sole purpose was to silence the leadership grumblings in the Liberal backbenches and among Martin supporters. The transparent stage-managing—plucking Brian Tobin out of Newfoundland into the cabinet, infusions of cash for health care, and accelerated tax cuts—was breathtakingly cynical. The shenanigans around the Auditor-General's report, and continued allegations of improprieties in the HRDC boondoggle (several criminal investigations were simultaneously underway in the Prime Minister's riding) completed the portrait of a party and a leader interested in nothing but power—winning it and keeping it. Indeed, the first poll released a week into the campaign showed the Alliance with 28 per cent of the decided vote to 45 per cent for the Liberals.[12] This was the highest level the Alliance or the Reform had enjoyed in their history, and the highest for any opposition party since Jean Chrétien won power in 1993. Pundits almost universally agreed that the Liberals had only a slim chance of a majority government, and that the most likely outcome would be a Liberal minority.

As readers know, Chrétien confounded those predictions. The Alliance polling numbers fluctuated slightly through the campaign, but essentially were stuck in the mid-20s, and remained there until election day (when the party attracted 26 per cent of the vote). While there are complex explanations for these outcomes, they also had to do to some extent with the dynamics of the campaign. True to the early intimations of his strategy at the Liberal convention in March, Chrétien began attacking the Alliance and Stockwell Day in the most uncompromising terms, focussing primarily on his definition of core Canadian values of sharing, health care, and support for the needy and for needy regions, and alleging that the Alliance had a secret agenda to undermine all that was good and true about Canadian life. He played the Alberta card—arguing that Day had been part of a government that had introduced private health care (through for-profit clinics) and that he would try to do the same in the rest of the country if Alliance were elected. He was even able to play the Quebec card: shortly before the election, two Bloc Québécois MPs had crossed the floor to join the Alliance, giving Chrétien a huge opening to plausibly claim that Day and his party were cozying up to the separatists.

Whereas the Liberal campaign was ruthlessly focussed, and moreover played to the leader's strength in allowing him to defend the broad principles of the policies for which he had fought all his political life, the Alliance campaign was wobbly from the start. Chrétien had calculated rightly that if he called an early election, the Alliance would have to scramble to put its organization into place. There were internal disputes in the Alliance team (for example, Tom Long, who had run for the leadership and had solid connections in Ontario, was hardly used at all), and the party made an early decision to focus almost exclusively on Day and his personality to the exclusion of the rest of the Alliance team. Possibly in an effort to defuse the charge that the Alliance was somehow 'scary', the party decided to take the high road and claim that it would fight a campaign of 'respect'—no personal attacks, only a focus on the issues and policy differences. In effect this did set the tone for the next six weeks, but in a way that was unintended: while the Liberals flailed away with personal attacks, innuendo, and outright lies (for example, about Alberta health care policy), the Alliance campaign bumbled along in a fog of platitudes. When it did sharpen its focus, the Liberals would adroitly seize on an Alliance campaign promise and watch the party tie itself into knots trying to defend itself. For example, in the second week of the campaign, the Alliance capitalized on the disgruntlement of Jewish voters with the Canadian government's decision to support a UN resolution sanctioning Israel. The Liberals responded by claiming (in speeches and in a series of attack ads) that the Alliance wanted to privatize health care. While Day was responding to this, several of his own senior party members mused in the media that some form of privatization might indeed be inevitable. The Liberals also were able to turn

Day's religious faith into a campaign issue by referring to his personal opposition to abortion and his pledge to have a free vote in the Commons on the issue, to the Alliance proposal for referenda on key policy issues (which again was linked to abortion, and was nationally ridiculed on the CBC TV comedy show, *This Hour Has 22 Minutes*), and to his evangelical Christian faith. The leaders' debates in early November were a cacophony of set speeches, and while Chrétien sometimes seemed bewildered at the blizzard of questions and attacks, he held his own and made no major mistakes. The campaign got more desperate in its last weeks. The Liberals made allegations that the Alliance was a haven for racists and Holocaust deniers, and then the Alliance obliged when one of its candidates was quoted as having referred to an 'Asian invasion'. Both the Alliance and the Progressive Conservatives pushed hard on allegations that Jean Chrétien had lobbied the Canadian Business Development Bank (a government agency) to extend loans to one of the Prime Minister's Shawinigan cronies. They demanded an investigation by the Prime Minister's Ethics Counsellor, who hastily provided a narrow procedural ruling that Chrétien had not been involved in any wrongdoing.

By election day the result seemed too close to call, though there seemed portents of a Liberal minority government. Virtually no one expected a strengthened majority, but that was precisely the rabbit that the Liberals, and especially Jean Chrétien, pulled out of their hats. When the votes were counted, the Liberals romped home with 172 seats, based on the support of 41 per cent of those who voted. This compared to 161 seats when the writ was dropped. In Quebec, they increased their percentage of the vote (from 36.7 to 44.2) and their seats (from 26 to 36). The Canadian Alliance won 67 seats, based on 26 per cent of the vote. This compared with the 58 seats Reform had commanded before the election. Alliance did win two seats in Ontario, but this was far from the breakthrough in that province that had been the raison d'être of the entire exercise of reinventing the party. The Bloc Québécois went down from 44 seats to 38. This was a delicious victory for Chrétien, and one that would eventually contribute to Lucien Bouchard's resignation as provincial premier and leader of the separatist Parti Québécois some months later. The Progressive Conservatives almost lost official party status, but managed miraculously to hang on to the necessary 12 seats with just 12 per cent of the vote. But this once proud national party was reduced to 9 seats in Atlantic

Canada, 1 in Quebec, 1 in Alberta, and 1 in Manitoba, making it essentially a regional party. Finally, the NDP, after a lacklustre campaign, lost 6 seats to win only 13, based on 9 per cent of the vote. Atlantic Canada gave it 4 seats, 4 came from Manitoba, 2 from Saskatchewan, 2 from British Columbia, and 1 from Ontario.

The magnitude of the Liberal party's victory, and the personal triumph of Jean Chrétien, cannot be overstated: this was the first time in 89 years that a prime minister had won three back-to-back majorities—the last had been Sir Wilfred Laurier, who governed from 1896 to 1911. The separatists had been slapped down, and the Conservatives and NDP contained even further in small, regional fiefdoms. The only party with any hope of defeating the Liberals had increased its seats, and had run second in 80 Ontario ridings, but its hopes had been dashed, its policy platform torn to shreds, and its leader made to look foolish and even a bit wonky.

The Liberals were back, and at the helm of a new policy agenda for a new mandate. Their election platform had laid out some general directions (largely echoing initiatives from previous years), but the start of a new Parliament on 29 January 2001 meant a Speech from the Throne (SFT) and a clearer idea of what power in transition might mean for the country as a whole. There were few surprises. The Liberals had had enough trouble coming up with an election platform—their Red Book was a slim effort compared with the first version in 1993—and understandably, since this Throne Speech followed so closely on winning a mandate based on that document, the Speech was closely modelled on promises the Liberals had made during the campaign. As pointed out in the Speech, the new government would pursue the aims of building a 'strong, ever more inclusive Canada and secure a higher quality of life for all Canadians' and in doing so it would 'carry out the commitments set out in its election platform.'[13] It would be easy to dismiss the Speech as mere rhetoric, especially since it parroted the Red Book, but in the Ottawa system of policy-making, the SFT (see the Lindquist chapter in this volume) is an important element of the priority-setting process. The highlights of the SFT tend to be the initial focus of any government.

Unlike the two previous SFTs, this one did not have an overarching theme, unless it was the vague notion of a 'Canadian Way for the Twenty-first Century'. This SFT had six main sections: economic policy, social and health policy, safe communities, environment, international aid, and citizenship and culture. The section on economic policy held no surprises: innovation and research were the key themes. After some self-congratulation on taxes and fiscal balance, the SFT urged Canada to 'become one of the top five countries for research and development performance by 2010.' The government promised to double its investment in research and development by that year, and to target that investment specifically on areas such as health, water quality, the environment, natural resources management, and oceans research. The government also promised to increase support for the development of new technologies to help Canadians with disabilities. Research in the life sciences would also be targeted, with special benefits for agricultural and rural economies. This would be supplemented by an emphasis on skills and learning, a key theme of the two previous Liberal governments. In the SFT the government promised to create Registered Individual Learning Accounts, which, in some unspecified way, would help Canadians finance their education. The usual list of target groups was added to this effort: youth, persons with disabilities, Aboriginals, and immigrants. Of course, the 'Connecting Canadians' initiative was profiled as part of the economic policy strategy, though again there was nothing new. The same was true of trade and investment, which consisted of warmed-over commitments on a Free Trade Agreement with the Americas and more Team Canada excursions.

Then came the 'Sharing Opportunity' section. Brilliantly, it provided a Liberal counterpoint to the previous section on 'creating opportunity'. In largely vacuous terms, it stressed the importance of Aboriginal peoples, children and families, the unemployed, and single parents. True to its importance in the election campaign, health care figured prominently in this section, which included proclamations of fidelity to the Canada Health Act and to previous commitments from the fall to pump more money into the system.

The environmental commitments were largely restatements of previous promises, though there were tantalizing hints of more investments in national parks, and, somewhat ominously, of 'restoring existing parks to ecological health'. Next came the commitment to strong and safe communities: the government would focus on organized crime, anti-gang laws, cyber-crime and terrorism, and young offenders. In moving to Canadian culture, the government promised (and this *was* a surprise) more money to the CBC and to book-publishing. This promise was coupled with a commitment to project Canadian values abroad, through increased support for overseas development assistance and continued leadership in international organizations whose aim is to provide opportunities for all.

The cherry on this rhetorical cake celebrated 'Canadian citizenship'—Liberal style. The nation was born of vision and will, and our prime virtue has been sharing. This sharing has been focussed on the full range of our compatriots: athletes, scientists, minority language groups, multicultural communities, immigrants, and so on. Thankfully, the Government 'will help Canadians to strengthen their bonds of mutual understanding and respect, to celebrate their achievements and history, and to exercise their shared citizenship.' The SFT's final hilarity in all this—from a government that has centralized power more than any other in Canadian history—was a pious promise to introduce a range of measures to enable 'members of Parliament to more effectively represent the views of their constituents.'

The SFT closed on an endearingly rousing note: 'Every Canadian is called upon to make a contribution to building our country. To ensure that the promise of Canada becomes an even greater reality in the 21st century. And to ensure that our Canadian Way remains the best example of what is possible when women and men of every race and creed come together in community in search of a better future.' Long live the Canadian Way.

AN OVERVIEW OF THE VOLUME

- **Geoffrey Hale** looks at what surely must be considered one of the great successes of the Liberal governments since 1993—its fiscal policy. The February 2000 budget and the mini-budget of October 2000 were, in Hale's view, driven as much by electoral considerations as by fiscal ones, and exemplified the careful balancing act Paul Martin has been able to achieve as finance minister. The centrepiece of those budgets, and indeed all four in the 1997-2000 mandate, was the formula of allocating half the fiscal dividend to new spending, and half to a mix of tax reduction and deficit reduction. Hale shows how, in fact, this formula was less a guide than a cover for expenditure and tax decisions being made by the government—the very complexity of budgetary proposals made it possible to package almost any combination in terms of the formula, and also served to balance different factions within the Liberal party. The chapter also outlines the creative use of financial management techniques that has marked the Martin years. After an initial round of priority-setting within a broad budgetary framework, Martin would then engage in a compensatory round using excess revenues to deal with different political pressure points. The chapter closes with an analysis of the politics of the October mini-budget, and the way its various provisions appeal to different groups and regions in order to pump up Liberal support going into the election.

- **Evert Lindquist**'s chapter explores the evolution of strategic planning in the federal government over the last two Liberal mandates. Rational or strategic planning had its heyday in the 1960s and 1970s, only to face growing derision as it constructed baroque decision-making systems that in the end seemed to have little impact on how decisions were actually made. Lindquist points out, however, that modern management theory has come to re-embrace strategy as a key aspect of decision-making in organizations, though the emphasis today is on collaboration and flexibility in the face of turbulence and increasingly complex policy issues. It is this new philosophy of strategic management that has gradually infused the Ottawa decision-making and planning cycle since the early 1990s. Lindquist outlines the federal government's planning cycle, which now includes transition advice, Speeches from the Throne (SFT), regular cabinet meetings and twice yearly retreats, the budget, and ongoing overviews of performance. He points out that these staples of the planning process have gradually been coordinated and integrated into an overarching process of mandate planning and adjustment. In the first mandate, of course, the government was fixated on the deficit, and the planning cycle was subsumed in the process of Program Review and budget cuts. The focus was inevitably short-term, so senior officials set in motion a series of innovations such as *La Relève* and the Policy Research Initiative. The second, post-deficit mandate required further changes, as the planning and policy cycle became much more a matter of considering new programs than simply a matter of cutting expenditures. Transition planning for the 1997 SFT wove together cabinet committee deliberations, the views of the senior mandarinate, and data from various other sources, to develop a more future-oriented, thematic, and even 'narrative' approach to outlining priorities. In Lindquist's view, this major shift in planning approaches between the first two mandates was accomplished without major changes in machinery—planning was simply integrated better, made more creative and horizontal in orientation, and driven by fresh commitments to collaboration and openness. It is too early to tell whether this approach will mark the third Chrétien government, but regardless, Lindquist draws the lesson that all governments, of whatever political stripe, need to pay attention to engaging citizens, making their transition advice more transparent and accessible, fostering policy research as a foundation for informed choices, ensuring fiscal prudence, and supporting cross-departmental initiatives.

- **Anne Perkins** and **Robert Shepherd**'s chapter focuses on changes in governance or public management at the federal level through the last two mandates. Tracking changes in administrative practices is a regular feature of *How Ottawa Spends*, and this chapter joins others from previous editions to provide an overview of what has gradually become a major shift in the way that the federal government conducts its business. Perkins and Shepherd argue that federal public sector management has been affected by four major trends: more partnering among government and non-government agencies, a growing commitment to services of good quality, a shifting of responsibilities in the form of decentralization, deconcentration, devolution, and deregulation, and an increased commitment to the use of information technologies in all aspects of governing. The chapter shows how these have emerged as major priorities in the Chrétien years, and provides illustrations of programs that express these new emphases.

The chapter closes with an analysis of the possible consequences of these changes for democracy and for decision-making in the federal government.

- **Gerald Boychuk**'s chapter examines the evolution of income maintenance programs—employment insurance (EI), children's benefits, and social assistance payments under the Canada Health and Social Transfer (CHST)—in the 1990s. Boychuk argues that under the Liberals these programs have gradually moved away from targeted assistance to lower income groups to something like a broad cushion for the middle class. This trend was further enforced by the pressures of electoral competition in late 2000. Employment insurance, for example, was dramatically revised in the mid-1990s as a program primarily for those with a sustained attachment to the labour force. High contribution rates also swelled federal coffers. In order to outflank opposition calls for reduced premiums or relaxed program provisions, the Liberals offered premium cuts just before the election as tax relief. The CHST barely makes any pretence any longer of providing funds to the provinces for social assistance—it is almost exclusively now a health transfer. But it was a central focus of the campaign, and once again the Liberals covered their flanks by pumping up transfers just before the election. Federal support for low-income earners is now delivered primarily through the Canadian Child Tax Benefit and the National Child Benefit, a package of programs that actually provides support right up the income scale, and is now sold (because it is a tax benefit) as tax relief, not support for the poor. Here too the Liberals cynically, if marginally, increased benefits in the lead-up to the campaign. Boychuk sees little political potential for change in EI in the new mandate, and relative stability in the CHST and the family/children's benefits packages. In his view, the evolution of these programs has been such that they are now more broadly based and strongly supported politically, even as they provide less help to the very poor. Moreover, in his view, the impact on women and youth has been particularly negative. Despite the robust political support these policies enjoy, Boychuk points out that they are now configured to provide support for good times—their resilience and responsiveness in an economic downturn remains to be seen.

- In her chapter, **Susan Phillips** explores the evolving relationship between the federal government and the voluntary sector. The federal government for most of the 1990s was pulling back from its relationships with groups and organizations in the voluntary sector. The first Chrétien government in 1993 was content to continue Conservative policies that cut funding to groups and provided support more through occasional project funding rather than through more stable core funding. In 1997, the government belatedly recognized the importance of the voluntary sector, both for building citizen trust and social capital, and for providing services. Phillips shows that the task of rebuilding the relationship between government and the sector has led to the design of a unique and distinctive process of 'joint tables', which appears to be truly collaborative, and benefits from participation from both sides at senior levels. The Voluntary Sector Initiative that was launched and will continue for several years is designed to address funding and governance issues in the broadest terms. Phillips points out some of the challenges that have arisen in this exercise—not least because of different resources and organizational cultures—but is generally optimistic that this shift in policy between the last mandate and the new one augurs well.

- **Michael Prince** explores the recent evolution of federal policies for Canadians with disabilities. He examines these policies in terms of five key elements of citizenship: the discourse of citizenship, legal and equality rights, democratic and political rights, fiscal and social entitlements, and economic integration. The 1998 joint federal-provincial policy framework on disability, entitled *In Unison: A Canadian Approach to Disability Issues*, articulated a new discourse and vision, according to which persons with disabilities should participate in all aspects of Canadian society. The other four elements of citizenship in this policy field have been reflected in reforms in criminal justice and human rights legislation that take into account the circumstances of the disabled, in revisions to the

Canada Elections Act, in enhancements to income security programs and the tax treatment of disabled Canadians, and in improvements to employment programs. Prince shows the great range and intensity of reforms in the last decade, but argues that progress has been slow. However, in 1999 Ottawa released its latest list of priorities for dealing with disability issues, a list that stresses improving policy coherence, developing a comprehensive knowledge base on disability issues, supporting the capacity of the disability community to participate in the policy process, addressing the needs of disabled Aboriginal Canadians, further improving income support and employment programs for the disabled, and promoting better health and the prevention of injury and disability. Prince ends with the hope that these priorities will become the foundation of improvements to disability policy in the Chrétien government's third term.

- **Sandra Burt** and **Sonya Hardman** explore the fate and fortunes of gender-based analysis (GBA) as the linch pin of federal policy toward women in the last several years. Their chapter shows that the evolution of federal policy toward women began early in the post-war period with the establishment of specific institutions such as the Women's Bureau in the Department of Labour, dedicated to research on the role of women in the Canadian labour market. By 1979 the Bureau had been elevated to a full branch within the department. The department of the Status of Women was created in the 1970s as well to monitor the integration of federal policy toward the status of women across all federal initiatives. Finally, the Women's Program of the Secretary of State was launched to provide support to feminist organizations, who then lobbied Ottawa for further policy changes to suit their agendas. This golden age began to wither under the economic and trade priorities of the Conservative governments of the 1980s. When the Liberals won the election in 1993, they continued to diminish or weaken much of the women's bureaucracy, but this time in the name of GBA as a broader government initiative. Status of Women Canada was given the responsibility of championing GBA across the government, and the Women's Bureau had the same responsibility in the newly created Human Resources Development Canada. But GBA was hobbled by several factors. The first was the culture of bureaucratic neutrality, which made it difficult for femocrats to lobby openly for women-oriented policies in Ottawa. The second was the broader Liberal policy agenda of budget cuts and management reform that characterized the first two Liberal mandates. Cuts to programs like Employment Insurance hit women the hardest, and GBA was nowhere in sight. Finally, the location of the Bureau and Status of Women in the labyrinth of the Ottawa policy machinery weakened their influence. While Burt and Hardman conclude that GBA has made some small differences in federal policy, it nonetheless has been overshadowed by the Liberal preoccupation with economic growth and trade. It does not seem likely to receive a boost in the new mandate.

- **G. Bruce Doern** and **Monica Gattinger** look at contemporary Canadian economic policy through the prism of Natural Resources Canada (NRCan) as it struggles to reposition itself and the natural resources industries to which it is connected as *new economy* sectors. Of course, NRCan and our resource industries have been stereotypically associated with the *old economy*, which was founded primarily on resource exports, and involved little research or value-added technology or production. It was the Canada of lumberjacks, miners, ranchers, and fishermen—noble sons of the soil and the sea who were the backbone of an economy that lived off its abundance of lightly processed resources rather than its wits. In the 1993 Red Book, the Liberals articulated a vision of a new economy based on innovation and sustainable development—both of these being paradigms in their own right that marked important departures from old-economy images. Economic policy had to shift from protecting sectors to encouraging innovation, research, and risk. The natural resource industries in the 1990s faced tremendous competitive international pressures from lower-cost exporters and declining raw material prices. To thrive, these industries would have to reinvent themselves—with government help, but help of a different kind—as knowledge-based and research-intensive. Doern and Gattinger trace the emergence and crystallization of the sustainable development and innovation paradigms through the first two Liberal mandates, and show how, after its creation in 1993, NRCan both absorbed and adapted them as it carved out an institutional niche for itself in official Ottawa. They end with a closer look at how NRCan has faced two recent issues: concerns about the health of the mining and metals industry, and the $100 million Sustainable Development Technology Fund (SDTF). In the mining case, NRCan has wrestled with positioning the sector as research-based, technology-driven, and global. In the SDTF case, NRCan had to grapple with the challenges faced when dealing with third-party research foundations and the university sector—in effect, it had to learn to work with partners to create innovation systems, whereas traditionally it had been expected simply to implement government programs.

- **Rodney Haddow**'s chapter explores Canadian regional development policy and the degree to which the consensus that surrounded it from its inception in the 1960s has begun to fray. Regional development policy was an item of sharp disagreement between the Canadian Alliance and the Liberals during the 2000 election campaign, which saw the Alliance challenging both its efficacy and its alleged use as a political pork barrel. In its origins in the 1960s, however, regional development policy evolved out of a growing agreement by Conservatives and Liberals that governments should act to improve the supply of capital and skilled labour in the poorer parts of the country. The chapter traces the way the alphabet soup of programs and agencies evolved over the next three decades, until almost every part of the country could claim 'regional development' monies. By 1993 the Liberals argued that regional development spending was unfocussed, and promised in their first Red Book to concentrate on infrastructure, commercial applications of research, and small- and medium-sized businesses. Both key opposition parties attacked the policy on principle—the first time that the cross-party consensus had been fractured. In part this reflected their concerns that the programs were being used to buy votes, but it reflected as well the growing scepticism concerning the efficacy of government interventions in the market. Indeed, academic criticism and research claiming that regional development programs actually impeded growth by tying up labour and resources in uneconomic ways continued to mount. The Liberals ignored this more fundamental critique, but did cut regional development expenditures significantly and redesigned their administration and delivery. Haddow points out that Liberal support, particularly in Atlantic Canada, dropped as a result. Unsurprisingly, by the summer of 2000 the Liberal government was promising new programs, such as the Atlantic Investment Partnership, along with gentler Employment Insurance provisions, and in November they won additional seats in the maritime provinces. Haddow concludes that this political success has not been matched by an equivalent policy success; key issues remain: how regional development programming should be administered, the objectives of policy, and the appropriate federal-provisional balance.

- The focus of this series is usually on how Ottawa spends money, but **Rainer Knopff**'s chapter reminds us that governments 'spend' a wide variety of resources, some material and some symbolic. In reviewing the Chrétien governments' relations with the courts, he shows both how the Supreme Court had become a major policy actor in the last decade, and how both the courts and government engage in a complicated strategic *pas de deux* around controversial policy questions. During the first two Chrétien mandates, the Supreme Court pronounced on constitutional issues, women's rights, sexual assault, gun control, search warrants, Aboriginal rights, same-sex unions, and child pornography. Knopff examines the 1995 *Secession Reference* and the 1999 *Sharpe* case on the possession of child pornography, illustrating how both the Court and the government engaged in strategic behaviour, and carefully husbanded their symbolic resources. The government in particular brilliantly exploited the Charter and the child pornography case during the election to paint the Alliance party—which supported the use of the section 33 override of the Charter—as appealing to the 'dark side' of human nature. Not only does the government enjoy fiscal surpluses, but it has managed to claim the Charter of Rights and Freedoms as its own, a huge political resource.

CONCLUSION: TRANSITIONS

The chapters in this volume clearly attest to the major transitions in public policy and administration that have occurred over the last two Liberal mandates, and which will doubtless continue in the third. Canadian Liberalism under Jean Chrétien has dedicated itself to the largely empty idea of 'balance', but as an ideological concept it has given his governments a tremendous amount of manoeuvring room. It was in the name of 'balance' that the Liberals attacked the deficit, reformed the Ottawa bureaucracy, cut taxes, reformed social programs, and faced up to Quebec separatism. This year's edition of *How Ottawa Spends* adds to the evidence that the Liberals have indeed shifted quite dramatically to the centre-right of the political spectrum, in part to address the threat of the Reform/Alliance, and in part to deal with the pathologies of federal governance that had become obvious to almost everyone by the early 1990s.

This transition of power and policy has evolved over the past decade, and as a shift to the right, probably peaked sometime in 1998-9, when the federal deficit was finally slain and money began to pour into federal coffers. The Liberals paid an electoral price for this shift and for getting Ottawa's fiscal and managerial house in order in their first mandate. They came within a whisker of being defeated in the 1997 election, a near-death experience that leading Liberals doubtless did not wish to see repeated. The 'balance' that marks contemporary Canadian Liberalism thus began to shift back toward the centre-left, with new monies for health care, children, economic programs, education, Aboriginals, and employment insurance. The transition was managed adroitly, and was profoundly comfortable for Jean Chrétien as he mused about the timing of the next election. His electoral campaign of 'values' was simply a crystallization of shifts the Liberals had been making, in the previous two years, back to their home base of activist government. It sent a message that was roundly rejected in most of western Canada, but that played well east of the Manitoba-Ontario border.

It must be said, however, that this delicate manoeuvring was much more than party politics. The Liberals managed, in their political rhetoric, to corner the market on virtually every political concept of the late twentieth century that resonates positively with voters. On the high plane of collective values, the Liberals seized on the concepts of opportunity for all, sharing, diversity, and unity. With respect to social policy, these values were transposed into support for a children's agenda, redistribution to disadvantaged individuals and regions, and education. With respect to economic policy, these values were enlisted to support innovation, research, education (again), and even tax relief. As the chapters in this volume show, one can take issue with the specifics of the programs and policies that the Liberals have implemented under this banner, but the rhetorical and strategic advantage of claiming this high ground cannot be underestimated. The 2000 election campaign is clear evidence of this. Organization mattered, of course, and the Liberals were superbly organized. But part of that organization was, in the parlance of electoral spin-meisters, being 'on message'. As well, claiming this rhetorical territory as their own meant that they could attack opposition proposals much more easily: if Liberals stood for opportunity for all, sharing, diversity, and unity, then the Alliance and Conservatives must have stood for opportunity only for the privileged, greed, racism, and decentralization and dismemberment of the country. The difficulty the Alliance in particular had in shaking these charges shows how completely the Liberals maintained their grip on these values. And, indeed, as long as these values do in some important way resonate, even if only at an emotional level, with most Canadians, any small-c conservative opposition will have an uphill battle. By definition, that side of the political spectrum champions a greater degree of individual responsibility, limited government, support only for the neediest in society, a core of social standards that may deny some groups their 'rights' (e.g., gay and lesbian marriage), and substantial decentralization to the provinces. There is nothing inherently repugnant in any of these ideological positions—as we noted, many voters in western Canada support them—but against a social tableau of 'Liberal' values, they give the appearance of mean-spiritedness.

This augurs well for the Liberals in their third term. Early indications from the Canadian Alliance as Parliament opened in January 2001 were not auspicious: several senior staff abandoned ship, attacks on the government were either anemic or disorganized, and Stockwell Day faced a barrage of criticism for accepting Alberta taxpayers' funds to bail him out of a legal claim for damages when he had been a minister in the Klein government. The NDP and the Progressive Conservatives were barely registering on the political radar, though Joe Clark mounted a relentless campaign in the House on what by late February 2001 was being called 'Shawinigate'—the Prime Minister's role and interests in financial dealings with cronies that also happened to involve government lending agencies.

Yet despite this disarray in the opposition ranks, several structural forces may still threaten Liberal hegemony. The first is the transition in leadership that will likely occur in this third term. The internecine battle among various factions in the party may strain its unity, though Liberals are usually disciplined about internal debates and party fractures. The second is possible challenges from a loose front of provincial premiers from Alberta, Ontario, and Quebec. For their own reasons, all three premiers may see some advantage in challenging Ottawa's dominance of social and economic policy. The third is that despite the government's acknowledged successes in dealing with the deficit, lowering taxes, and perhaps even stimulating economic growth (or at least not impeding it), there are worrisome signs on the horizon that the country will face some major challenges for which the government seems unprepared. Canada's productivity rates still lag behind those of the United States. As a result, living standards have been under substantial pressure, and getting ahead or even staying above water for many Canadian families routinely requires at least two incomes. The Bush administration's apparent focus on Mexico may be a harbinger that Canada's favoured relationship with the richest and most powerful country on the planet may be changing. The health care system will surely come under more strain as the population ages. In the face of all these challenges, the Chrétien government seems incapable of doing anything beyond repeating the mantras of its last two administrations.

The fourth factor is partly peculiar to the Liberals as a party, and partly a function of their electoral success—the growing unease about

Canadian democracy. Simply having had the Liberals in power as long as they have will generate a taste for change by 2004. But the Liberals under Jean Chrétien have been unwilling to consider major changes to Canadian parliamentary and federal institutions and processes that would make our democracy more transparent and less controlled from the centre. It is too much, of course, to expect incumbent governments to hand power over to their opponents. However, the sense that the Prime Minister rules with an iron fist, combined with continued charges that he abused his powers to aid his friends, may eventually dent the government's teflon coating.

NOTES

1 Department of Finance Canada, *The Budget Plan* (Ottawa, 28 Feb. 2000).
2 Robert Fife, '"It's Almost like a Coup d'état": Chrétien's Circle Angered by Martin's Plan to Steal Leadership from Prime Minister', *The National Post*, 20 Mar. 2000, A1.
3 Jim McNulty, 'The Sun is Shining ... I'm Running', *The Province* [Vancouver], 19 Mar. 2000, A36.
4 Paul O'Neil, '"There Will Be No Doubt" Chrétien Will Lead Liberals', *The Vancouver Sun*, 20 Mar. 2000, A1.
5 Jim McNulty, 'The Sun is Shining ... I'm Running'.
6 Jim McNulty, 'Day's First Challenge—Bringing All Camps into His Alliance Fold', *The Province* [Vancouver], 10 July 2000, A9.
7 Lawrence Martin, 'Chrétien May Be Taking the Gamble of His Career', *The Calgary Herald*, 25 Aug. 2000, A18.
8 Joan Bryden, 'Chrétien's Caucus Buoyed by Latest Polling Data: But the Liberals Are Warned Not to Take Victory in the Next Federal Election for Granted', *The Vancouver Sun*, 31 Aug. 2000, A9.
9 Duart Farquharson, 'Liberals Already Have a Winner: Party is Heading for Trouble if It Doesn't Get Firmly Behind Chrétien', *The Edmonton Journal*, 4 Sept. 2000, A12.
10 For a copy of Auditor-General's report, see web site: www.oag-bvg.gc.ca/domino/reports.nsf/html/00menu_e.html
11 Minister of Finance, *Economic Statement and Budget Update* (Ottawa, 18 Oct. 2000). See web site: www.fin.gc.ca/toce/2000/ec00e.htm
12 Ipsos Reid, *The Globe and Mail* [Toronto], CTV poll, released 1 Oct. 2000. See web site: www.angusreid.com/media/content/displaypr.cfm?id_to_view=1084
13 Speech from the Throne to Open the First Session of the 37th Parliament of Canada (Ottawa, 30 Jan. 2001). See web site: www.sft-ddt.gc.ca/sftddt_e.htm

2

Priming the Electoral Pump: Framing Budgets for a Renewed Mandate

GEOFFREY E. HALE

> Election campaigns are no time for the serious discussion of policy issues.
> — former Prime Minister Kim Campbell, 1993 election campaign

The policy framework for the 2001-2 federal budget was shaped by Prime Minister Chrétien's decision to pre-empt the fall session of Parliament and obtain a new mandate from the Canadian people in the election of 27 November 2000. With the Canadian economy growing at an annual after-inflation rate of almost 5 per cent, the preparation of the two pre-election federal budgets has focussed at least as much on 'priming the electoral pump' as on short- or medium-term economic policy considerations. While subsequent projections of an economic slowdown in the United States have strengthened arguments for significant tax cuts, hard-nosed political calculations appear to have counted rather more in the government's policy priorities than crystal ball-gazing.

Under normal circumstances, a pre-election budget such as Paul Martin's *Economic Statement and Fiscal Update* of 18 October 2000 would have been the centrepiece of the Chrétien government's political and economic agenda. A government that had presided over consistent economic growth, growing personal incomes, and rising levels of employment (see Table 2.1) could have been expected to seek re-election on its record of successful economic management. During the summer of 2000, Prime Minister Chrétien also hinted that an election campaign could provide the opportunity for a national debate over the use of the fiscal dividend—the huge surpluses that would result from projected levels of economic growth at current levels of spending and taxation.

However, the campaign recalled former Prime Minister Kim Campbell's astute, if ill-timed, comments from the 1993 election that 'election campaigns are no time for the serious discussion of policy issues.' The accelerated tax reductions promised in Martin's *Fiscal Update* and the modest spending plans announced during the campaign effectively blurred the distinctions among the policy alternatives outlined by the Liberals, by their principal challengers, the Canadian Alliance, and by the Progressive Conservatives, leaving the party leaders to pursue the politics of personal destruction.

Ironically, Prime Minister Chrétien's generally cautious, incremental approach to the management of Ottawa's political agenda during the short life of the last Parliament may offer a plausible explanation for

Table 2.1

The Economy On A Roll

	1997	1998	1999	2000
Unemployment rate	9.1	8.3	7.6	6.8
Participation rate	64.9	65.1	65.6	65.9
Real GDP Growth	4.4	3.3	4.5	5.0 [projected]
Inflation Rate: CPI	1.6	0.9	1.7	3.2 [projected]

Source: Statistics Canada, 25 January 2001.

the budget's low political profile during the election campaign. The Prime Minister decided to protect both his flanks. First, he negotiated with the provinces a pre-election agreement on health funding that restored previous federal transfer cuts. Second, he accelerated planned personal and business tax reductions to steal the tax cut thunder of the Canadian Alliance. This latter initiative was clearly aimed at depriving the opposition of its main election platform, while attempting to demonize it as a supposed risk to Canada's social programs and fiscal stability. Unlike the Prime Minister's electoral rhetoric, this approach was consistent with the government's generally cautious approach to the management of fiscal and budgetary policy during its second term in office.

This chapter examines the fiscal track record of the Chrétien government's second mandate, the balancing of party factions and policy priorities reflected in Paul Martin's four budgets during this period, and the effects of the 'electoral business cycle' on the latter's pre-election budget of October 2000. It assesses the political balancing act of the Chrétien-Martin 'team' during the past fiscal year and its efforts to cover the government's political flanks by allocating a rapidly growing fiscal dividend to a number of projects, notably debt repayment, taxation, Employment Insurance, health transfers to the provinces, and children's services. Finally, it considers the outcomes of the 2000 election campaign and their implications for federal fiscal policies in the foreseeable future.

THE CHRÉTIEN STYLE AND THE POLITICS OF BALANCE

The Chrétien government ran for re-election in 1997 as the party of political and social balance, a party that combined the managerial competence that had enabled it to come within reach of eliminating the $43 billion deficit inherited from the Mulroney government in 1993 with a policy of selective activism, which allowed it to redirect social and economic spending so as to meet key social and economic priorities.

This approach to fiscal and budgetary policy reflects Chrétien's efforts to balance the two different approaches to contemporary liberalism that are reflected in his cabinet and caucus. 'Distributive liberalism'—more closely identified with the Prime Minister's political style and rhetoric—recalls an older school of politics that advocates the use of political power to advance the claims of a broad range of social and economic interests to a growing share of government revenues and protective government regulations. Politicians are expected to 'bring home the bacon' to constituents. Political intervention is expected to deliver grants and subsidies for economic development, job creation, and business expansion; politically advantageous public works contracts for 'infrastructure'; and tax policies that both target economic benefits to politically important groups and facilitate the redistribution of income.

Distributive liberalism is closely identified with the politics of clientelism—the use of public policy to generate political loyalty and gratitude rather than specific policy outcomes.[1] Examples are scattered through the reports of the Auditor General—most notably his recent scathing criticism of a series of Human Resources Development Canada (HRDC) employment programs initiated to soften the blow of the government's Employment Insurance reforms of 1996-7.[2]

'Managerial' or 'technocratic' liberalism, personified by Finance Minister Paul Martin and his allies on the Commons Finance Committee, has consistently sought to implement the neo-liberal fiscal, economic, and social paradigm outlined in the government's 'Purple Book' of 1994.[3] These policies have emphasized fiscal discipline and, since 1997, the careful investment of most surplus revenues in a series of targeted tax and spending measures seen to be most likely to promote economic growth, facilitate skills acquisition and workplace attachment, and encourage research and innovation. Cumulatively, they are intended to facilitate the integration of Canada and Canadians into the emerging 'knowledge-based economy', while targeting the largest income transfers to those families 'in greatest need'. More recently, they have sought to provide all income groups with higher standards of living as a result of ongoing and sustainable tax relief.

Another perspective on Martin's managerial liberalism is that it seeks to empower decision-making elites within the federal government, particularly within the Department of Finance, in balancing the competing claims of social and economic interests over a growing fiscal dividend. Faced with demands from the populist left for increased public spending and new national social programs, from the populist right for large-scale, broadly-based tax cuts for individuals and families, and from both for the immediate restoration of federal transfer payments to the provinces, managerial liberalism requires a significant degree of autonomy for technocratic elites in balancing these competing claims without yielding control over federal priorities or the fiscal framework[4] to either. Centralized Finance Department control over Ottawa's fiscal framework has been a key factor in fostering the fiscal self-discipline needed to promote economic growth together with sustainable and effective social programs in an open, 'globalized' economic system.

Chrétien and Martin's ability to balance these objectives has relied heavily on the principle and practice of 'triangulation'—the use of complementary policy instruments to contain and accommodate the claims and expectations of competing interests or policy goals. The centrepiece in the communication of the government's strategy of political and fiscal balance during the last four years has been its so-called '50-50' plan.

FISCAL POLICY 1997-2000: THE '50-50' PLAN AND THE POLITICS OF 'BALANCE'

The Liberals' 1997 election platform committed the government to allocating half of future budget surpluses to increased program spending over the life of its mandate, and the other half to debt reduction and tax relief.[5] This commitment provided a simple, easily understood formula to discipline competition among competing factions of the Liberal party in their attempts to control the fiscal dividend. It allowed 'core program spending' to grow with inflation and overall population levels. Tax relief was initially to be targeted to 'lower- and middle-income families', with more broadly-based tax reductions to follow once they could be 'sustained' through the fluctuations of the business cycle without resorting to deficit spending.

In addition to disciplining competing external demands for policy change, the commitment still gave the government the flexibility it needed to respond to political and economic circumstances from year to year. The concepts of 'new spending' and 'tax relief' were sufficiently flexible that Martin could package rising tax credits for children and selective tax breaks as 'tax relief' in one budget and 'new spending' in another to show the government's continued commitment to its 50-50 plan (see Table 2.2).

Key Fiscal and Economic Promises from the 1997 Liberal Platform

We will
* allocate our budget surpluses so that, over the course of our mandate, one half will be spent to improve our programs, and one half will go to tax cuts and reduction of the debt [28].
* ... put the debt to GDP ratio on a permanent downward track [30].
* ... [make] strategic investments in youth, small business, tourism, infrastructure, trade, innovation and technology [31] ... [and apply] substantial new resources to investments in jobs, health care, our children's future, and education and knowledge [32].
* ... [make more] selective tax cuts. The time for a broad-based tax reduction will come, when we can afford it as a society and when Canadians can be assured that such cuts can be permanent [32].
* ... ensure that Canada continues to provide one of the most favourable tax regimes for R&D in the world [32].
* ... invest $800 million a year in active employment benefits, while reducing the overall cost of the [EI] program [by 2000] [63].

Source: Liberal Party of Canada, *Securing Our Future Together: Preparing Canada for the Twenty-First Century: Red Book II:The Liberal Plan* (Ottawa, 1997).

However, close observers of the process suggest that the 50-50 principle was more a means of packaging the government's policy decisions—described elsewhere as the 'public budgetary process'[6]—than of shaping the priorities of senior budget decision-makers. One senior official contacted by the author comments that the policy had 'no importance for policy decisions', but was used primarily to show how the government's actions lived up to it after the fact.[7]

Finance Minister Martin tabled four budgets during the government's three-and-a-half-year life. Each one was organized around specific policy themes that emphasized particular elements of the government's medium-term policy agenda of projecting 'leadership' in social and economic policy and increasing the government's relevance to the day-to-day lives of individual Canadians. The focus shifted from an emphasis on targeted and continuing spending increases in Martin's early budgets (intended to offset the spending reductions needed to

Table 2.2

The '50-50' Deficit Reduction Plan In Retrospect

	Tax Expenditures as tax relief $ billions	% of total	as spending $ billions	% of total
New Spending*	55.2	43.1	64.7	50.5
Tax Expenditures				
Canada Child Tax Benefit and other social policy	7.8	6.1		0.0
Research and innovation	1.5	1.2		0.0
Tax fairness measures	0.2	0.2		0.0
Tax and EI reductions	48.2	37.6	48.1	37.5
Total tax measures	57.6	44.9	48.1	37.5
Debt reduction				
until 1999-2000	6.4	5.0	6.4	5.0
applying $3 billion annual contingency funds to debt	9.0	7.0	9.0	7.0
Potential debt reduction	15.4	12.0	15.4	12.0
Total discretionary changes	**128.2**	**100.0**	**128.2**	**100.0**

*'New spending' in addition to annual 3% funding increases in existing programs to reflect inflation and population growth. Does not include future in-year spending increases due to windfall revenue above forecast levels.

Note: Numbers may not add be exact due to rounding. Assumes 10% per year reduction in EI employee premium rates for 2001, 2002, 2003; assumes $3 billion contingency fund applied to debt reduction.

Source: Paul Martin, *Budget 2000*, Table A.1.1; author's calculations.

balance the federal budget between 1993 and 1997) to a greater emphasis on tax reduction in his two most recent budgets. While the February 2000 budget was carefully ambiguous with respect to the timing of most of Martin's proposed tax reductions, so that the government could retain as much flexibility as possible, his October 2000 mini-budget owed far more to the demands of partisan political competition and the impending federal election.

The centrepiece of Martin's February 1998 budget was the so-called 'Canadian Opportunity Strategy', which combined seven distinct elements intended to project federal leadership in improving access to skills, education, and youth employment, and included a number of housekeeping measures dealing with previous government commitments.[8]

The 1999 budget continued the incremental extension of tax relief, family benefits, support for education, and support for research and innovation while promising the partial restoration of federal health care transfers to the provinces over five years.[9] This approach enabled Martin to maintain control over federal finances by allowing for gradual increases in federal transfers, while offering the provinces the carrot of further transfer growth if they cooperated with Ottawa in developing a comprehensive strategy for the adaptation of health care systems to new technologies and the demands of an aging population. While the 'Social Union' agreement negotiated in February 1999 provided a framework for ongoing federal-provincial diplomacy over social policy and transfer payments, the provinces skilfully manipulated the public debate by emphasizing the effects of past federal funding cuts while leading public opinion in a chorus of 'show us the money.'[10]

Martin emphasized the government's new spending initiatives in his first two budgets while holding tax relief to a minimum—even though much of the 'new' spending involved a reallocation of existing funding commitments (see Table 2.3). However, growing federal surpluses increased political pressures on Martin to make the kinds of long-term commitments on specific tax relief measures that he had made previously to increase funding for education, research, child benefits, and health transfers to the provinces.

Critics noted that much of Martin's incremental tax relief, especially for middle-income families, had been offset by sharp increases in Canada Pension Plan premiums and the cumulative effects of bracket creep.[11] Both the Reform and Conservative parties tabled ambitious five-year tax cut agendas in an effort to outbid the Liberals for the support of middle-class voters in Ontario and Quebec in a pre-election year. Martin responded in his February 2000 budget by re-indexing income taxes to inflation and announcing plans for broadly-based personal and business tax reductions totalling $58.5 billion over five years.[12] While proposed tax reductions included modest reductions in

Table 2.3
Summary of Spending and Tax Actions
1998, 1999, 2000 Budgets and 2000 Budget Update
($ millions)

Spending Initiatives	1997-8	1998-9	1999-2000	2000-1	Total	Per cent
Health spending						
Increased CHST Transfers	200	4,400	4,000	2,500	11,100	31.6
Other health initiatives	800	368	260	1,947	3,375	9.6
Education and research related spending						
Canadian Opportunities Strategy	2,555	763	2,829	3,069	9,216	26.3
Other spending						
Other social spending	483	697	1,054	3,003	5,237	14.9
Economic adjustment		1,241	645	152	2,038	5.8
Other public services			1,974	2,167	4,141	11.8
Total	4,038	7,469	10,761	12,837	35,103	100.0
Change in program spending in relation to previous year	3,933	2,640	370	7,900 [projected]		
Change in total spending in relation to previous year	-109	3,103	623	8,500 [projected]		
Tax expenditures and general relief						
General tax relief		880	2,975	8,355	12,210	53.8
EI premium reductions	235	1,025	2,320	3,467	7,047	31.1
Canada Child Tax Benefit			320	1,450	1,770	7.8
Education and youth-related tax measures		120	360	460	940	4.1
Other selective tax changes		125	255	340	720	3.2
Total	235	2,150	6,230	14,072	22,687	100.0

Sources: *Economic Statement and Fiscal Update* (Ottawa, 18 Oct. 2000), 27, 134: *Fiscal Reference Tables* (Ottawa: Department of Finance, Sept. 2000), 15.

capital gains tax rates and the gradual elimination of the upper-income surtax, the bulk of tax relief was directed to lower- and middle-income earners, as was consistent with earlier Liberal promises. Both the restoration of indexing and the major expansion of the Child Tax Benefits over five years were consistent with the government's previous strategy of using incremental change and the federal tax system to combine a disciplined approach to fiscal policy with visible commitments to the government's key political constituencies. Continued growth in employment and economic activity allowed Martin to apply a record $12 billion to debt reduction—rather than the $3 billion projected in his February budget.[13]

However, the Chrétien government departed from this process of cautious incrementalism in Martin's fourth budget, tabled in October 2000 in the shadow of an impending election call. While the government enjoyed a commanding lead in public opinion polls, it faced contradictory pressures, for higher spending and tax reduction, from both the political opposition and the provinces. The budget included a five-year, $23-billion agreement with the provinces for the increase in federal health transfers negotiated by Health Minister Allan Rock in September. It also confirmed the government's plans to appeal to Atlantic voters by rolling back many of the 1996 changes to the Employment Insurance system, and by committing $700 million to 'new economy' subsidies over the next four years. Martin also accelerated the rate of tax reductions announced in his February budget, and introduced a series of new tax cuts to neutralize the growing appeal of the Reform opposition—recently reorganized as the Canadian Alliance under its new leader, Stockwell Day.[14] The details of this 'mini-budget' will be examined later in this chapter.

The Liberals' 50-50 plan from the 1997 election served its purpose during the Chrétien government's second term. It allowed Prime Minister Chrétien to hold the balance between supporters of more aggressive tax reduction and supporters of more activist government within his caucus, while delegating the technical details of this balancing act to his Finance Minister. Its calculated ambiguity enabled Martin to use the tax system as a vehicle for maintaining federal government—and Finance Department—control over the fiscal framework rather than making open-ended commitments either to tax reduction, federal transfers to the province, or the creation of new national social programs.

It has also enabled Martin and his officials to build periodic 'consolation rounds' into their budget processes in a way that allowed them to pursue their medium- and long-term fiscal policy goals while using periodic fiscal windfalls to accommodate short-term policy corrections and political pressures for greater spending.

MAXIMIZING POLITICAL AND FISCAL FLEXIBILITY: MARTIN'S THREE-STAGE BUDGET PROCESS

The budgetary process of Canadian governments has evolved into a year-round activity. It involves the continuous monitoring and evaluation of economic activity and fiscal performance so that governments can anticipate and respond to changing circumstances without disrupting either the effective provision of public services or the efficient working of the economy. It also requires a sensitivity to public expectations that enables political leaders to respond to citizens' short-term priorities while attempting to strike a coherent balance among competing and often conflicting policy goals over the medium term. Maintaining a degree of fiscal flexibility provides governments with the margin of error necessary to carry out this political and administrative balancing act without being thrown onto the defensive by short-term political pressures or unforeseen economic circumstances.

Achieving and then maintaining this political and fiscal flexibility has been the major tactical goal of Paul Martin's budgetary strategy since he became minister of finance in 1993. Martin's use of budget targets to shape public expectations and to discipline the demands of his political colleagues and assorted interest groups has been central to his ability to control Ottawa's fiscal framework. So has the continued support of Prime Minister Jean Chrétien, whatever the reports of their political differences. A number of senior participants in the budget process confirmed that differences in outlook between the two men have usually been quite minor, and that Chrétien 'gave Martin rock-hard support in virtually everything.'[15]

Martin's creative use of financial management techniques to give the government greater flexibility in responding to unforeseen political and economic circumstances ('fiscal illusion')[16] allowed him to meet or exceed his budget targets in each year of the government's second mandate. At the same time, it gave him the necessary leeway to build in one, and sometimes two, 'consolation budget rounds' to accommodate political pressures for increased spending without losing control of the government's finances. This section examines Martin's innovative use of a three-stage budgetary process to maximize both his fiscal and his political flexibility during the last four years.

Stage I: An initial round, in which priorities are set. At this stage, the government commits itself to a modest increase in spending, and to a reduction of taxes in selected sectors; at the same time, it uses the techniques of fiscal illusion to retain the flexibility needed to respond to changing political and economic circumstances.

Martin's annual budget speeches consistently projected 'balanced budgets', based on 'prudent economic forecasts', with 'contingency reserves' of $3 billion that could be applied to debt reduction if not needed to meet his budget targets. In practice, the combination of Martin's cautious forecasts and steady growth in levels of employment, economic activity, and corporate profits since 1997 resulted in federal revenues averaging $9.7 billion more than budgeted between 1997 and 2000. As the actual costs of financing the federal debt averaged $2.9 billion less than forecast during the same period, Martin's combination of craft and luck gave him $37.7 billion more to work with than originally budgeted. Given that surplus revenues of more than $11 billion are projected during the current fiscal year, Martin's annual fiscal windfall will have averaged close to $12 billion between 1997 and 2001 (see Table 2.4).

Stage II: The 'consolation budget round'. At this stage, in-year spending commitments are made that use revenues in excess of budget projections to deal with political pressure points.

The 'consolation budget rounds' usually resulted in a series of new spending announcements at different times during the budget year. The combination of Martin's cautious budget projections, continued fiscal discipline, and creative accounting practices enabled the canny Finance Minister to finance most of his new spending commitments over the past three budgets from 'savings' that materialized as a result of improved economic growth and lower than anticipated interest rates. However, unlike previous governments, which have tended to treat budgetary windfalls as excuses for comparable spending increases,

Table 2.4
The Fine Art of Fiscal Forecasting: 1997-8 to 2000-1
In-year changes in federal budgets

	1997-8 ($ billions)	per cent	1998-9 ($ billions)	per cent	1999-2000 ($ billions)	per cent	2000-1 ($ billions)	(prelim.) per cent
Budgetary revenues	15.4	11.2	4.7	3.1	9.0	5.7	11.7	7.2
Program spending	3.0	2.8	6.9	6.6	0.6	0.5	3.7	3.2
Operating balance	3.9	9.6	-2.2	-4.7	8.4	18.5	8.0	17.4
Public debt charges	-5.6	12.0	-2.1	-4.8	-0.9	-2.1	0.2	0.5
Underlying balance	17.5	-125.0	0.1	-3.3	9.3	310.0	7.9	97.5
Contingency reserve	0.0	0.0	-0.1	-3.3	0.0	0.0	0.0	
Net surplus/ (deficit)	20.5	-120.6	2.9	-3.3	12.3	410.0	11.9	

Sources: Paul Martin, Minister of Finance, *The Budget Plan: 1997* (Ottawa, 18 Feb. 1997); Martin, *The Budget Plan: 1998* (Ottawa, 24 Feb. 1998); Martin, *The Budget Plan: 1999* (Ottawa, 16 Feb. 1999); Martin, *The Budget Plan: 2000* (Ottawa, 28 Feb. 2000); Department of Finance, *Annual Financial Report: 1999-2000* (Ottawa, 20 Sept. 2000); author's calculations; Martin, *Economic Statement and Budget Update* (Ottawa, 18 Oct. 2000). Figures may be inexact because of rounding.

Table 2.5

Budget Consolidation Rounds—1998-2000

	1997-8 prelim.	1997-8 final	1998-9 prelim.	1998-9 final	1999-2000 prelim.	1999-2000 final
In-year 'spending increases' ($ billions)	3.2		5.4		5.9	
In-year tax reductions ($ billions)	0.2		0.3		0.3	
Per cent reallocated from existing spending	248.2%	180.3%	0%	0%	42.0%	103.4%
Per cent of unbudgeted revenue surpluses assigned to net growth of in-year spending	0.0%	0.0%	101.8%	102.1%	70.5%	0.0%

Sources: *The Budget Plan: 1997, 1998, 1999, 2000*; Department of Finance, *Annual Financial Report: 1999-2000*; author's calculations.

Martin has limited unbudgeted spending increases to an average of $3.5 billion—or 29 per cent of available funds. In 1997-8 and 1999-2000, in-year spending increases were financed entirely from in-year savings that resulted from lower than expected interest rates and unemployment levels (see Table 2.5).

Stage III: Martin's 'third round' often coincides with his next budget. Under accrual accounting rules,[17] unbudgeted revenues not previously committed to in-year spending increases may be allocated to spending on specific projects in future years if funds are transferred to special accounts created for that purpose and the government effectively gives up control over them. Surplus revenues on income earned during the preceding year that exceed levels forecast in the next budget are normally allocated to debt reduction.

Unbudgeted surpluses in 1997-8 helped to pay for Chrétien's personal project, the 'Millennium Scholarship Fund'—even though funds were only dispersed to the provinces in subsequent years. Surplus revenues of $3.5 billion in 1998-9 and $2.5 billion in 1999-2000 were allocated to supplementary transfers to the provinces for health care—with funds to be disbursed over a period of up to five years.

However, the unpredictable character of government revenues—especially those resulting from taxation of investment income and corporate profits—may result in final revenues significantly higher than those contained in revised budget forecasts. In 1999-2000, an end-of-year revenue 'surge' resulting from higher than projected growth levels enabled Martin to pay a record $12 billion rather than the budgeted $3 billion toward debt reduction.[18] Along with his commitment to apply $10 billion in 2000-1 to debt reduction, this is probably the single most significant departure from the 'cautious incrementalism' of the Chrétien-Martin era.

The 50-50 plan and the politics of balance: a shifting target
The government has shifted its 50-50 goalposts over the past three and a half years. In 1997-8 and 1998-9, budgets credited refundable tax credits to the government's tax reduction targets to demonstrate its efforts at balance. In 1999-2000, the 'spending' component of refundable tax credits was acknowledged as the government shifted

toward an emphasis on more broadly-based tax reduction. In 2000-1, any pretense that the 50-50 formula would be honoured appears to have gone out the window. Fiscal projections at mid-year anticipate a $15 billion surplus in 2000-1.[19] With slower growth rates anticipated in 2001 and 2002, Martin has sensibly allocated two-thirds of this amount to debt reduction—thus releasing at least $700 million in annual debt interest payments for other public purposes. While this has opened the government to criticism from some quarters, it illustrates the practical limitations of governing by slogan.

Kneebone and McKenzie have suggested that Canadian governments tend to exercise considerable fiscal discipline relative to the overall business cycle in the early years of their electoral mandates, while running 'looser' fiscal policies as an election approaches.[20] However, an examination of Paul Martin's budgetary policies over the last four years suggests a more complicated picture. Federal spending has increased only slightly faster than inflation and the growth of population since 1997-8—and most of that increase occurred in 2000-1. Despite sizable tax reductions in the current year, federal revenues have increased faster than spending, with the result that more than $22 billion in federal debt has been repaid during the past year. At the same time, the federal government committed itself in its pre-election budget to tax reductions totalling close to $100 billion during the next five years. Spending announcements made before and during the election campaign totalled $50 billion.[21]

While the government's commitments to fiscal discipline and the preservation of fiscal flexibility appear to have been alive and well during most of its second mandate, its pre-election budget clearly was directed toward priming the electoral pump.

PRIMING THE ELECTORAL PUMP: THE PRE-ELECTION BUDGET OF OCTOBER 2000

Martin's pre-election budget contained four major components, each of which was consistent with the government's overall policies of political triangulation—the use of complementary policy instruments to contain and accommodate the claims and expectations of competing interests or contradictory policy goals. The government entered the election far ahead of its main opposition, according to published polls.

However, faced with lukewarm support from many voters, it acted decisively to address potential challenges to its re-election in four ways:

- by restoring health care funding and other transfers to the provinces—the single most pressing issue in virtually every pre-election poll;
- by restoring Employment Insurance benefits, lowering access requirements, and increasing subsidies for regional economic development in order to expand its political base in Atlantic Canada and Eastern Quebec, and offset potential electoral losses in Ontario;
- by accelerating and deepening promised personal income tax reductions in order to neutralize the appeal of sharp tax reductions promised by the Canadian Alliance to middle-class voters; and
- by matching opposition promises of more rapid tax cuts for corporations and investors, while expanding business subsidies—especially for firms in the 'knowledge-based economy'—and committing as much as $10 billion from the current year's surplus to debt reduction.

These policies reflect a mix of managerial and distributive liberalism calculated to secure as wide a swath of public support in the centre of Canada's political spectrum as possible, simultaneously offering middle-class voters most of the tax benefits offered by the Canadian Alliance and appealing to soft liberal and social democratic voters to rally against the 'two-tiered monsters'[22] on the right. Rising budget surpluses and economic growth projections created an opportunity to pre-empt the opposition and make longer-term fiscal commitments than Martin had been willing to hazard in past budgets.

Increasing Health and Other Transfers to the Provinces
To prevent the loss of small-l liberal supporters to the New Democratic Party and to position itself as a defender of Canada's health care system, the government signed an agreement with the provinces promising to restore, over a period of five years, federal health transfers that had been cut between 1995 and 1997. The September 2000 agreement provided for increased federal transfers of $18.9 billion to

be added to the Canada Health and Social Transfer (CHST) to the provinces. Health Minister Allan Rock also added $2.3 billion to Health Transition Funds for new medical equipment, health information technology, and primary care. The government also committed an additional $2.2 billion to the CHST to finance early childhood development projects.[23]

The funding agreement addressed two major areas of political vulnerability for the Liberals while reinforcing a series of incremental programs to address specific issues within the health care system, and largely respecting provincial jurisdiction over health care administration. The provincial governments, particularly Ontario, had attempted systematically over several years to shift the blame for stresses in their health care systems onto the federal government—citing its overall reduction of 25 per cent in transfer payments to the provinces since 1995. All four federal opposition parties had taken up the underfunding chorus, responding to polling data that consistently showed increased health spending as the public's top spending priority.[24]

Martin's 1999 and 2000 budgets had provided short-term band-aids of $3.5 billion and $2.5 billion, payable over five years. However, they signalled that large-scale funding increases would depend on provincial cooperation with Ottawa in developing sustainable reforms of their health care systems and accommodating federal priorities such as improvements to home care and drug benefit plans. The September agreement with the provinces provided additional funds for health care, with incremental funding increases for a number of projects specifically related to the federal agenda. It also contained a federal commitment to provide $2.2 billion through the CHST to fund a variety of provincial initiatives related to early childhood development (see Table 2.6).[25]

Past federal efforts to initiate new national programs in this area had been pre-empted by federal budgetary considerations, particularly the priority given to expanding the National Child Benefit, issues of federal-provincial jurisdiction, and the widely differing priorities of provincial governments in delivering services to families and children. The emphasis on children's benefits acknowledged political pressures from social liberals in the government caucus. However, Martin used his control over the budgetary process to allocate these funds directly to lower- and middle-income families through the tax-transfer system

Table 2.6
Expanded Federal Funding for Health, Early Childhood Development
September 2000
($ billions)

Category	2000-1	2001-2	2002-3	2003-4	2004-5	2005-6	Total new cash
Canada Health and Social Transfer							
Current cash[a]	15.5	15.5	15.5	15.5	15.5[b]	15.5[b]	--
General cash increase	--	2.5	3.2	3.8	4.4	5.0	18.9
Early childhood development	--	0.3	0.4	0.5	0.5	0.5	2.2
TOTAL CHST CASH	**15.5**	**18.3**	**19.1**	**19.8**	**20.4**	**21.0**	**--**
Medical Equipment Fund	0.5	0.5	--	--	--	--	1.0
Health Information Technology	0.5	--	--	--	--	--	0.5
Health Transition Fund for Primary Care	--	0.2	0.2	0.2	0.2	--	0.8
TOTAL CASH	**16.5**	**19.0**	**19.3**	**20.0**	**20.6**	**21.0**	**23.4**

a   Total cash includes CHST supplements of both Budget 1999 ($3.5 billion) and Budget 2000 ($2.5 billion).
b   Existing legislation extends to 2003–4. $15.5 billion is base cash for subsequent years.

Source: Privy Council Office, 11 Sept. 2000.

rather than commit the government to a new national shared-cost program to finance child care services, as desired by much of the social policy lobby. While the funding commitment removed a symbolic irritant, negotiations on a framework agreement will continue between Human Resources Development Minister Jane Stewart and her provincial counterparts.

While all four opposition parties aggressively sought to capitalize on the government's belated restoration of federal transfers during the election campaign, the funding commitments in the September 2000 agreement and the government's effective demagoguery on the alleged threat of 'two-tier' health care should its opponents prevail neutralized the issue.

Subsidies Galore

Atlantic Canada sharply rebuked the Liberals for the effects of their deficit reduction program during the 1997 election—it returned only 11 Liberal members compared with 32 in the previous election, along with 14 Conservatives and 7 New Democrats. Changes to the Employment Insurance program that reduced benefits for most repeat users and increased qualifying periods were bitterly resented, especially in rural Atlantic Canada, which continues to be heavily dependent on seasonal employment closely integrated with the availability of EI benefits.

Recovering the seats lost in Atlantic Canada was one of Prime Minister Chrétien's key strategies in his pursuit of a third majority government—particularly if the government failed to maintain its unprecedented control of more than 100 seats in Ontario. Despite reported opposition from senior economic cabinet ministers, Chrétien decided by mid-year that with the government's finances far stronger than expected, the potential of 15 to 20 additional seats in Atlantic Canada well justified an investment of about $2.15 billion over five years to roll back to the most unpopular reductions in regional benefits.

Bill C-44, introduced on September 28 with the House of Commons in full pre-election mode, proposed the repeal of the EI intensity rule, which reduced benefit rates by 1 to 5 per cent for claimants who had used the program during the previous five years, and proposed as well the reduction of the experience-rated clawback of EI benefits for workers earning more than $48,750 a year. It would also increase accessibility to EI benefits for fishers, new labour force entrants, and recipients of parental leave benefits.[26]

Human Resources Development Minister Jane Stewart claimed that the intensity and clawback rules had 'proven to be less effective than we had anticipated and in some cases punitive, particularly to seasonal workers and women.'[27] While some policy observers may have disputed her analysis, the restoration of EI benefits responded to the concerns of social policy lobbyists and numerous Liberal MPs, who had pressured the government to use a share of its huge EI surplus to roll back at least a portion of the 1996 reforms.[28]

Earlier in the summer, Chrétien also announced plans to spend $700 million over five years to promote research, innovation, and high-technology industries through a new 'Atlantic Innovation Fund'. In a symbolic gesture, part of this money was diverted from the job creation programs whose slipshod administration had embroiled the government in the controversy over HRDC grants.[29]

While other regions, particularly Eastern Quebec, Northern Ontario, and the British Columbia interior also benefited from the government's change of heart, the government's strategy was clearly targeted at the restoration of its political dominance of Atlantic Canada. To remove any doubt on this point, just before calling the election Chrétien announced the return of Newfoundland Premier Brian Tobin to federal politics and his appointment as Minister of Industry—responsible, of course, for doling out regional development grants.

While Liberals saw their huge pre-election lead in the polls reduced somewhat in Atlantic Canada as in most other regions of the country, the end result was an increase of eight seats—rather more than enough to offset the modest Liberal losses in other parts of the country.

However, the centrepiece of Martin's pre-election budget was his announcement of more than $40 billion in planned tax cuts over the next five years—broadening and deepening the tax reductions promised in his previous budget.

My Tax Cut Is Better than Your Tax Cut
In his February 2000 budget, Paul Martin announced plans to allocate $58 billion of a projected $95 billion fiscal dividend to tax reduction over a period of five years, while continuing to make specific

commitments in the context of the rolling two-year fiscal plans used in his six previous budgets.

The February tax reductions, most of which were anticipated to some degree by the December 1999 report of the Commons Finance Committee,[30] were intended to serve a mix of medium-term policy goals as well as reinforce the government's main policy objectives—as is consistent with Martin's policy of 'managerial liberalism':

- using 'targeted tax relief' in order to direct the bulk of tax reductions to lower- and middle-income Canadians, while 'ultimately benefit(ing) all Canadians';
- emphasizing the reduction of income taxes as the area in which overall Canadian tax levels are most significantly above those of its international competitors;
- maintaining business taxes at internationally competitive levels;
- not borrowing money to finance broadly-based tax relief.[31]

Martin consistently promised that the government would accelerate its timetable for tax reduction to the extent that these reductions could be sustained in the event of an economic downturn. The pre-election mini-budget tabled on October 18 accelerated the Liberal timetable for tax relief and deepened planned tax reductions for some groups in response to three main factors.

Increased economic growth had pushed estimates of the fiscal dividend between 2001 and 2005 from approximately $95 billion to approximately $150 billion.[32] While the uncertainties of economic forecasting mean that this windfall is far from guaranteed, these projections prompted both the Canadian Alliance and Progressive Conservative opposition parties to propose much more aggressive timetables for tax reduction for all income groups. As all parties were projecting that the largest group of swing voters in the coming election would be middle-class voters in Ontario and the lower mainland of British Columbia, Martin sought to neutralize the potential appeal of the opposition tax plans by committing the government to significant tax reductions for all income groups in 2001.

The government also sought to pre-empt the Alliance's initial proposal of higher income tax exemptions and a single rate tax of 17 per cent on the remaining income by reducing income tax rates for lower- and middle-income earners, creating a new, lower 'upper-middle income' tax bracket for persons earning between $61,500 and $100,000, and eliminating the remaining surtax (see Table 2.7) on upper-income earners. This policy served the government's political objectives—to target significant tax reductions toward the lower- and middle-income earners, who account for approximately 80 per cent of Canadians paying income tax.

At the same time, it responded to the concerns of Finance Department officials that the sharp progressivity of Canada's income tax

Table 2.7

Accelerating, Deepening Personal Tax Reduction: February vs. October 2000

	February	**October**
Basic personal exemption/ spouse	$7,231 / $6,140 including indexing	$7,412 / $6,294 including indexing
Tax rate on first $30,000 of income	17 per cent	16 per cent
'Middle income' tax rate	23 per cent in 2001 (from 26 per cent in 1999)	22 per cent
Upper-middle income tax rate (incomes of $61,509 to $100,000)	29 per cent	26 per cent
Upper income surtax (and threshold)	5 per cent on incomes over $85,000 to be phased out over 5 years	Eliminated
Canada Child Tax Benefit (CCTB)	$70 increase for all eligible families (indexed)	

Source: Paul Martin, *Budget Plan 2000*, 82-90; Paul Martin, *Economic and Budget Update*, October 2000, 91-3

Table 2.8

Personal Top Marginal Income Tax (MIT) Thresholds

Canada	**(1999)**	**$60,000**	France	(1996)	$262,000
Britain	(1996)	$61,000	Italy	(1996)	$269,000
Canada	**(2001)**	**$100,000**	Japan	(1996)	$354,000
Germany	(1996)	$106,000	United States	(1996)	$371,000

Source: Don Drummond, 'Can a Mini-budget Offer "Vision"?' (Toronto, TD Economics, 11 Oct. 2000), 4.

system was undermining economic growth and reducing work incentives for entrepreneurs, skilled professionals, and the most highly skilled industrial workers (see Table 2.8).[33] The government's decision to commit almost two-thirds of its projected fiscal dividend to tax reduction also suggests a reversion to Finance's traditional strategy of disciplining pressures for increased spending by committing itself to tax reduction targets that it may implement promptly or defer, depending on the state of the economy and the government's finances. While flexible commitments for debt reduction and allowances for 'economic prudence' remain Finance's ultimate 'fudge factors' in managing its fiscal framework, its decision to create public expectations of tax reductions totalling close to $100 billion over six years (including those contained in the February 2000 budget) marks a significant departure from its ultra-cautious budgetary policies of recent years.

However, the promised tax reductions appear to have served their political purpose. Martin's budget proposals, combined with the Alliance's pre-election decision to retain a 25 per cent top marginal tax rate on personal income over $100,000 for at least five years, blurred the distinctions between the two parties' proposals sufficiently that they did not become a major issue during the election campaign.[34] A study published by the left-leaning Canadian Centre for Policy Alternatives during the campaign noted some degree of convergence on the overall scale of tax reductions among the Liberals, Alliance, and Progressive Conservatives, with the New Democrats alone challenging the policy consensus by allocating 72 per cent of the fiscal dividend to increased spending (see Table 2.9).[35] Some differences remained—notably the balance between tax reduction and spending, the number of lower-income families exempted from taxation, the relative size of tax reductions for upper-income families—but they lacked the political visibility or transparency to shift large numbers of votes from one party to another.

While the parties traded accusations of fiscal irresponsibility during the campaign, these were largely neutralized by the largely technical nature of the discussion and the admission by Liberal candidate and former Royal Bank Chief Economist John McCallum that the government's own proposals risked a return to deficit financing.[36]

Taking Care of Business

The October 2000 budget's treatment of business issues reinforced the emerging bi-partisan and federal-provincial consensus on business taxation and the taxation of investment income, while drawing significant distinctions between the Liberals and the Alliance on support for research, innovation, and high-technology industries. Responding to the growing mobility of capital, the budget accelerated the planned reduction of corporate income taxes and reduced the inclusion rate for capital gains[37] to 50 per cent of taxable income.

Table 2.9

Total Costs of Party Platforms over a Five-Year Horizon ($ billions)

	Liberals	**Alliance**	**PC**	**NDP**
Tax Cuts	100.5	115.4	121.9	33.2
Spending	49.9	11.3	7.4	125.1
Debt reduction	22.0	30.0	25.1	16.0
Economic prudence	9.5	9.5	none	none
Total platform	**181.9**	**166.2**	**154.4**	**174.8**

Source: A. Yalnizyan, 'What Would They Do with the Surplus?' (Ottawa: Canadian Centre for Policy Alternatives, November 2000), 8.

Martin's February 2000 budget had committed the government to reducing general corporate income taxes from the current 28 per cent to 21 per cent—the current level for manufacturing industries—by 2005, while proposing a token 1 per cent reduction in 2001 and leaving the schedule for future cuts vague. The October 2000 budget announced the government's plans to reduce corporate income taxes by 1-2 percentage points annually over four years, effectively matching the tax cut schedule previously tabled by the Canadian Alliance. These changes responded to criticisms by market-oriented economists and business groups that marginal corporate tax rates were increasingly out of line with those of Canada's major trading competitors. They also reflected concerns raised by Finance Department research that growing numbers of corporations were locating a larger share of their high value-added activities outside Canada, while shifting low-margin activities to Canada to take advantage of the differences between Canadian tax rates and those of its trading partners.[38]

The capital gains tax cuts were a response to persistent lobbying by high-technology industries, many of whose highly mobile employees are compensated with stock options, and to the recommendations of prominent economists to reduce taxation of capital income to levels comparable to those of the United States. These changes also matched the reductions in capital gains inclusion rates announced in Ontario's May 2000 budget—bringing Canadian capital gains taxes into rough parity with the taxation of long-term capital gains in the United States, and matching the policy proposals advanced earlier by the Alliance. In a practical gesture to both small business owners and venture capitalists, Martin also extended the capital gains free rollover on investments, originally introduced in his February budget, from $500,000 to $2 million for businesses with assets under $50 million.[39]

Martin also used the budget to highlight the differences between the Liberal government's approach to promoting research and innovation in the 'new economy' and that of the Alliance—emphasizing its support for high-technology industries, university research, export-oriented industries, and access to skills training and education. While most of these announcements reflected incremental changes in existing policies, they reinforced the politics of selective activism whereby the government has sought to focus much of its increased spending on policies intended to promote the extension of the knowledge-based economy and improved access to education and skills training. These measures are consistent with the politics of managerial liberalism pursued by Martin in his budgets since 1997.

The October 2000 budget also promised to allocate $10 billion of the anticipated $15 billion surplus for the 2000-1 fiscal year to debt reduction, while reiterating the government's promise to maintain its annual $3 billion contingency fund—the source of its previous payments against the debt. Martin's gesture was intended to fend off criticisms from the financial community and the Alliance opposition that the government is not really serious about debt reduction, while making use of unusually high levels of economic and revenue growth to offset growing inflationary pressures.[40]

CONCLUSION

The fiscal windfall resulting from Martin's careful stewardship over seven years and the higher than expected growth of the North American economy during the past year provided him with sufficient surpluses to prime the Liberals' electoral pump while continuing to pursue the medium-term policy goals of more competitive taxes, reduced debts, and targeted spending increases suggested by managerial liberalism.

Even though the Liberals chose not to emphasize either their fiscal record or their proposed tax cuts in the recent election campaign, Martin's budgets represent a clear attempt to set the national agenda in fiscal, economic, and social policy while retaining control over the levers of power. While yielding to political pressures from his colleagues for significant increases in public spending, he has succeeded in targeting much of these to activities that are, for the most part, consistent with his overall policy goals. The increased transfers contained in his February 2000 promises of increased child tax benefits dwarf the much smaller amounts earmarked for parallel provincial programs. Martin's changes to personal income taxes, while consistent with the Liberal rhetoric of 'targeting', have begun to reverse the decline in living standards experienced by many middle-class Canadians as a result of stagnant income growth and higher taxes during the 1990s. His acceleration in tax reductions to businesses and investors, while having limited political appeal outside business circles, reduces the threat of capital flight that has forced most major industrial countries to pursue similar measures in recent years.

Martin's careful balancing of interests is a far cry from the inflammatory rhetoric and political polarization that characterized the 2000 election campaign. However, by making it serve both the political objectives of the government's re-election campaign and the continuing policy objectives of managerial liberalism, Martin has established his claim to be not only the longest-serving finance minister of the postwar era, but also the most effective.

The looming slowdown in the American economy, which has led most economists to reduce their forecasts for Canada's economic growth in 2001 (see Table 2.10), reinforces the timeliness of Ottawa's personal tax cuts, which are intended to stimulate the domestic economy just as export-driven growth begins to falter.[41] However, the federal government's ability to deliver on its tax reduction promises without resorting to deficit spending will depend on its willingness to limit the overall growth of its spending within the annual 3 to 4 per cent range for inflation and population growth outlined in its February and October 2000 budgets.

It remains to be seen whether either Martin or Prime Minister Chrétien will remain in office long enough to implement the fiscal strategy outlined in the October 2000 budget—or whether the

Table 2.10

Spinning the Economic Crystal Ball
Consensus Private Sector Forecasts for Real GDP Growth

	February 2000 Federal budget	**October 2000** Federal budget	**January 2001***
	— per cent —		
2000	3.5	4.7	5.0
2001	2.9	3.5	3.0
2002	n/a	3.1	3.6

* Average of January 2001 forecasts by Canada's five largest chartered banks.
Sources: *Budget Plan, 2000*; *Economic and Fiscal Update*, October 2000.

competition among Liberal factions seeking to influence the possible leadership succession will disrupt their carefully calculated balance between the demands of managerial and distributive liberalism. However, if their track record of the past seven years is any guide to future performance, it is not unreasonable to expect the continuation of the cautious managerial liberalism, combined with a series of incremental policy changes in response to changing political and economic circumstances.

NOTES

1 James Q. Wilson, ed., *The Politics of Bureaucracy* (New York: Basic Books, 1980); Theodore Lowi, *The End of Liberalism* (New York: W.W. Norton, 1985).
2 Canada, *Office of the Auditor General, Human Resources Development Canada: Grants and Contributions* (Ottawa, Oct. 2000), chap. 11 .
3 Canada, *Agenda: Jobs and Growth–A New Framework for Economic Policy* (Ottawa, Oct. 1994).
4 The fiscal framework consists of the specific targets for revenues, spending, and budget balances that provide the financial context for government budgets, and the economic assumptions that assist governments in setting them.
5 Liberal Party of Canada, *Securing Our Future Together: Preparing Canada for the Twenty-First Century* ['Red Book II: The Liberal Plan'] (Ottawa, 1997), 28.
6 The public budgetary process is the process of testing and mobilizing public and interest group opinion to frame, communicate, promote, and legitimize economic and social agendas outlined in budget speeches and related legislation. Geoffrey Hale, *The Politics of Taxation in Canada* (Peterborough, ON: Broadview Press, forthcoming), chap. 5.
7 Correspondence, senior Finance Department official.
8 Canada, *The Budget Plan 1998: Strong Economy & Secure Society*, (Ottawa, 24 Feb. 1998), chap. 4.
9 Canada, *The Budget Plan 1999: Building Today for a Better Tomorrow* (Ottawa, 16 Feb. 1999).
10 Government of Canada and the Governments of the Provinces and Territories, *A Framework to Improve the Social Union for Canadians* [First Ministers' Meeting, Ref.#800-037/01] (Ottawa: Canadian Intergovernmental Conference Secretariat, 4 Feb. 1999); 'Canada's Social Union', *Policy Options/Options politiques* 19, 9 (Nov. 1998); 'Improving the Competitiveness and Standard of Living of Canadians: Common Position of Provincial and Territorial Finance Ministers', 2 Dec. 1999.

11 Geoffrey Hale, 'Only a Small Step Toward Restoring Living Standards', *Policy Options/Options politiques* (Mar. 1999): 51-4; Ken Battle, 'Credit Corrosion: Bracket Creep's Evil Twin' (Ottawa: Caledon Institute, Dec. 1999); Geoffrey Hale, 'Managing the Fiscal Dividend: The Politics of Selective Activism', in Leslie A. Pal, ed., *How Ottawa Spends 2000-2001: Past Imperfect, Future Tense* (Toronto: Oxford University Press, 2000), 59-94.

12 Monte Solberg, MP, 'The Single Rate Tax' (Ottawa: Reform Party of Canada, 27 Jan. 2000); Scott Brison, MP, 'Creating a Culture of Opportunity' (Ottawa: Progressive Conservative Party of Canada, 2 Feb. 2000); Canada, *The Budget Plan 2000: Better Finances, Better Lives* (Ottawa, 28 Feb. 2000).

13 Hale, 'Managing the Fiscal Dividend'; Canada, *Annual Financial Report of the Government of Canada, Fiscal Year 1999-2000* (Ottawa: Department of Finance, 20 Sept. 2000).

14 Canada, *Economic Statement and Budget Update* (Ottawa, 16 Oct. 2000).

15 Correspondence, senior Finance Department official; interview, Prime Minister's Office. These contacts reinforce Donald Savoie's findings in *Governing from the Centre* (Toronto: University of Toronto Press, 1999), chap. 6.

16 Hale, 'Managing the Fiscal Dividend', 70-4.

17 In accrual accounting, income and expenses are reported for the year in which they are earned and incurred, respectively, even though cash receipts and payments may take place during another fiscal period. A business or self-employed person normally 'earns' income in the fiscal period in which goods or services are invoiced to a customer, not that in which payment is received.

18 *Annual Financial Report, 1999-2000*.

19 Don Drummond, 'Can a Mini-budget Offer "Vision"?' (Toronto: TD Economics, 11 Oct. 2000), 1.

20 Ronald D. Kneebone and Kenneth J. McKenzie, 'Fiscal Policy in Canada', *Canadian Public Policy* 25, 4 (Dec. 1999): 483-502.

21 Armine Yalnizyan, 'What Would They Do with the Surplus?' (Ottawa: Canadian Centre for Policy Alternatives, Nov. 2000), 8.

22 The Liberals' successful effort to demonize the Alliance during the election was noted by many commentators, some with approval, others more sardonically. Charles Gordon, 'Ontario Voters Slay the Two-Tiered, Creationist Monster', *The Ottawa Citizen*, 28 Nov. 2000.

23 Canada, Privy Council Office, 'New Federal Investments to Accompany the Agreements on Health Renewal and Early Childhood Developments' (Ottawa, 11 Sept. 2000); Health Canada, 'Minister Rock Releases Final List of Health Transition Fund Projects', Release # 2000-100 (Ottawa, 13 Oct. 2000).

24 'Healthcare (64%) continues to be the issue which Canadians feel should receive the greatest attention from Canada's leaders. Education (24%) is second, followed by deficit/debt/government spending (18%).' Ipsos-Reid Ltd., 'Federal Election Poll November 12, 2000'. See web site: www.ipsos-reid.com/media/content/displaypr.cfm?id_to_view=1111

25 'Provincial and territorial governments will use this increased funding to promote healthy pregnancy, birth and infancy; improve parenting and family supports; strengthen early childhood development, learning and care; and strengthen community supports.' 'Supporting Families and Children: Government of Canada Initiatives' (Ottawa: Human Resources Development Canada, 20 Sept. 2000).

26 Kevin B. Kerr, 'Bill C-44: An Act to Amend the Employment Insurance Act', LS-373E (Ottawa: Library of Parliament, 5 Oct. 2000); Alice Nakamura, 'Make EI Fairer' (Toronto: C.D. Howe Institute, 17 Oct. 2000).

27 'Proposed Changes to Employment Insurance Legislation', Release # 00-66 (Ottawa: Human Resources Development Canada, 28 Sept. 2000).

28 Sherri Torjman, 'Employment Insurance Isn't Doing Its Job', *The Globe and Mail* [Toronto], 17 Feb. 2000, A15; S. McCarthy, 'Liberals Planning to Restore Money to UI Program', *The Globe and Mail* [Toronto], 20 Mar. 2000.

29 Giles Gherson, 'Cabinet Split Stays PM's Hand on EI Changes', *The National Post,* 29 June 2000, A10; Yalnizyan, 'What Would They Do with the Surplus?' 28.

30 Standing Committee on Finance, *Budget 2000: New Era ... New Plan*, First Report (Ottawa, House of Commons, Dec. 1999), chap. 2.

31 Paul Martin, *Economic and Fiscal Update*, 2 Nov.1999, 17-18.

32 Private sector economists advising the Department of Finance projected budget surpluses over five years of $121 million in October 2000, not including $23 billion in additional spending contained in the federal-provincial agreement of September 2000 or $3.5 billion in additional EI benefits announced earlier. Eric Beauchene, 'Surpluses to Total $121B by 2006', *The Ottawa Citizen*, 11 Oct. 2000.

33 Interviews, Department of Finance; Don Drummond, 'Formulating the Federal Budget', presentation to Canadian Centre for Management Development conference (Ottawa, mimeo, May 2000); Drummond, 'Can a Mini-budget Offer "Vision"?'

34 Opinion polls published during the campaign suggested that the budget had largely pre-empted the Alliance's goal of 'owning' the tax cut issue, especially in Ontario and Quebec. Ipsos-Reid Ltd., 'Federal Election Poll November 2, 2000.'

35 Yalnizyan, 'What Would They Do?', 8.

36 Alan Toulin, 'Liberal Candidate Backtracks on Red Book Spending', *The National Post,* 9 Nov. 2000.

37 Inclusion rate for capital gains: the capital gains made on the sale of property and other assets have been subject to income taxation in Canada since 1971. To reduce double taxation and the effects of inflation on gains held over an extended period, taxes were only applied to 50 per cent of capital gains between 1971 and 1987. This is the 'inclusion rate'. Increased U.S. taxes on capital gains permitted the Canadian government to increase the inclusion rate on capital gains to 75 per cent between 1988 and 1990. Following changes to U.S. capital gains tax rules, economists estimate that an inclusion rate of 50 per cent would result in a roughly equal tax rate on capital gains for upper-income earners in Canada and the United States. Jack M. Mintz and Thomas A. Wilson, 'Capitalizing on Cuts to Capital Gains Taxes', (Ottawa, Oct. 2000) *Commentary # 137* (Toronto: C.D. Howe Institute, February 2000).

38 Interview, Department of Finance. For recent discussion of the competitive business tax environment, see David Conklin and Darroch A. Robertson, 'Tax Havens: Investment Distortions and Policy Options', *Canadian Public Policy* 25, 3 (Sept.1999): 333-44; Jack M. Mintz, 'Why Canada Must Undertake Business Tax Reform Soon' (Toronto: C.D. Howe Institute, 4 Nov. 1999); Duanjie Chen, 'The Marginal Effective Tax Rate: The Only Tax Rate That Matters in Capital Allocation' (Toronto: C.D. Howe Institute, 22 Aug. 2000).

39 Capital gains free rollover is a tax preference intended to foster venture capital investments in small Canadian businesses by allowing investors and business owners to defer up to $2 million in capital gains taxes when selling their shares in eligible small businesses if these profits are reinvested in another eligible small business within four months. *Budget Plan, 2000*, Annex 7, 233-6; 'Notice of Ways and Means Motion to Amend the Income Tax Act' (Ottawa: Department of Finance, 18 Oct. 2000), paragraph 15.

40 Don Drummond, a former senior Finance Department official recently appointed Chief Economist of the Toronto-Dominion Bank, notes that 'at 86 per cent, the combined federal and provincial debt ratio is 12 percentage points higher than it was 10 years ago. ... We were pretty much considered a fiscal basket case at that time, so we shouldn't be breaking out the champagne yet.... A substantial amount of debt should be retired this year and next while the surpluses are large and the economy hot.' Drummond, 'Can a Mini-budget Offer "Vision"?', 1-2.

41 'Probably the most important contributor to the performance of the Canadian economy over the near-term are the spate of tax cuts announced by the Minister of Finance just before the election.' John Clinkard, 'Outlook for Canada', (Toronto: CIBC Economics, 11 Jan. 2001), 2.

3

How Ottawa Plans: The Evolution of Strategic Planning

EVERT A. LINDQUIST

> Planning attempts to relate and compare policies and programs originally developed within various sectors, as an ensemble. Planning implies political choice of overriding criteria within which the competing claims of different sectors to the limited resources of government will be rationalized. It implies the identification by ministers of dominant concerns to which policies and programs conceived within the parochial context of a given sector must be bent.
>
> Richard French,
> *How Ottawa Decides*, 1980

With great pomp and circumstance, at the beginning of each session of Parliament, the Governor General of Canada reads the Speech from the Throne (SFT), which outlines the government's legislative intentions for that session. The event occasions a great flurry of interest among ministers and top officials and fleeting interest in the media, and then seems to be quickly forgotten. At the very least, observers see the reading of the Speech as one of the great symbolic moments in Ottawa; at the very most, they see it as a tactical opportunity, where proponents of certain policy ideas gain momentary advantage.

At the highest levels of the federal government, however, the SFT is now understood as an important part of a broader, rolling process of strategic planning within the government of Canada. From an outside perspective, how Ottawa plans may not appear to have changed much over the years. Many of the traditional high-water marks of the budgeting and legislative cycle persist: Speeches from the Throne, cabinet committee meetings and retreats, transition management, and the budget. Despite the concerns about the liabilities of the formal priority-setting and planning systems of the early 1970s and in the early 1980s, strategic planning is alive and well in Ottawa, and constitutes a critical part of public management and governance. A critical question that has confronted senior officials is how to adapt planning processes designed in the 1960s and the 1970s to deal with a fundamentally different political environment, which is faster-paced, more complicated, and arguably more transparent. Indeed, a crucial question for those responsible for guiding this process is how to use these 'traditional' occasions in a more strategic manner in order to deal with the evolving complexities and challenges of government.

Much of the literature concerning policy-making in the federal government focusses on how individual decisions are made—what could broadly be termed the operational side of government—factors such as the composition of cabinet, how documentation is prepared for cabinet meetings, how those meetings are chaired, and how ministers develop specific policy proposals and move them through the cabinet committee process to reach a final decision and obtain funding in the budget.[1] However, less has been written on the government of Canada's strategic planning function—that is, how the government sets its overall priorities in the first place. Generally, it is these priorities that tend to dictate which types of policy proposals get developed and funded over the course of a mandate.

This chapter begins with a brief review of the literature on strategic planning in the federal government and more general theories of planning. It then examines the key institutions and the planning cycle, and reviews the most recent two rounds of the planning cycle under the Liberal government, particularly with respect to managing the transition from deficits to surpluses. It concludes by reviewing the recent experience with strategic planning and considers the implications for future governments.

THE RISE AND FALL OF PLANNING: FROM RATIONAL TO STRATEGIC PERSPECTIVES

Any attempt to discuss the state of 'strategic planning' in the government of Canada is a daunting task: at any given time, strategic planning proceeds at different levels within and across the many organizations that comprise the federal government. Moreover, one must be precise when invoking the term 'planning', since in Ottawa the concept can quickly lead to unpleasant flashbacks about experiments with ambitious and flawed planning systems designed during the 1970s. Following Richard French's epigraph to this chapter, we want to assess the systems currently in place to mesh political priorities with the plans of the federal public service, and this implies focussing on, but not limiting the analysis to, the role of the Plans and Consultation Division of the Privy Council Office (PCO). Later, the chapter will describe in more detail the actors and processes involved in strategic planning.

The Rise and Fall of Rational Planning in Ottawa
For many practitioners and students of Canadian public administration, strategic planning will forever be associated with the late 1960s and the 1970s, when successive governments formalized different facets of the cabinet decision-making process and also expanded associated bureaucratic capacities. Formalization was secured first by creating a Planning committee of cabinet (later, Planning and Priorities [P&P]), and then by introducing more systematic procedures for identifying priorities, submitting documents for consideration by cabinet, and ensuring that issues were vetted by relevant ministers and departments. In 1969, Michael Pitfield was appointed as the first Deputy Secretary of the Plans Division of the PCO; he then created a Planning and Priorities secretariat (PPS).[2] More generally, the central machinery of government was growing with the creation of the

Treasury Board Secretariat (TBS), the expansion of secretariats within the PCO, and, in the early 1970s, the emergence of several ministries of state.[3]

These developments were informed by systems and planning theory, cybernetics, and program, planning, and budgeting systems then in vogue, which suggested that governments think broadly about problems, however defined (economic, social, environmental, international, health, etc.), and develop comprehensive perspectives on how to intervene to solve them. Moreover, ministers and officials were to acquire information, identify priorities, and develop policy responses in a more orderly, systematic, and coordinated manner. Efforts were made to rank priorities, undertake policy reviews, and to ask questions like 'What kind of Canada do we want in the year 2000?'[4] Finally, there was considerable optimism about the potential for applying 'knowledge' from the rapidly expanding sciences and social sciences disciplines to the practical problems that confronted governments. A crucial implication for governments was that requisite capacities had to be installed at the centre in order that these ambitions and potentialities be realized.

The early optimism about more formal planning was soon tempered by experience. Systematic efforts to have the cabinet and the PPS identify priorities and develop long-range plans were challenged by unanticipated problems and the hurly-burly of electoral politics during the early 1970s. Under the minority government from 1972 to 1974, the time-frames for 'planning' were shortened and the goals became more pragmatic.[5] The early attempt to bring rational and comprehensive planning to Ottawa culminated in the Priorities Exercise of 1974-5, which followed the July 1974 election.[6] This process, which began with interviews of ministers by Prime Minister's Office (PMO) and PCO officials to identify priorities, then engaged ministers at a cabinet retreat, the Liberal caucus, P&P, the full cabinet, each department, and deputy ministers as a collectivity. Teams of TBS and PCO officials recombined departmental initiatives in the different priority areas, and then forwarded them as memoranda to cabinet in July 1975, where they were subsequently ignored. The result was that 'planning' was seen as excessively bureaucratic and largely irrelevant.[7]

Following the introduction of wage and price controls in the early 1970's, and the unilateral announcement by Prime Minister Trudeau of significant budget cuts after the Bonn Summit in 1976, the Policy and Expenditure Management System (PEMS) was introduced in 1979 to provide greater fiscal discipline and to better connect priority-setting and resource allocation decisions.[8] PEMS was designed to be a planning system premised on 'workable rationality', which decentralized decision-making even as it sought more strategic coherence between the policy, budgeting, and planning functions.[9] But the experience of the early 1980s quickly revealed a system too complicated and unwieldy for ministers and officials alike, and too easily subverted by skilful political and bureaucratic entrepreneurs and by intervening events. Beginning with Prime Minister John Turner in September 1984, and then under both governments led by Prime Minister Brian Mulroney, virtually all of the key features of PEMS were dismantled, with the exception of the department-based strategic overviews and multi-year operational plans.[10]

In short, Ottawa's experiments with planning systems during the early 1970s and the early 1980s were swept along with the broader indictment of 'rational, comprehensive, synoptic decision-making', which is usually associated with big, inefficient government.[11] The view was that the 'weight' of these systems, the proliferation of rules and actors, did not produce sufficient benefits and sufficiently greater strategic direction.[12]

New Conceptions of Strategic Planning in the Private and Public Sectors

Despite the decline in confidence in formal systems for strategic planning, the planning function remains an integral part of policy-making for large-scale organizations of all kinds: their leaders must identify medium-term challenges, establish priorities over the planning horizon, and ensure that the organization stays on track to meet key priorities or adjusts course in rapidly shifting decision-making environments. This has led to new perspectives on strategic planning in the private sector and the public sector.

Private sector theorists now emphasize more flexible, collaborative approaches to planning. Mintzberg has argued that formal planning is typically about 'programming' and monitoring performance, which only works under certain conditions.[13] He sees planning as simultaneously a retrospective and a forward-looking activity. He suggests that strategic planning involves discerning or finding *emergent* strategies, analysing and forwarding options for consideration by decision-makers, and promoting strategic thinking through challenge, scenario-building, and creativity.[14] Others argue that planning must anticipate uncertainty, or otherwise be undermined or discredited.[15] Stacey calls on leaders to balance the need for order and stability with the need to deal with uncertainty and to generate new ideas and strategies—this affects how organizations are designed, and what cultures need to be fostered within them. He recommends flexible structures, a commitment to learning (as well as 'contention and dialogue'), a willingness to embrace intuition and alternative perspectives, and modesty about capacities and strategies. Floyd and Wooldridge characterize 'large, established companies in technologically dynamic, complex, and competitive business environments' as requiring breakthrough ideas.[16] In their view, this 'puts a new premium on new ideas generated at the operating level and creates a shift in the "strategic" responsibility within organizations.'[17] Accordingly, middle managers must see how their ideas connect to broader strategic possibilities, and executives must function more as 'strategic architects' (as opposed to innovators), dedicated to increasing the chances that ideas gain support from elsewhere in an organization. This literature suggests that in a rapidly changing world, organizations can be more strategic by better sharing of information, by anticipating different possibilities, by building flexible capacities and plans, by increasing levels of trust and sharing values, and by devoting time for dialogue, exploration, and commitment-building.

Several observers have proposed new lenses for describing the strategic and other work of central agencies, including network perspectives. Lindquist suggests that central agencies can be seen as 'organizational baskets' of smaller bureaus at the nodes of distinct administrative networks that span a public service, and that these networks lever the resources of other actors.[18] Rhodes argues that central institutions are no longer fulcrums for power, because the state has been 'hollowed-out' with the advent of alternative service delivery models, deficit reduction, globalization, trade agreements, and new international bodies.[19] The Organisation for Economic Co-operation and Development's (OECD) Public Management (PUMA) Service observes that all governments are now challenged by less stability, fewer well-defined boundaries, less robust concepts, and globalization. Consequently, governments and their central institutions have the challenge of 'managing multiple layers of policy making without losing sight of their own national policy agendas', and their main role is increasingly that of 'strategic enabler and co-ordinator of other actors in public policy processes.'[20] PUMA suggests that governments should (1) create coherence in the face of complexity in order to promote strategic direction and consistency, and to manage horizontally; (2) accept the fact that democratic politics produces incoherence; and (3) create sufficient capacity to achieve coherence through process, which entails strong centres, organizational flexibility, the linking of policy priorities to budget constraints, increasing cross-sectoral co-operation, and the gathering, filtering, and sharing of information.[21]

The challenges for strategic planning outlined by PUMA are strikingly similar to ideas from the literature on strategic planning in the private sector. Less stock is put on structural change and formal planning, and more on increasing flexibility in the face of turbulence, developing vision and coherence, cultivating relationships, sharing information, and using existing processes to achieve strategic objectives more effectively.

AN OVERVIEW OF OTTAWA'S PLANNING CYCLE

Before discussing the current strategic planning cycle, it is necessary to present some background concerning key bureaus. The PCO functions as the prime minister's department, serving as a source of professional, non-partisan public service advice on the complete range of issues, social, economic, international, security, machinery of government, and others. The PCO coordinates how policy proposals move through the cabinet committees and cabinet, and assists with monitoring their implementation. It has two major branches that oversee strategic planning: Operations, and Plans and Consultation. The other branches, which we cannot review in detail here, include Intergovernmental Affairs, Security and Intelligence, and Privy Council and Counsel, respectively led by a deputy minister, a deputy secretary, and a deputy clerk[22] (see Figure 3.1).

The Plans and Consultation branch undertakes strategic planning and advises the prime minister on the overall management of the policy

68 HOW OTTAWA SPENDS

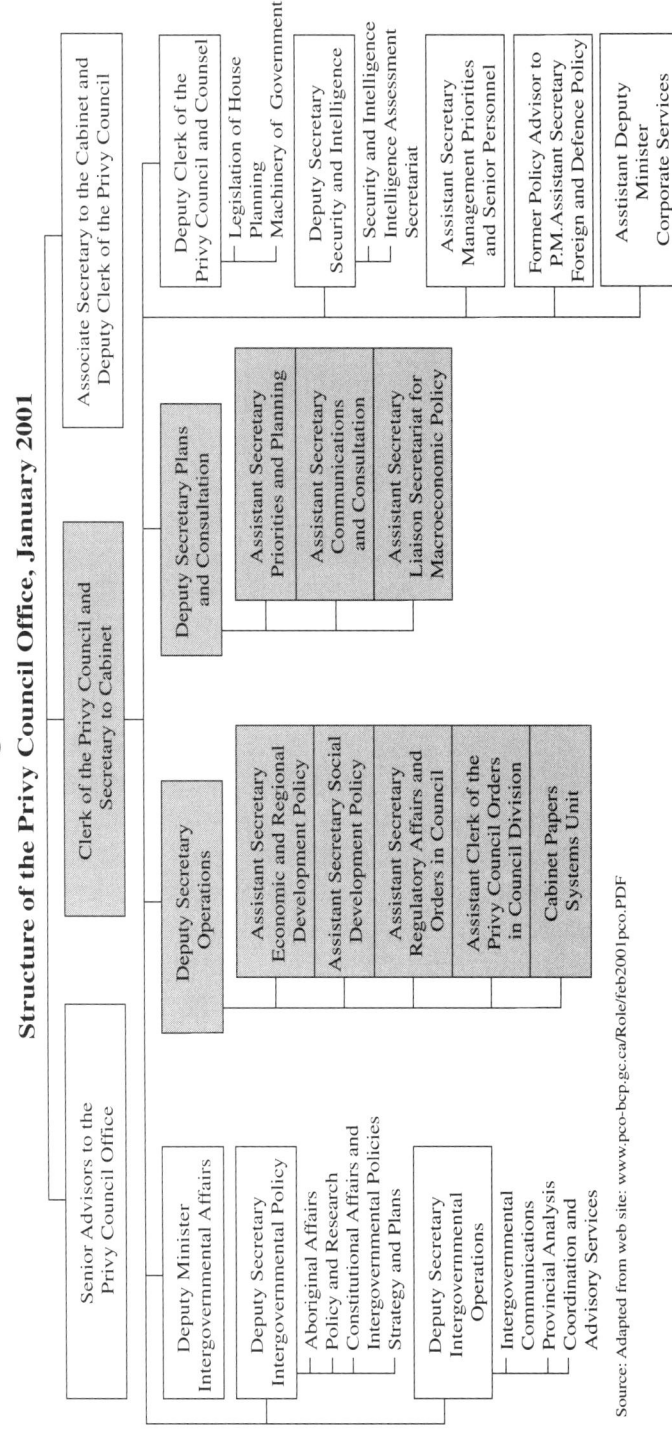

Figure 3.1

Structure of the Privy Council Office, January 2001

Source: Adapted from web site: www.pco-bcp.gc.ca/Role/feb2001pco.PDF

agenda. It manages the weekly meetings of full cabinet, which generally considers issues of broad strategic importance, and bi-annual cabinet planning sessions. The branch is comprised of three small secretariats:

- the Communications and Consultations secretariat provides advice on strategic communications planning, the cross-departmental coordination of communications, and outreach with citizens;
- the Liaison Secretariat for Macroeconomic Policy communicates with the Department of Finance and provides advice to the prime minister on economic and fiscal issues, federal budget planning, and expenditure management; and
- PPS consists of a deputy minister and several senior policy analysts. It handles strategic planning, and gives strategic policy advice to the prime minister and cabinet, assistance in the development of SFTs, and support for full cabinet and bi-annual planning sessions. PPS also prepares the Clerk for the meetings of the Coordinating Committee of Deputy Ministers policy committee and the weekly Deputy Ministers Breakfasts.[23]

The Operations branch manages day-to-day cabinet committee business. Policy proposals are considered in detail in the Cabinet Committee on the Social Union, the Cabinet Committee on the Economic Union, and the Special Committee of Council—not in meetings of the full cabinet.[24] The three committees are served by three secretariats: Social Development Policy, Economic and Regional Development Policy, and Regulatory Affairs and Orders-in-Council. The branch coordinates the inputs of departments and central agencies on cross-cutting issues, and the Cabinet Papers Systems Unit controls the flow of documents. As Schacter and Haid suggest, the Operations branch is more concerned with specific 'transactions' associated with policy decision-making, whereas Plans and Consultations deals with the 'strategic' issues confronting governments, although there are important linkages and overlaps between these functions.

Figure 3.2
The Planning Cycle at a Glance

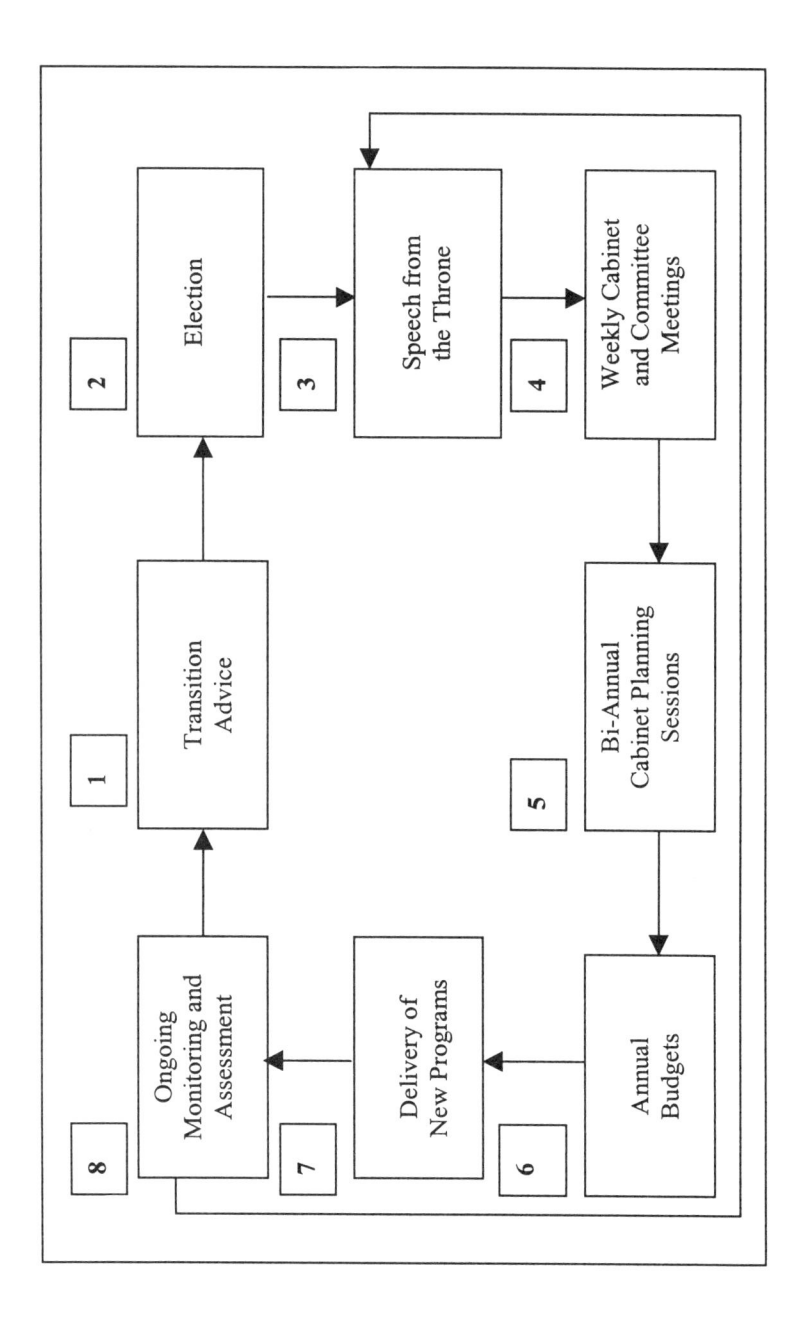

1. Transition Advice
2. Election
3. Speech from the Throne
4. Weekly Cabinet and Committee Meetings
5. Bi-Annual Cabinet Planning Sessions
6. Annual Budgets
7. Delivery of New Programs
8. Ongoing Monitoring and Assessment

Strategic planning by the federal government follows a reasonably well-defined cycle (see Figure 3.2), which includes preparing for government transitions, the SFT, regular meetings of the cabinet and its committees, twice-yearly cabinet retreats, the annual budget of the minister of Finance, and ongoing assessment of progress on government priorities.

Developing Transition Advice
Perhaps counter-intuitively, the planning cycle for the public service begins when an incumbent government nears the end of its electoral mandate (political parties engage in their own internal planning exercises before an election, including developing a policy platform and, in some cases, appointing a transition planning team). Immediately after taking office, the new or returning prime minister can expect from the Clerk of the Privy Council a detailed series of briefings on key issues for the government over the course of the new mandate. The material that the PCO prepares for these briefings, and the briefings that ministers receive from their respective deputy ministers, constitute the public service's transition policy advice.[25] PPS coordinates and rolls up this advice, which in recent years consists of detailed assessments of major trends and pressures facing the country and its citizens, key policy challenges and gaps, and proposed policy directions. Not only does this assist the new or incumbent prime minister with managing the transition, it is also intended to provide a 'road map' for managing the policy agenda over the course of the mandate. As is discussed later in more detail, developing this policy advice requires sustained effort and collaboration across government. Hence, the nine-month to one-year period leading to an anticipated election is a time of intense activity within PPS, as the secretariat works to develop this advice, often in close consultation with other central agencies and operating departments.

Preparing the Speech from the Throne
After proffering transition policy advice to the prime minister, the PCO turns to drafting the SFT. Read by the Governor General in the Senate chamber, the SFT officially opens each session of Parliament. It sets out the broad goals and directions of the government, and outlines its strategy to accomplish those goals. The PPS provides the public service's support to the PMO in the drafting of the SFT. Unlike preparing

transition advice, drafting the SFT involves extensive political input and direction: whereas the former represents the advice of public servants, the latter represents the government's undertakings to Canadians. The PMO and the PPS revise and refine the SFT on the basis of the party platform, campaign commitments, bilateral discussions with ministers and senior department officials, and other informal consultations. The Governor General's input is also sought. The full cabinet reviews the complete text of the speech and offers its final direction prior to presentation. Ultimately, there should be a synergy between the proposed policy directions recommended by the public service and the directions set out in the SFT. Transition policy advice is considered successful for PPS if it becomes the basis or key reference for drafting the SFT. If the transition advice received from the public service is sound, the government is more likely to accept the associated policy directions, and bilateral discussions between political leaders and the PCO will be more productive and forward-looking.

Cabinet and Cabinet Committee Meetings
Once the government articulates its commitments to citizens and its over-arching priorities for the mandate in an SFT, the focus turns to designing and implementing specific initiatives. Typically this is handled through the cabinet committee process, which is supported by officials in the Operations branch. Ministers direct their departments to develop detailed policy proposals that respond to the directions and specific commitments outlined in the SFT (although over the course of a mandate ministers will develop additional proposals in response to evolving demands). Such proposals are brought forward to one of the two policy Committees of Cabinet—the Cabinet Committee for the Economic Union for matters relating principally to the economic sphere, or the Cabinet Committee for the Social Union for primarily social issues—for debate and discussion of the various available options. For example, to meet a government commitment to enhance the well-being of Canadian children, the minister of Human Resources Development Canada might, following consultation with the ministers of Health and of Indian and Northern Affairs, bring forward to cabinet committee a proposal to enhance community supports for early childhood development. In some cases, a proposal will be reviewed in a joint meeting of the committees (see Figure 3.3). Once a committee reaches

a decision, the recommendation is transmitted to the full cabinet for ratification. In addition to its role as final arbiter of the recommendations flowing from cabinet committees on specific policy initiatives, the cabinet provides a venue for consideration of broader strategic issues that hold the potential to affect the entire agenda. Full cabinet also provides a forum for discussion of issues that are neither primarily economic nor social, such as foreign and defence issues.

Bi-Annual Cabinet Planning Sessions
Twice a year, the cabinet meets for a two-day planning session, once in late spring and again in late fall. These sessions provide an opportunity for the cabinet to take stock of the government's progress on key commitments and to plan for the future. Economic and fiscal updates, as well as political updates and polling information, are presented. PPS works with relevant departments to develop presentations that take stock of the government's progress on key agenda priorities, the gaps that remain, and possible future policy directions. Together, this information provides a sense of the scope for government action on stated priorities. Ministers and all secretaries of state are given the opportunity to speak and comment on issues.[26] Although retreats typically do not yield decisions, the prime minister uses them to gauge views on priority issues and to receive the advice of his colleagues. These discussions are important for the Clerk and PPS officials to monitor; it is a means of discerning themes that may inform strategic and operational planning as well as define a concrete work agenda for central officials and deputy ministers. For example, following a spring retreat, officials are in a position to identify their 'summer' work priorities so that they can prepare for the fall session of Parliament.

Annual Budgets
Since the late 1980s, the budget is typically tabled in late February of each year.[27] It sets the fiscal framework within which departments must work to deliver on government priorities, and provides a high-profile moment when governments can 'deliver' on commitments identified in the SFT. The budget announces the launch of new initiatives and sets aside the funds required for their implementation. In most cases, the lead ministers and their departments will flesh out more detailed policy proposals for these new initiatives and bring them to

Figure 3.3
The Committees of Cabinet (January 2001)

Economic Union	Social Union	Special Committee of Council
Chair: Ralph Goodale (Natural Resources) *Vice-Chair*: Arthur Eggleton (Defence) *Members*: David Collenette (Transport) David Anderson (Environment) Brian Tobin (Industry) Sheila Copps (Canadian Heritage) John Manley (Foreign Affairs and International Trade) Anne McLellan (Justice) Alfonso Gagliano (Public Works and Government Services) Martin Cauchon (National Revenue) Jane Stewart (Human Resources Development) Pierre Pettigrew (International Trade) Don Boudria (House Leader) Lyle Vanclief (Agriculture and Agri-food) Herb Dhaliwal (Fisheries and Oceans) Ronald Duhamel (Veterans Affairs, Western Economic Division, Francophonie) Claudette Bradshaw (Labour) Robert Thibault (Atlantic Canada)	*Chair*: Anne McLellan (Justice) *Vice-Chair*: Allan Rock (Health) *Members*: David Anderson (Environment) Ralph Goodale (Natural Resources) Sheila Copps (Canadian Heritage) Lawrence MacAulay (Solicitor General) Alfonso Gagliano (Public Works and Government Services) Jane Stewart (Human Resources) Stéphane Dion (Intergovernmental Affairs) Pierre Pettigrew (International Trade) Ronald Duhamel (Veterans Affairs, Western Economic Division, Francophonie) Claudette Bradshaw (Labour) Robert Nault (Indian Affairs and Northern Development) Maria Minna (International Cooperation) Elinor Caplan (Citizenship and Immigration)	*Chair*: Herb Gray (Deputy Prime Minister) *Vice-Chair*: Anne McLellan (Justice) *Members*: Alfonso Gagliano (Public Works and Government Services) Lucienne Robillard (Treasury Board) Don Boudria (House Government Leader) Lyle Vanclief (Agriculture and Agri-food) Herb Dhaliwal (Fisheries and Oceans) Ronald Duhamel (Veterans Affairs, Western Economic Division, Francophonie) Robert Nault (Indian Affairs and Northern Development) Sharon Carstairs (Senate Government Leader)

Treasury Board

Chair: Lucienne Robillard (Treasury Board)
Vice-Chair: Paul Martin (Finance)

Members:
Brian Tobin (Industry)
Arthur Eggleton (Defence)
Alfonso Gagliano (Public Works and Government Services)
Herb Dhaliwal (Fisheries and Oceans)

Alternates:
Herb Gray (Deputy Prime Minister)
Ralph Goodale (Natural Resources)
Anne McLellan (Justice)
Lawrence MacAulay (Solicitor General)
Don Boudria (House Government Leader)
Elinor Caplan (Citizenship and Immigration)
Sharon Carstairs (Senate Government Leader)

Secretaries of State:
Ethel Blondin-Andrew (Children and Youth)
Hedy Fry (Multiculturalism) (Status of Women)
David Kilgour (Latin America and Africa)
James Scott Peterson (International Financial Institutions)
Andrew Mitchell (Rural Development) (Federal Economic Development Initiative for Northern Ontario)
Gilbert Normand (Science, Research and Development)
Denis Coderre (Amateur Sport)
Rey Pagtakhan (Asia-Pacific)

Note: The Deputy Prime Minister, the Minister of Finance, and the President of the Treasury Board are ex-officio members of the following committees: Economic Union, Social Union, Special Committee of Council. The Leader of the Government in the House of Commons is an ex-officio member of the Social Union Committee.

Sources: Web site: www.canada.gc.ca/howgoc/cab/cab-com_e.html and www.canada.gc.ca/howgoc/cab/mini_e.html

cabinet committee for review. If the committee is satisfied that the policy is sufficiently developed to match the available funding, the package is sent to full cabinet for final ratification. In other instances, the budget provides funding for initiatives already supported by a Cabinet Committee earlier in the year, but for which no source of funding was identified at the time. The sponsoring minister effectively asks colleagues to provide 'approval in principle' to the detailed policy work supporting a proposed but 'unfunded' initiative, recognizing that without a source of funding it will not proceed to ratification by the cabinet and implementation.

Ongoing Monitoring and Assessment
At least twice a year, prior to the fall and spring sittings of Parliament, PPS develops 'six month notes' to brief the prime minister on key events and issues the government can expect to encounter over the next half year, and proposes strategies for managing the agenda. As needed, PPS prepares briefings for the prime minister on emerging issues that have the potential to affect the overall policy agenda. Along with reviews at the planning sessions, this ongoing monitoring and assessment informs the prime minister's decision to call an election, to develop a new SFT (which is often done at mid-mandate as a means of refreshing the government's agenda by launching a new session of Parliament), or to accelerate the government's efforts on certain issues.

THE RECENT EVOLUTION OF STRATEGIC PLANNING: PROGRAM REVIEW AND THE POST-DEFICIT AGENDA

Most students of public administration will be familiar with the elements of the planning cycle outlined above. They have been staples of planners and observers for close to three decades. What has changed in recent years, however, is the extent to which these enduring 'events' are integrated into an overarching process of mandate planning and adjustment. This section reviews how planning changed during the first two mandates of the Liberal governments led by Prime Minister Jean Chrétien in order to deal with the challenges associated with, first, deficit reduction and program restructuring (1994 to 1996), and then the post-deficit agenda (1997 to 2000).

The First Mandate: The Program Review and Deficit Reduction
The need to improve the state of federal government finances drove strategic planning during the first mandate, and this resulted in concerted medium-term planning through the Program Review process that affected all programs and resulted in the articulation of a new Expenditure Management System (EMS). During this process, however, the Clerk and the PPS set in motion several initiatives designed to anticipate priorities beyond the planning horizon associated with Program Review. Otherwise, aside from an improvement in communications between the Plans branch and the Operations branch, the main features of the planning cycle remained intact.

When the Chrétien government took office in 1993, the political environment was characterized by rising public attention to the federal deficit and debt. The annual federal deficit had reached $42 billion in the 1992-3 fiscal year, with the combined federal-provincial debt burden reaching 96 per cent of GDP. In addition, there was growing concern about the possibility of another referendum on Quebec sovereignty, and tensions in the federation concerning federal-provincial fiscal issues.[28] Consequently, the transition policy advice to the government focussed on resolving the fiscal crisis, scrutinizing and modernizing existing programs, and promoting national unity.

The government's planning was conditioned by the immediacy of the challenges facing the country, the restructuring of the public service by the previous government, and the well-articulated commitments in Liberal Red Book I. Accordingly, the PPS focussed on identifying and assembling relevant briefing materials from the Operations Branch secretariats, and from departments and agencies, to provide transition advice on immediate 'hot issues' rather than on medium- to long-term plans. In addition to initiating several sector-specific policy reviews, the prime minister announced a government-wide Program Review in February 1994. Beyond the deficit-reduction strategy and fiscal policy, this was the primary cross-government activity of the first mandate.

The Program Review was a strategic exercise designed to address the expenditure side of deficit reduction through a comprehensive review of all government programming; it was hoped that this might provide an opportunity to modernize the role of the federal government. Launched in the February 1994 budget speech, the initiative did not gather steam until mid-summer 1994; the final decisions about the three-year program reduction targets were announced in the February 1995 budget.[29] Although Program Review spanned the range of government programs, from a PPS perspective the challenge was to ensure coordination across departments, rather than to guide a horizontal policy-making exercise. Each department was given an expenditure reduction target by the Department of Finance that was consistent with the government's broad priorities, but specific proposals were developed by ministers and their respective departments.

Many central agencies and bureaus played important roles in the Program Review. PPS developed the underlying approach and policy tests, with input from the Machinery-of-Government secretariat, while staff from the TBS and the department of Finance provided perspectives on the department proposals. The department of Finance had identified specific expenditure targets for each department.[30] Department proposals were reviewed first by a committee of deputy ministers and then by a committee of ministers, both supported by a temporary secretariat in the PCO.[31] The government's expenditure management rules were tightened significantly. Under the EMS announced in the February 1995 budget, no policy proposal could be brought forward to Cabinet Committee without a source of funding identified in advance—whether through the budget, or through ministers' deciding to reallocate existing resources from other areas of their portfolio.

After the Program Review was set in motion, concern emerged that despite its commitment to achieving long-term stability in government finances it would foster short-term and department-specific perspectives on how to deal with a range of policy challenges. There was also worry about the erosion of the ability of the government to undertake medium- to longer-term policy development after a decade of austerity within the public service, which had focussed on streamlining 'overhead' at headquarters. In 1995, in response to these and other concerns, the Clerk launched several deputy minister task forces, including one on policy capacity and another on horizontal policy development.[32] The task forces presaged several initiatives in 1996, such as La Relève, and what would later be known as the Policy Research Initiative (PRI).[33] The latter effort is particularly pertinent to this chapter: the Clerk appointed two deputy ministers in October 1996 to lead more than 20 assistant deputy ministers (collectively called the Policy Research Committee) from across the public service to assess the main trends and pressures facing the country in the medium term.[34]

Preparation for the 1994 and 1996 SFTs followed the standard process: the PCO and the PMO canvassed departments for possible initiatives that could be included in the text of the speech, but departments were not further engaged by the centre. Priorities and themes for both SFTs emerged from a guarded drafting process involving PMO and PPS representatives. However, during 1996 PCO officials also agreed to encourage more regular communications between the Plans and the Operations branches. Weekly meetings were held, usually close to a week before meetings of the full cabinet. Moreover, PPS ensured that, depending on the substantive issues under consideration, the appropriate Operations staff would be involved in the preparations for important events in the planning process, such as cabinet retreats.

Preparing for the Second Mandate:
Determining the Post-Deficit Agenda
Planning for the next mandate began before the election, in late 1996. The prospect of a modest budget surplus meant that the overall policy agenda would no longer have deficit reduction as an integrating theme. PPS had to work with the government and the public service to articulate a new vision and policy agenda for the country. This involved tapping into the public service in new ways for the identification of challenges and priorities, and led to adjustments to the EMS.

In fall 1996, the Prime Minister requested that each of the chairs of the policy committees of cabinet work with colleagues to discuss and recommend priorities for the government over the next three years. The chairs prepared short discussion notes to inform the meetings of each committee. The results of these deliberations were presented by the respective committee chairs to ministerial colleagues at the November 1996 cabinet retreat. These deliberations informed budget decisions of the Minister of Finance and the Prime Minister, and identified possible priorities for election themes and the next mandate.

The political environment for strategic planning was markedly different in 1997. There was a consensus that the deficit was under control and even optimism about an emerging fiscal dividend. The prospects for federal-provincial collaboration appeared to be improving, following overtures by the federal government to address provincial concerns about the spending power and overlap and duplication. Increased fiscal flexibility, coupled with greater scope for collaboration, expanded the policy choices available to the government and had important implications for government-wide strategic planning. On the process side, this meant that collaboration would need to become an essential ingredient of strategic planning.

Following the cabinet retreat, PPS organized a retreat of deputy ministers in mid-November 1996 to take stock and to prepare for the next federal election. These deliberations were informed by three streams of information: summaries of the priorities identified by ministers at the cabinet retreat, presentations from deputy ministers about what they believed to be key issues and pressures confronting the country and the government, and a draft interim report from the Policy Research Committee.[35] This differed considerably from the system of submitting department-based ideas for consideration in the SFT. PPS officials took the results from both the cabinet and deputy minister retreats to develop a work plan for early 1997.

When developing transition policy advice in early 1997, PPS met with departments more than a hundred times over a two-month period. These meetings sought to build a shared framework for situating proposed policy directions. Immediately following the deputy ministers' retreat, the Policy Research Committee accelerated its activities along five broad thematic lines and several sub-committees were formed to probe particular topics within each area. The sub-committees were led by assistant deputy ministers from across the public service, and each had representation from many departments. The Deputy Secretary of Plans sat on the steering committee.[36] Interim reports were available by early spring, most notably the *Canada 2005* report. All of this would inform the transition advice for the prime minister, the drafting of the SFT, and broader mandate planning. It also would inform the transition advice given to newly appointed ministers by departments.

The federal election of 2 June 1997 returned the Liberal government to power. As was the case with the transition policy advice, PPS modified how the SFTs were crafted in 1997 and 1999. PPS sought to avoid the past practice of canvassing departments for 'lines' or initiatives for possible inclusion in the speech; rather, the goal was to work from the framework and assessments that informed the transition. PPS staff believed, first, that the complexity of the longer-term issues facing the country (such as Aboriginal and environmental issues) required cross-cutting work on solutions by departments. Second, if government choices would no longer be constrained by deficits, PPS felt that the leaders of the public service needed to develop a shared sense of why they were recommending certain sets of choices for the new mandate over others. Finally, PPS believed that the government should also consider adopting a similar approach to justify its strategic choices to citizens.

PPS argued that the SFT should develop and offer a vision for the future rather than a list of promises—thus, some effort was taken to reduce the litany of new or specific initiatives, since this might detract from communicating the overall story lines. The three SFTs since 1997 reveal a discernible difference in style, with more attention directed to citing accomplishments and goals to be pursued, and greater effort to develop themes across what would have previously been seen as distinct policy domains.[37] Rather than constituting a detailed set of commitments, the recent SFTs read more as a description of broad strategy. Since the SFTs were partly based on the transition advice, previous consultations with departments influenced the major policy directions set in the speech as well as any specific initiatives that were identified.

The evolution in strategic planning was linked to changes in the government's EMS and preparations for the Minister of Finance's budget. Under the EMS, which was formally introduced in the February 1995 budget, unfunded policy proposals could not be considered by cabinet committees.[38] Ministers first had to obtain funds, either in the budget or by re-allocating existing departmental resources. This limited the ability of ministers to propose new initiatives, test ideas, and prepare for contingencies.[39] Such restrictions made less sense in an era of fiscal surplus.

Several adjustments were made to the EMS rules in 1998. First, unfunded policy proposals could be reviewed by cabinet committees, which could be 'approved in principle' should sufficient funds become available in the future. Second, as the number of unfunded policy proposals mounted (partly flowing from the Liberal party's Red Book II), two rounds of priority-setting were instituted, one in the late fall and the other in the late spring, by means of Joint Cabinet Committee meetings. The rankings, assessments, and advice on timing of initiatives to address the most pressing priorities served as input for the Prime Minister and Minister of Finance as they made decisions on budget planning for the very limited 'space' available in the February 1998 budget (which could accommodate one or two new priorities), and for advance deliberations on the directions to be taken with the February 1999 budget.

IMPLICATIONS OF RECENT APPROACHES TO STRATEGIC PLANNING

Every Clerk, working with the Deputy Secretary of Plans and Consultation, attempts to adapt strategic planning practice to respond to the agenda of the prime minister and the government and to anticipate emerging challenges, sometimes years in advance. This involves preparing for and utilizing the key moments in the strategic planning cycle as shrewdly as possible. Ultimately, this is a balancing act that depends crucially on the style and priorities of the prime minister and key advisors, the state of finances and federal-provincial relations, the approach of the Clerk and top PCO officials, and the level of trust between the government and the senior public service.

The challenges and policy agendas of the first and second Chrétien governments were radically different, and these differences led to the adoption of different strategic orientations by PPS. The changes are subtle, but they make a significant difference when ministerial time continues to be at a premium and issues are ever more complicated.

Planning, not machinery, adjusted to new imperatives. As the government moved from a period of fiscal restraint to one of surplus, it had to identify new priorities and modify how it approached strategic planning. However, the government did not extensively change the machinery of government with respect to structure or process. Much was achieved by encouraging more open discussion of how best to allocate the fiscal dividend, and these changes contributed to improved collective cabinet decision-making, even while continuing to respect the prerogatives of the prime minister and the minister of Finance.

Planning began with preparing for transitions. More effort was taken to prepare advice and build a shared sense across departments of the priorities of future governments. PPS adopted a collaborative approach to identifying problems and opportunities, and more openness when developing strategic policy advice for a new government, even though the final briefing materials provided to a new prime minister were treated, of course, as secret. However, the underlying rationale for the recommended policy directions were widely understood by deputy ministers and communicated to all other interested parties.

The planning cycle was more integrated. The connection between different phases of the policy cycle was tighter. In part, this flowed naturally from a more regular, and more open, budget process. It is easy to forget that before the late 1980s, ministers of finance could announce budgets at any time.[40] A regular budget process means that governments and the public service can develop a broader rhythm to mandate planning and better utilize transition preparations, SFTs, cabinet retreats, and cabinet committee deliberations to identify priorities and to allocate resources through the budget process. A more open budget process also results in fewer policy 'surprises' for ministers and deputy ministers alike.

Creativity was used in conveying complex information. An enduring challenge for PPS is how to convey complex information for the prime minister and other ministers. PPS continues to experiment with graphics and layered ways to present detailed information in a succinct manner. This involves a constant dialogue with ministers and their staff about the most productive approaches. During the period under review, attempts were also made to build 'coherence' by developing meta-narratives to embrace a range of complex issues.[41] Not only can such narratives frame the government's policy choices, they can also be important means for communicating these choices to citizens. Dominant issues, such as deficit reduction, supply their own narratives. With choice and a multiplicity of possible initiatives, governments must construct integrating narratives and speak with 'one voice' to ensure that departments and citizens alike see the overall agenda.

Strategic planning became more horizontal, and deeper. Identifying government-wide policy objectives, and developing policy responses, necessarily involves collaboration across departments. But the efforts of PPS during the late 1990s to increase collaboration in support of transition planning, drafting SFTs, and priority-setting did not proceed in isolation—they were part of a public service-wide movement. Strategic planning proceeds at many levels of the government and its public service, and this also holds for horizontal management.[42] Even the PRI, for example, can be seen partly as an attempt to reach beyond the apex of the public service for ideas about the challenges confronting governments, and thus constitutes a step toward engaging both the 'middle' and 'outside experts' for strategic purposes. However, while progress was made with respect to better informing transition advice and preparing SFTs, some concern has emerged about whether there is sufficient collaboration across departments in support of specific proposals brought before Cabinet committees.

A role was established for medium-term policy research. The PRI did inform environmental scanning, which contributed to transition planning and to priority-setting by the government. Further efforts have been made to galvanize the government's policy research community, by encouraging collaboration, sharing findings, identifying new research priorities, and establishing a dedicated Secretariat. This stands in deep contrast to previous governments, which relied on instruments such as government councils and royal commissions to undertake policy research and provide medium- to long-term advice, which were substantial undertakings. Several initiatives have proceeded in collaboration with think tanks, universities, and the Social Sciences and Humanities Research Council to sponsor a sustained, wide-ranging agenda for policy research, even if this work focussed more on identifying trends and issues than on developing specific policy interventions.[43]

Collaboration and prudent openness were encouraged. Even though the principles of cabinet secrecy and ministerial responsibility remain foundation principles of parliamentary government, new demands have led ministers and officials alike to work in new ways. Good strategic planning must anticipate uncertainty, tap into information from many sources, and develop a shared vision from diverse perspectives. Ministers and officials chose to work across boundaries in a more co-operative manner, and yet to respect the expertise, mandate, and authorities of others. These principles seemed to apply when working across the branches within the PCO, across the central institutions of government, or across the deputy minister community. This may seem like a rosy, 'new-age' interpretation, but inculcating this disposition among public servants emerged as an expectation during this era, and many of the developments in government-wide strategic planning could not have been made without such collaboration.

CONCLUSION: PROSPECTS AND CHALLENGES

During the mid- to late 1990s, strategic planning at the apex of the Canadian government was notably different from that of the 1970s and the early 1980s. Rather than adopt elaborate formal planning systems, the Prime Minister opted for a leaner cabinet decision-making system and greater integration of the planning cycle, and, in the post-deficit environment, endorsed a rolling process that encouraged broader input from ministers and public service executives on strategic policy priorities.

It is intriguing that PPS, during the late 1990s, saw its role as developing a 'story' or a meta-narrative to inform and guide strategic planning, an approach consistent with Mintzberg's conception of searching for deliberate and emergent strategies. Developing a meta-narrative, of course, could be interpreted as 'spin' or 'packaging' in the name of gaining and holding onto power. Even French, in his indictment of planning, worried about the shift from 'analysis to process, from policy to positioning, from modern to postmodern government.'[44] Rival political parties or citizens did not necessarily agree with the narratives that arose from strategic planning as it was practised in Ottawa during the late 1990s—politics is inherently about contesting existing policy visions and developing alternatives. However, given the complexities and interconnectedness of policy challenges confronting the country, and given that citizens seek coherence from those who govern, any government would do well to develop a political vision and meta-narrative that ties in specific policy approaches. Moreover, the leaders of professional public services should continue to think in these terms as they prepare to advise new governments.[45]

Since this chapter was first drafted, Prime Minister Chrétien was returned to power with a third majority Liberal government on 27 November 2000. There has also been turnover in top appointments in PMO and PCO during the last year. A fair question to ask, then, is this: to what extent does this chapter's rendering of the evolution of strategic planning during the late 1990s reflect the current system?

There are preliminary indications that the transition management and the drafting of the 30 January 2001 SFT were more closed than before, though any final assessment should be based on interviews as well as an assessment of how critical planning occasions are utilized in the future to develop and announce new priorities. The 2001 SFT has many of the hallmarks of its immediate predecessors, with respect not only to style but also to key themes, although the emphasis on skills in the knowledge economy and on the need to address the problems and aspirations of Aboriginal communities seems to carry greater urgency.[46] More intriguing was the decision of the Liberal government to announce a mini-budget on 18 October 2000, before the election, and a determination not to introduce another budget in February 2001.[47] Contrary to interpretations proffered in the media, however, this does not mean that the normal planning cycle has been interrupted: the Estimates process (which deals with the expenditure side of the budget) remains intact, and both the Minister of Finance and the President of the Treasury Board will make their normal statements in the House of Commons in early spring, even if the Finance Minister, rather than introduce a budget announcing new policy directions, simply uses the occasion to announce updates and adjustments to the current fiscal plan.

It is interesting to speculate, however, on the directions that strategic planning could take in the future. One view is to see the changes in strategic planning during, and in anticipation of, the second mandate of the Chrétien government as episodic, reflecting not only the concerns of key personalities but also the dire need of the government and the public service to find bearings after an era of concerted restructuring and a single-minded focus on dealing with the deficit. A change in course, and the search for new approaches, required that the Clerk and the Deputy Secretary of Plans and Consultation reach beyond the 'jurisdiction' of the branch and PPS. In this view, with a robust strategic vision and a new mandate, a third-term Liberal government will require a similar canvassing of possibilities among ministers and across departments, and planning practice can revert to the practice of the early 1990s. Alternatively, one might see the strategic planning of the late 1990s as an 'inherent' and necessary approach to modern governance, but inevitably subject to adaptation in light of new priorities, circumstances, and personalities. In this view, the complex and ever-changing policy and political landscape will drive most governments and public service organizations toward more collaborative, horizontal, and open approaches, even in the face of the prerogatives and traditions of parliamentary and prime ministerial governance. This may require deeper changes in how the public service organizes itself to proffer advice on specific issues and proposals to ministers as a collective.

Regardless of which hypothesis holds true, there are several matters that deserve further consideration as a matter of public policy and of academic inquiry. They include:

Engaging citizens. Ministers and public service executives may have recently worked together with shared, relatively more coherent narratives, but it is not clear that these narratives are well understood by citizens (and, for that matter, most rank and file public servants). Canadians have been 'bewildered' by the pace of change during the 1990s. The degree to which our country has changed and our capacity to experiment with different policy and administrative regimes are insufficiently understood. This limits the scope for constructive debate on how to deal with the stark challenges outlined elsewhere in this volume.[48] Conveying the nature and complexity of change to citizens remains an important challenge for governments.

Transparent transition advice. One way to better inform citizens is simply to give them access to the background material that underpins specific transition advice to governments. Cameron and White recently recommended that governments should publicly release transition briefing books as a way to improve transition planning and to better inform journalists, opposition members, and citizens about the challenges and complexities confronting new governments.[49] The transition advice tailored for a particular party, though, should be proffered in confidence.

Fostering policy research. It has long been recognized that policy research, undertaken inside and outside government, has a potentially important role in informing government priority-setting and planning. Indeed, good policy research not only helps to create meta-narratives, but inevitably challenges them and constitutes one important 'early warning' capacity. While governments will want to enhance the quality, quantity, and relevance of such policy research conducted inside and outside the public service, such research must strike a balance and assiduously preserve its independence, since its value lies in identifying unanticipated issues and challenging preconceived notions.

Adapting expenditure management. There is not the space here to delve into the EMS, but the prospect of continued, possibly expanding, budgetary surpluses will mean continued pressure to ensure that new policies and programs reflect ministerial and caucus priorities, and that fiscal discipline be maintained. While a repeat of the Program Review is not likely, there needs to be developed a better capacity— possibly a horizontal one—for reviewing and challenging how existing programs are delivered, and to test if they are fully aligned with government priorities and with programs delivered by other departments and governments.

Supporting horizontal initiatives. Strategic planning by PPS is, in part, yet another example of horizontal management in the Canadian government. Encouraging this disposition takes time, leadership, and an ability to demonstrate that working in new ways can produce results worthwhile to all involved. However, the rhetoric about managing horizontally should not outstrip the capacities (time, resources, competencies) of public servants. In the case of strategic planning, the changes overseen by PPS were evolutionary and well supported by public service executives. The lesson here for other horizontal initiatives is that it is crucial that those who expect improved results anticipate and install requisite capacity. If the government seeks to improve horizontal policy development, it must go beyond announcing procedural changes for cabinet submissions and ensure that new capacities are created at the centre and in departments in support of higher quality analysis and collaboration.

Clearly this chapter has only scratched the surface of how 'the centre' now operates in Ottawa. This chapter focussed on the government-wide 'priorities and planning' function of the government and the PCO. Similar chapters could have been drafted on the strategic planning associated with other functions, such as intergovernmental affairs, the machinery of government, senior personnel and human resource challenges, intelligence assessment, expenditure management, the coordination of macroeconomic policy, information technology, and service innovation, to name just a few. Careful analysis of such practices and developments will not only produce more up-to-date accounts of our central institutions, but, as is the case with substantive policy-oriented research, will also produce state-of-the-art conceptual frameworks for better understanding and facilitating the evolution of governance.

NOTES

I would like to extend thanks to Samy Watson, Simon Kennedy, Jonathan Will, and Linda St. Amour for their assistance. I greatly appreciate the insightful comments received from Jocelyne Bourgon,

Ian Clark, Ruth Dantzer, Raymond d'Aoust, Maurice Demers, Geoff Dinsdale, David Good, Chaviva Hosek, Carole Swan, and, of course, Leslie Pal. The views in this chapter are those of the author and do not represent in any way the views of the government of Canada. Any errors in fact or interpretation are mine alone.

NOTES

1 See Donald Savoie, 'The Privy Council Office: A Safe Pair of Hands', in *Governing from the Centre: The Concentration of Power in Canadian Politics* (Toronto: University of Toronto Press, 1999), 109-55; Mark Schacter and Phillip Haid, *Cabinet Decision-Making in Canada: Lessons and Practices* (Ottawa: Institute on Governance, Apr. 1999); and Glen McGregor, 'When Cabinet Meets', *The Ottawa Citizen*, 17 Dec. 2000, A14.

2 Richard D. French, *How Ottawa Decides: Planning and Industrial Policy Making 1968-1984*, 2nd ed. (Toronto: Lorimer, 1984), 46. These changes followed the early elaboration of the 'modern' PCO under Prime Minister Pearson, which first included the appointment of four assistant secretaries, who functioned as subject-matter specialists (in a secretariat later to be referred to as 'operations'), and soon after, of the science and special planning secretariats. Pitfield's appointment as deputy secretary for plans was complemented by similar appointments for operations and for federal-provincial relations. See also G. Bruce Doern, 'The Development of Policy Organizations in the Executive Arena', in G. Bruce Doern and Peter Aucoin, eds, *The Structures of Policy-Making in Canada* (Toronto: Macmillan, 1971), 39-78.

3 A few years earlier, the Economic Council of Canada (1963) and the Science Council of Canada (1966) were created to undertake applied policy research.

4 French, *How Ottawa Decides*, 46-58.

5 Richard W. Phidd and G. Bruce Doern, *The Politics and Management of Canadian Economic Policy* (Toronto: Macmillan, 1978).

6 For details, see French, *How Ottawa Decides*, 75-85.

7 French described it as 'a highly formal, rigid, rational, systematic and ultimately sterile attempt to frame the current and future actions of government' (Ibid., 18).

8 This was done by assigning 'envelopes of funds' to the policy cabinet committees, each with its own secretariat or ministry of state, layered over the existing array of central agencies. These new entities were to roll up the annual strategic overviews and detailed multi-year operating plans that were required from each department in the form of sectoral overviews for each policy sector to guide the use of expenditure envelopes, which, in turn, were to be linked to the government's fiscal plan.

For one account among many, see Richard Van Loon, 'Planning in the Eighties', in French, *How Ottawa Decides*, 157-90.

9 See Sandford Borins, 'Ottawa's Expenditure Envelopes: Workable Rationality at Last?' in G. Bruce Doern, ed., *How Ottawa Spends Your Tax Dollars: 1982* (Toronto: James Lorimer, 1982), 63-86.

10 For more detail on this era, see Richard Van Loon, 'The Policy and Expenditure Management System in the Federal Government: The First Three Years', *Canadian Public Administration* 26, 2 (1983): 255-85, and Ian D. Clark, 'Recent Changes in the Cabinet Decision-Making System in Ottawa', *Canadian Public Administration* 28, 2 (1985): 185-201.

11 See, for example, David Braybrooke and Charles E. Lindblom, *A Strategy of Decision* (New York: Free Press, 1963).

12 The irony, however, is that many of the *logistical* innovations associated with these systems were retained, such as the procedures for preparing cabinet documents, the expanded capacities of the PCO, and improvement in reporting to Parliament. Even 'mandate planning', often perceived as an innovation of the 1990s, was first introduced under the guidance of Michael Pitfield, when he was Deputy Secretary, Plans. See French, *How Ottawa Decides*, 77.

13 Mintzberg distinguishes between *intended* strategy (which divides into 'unrealized' and 'deliberate' components) and *realized* strategies (which are a mix of 'deliberate' and 'emergent' strategies). See Henry Mintzberg, *The Rise and Fall of Strategic Planning* (New York: Free Press, 1994), 333-51.

14 Ibid., 361-91.

15 See Ralph D. Stacey, *Managing the Unknowable: Strategic Boundaries Between Order and Chaos* (San Francisco: Jossey-Bass, 1992). See also James Gleick, *Chaos: Making a New Science* (New York: Penguin, 1987), and Mitchell Waldrop, *Complexity: The Emerging Science at the Edge of Order and Chaos* (New York: Simon and Schuster, 1992). This work was anticipated by Michael Cohen, James G. March, and Johan P. Olsen, 'A Garbage Can Theory of Organizational Choice', *Administrative Science Quarterly* 17 (1972): 1-25, a seminal article that recognized that random or unpredicted events are an inherent part of decision-making in organizations. On chaos-like principles applied to agenda-setting and public policy change, see John W. Kingdon, *Agendas, Alternatives, and Public Policies*, 2nd ed. (New York: HarperCollins, 1995); Paul A. Sabatier and Hank C. Jenkins-Smith, eds, *Policy Change and Learning: An Advocacy Coalition Approach* (Boulder: Westview, 1993); Frank R. Baumgartner and Bryan D. Jones, *Agendas and Instability in American Politics* (Chicago: University of Chicago Press, 1993). Unlike Stacey, these authors do not probe the implications for strategic planning and organizational change in the public sector.

16 Steven W. Floyd and Bill Wooldridge, *Building Strategy from the Middle: Reconceptualizing Strategy Process* (Thousand Oaks, CA: Sage, 2000), 15.
17 Ibid., 14. Such a view stands in contrast to previous work that saw the role of managers as 'buffering the technical core'. See James D. Thompson, *Organizations in Action* (New York: McGraw-Hill Ryerson, 1967).
18 See Evert A. Lindquist, 'New Agendas for Research on Policy Communities: Policy Analysis, Administration, and Governance', in Laurent Dobuzinskis, Michael Howlett, and David Laycock, eds, *Policy Studies in Canada: The State of the Art* (Toronto: University of Toronto, 1996), 227-34, and Evert A. Lindquist, 'Reconceiving the Center: Leadership, Strategic Review and Coherence', in Organisation for Economic Co-operation and Development (OECD), *Government of the Future* (Paris: OECD, 2000), 149-83.
19 Indeed, Rhodes defines the core executive as the set of networks that police the functional policy 'networks'. See R.A.W. Rhodes, *Understanding Governance: Policy Networks, Governance, Reflexivity and Accountability* (Buckingham: Open University Press, 1997), 13-14.
20 OECD, PUMA Service, 'Building Policy Coherence: Tools and Tensions' (1996), at web site: www.oecd.org/puma/gvrnance/strrat/cohernc.htm
21 Many of these themes were echoed in a symposium on 'Government of the Future: Getting from Here to There', held in Paris, 14-15 Sept. 1999. For the proceedings, see OECD, *Government of the Future*. This and supporting country reports for the symposium are at web site: www.oecd.org/puma
22 For more details, see Privy Council Office, *The Role and Structure of the Privy Council Office* (Ottawa: Information Services Division, Feb. 1999).
23 For details, see Savoie, *Governing from the Centre*, 119-20.
24 For details, see 'Managing Cabinet Committees: The Role of the Operations Sector in PCO', in Schacter and Haid, *Cabinet Decision-Making in Canada*, 11-15.
25 J.L. Manion and Cynthia Williams, 'Transition Planning at the Federal Level in Canada', in Donald J. Savoie, ed., *Taking Power: Managing Government Transition* (Toronto: Institute of Public Administration of Canada, 1993), chap. 4, 99-113.
26 Cabinet retreats typically include all ministers and secretaries of state. The presence of all secretaries of state is interesting, because usually no more than three secretaries of state are invited to participate in full cabinet meetings.
27 Evert A. Lindquist, 'Citizens, Experts and Budgets: Evaluating Ottawa's Emerging Budget Process', in Susan D. Phillips, ed., *How Ottawa Spends 1994-95: Making Change* (Ottawa: Carleton University Press, 1994), 91-128.

28 Edward Greenspon and Anthony Wilson-Smith, *Double Vision: The Inside Story of the Liberals in Power* (Toronto: Doubleday, 1996).
29 See Gilles Paquet and Robert Shepherd, 'The Program Review Process: A Deconstruction', in Gene Swimmer, ed., *How Ottawa Spends 1996-97: Life Under the Knife* (Ottawa: Carleton University, 1996), 39-72.
30 Ministers with their departments developed proposals to meet spending reduction targets for their portfolios against six tests. The six tests were whether a given program was in the public interest, whether there was a legitimate and necessary role for government, whether the program could be better provided by a different order of government, whether the service could be better provided by the private or voluntary sector, whether the program was efficient and effective, and whether the program was affordable.
31 Proposals accepted by the committee of ministers were forwarded to the prime minister for approval.
32 Privy Council Office, *Strengthening Policy Capacity* (Dec. 1996) and *Management of Horizontal Policy Issues* (Dec. 1996). See web site: www.ccmd-ccg.gc.ca/publications_e.html. The other task forces were on service delivery models, overhead services, federal presence, federal presence abroad, policy planning, values and ethics, and scenario-building. For a summary of several of these task forces, see web site: www.ccmd-ccg.gc.ca/pdfs/summarye.pdf
33 See Canada, *La Relève: Renewal in the Public Service of Canada: A Virtual Showcase of Key Documents* (Ottawa: Canada Communications Group, 1998), and Herman Bakvis, 'Rebuilding Policy Capacity in the Era of the Fiscal Dividend', *Governance* 13, 1 (2000): 71-103.
34 The key trends and pressures identified included globalization and North American integration, demographic changes, technological change and the information revolution, environmental pressures, and the fiscal context. The PRI web site is at www.policyresearch.schoolnet.ca/. For a detailed review and critique, see Bakvis, 'Rebuilding Policy Capacity'. Overviews of the results of the Trends Project can be found in *Canadian Public Policy* (Aug. 2000), Special Supplement 26.
35 See 'Progress Report: Overview' (Apr. 1997) at web site: policyresearch.schoolnet.ca/ under 'Key Documents'.
36 Policy Research Committee, *Canada 2005: Global Challenges and Beyond*, Draft Interim Report (Ottawa: Policy Research Secretariat, Feb. 1997). See web site: www.policyresearch.schoolnet.ca/ under 'Key Documents'.
37 For links to the last four Speeches from the Throne, see web site: www.pco-bcp.gc.ca/relate_e.htm
38 Canada, *The Expenditure Management System of the Government of Canada* (Ottawa: Minister of Supply and Services, 1995).

39 For example, ministers could not bring forward a policy proposal for discussion to deal with an anticipated crisis unless funds were already available, and thus they could not work out the policy and debate it among colleagues.
40 Evert A. Lindquist, *Consultation and Budget Secrecy* (Ottawa: Conference Board of Canada, 1982).
41 See Emery Roe, *Narrative Policy Analysis: Theory and Practice* (Durham, N.C.: Duke University Press, 1994).
42 Cases recently reviewed by the Canadian Centre for Management Development's Roundtable on the Management of Horizontal Issues demonstrate that horizontal approaches can be uncovered across the public service, and in all parts of the country, and involve new ways of working with other governments with the private and voluntary sector, and with citizens.
43 See Policy Research Committee, 'Meeting of Policy Research Organizations: November 13, 1997, Report' (Ottawa: Policy Research Secretariat, 1997); Public Policy Forum and Canadian Policy Research Networks, 'Improving Relationships Within the Policy Research Community: Report from a Joint Project by Canadian Policy Research Networks and the Public Policy Forum for the Policy Research Network and the Treasury Board Secretariat' (Ottawa, 29 May 1998); and Policy Research Secretariat, 'Policy Research in Canada: A Capacity for the Future: A Discussion Document' (Ottawa: Policy Research Secretariat, Mar. 1999 Draft).
44 See Richard D. French, 'Postmodern Government', *Optimum* 23, 1 (Summer 1992): 43-51; and, for a rejoinder, see Evert A. Lindquist, 'Postmodern Politics and Policy Sciences', *Optimum* 24, 1 (Summer 1993): 42-50.
45 See Roe, *Narrative Policy Analysis*, for a discussion on how building and analysing narratives should be an essential tool of policy analysts and researchers, particularly for dealing with complex policy problems.
46 See web site: www.sft-ddt.gc.ca/sftddt_e.htm
47 See Canada, Department of Finance, *Economic Statement and Budget Update (Oct.18, 2000)*, at web site: www.fin.gc.ca/access/budinfoe.html
48 Evert A. Lindquist, 'The Bewildering Pace of Public Sector Reform in Canada', in Jan-Erik Lane, ed., *Public Sector Reform: Rationale, Trends and Problems* (London: Sage, 1997), 47-63.
49 See David R. Cameron and Graham White, *Cycling into Saigon: The Conservative Transition in Ontario* (Vancouver: University of British Columbia Press, 2000), 158.

4

Managing in the New Public Service: Some Implications for How We Are Governed

ANNE PERKINS

ROBERT P. SHEPHERD

Over the past decade, traditional public administration has gradually fallen into disfavour, and has been replaced by a different understanding of the role of government, alternative ways of organizing, and a more business-like approach to managing the public sector.[1] The reasons for the change are many and complex. The need to deal with the deficit and the debt has been a key factor. Another has been the public's apparent loss of confidence in government, which is due in part to its inefficiency and lack of responsiveness. Early on, government itself recognized that Canadians would continue to want more and better services for less cost, and that a client-oriented, high-quality public service culture would have to be created—one that would be more adaptable, more innovative, and more creative than traditional bureaucratic structures usually allow.[2]

In 1993, Program Review was initiated to deal with the crisis in public finances and with the demands for changes in the structure and functioning of the federal government and its institutions.[3] When it ended in March 1999, Canada had conquered the deficit, the first of the G-7 countries to do so. The Chrétien government has recently promised to work harder to reduce the national debt of more than $580 billion during its new mandate. While there is disagreement as to whether Program Review was responsible for generating the reforms needed to make government more effective, responsive, and businesslike, one thing is clear. The strong move toward a client service orientation, alternative service delivery (ASD), and other trends that have been identified with the 'new public management' was given a decisive push when government was forced to search for new and better ways to ensure that public needs and the needs of targeted customers and clients could be met, despite the radical downsizing of the public service that had occurred. Therefore, while traditional bureaucracy has not actually disappeared, the federal public service of the second Chrétien mandate had begun to function quite differently in several key respects from the way it had previously.

THE CHANGING LANDSCAPE

The purpose of this chapter is to examine some key trends in the way the federal public service and, indeed, public services throughout the country and abroad now operate and to consider how they may eventually affect certain aspects of how we are governed. We will investigate four of these trends, drawing on public service documents and on our own experience consulting with central agencies, line departments and agencies, and regional offices:[4]

- *partnering* in policy-making, management, program development, and the delivery of goods and services within and across departmental and agency boundaries, between orders of government, and across sectors;
- the ongoing development of and commitment to a *service-to-the-public* focus as one critical factor of an effective public sector;
- the *shifting of responsibilities* from one authority to another, as evidenced by increased decentralization, deconcentration, devolution, and deregulation in favour of the market and self-regulation; and

- the increased commitment to and dependency on *information technologies* in all aspects of governing, from political policy- and decision-making, to the management of programs, to the delivery of goods and services to clients, customers, and the general public.[5]

This first section examines how the four trends have developed and are being implemented in the federal public service. In the second section, we are interested in the impact these may have on the operations of Parliament, the executive and senior management, and the electoral process, especially insofar as each is essential to the representing and representative functions of government,[6] and to its policy- and decision-making structures and processes. In the final section, we speculate about what may happen with these trends during the third Chrétien mandate.

Partnering
Partnering is a process by which formal or informal relationships are developed and maintained within or between government departments and agencies, between one order of government and others, and/or between government and the private sector, and through which the parties work together to achieve agreed-upon results. *Working together* implies that each partner should expect to benefit in some way from the relationship, and will have a direct role in helping to ensure that desired results are achieved by sharing in decision-making and risk-taking, and by contributing financial and/or other resources. The *partnerships* that result may be agreements on principles (the Social Union Framework, for example[7]), or information exchange networks. They may be temporary interdepartmental or inter-governmental committees working together to deal with cross-jurisdictional policy or program delivery issues; organizations with their own mandates, strategic directions, expectations with respect to results, dedicated resources, and other trappings of permanence; or something in between.[8]

Partnering as a strategy for governments to get things done is not new. It is implicit in the very nature of the Canadian federal state, where the Constitution (in the case of shared jurisdictions such as agriculture or immigration) or circumstance and practice (e.g., health, education, social welfare) make such arrangements appropriate.

Partnering with the private sector has also been relatively common since Confederation, especially for mega-projects such as the building of the railways and the St. Lawrence Seaway (which also had cross-national government partners), and for the exploration and development of natural resources where private sector resources and expertise were needed.

What is new today, however, is the extent to which the federal government is encouraging the use of partnerships for dealing with a variety of matters, including management, the development and delivery of programs and services, and policy-making. Developing partnership relationships within government, between governments, and with the private (profit and not-for-profit) sector has been a recurring theme in central agency reports and in departmental and agency studies since the early 1990s.[9] During the second Chrétien mandate, partnering emerged as a policy instrument of choice.

There are several reasons for this. As in the past, there is a need to spread the financial burden of public programs and services, and to have access to expertise and other resources found in another order of government or in the private sector. It is now also recognized that those who receive government services, locally-based public servants, and community groups and businesses are often in the best position to know what is required with respect to programming and service delivery, and are the most likely to be committed to making it all work. Creating community-based partnerships is a very effective way of dealing with local needs and wants. Partnerships between departments and agencies or orders of government may also reduce duplication and, at the same time, provide citizens and clients with more effective programs and services. Finally, partnering is being used as a strategy because most public problems are difficult, complex, and interrelated, and therefore need to be addressed from several different perspectives in an integrated way.[10] Partnering provides an opportunity to bring these different perspectives together.

Government partnerships come in a variety of configurations. There are several interdepartmental partnering relationships within the federal sphere. Some are concerned with single or closely-related policy and/or program issues. One such partnership is Team Canada Inc (TCI), which brings together 23 federal departments and agencies that have some aspect of trade promotion as part of their mandates. The purpose of the partnership is to coordinate the development of federal trade promotion policy, and to provide one-stop access to business programs and information services that help Canadian business compete in the global marketplace.[11] Others have been created as learning networks to share insights and best practices in public management. The Partnership for International Co-operation, for example, was initiated in April 2000 by the Canadian Centre for Management Development (CCMD) to bring together expertise from within the federal public sector to assist international organizations and government institutions in other countries. Its partners are federal departments and agencies, tribunals, and parliamentary institutions.[12]

Cost-sharing arrangements usually characterize partnering between orders of government. Increasingly, however, intergovernmental partnerships have moved beyond cost-sharing to involve all or most partners directly in the development of common or complementary policies or planning strategies, and operational concerns such as the design, management, and delivery of programs and services. The recently-proposed partnership for urban planning between the federal National Capital Commission (NCC), the new city of Ottawa, and the municipalities of La Communauté Urbaine de l'Outaouais (CUO) is a case in point.[13] Some of the costs involved in local planning will be shared, as will some of the decision-making and coordination of land use and related development priorities (see box below).

Partnerships that involve the private sector are also becoming more commonplace. Many involve a number of interdepartmental and intergovernmental partners. Legal aid programs, the Urban Aboriginal Youth Centres Program, and some of the Service Canada initiatives, such as the Oxford County Integration Network (COIN), are good examples of what are often complex, multi-layered arrangements. Although all partnerships are challenging, those involving the private sector and government partners may be among the most difficult to manage, if only because of the sheer number and variety of partners. Private sector partners, whether they are profit-oriented organizations, or non-profit or volunteer organizations, professional groups, pressure groups, or individual clients and client groups, generally expect the partnership to be a truly collaborative effort, in which risk-taking and responsibilities for planning and decision-making are shared to some extent. Then, too, significant differences in corporate culture between

> **Team Canada Inc**
> Team Canada Inc (TCI) has some of the trappings of an independent agency. Although each partner retains control over its own trade-related programs, TCI has a governance structure, an annual budget of about $1.6 M raised through partnership fees, an official business plan, and a dedicated staff (the Information Products and Marketing Group) that is responsible for marketing its services, developing the website and other products, and secretariat services. *TCI Business Plan 1999-2002*
>
> **Complex Cross-sectoral Partnerships**
> The Urban Aboriginal Youth Centres (UAYC) program in Winnipeg is one component of the federal Urban Aboriginal Strategy. Its purpose is to 'improve the economic, social and personal prospects of Aboriginal youth, and to provide them with greater access to existing and value-added programming, in order to meet their expressed needs and those of their community.'
>
> Although still in its infancy, UAYC will eventually involve a wide range of partners: federal departments, the government of Manitoba, the city of Winnipeg, local Aboriginal NGOs, social agencies, and businesses. Some will be involved in policy-making and some in program development and delivery or program evaluation. Others will provide resources. Some will be involved in all of these. *Service Canada Cases (TBS), March-July 2000*
>
> **From Personal Commitment to Accountability**
> 'Although we have not yet developed formal accountability agreements for Oxford County Integrated Network and The Livingston Centre, we are well aware that without such agreements, we are flirting with disaster if and when those of us who are so personally committed to the projects leave or retire.' *A partner in The Livingston Centre and COIN initiatives in Oxford County Ontario.*

sectors may exist, and must be taken into account. Strategic directions, expected results, roles and responsibilities, and accountability relationships may not be clear at first because the parties involved must expend a great deal of energy learning to work with one another—both as individuals and as representatives of their respective organizations.[14] This is not time wasted. The personal commitment of partner representatives is often critical to the success of these endeavours, because they will likely have to invest a great deal of their own time in making the partnership work.

Even with the best of intentions, however, such partnerships will be successful only if several key questions are addressed. How should the partnership be organized, and how should it be governed? What will/should each partner contribute (resources, time, roles, expertise, etc.), and under what conditions? Which partner(s) will be responsible for what? Even though the partners may share common goals and want to achieve the same results, each has other separate sets of responsibilities and objectives that may, at one time or another, conflict with those related to the partnership. From the perspective of the federal government, what skills do its people need in order to deal with (or 'manage') the other partners? Have the risks and benefits been clearly identified, and how are the risks to be managed? Who is ultimately to be held to account if things go awry when responsibilities have been clearly assigned to a non-government or another government party? In what areas and to what degree should non-government partners have decision-making responsibility? Who should decide who is to be included in the partnering arrangement and who is not? How can we prevent one partner or set of partners from exerting undue influence on the arrangement?

Building trust in partners' abilities and ways of operating is critical to the success of partnerships, whether they be relatively simple interdepartmental or intergovernmental arrangements or complex, multi-layered, cross-sectoral ones. As government's experience working with partnerships under different circumstances grows, it is likely that it will use them with increasing frequency.

Providing Service to the Public
The commitment to create a client-oriented public service was part of the Public Service 2000 initiative, in which service to the public was used to describe service to ministers, the Canadian public, and individual clients 'in support of the national interest'. This represented a major change in attitude—Canadians were now to be treated as clients and customers, as well as citizens. Moreover, deputy ministers were to be held accountable for ensuring that the measures required to make service to the public and a client orientation possible were put in place. These included such things as service standards, client feedback mechanisms, complaint procedures, and effective consultation strategies.[15]

Despite the strong personal commitment of then Prime Minister Brian Mulroney and key deputy ministers, several of whom were directly involved in writing the Public Service 2000 Task Force report on service to the public,[16] a client-service approach did not really begin to take hold until the new Chrétien government announced, as part of its February 1994 budget, that service standards would be implemented government-wide. In response, the Treasury Board Secretariat, with the volunteer participation of many individuals from across the public service, developed the Quality Services Initiative. Its purpose was to improve client satisfaction and the quality of accessible, affordable, and responsive services to Canadians in a measurable way[17] (see box below).

Quality service delivery and client satisfaction remain priorities for the Board. Under the Service Canada initiative, the federal government is expanding its commitment to service delivery of high quality by organizing access to government services in ways that reflect the needs of those Canadians who actually use them. During the past two years, several pilot projects have been launched under the auspices of Service Canada at departmental service sites across the country. The Livingston Centre and COIN projects in western Ontario combine single-service locations ('single-windows') and electronic access to government and other services. In Manitoba a Single Windows initiative coordinated by Service Canada through Canadian Heritage will provide integrated federal programs and services in the French language at easily-accessible community-based, client-oriented sites in St-Boniface

---

Service Canada in Oxford County

Human Resources Development Canada (HRDC) and Industry Canada are partners in the 'seamless' delivery of federal services to the citizens of Tillsonburg and surrounding Oxford County, Ontario. Services are delivered on site at the Livingston Centre in Tillsonburg and at 13 other community sites. There are plans to make services available on-line directly to residences in the area using a local cable supplier, which is a new partner of the County's high-speed network for communication and information exchange, known as COIN.

COIN connects public service agencies throughout the area to one another, to their targeted clients, to local citizens, and to individuals and organizations beyond its borders. As committed members of the community, key individuals from local HRDC offices and the Livingston Centre are active with the founding partners in COIN decision-making as informal operating partners. *Service Canada Cases (TBS), March-July 2000.*

and five other communities with a high concentration of Franco-Manitobans. Provincial, municipal, and private sector partners are also involved in these particular projects; in fact, the Manitoba Single Windows project actually began as a provincial initiative.[18] Through initiatives such as these, Canadians across the country will eventually be able to contact government directly—in person at an integrated service centre, by telephone using the *1-800-0-Canada* numbers, or electronically through the Internet and e-mail—to get information, download forms and complete transactions (e.g., pay taxes, submit applications), and receive help in identifying their needs and other federal resources that are available to them. In many cases, the citizen-client will also have access to service providers in the provincial and local government and in the private sector through the same access points.

It would seem that what appeared to be a passing phase in the early 1990s has become a core public service value and a primary focus of public service interest and activity.[19] The general public and individual Canadians now expect to be treated as clients and, in some cases, to be able to influence service delivery, program development, and even public policy-making in a direct way through the 'service window'. The focus on client service has, in turn, been a powerful force behind the further development of e-government and ASD strategies such as partnering—so that government might better serve the increasing needs and wants of Canadians, as both citizens and individuals.[20]

Shifting Responsibilities and Authorities

Another key trend has been the shifting of responsibilities and authorities from one part of an organization to another or from one jurisdiction to another, usually to improve efficiency and/or effectiveness, increase access to resources, or reduce costs. Program Review re-examined the activities of government to determine which should be retained and which could be assigned elsewhere, keeping in mind that they might still be valued by the public and that government ought perhaps to remain involved in some way. Four processes have been used to shift responsibilities: deconcentration, decentralization, devolution, and deregulation. Some have been used for a while and others are of more recent origin.

The decision to shift responsibilities and/or authorities from one jurisdiction to another may be made at political or bureaucratic levels; the decision to shift responsibilities and/or authorities within an organization is usually made by senior management. The decision is likely be a political one if the issues or circumstances addressed by the shift are essentially political in nature, or if there is concern that the change will cause a politically-significant reaction on the part of the Canadian public, government clients or customers, another order of government, or private interests. The decision *must* be a political one when it is precedent-setting, when it significantly changes how the government operates in the area, and/or when it is expected to alter the machinery of government in some fundamental way. Because making changes in the machinery of government is a prime ministerial prerogative, the prime minister, usually on the advice of the relevant minister(s), cabinet, and the senior public service, may elect to make the decision. Or, alternatively, Parliament may be asked to legislate the new arrangement. Once the decision to go ahead is made, consideration is given to the amount of decision-making authority that must be delegated if the assigned responsibilities are to be carried out.

Deconcentration, decentralization, devolution, and deregulation form a continuum based on the type and degree of authority delegated. At one end, deconcentration usually involves the physical dispersal of members of an organization, with most of the decision-making authority remaining with the centre. Decentralization also involves the dispersal of organizational members, but gives local authorities more discretion over local decision-making than is the case with deconcentration. Devolution involves the passing of specific responsibilities and the decision authority that has been associated with a subordinate part of the organization across the organizational boundary to an independent agency, although regulation and standards continue to be maintained by the centre. Finally, at the other end of the spectrum, the process of deregulation reduces or eliminates government regulatory control over a private market (although there has been deregulation within government, also), so that it has the requisite authority to be able to operate under competitive conditions. Each of these processes is discussed below.

Deconcentration and decentralization have been used to shift government responsibilities within government departments and agencies since Confederation. Deconcentration has always applied to customs, postal services, and military recruitment, whose facilities have always been established in the regions for reasons of geography, although a high degree of decision-making authority continued to be maintained at the centre. In the past few years, a degree of decision-making authority has been delegated to these local offices in conjunction with the move toward more effective client service and service-to-the-public strategies. Local public servants are now given more discretion to make decisions on the cases under their purview in the interests of greater responsiveness, efficiency, and cost-effectiveness. The moving of the public servants who administer the GST from Ottawa to Summerside, Prince Edward Island is a recent example of decentralization.

There are at least three strategic choices associated with the use of decentralization. The first is between political decentralization, in which authorities are transferred to elected officials (e.g., the transfer of social welfare from provincial to local governments), and administrative decentralization, in which authority is transferred to an appointed body. The second choice is between transferring authority to a body by competitive means (e.g., contracting out, as in the GTS Katie case)[21] and doing so by non-competitive means (e.g., postal services). The third is between the internal decentralization of authority and responsibility to lower levels of the hierarchy, and external decentralization to other bodies, as is the case with the devolution of responsibilities under Aboriginal self-government.[22] The Chrétien Liberals have tended to be cautious about contracting out and devolution, showing a marked preference for internal decentralization to the regions, and for administrative decentralization through the creation of agencies.

The Canadian Food Inspection Agency (CFIA), the Parks Canada Agency, and the Canada Customs and Revenue Agency (CCRA) are three examples of administrative decentralization. Several reasons have been given for their creation. It is thought that they are able to be more adaptable than regular government departments, which are perceived to be inflexible and governed by process-driven rules. Other reasons include improved quality of service to clients, customers, and/or citizens; reduction in the size of government; the ability to identify and separate policy and operational roles more clearly; and the involvement of private sector organizations in service delivery. From an operations perspective, more flexible human resource management and the ability to motivate employees more easily are also key factors. This is particularly true with respect to science-based organizations such as the CFIA, where a flexible working environment is a principal motivating factor for employees. With respect to the Canadian Tourism Commission, the ability to involve private sector specialists in tourism marketing, which, in turn, has encouraged buy-in from industry participants, was also a key consideration in its creation[23] (see box below).

The most notable application of devolution has been the negotiation and implementation of Aboriginal self-government and justice. The process of devolving responsibilities began in the 1970s with the negotiation of administrative instruments designed to increase local control. By the late 1980s, various funding agreement mechanisms were created that gave native public servants principal responsibility for program design and delivery. A significant shift had taken place—

Canadian Food Inspection Agency

"[B]ureaucracy as a method of organization and service delivery is outmoded and bankrupt in the contemporary globalized, service-based economy of modern nation-states. A radically different way of doing the business of the public is therefore needed, a way that is entrepreneurial in outlook and approach.... A factor shaping the creation of the CFIA was the pervasive belief within the food safety policy community that the federal inspection and regulation function ought to remain within the federal government domain." *Michael Prince, "Banishing Bureaucracy or Hatching a Hybrid."*

Canadian Tourism Commission

"Our 'industry-led, market-driven' approach works. Industry watchers consider the Commission an essential forum for the broad range of players to address common issues facing the tourism industry in Canada." *Hon. Judd Buchanan, Chairman of the CTC.*

Devolution and the Nisga'a Treaty

"Today, the Nisga'a people became full-fledged Canadians as we step out from under the Indian Act forever.... We remain self-governing today, and we are proud to say that this inherent right is now clearly recognized and protected in the Constitution of Canada."
Chief Joseph Gosnell Sr., Ottawa, Ratification Day in the House of Commons, 13 April 2000.

Indian and Northern Affairs Canada (INAC) had become primarily a funding agency rather than a deliverer of programs and services. First Nations clearly supported this move because they wanted greater control over their communities.

From an administrative standpoint program effectiveness is enhanced through devolved decision-making, because it gives First Nations greater flexibility to address individual community challenges. It is also impossible for a centralized bureaucracy to administer effectively the ever-wider range of policies and programs to geographically and culturally diverse Aboriginal communities. As a result, important questions have arisen about how responsibilities are to be shared and who is to become accountable to whom for what. Moreover, the political, financial, and administrative risks of sharing responsibilities are increasing. Recent reports of excessive salaries for Chiefs and Councils illustrate the challenges of moving from a situation in which one government is in a position of power to a sharing of power with First Nations governments. They also raise more practical questions about who is ultimately responsible for the stewardship of public funds in such relationships.

In this case of deregulation, government makes a decision to shift responsibility for industry regulation and behaviour from the public sphere to an outside industry body or professional organization. Since the 1970s, deregulation has been used extensively to reduce red tape and to privatize public assets where it was believed the market could operate as well as or better than the public sector. The Mulroney government made the greatest use of deregulation in this sense, firmly believing that state intervention in the lives of individuals and the market was excessive.[24] By the late 1980s, sweeping deregulation had been introduced in the financial services, in communications, and in the energy sector. Several government-owned corporations had also been privatized, particularly in the resource and transportation industries, with the result that the extent of regulation in these sectors has been reduced.

In his first mandate, Chrétien continued to deregulate—even using the same rhetoric as his predecessor. By the beginning of the second mandate, however, the rhetoric of deregulation had been transformed into the rhetoric of *facilitation*, in support of the growth and development of small and medium-sized businesses, industry competitiveness, private sector innovation, entrepreneurship and risk-taking, and the expansion of opportunities for Canadians in the labour market. Through such institutions as the Competition Bureau within Industry Canada, the Chrétien government has committed itself to promoting competition and economic efficiency. Because it is considered only a short-term strategy for creating and facilitating access for firms in sectors characterized as monopolies or oligopolies, the use of regulation has diminished as an instrument of choice[25] (see box below).

More recently, the term deregulation has been used to describe changes within government itself. Central agencies have moved from dependency on rules and regulations to more open guidelines and frameworks, especially in the areas of human resources management, management control and comptrollership, and the management of information systems. The Modern Comptrollership Initiative (1997–present) is one example. It focusses primarily on improving control and comptrollership by improving management practices and performance evaluation frameworks, rather than by applying standardized financial and other rules and regulations from the centre. At the time of writing, several pilot departments were carrying out capacity checks to assess their modern management practices and to determine how they might be improved.[26]

Supporting Small Business

"The Liberal government has made capital, export assistance, and information available to small and medium-sized enterprises to help them grow, trade and develop innovative ideas that create jobs and growth.... The 1997 budget lightened the paper and regulatory burden on the small-business community.... [It] also announced changes in the rules for labour-sponsored venture capital corporations, to encourage them to invest more actively in small businesses, thereby helping them create jobs." *Liberal Red Book II, Pages 42-3.*

The Use of New Technology and E-government
The federal government is committed to helping the country move to a knowledge-based economy premised on partnerships and other cooperative arrangements. Accordingly, it has made the wise use of technology a key priority in linking program design, delivery, and results.

Since the 1970s the federal government has used electronic means to store and retrieve information. The new challenge is to keep citizens informed and to deliver programs *through* technology in order to improve administrative efficiency and to create direct connections with citizens. There are at least four reasons why the government is embracing modern information technologies:

- to support transactions and the dissemination of information within government, thereby improving its own efficiency, and reducing overlap and duplication;
- to attract and retain innovative and creative employees by making technology a key component of the work environment;
- to support and expand service to the public through e-government via such models as single-window service delivery; and
- to use technology as a means of reaching, consulting, and relating to citizens and targeted publics insofar as they are the 'governed' (i.e., e-democracy).

With respect to the first purpose, all orders of government are committed to improving the way they use public resources and to reducing overlap and duplication within and between jurisdictions. Technology is regarded as a tool for linking similar programs and services, carrying out financial and program delivery transactions, disseminating information, and consulting organizational members about various aspects of policy and program initiatives. At present, most government departments have been in the process of digitizing information. A number also have web sites, but these are often not organized by subject or service, nor are they linked to one another. There have been some innovations, however, such as the on-line auction of two bands of the radio spectrum under the Canadian Radio Television and Telecommunications Commission (CRTC).[27] The first step toward linking the public sector to citizens is to make the most effective and efficient use of technology within government.

With respect to the second purpose—remaining competitive in the labour market—the effective use of technology is regarded by new public employees as fundamental. The federal public service has always had difficulty acquiring the technology and expertise to build up-to-date working environments that are technologically superior, and that value efficient communication and project management strategies. Public servants want and, indeed, expect a work environment that values creativity and innovation and encourages the free flow of information within government and between partners. This requires some rethinking about how best to use technology to link programs and services in a collaborative way that may not be consistent with those organizational structures that still rely on vertical command and control models.

Regarding the third purpose—to support and expand service to the public through e-government—the federal government is committed to becoming a model user of information technology and the Internet, to being known around the world as the government most connected to its citizens, and to being able to give its citizens access to government information and services on-line at the time and place of their choosing.[28] To facilitate this, the Information Highway Advisory Council was created in 1994 to conduct research into three areas where technology could be used: for job creation, in support of Canadian sovereignty and cultural identity, and to ensure universal access at a reasonable cost.[29] Its 1995 Report concluded that the federal government would have to deal with several issues, including those related to service to the public, access and social impacts, and security and privacy. Three years later, the federal government set out a six-pillar connectedness agenda, one key aspect of which was access to government (the single-window service delivery initiative).

Achieving the final purpose—using technology to reach, consult, and relate to Canadians (e-democracy)—is still a long way off, given the daunting technical issues, differences in access among Canadians (the so-called 'digital divide'), and the need to reorganize the way government approaches public consultations. For example, it is still not possible to e-mail all public servants internally, let alone give the public on-line access to debates and discussions concerning various public policy questions. There are also significant privacy and security issues, policy and legal frameworks to develop, and the challenge of educating the public about technological access. Some pilot projects have already been instituted with respect to e-democracy, such as Natural Resources Canada's (NRCan) on-line conferencing in 2001 to exchange information on pipeline reliability. And Elections Canada commissioned a study by two consulting firms, KPMG and the Sussex Circle, that examined the possibility of amendments to the Canada

Elections Act with respect to the introduction of electronic voting and other e-government applications.[30]

POSSIBLE IMPLICATIONS

In this section, we examine some of the effects of these trends in management and governance on Parliament, on the executive and the public service, and on the electoral process, and we do so from two perspectives: government's role as representing and representative, and its policy- and decision-making structures and processes.

Government as Representing and Representative
In Canada, Members of Parliament are elected to represent their constituents. Interest and lobby groups also may—and are often encouraged to—deal directly with parliamentarians, cabinet ministers, and senior public servants when they want to have an impact on public policy and its implementation. In addition, a great deal of effort goes into ensuring that the various elements of the machinery of government reflect the variety of cultures and individuals in Canada. The prime minister attempts to get his cabinet to be as representative of the regions, religions, genders, cultures, and other key elements of the population as possible, even though convention requires that he must choose its members from his caucus. Similarly, attempts have been made to ensure that the public service, courts, and other national institutions represent the breadth and depth of Canadian society. In this section, we are examining the potential implications of management and governance trends on government's role as representing and representative. We have identified five sets of implications.

1. Representing Group Interests
The trends have at least four related implications in relation to the representation of various group interests at the national, regional, and local levels.

Partnering and other ASD strategies are considered to be moves away from support for interest criticism and advocacy to an emphasis on service delivery and implementation. Although such strategies may save money and enable governments to offer programs and services that would not otherwise have been possible, the political emphasis on reducing expenditures has meant fewer resources for certain groups, including First Nations, women, and visible minorities, to voice public criticism.[31] In effect, partnerships and other ASD strategies have reduced the need for government to financially support some of these groups, because they are now receiving financial and other resources from their various partnerships.

The move away from criticism and advocacy toward service delivery and implementation has at least two more consequences. First, the federal government may focus more on the concerns of the partnership as a whole than on the specific concerns of individual members. Second, as partnerships and other arrangements become the preferred mode of responding to the needs and wants of the public, clients, and customers, the voice of groups and interests as individual members in these arrangements may be drowned out, because they become one among many members. This does not mean, however, that partners are necessarily precluded from voicing their opinions outside of the confines of the partnership, although their effectiveness in doing so may be diminished.

2. Increased Involvement in the Electoral Process
As particular interests find that their influence on the day-to-day operations of government is diminishing, their involvement in the electoral process may increase. A major implication of building partnerships between government and minority groups, citizens, clients, or customers is that *buy-in* is created. Along with buy-in comes the expectation that the government's side of the bargain will be maintained and upheld. If it is perceived that these relationships or arrangements are threatened by the stated policies or positions of opposition political parties, some groups may find it necessary to become more involved in the electoral process in order to preserve the integrity of current arrangements. For example, First Nations felt threatened by the Canadian Alliance party's election promise that it would re-evaluate current self-government policy. The Assembly of First Nations and several provincial Aboriginal organizations campaigned openly against the party and in support of the Liberals in the 2000 election.

3. Parliament's Watchdog Role
The watchdog role of Parliament and of individual MPs may also be affected by the public sector's reliance on partnering and by shifting responsibility strategies. As responsibilities are shifted, parliamentarians

may wish to become more rigorous in the exercise of their oversight responsibilities through parliamentary committees. Parliament's right to seek answers about the stewardship of public funds may become more difficult to satisfy as access to and availability of information from outside partners becomes complicated by partner concerns over issues related to independence, competitiveness, and privacy.

With respect to the watchdog role of individual MPs, their importance as representatives of individual constituents and of local interests may increase. Constituents and local interests may be inclined to take their complaints about programs and services to the local member, as well as to the service-provider. The MP may, therefore, have to become a more effective watchdog over the way in which government programs and services are being delivered locally and represent those concerns to caucus, to the public service, and to the executive. MPs may also find they have to take a more active role in finding solutions and in resolving disputes between their constituents and the government.

4. Local Public Servants as Representing and Representative

Public servants are also well equipped to represent the interests of the communities in which they live and work, because partnerships and other ASD strategies require their direct participation. As is the case with the local MP, these public servants are representative of local values and challenges. They are committed to making sure that arrangements work effectively, and, in fact, may give much of their own time, over and above that required by their official positions, to achieve this end. In this way, they represent the needs and wants of local communities up the line, through their departments. Although this may be very positive, it has led public servants, in some cases, to believe that they are directly accountable to their clients.

5. The Role of Information Technology

The current state of information technology also makes it possible for the direct participation of citizens in the democratic process. But the technology has its limitations. It does not aggregate interests in an orderly way. Moreover, the relative speed and frequency with which technology allows individuals and groups to communicate their opinions and demands—and change their minds—cannot provide the relatively stable set of views government needs in order to develop policies and programs and eventually measure their effectiveness. The electoral process and party system, Parliament and its individual members, and the government of the day collectively fill these roles. At the same time, the very possibility of direct citizen involvement through e-government puts pressure on the usual modes of representing to become more effective in aggregating and responding to the needs and wants of Canadians.

Policy- and Decision-Making Structures and Processes
Parliament, the executive, and the public service all have significant policy- and decision-making responsibilities. How well they are able to meet these responsibilities depends on several factors. We have identified four of these factors relative to the trends we have been discussing.

1. Public Service Accountability
Service to the public and ASD initiatives are challenging the traditional concept and practice of accountability—that is, that public servants are accountable, up the line, through the bureaucracy, to their deputy, the minister, cabinet, the prime minister, and Parliament. Time and again we have been told by front-line public servants and, sometimes, by more senior managers, that they are somehow accountable to their clients. The implication is that clients and customers somehow have the *right* to sanction or reward individual public servants *directly* for their performance, and that accountability up the line ought, perhaps, to be a secondary consideration. We have also found that public servants at all levels seem to be confused about how accountability works within partnerships, and between individual public sector partners and their own departments or agencies. How public service accountability should be applied in the context of service to the public and ASD needs to be clarified.

2. Leveraging, Control, and Influence
By partnering, government is able to leverage relatively small amounts of resources into more substantial ones, or get different, more, and/or better results from limited resources. There is an associated cost, however. When government has full control over support and delivery of its programs and services, it has the option, if it so wishes, of making policy and day-to-day decisions virtually unopposed. But as one partner among others, government can exert direct control only over those

resources it has contributed to the partnership and those aspects of the activities or outcomes for which it has taken responsibility. Otherwise, government must depend on its ability to influence the other partners. How successful it is at doing this depends directly on whether its participation is essential to the partnership, and the respect the other partners have for it.

3. Today's Decisions in the Future
Partnerships inevitably bind government, implicitly or explicitly, to certain obligations and/or expectations about what decisions are within an acceptable range. A partnership agreement sets out the nature of the relationship and the conditions under which it will operate, and the partners are bound by them. From time to time, however, government will find it no longer wants to be involved, because of changes in circumstances, new policies, and/or different public priorities. It needs to determine how best to deal with this eventuality *before* entering into partnership agreements, and to do so in a way that does not undermine the possibility of developing good working relationships with those involved.

Some departments have tried to deal with this challenge by specifying that their partnership agreements be evaluated yearly on the basis of performance, and that their involvement has a five-year limit. Although this might be a good idea in some cases, it might well discourage businesses from becoming active partners in projects involving a great deal of time and money, like rapid transit or other capital-intensive projects.

4. The Need for New Skills
As public sector organizations continue to evolve from bureaucratic to post-bureaucratic forms, both politicians and public servants will require new skills. Public servants who are already weary of having to deal with change are now being asked to manage risk and relationships that are increasingly decentralized. They are also being asked to manage services that are results-oriented as opposed to administering programs according to established rules, regulations, and budgets. In addition to exercising the traditional skills of planning, organizing, budgeting, and supervising, they are required to manage and facilitate relationships with clients and citizens. This demands leadership, communication and negotiating skills, and working in cross-jurisdictional

teams in a competitive and results-oriented environment. In this regard, it is significant that one of the key sets of competencies now required by senior public servants is that associated with partnering.[32]

Similarly, politicians may have to acquire a new set of skills. There may be pressure, for example, to rely less on partisan politics and concentrate more on skills associated with facilitating results, such as negotiation, dispute resolution, listening, and the like. They will also likely have to work more regularly with politicians in other jurisdictions in a non-ideological way.[33] There is, in fact, evidence that this is already happening in some jurisdictions. For example, in Ottawa and Vancouver, politicians from all levels of government are beginning to come together to address quality of life and infrastructure issues.[34]

REFLECTIONS ON THE NEW MANDATE

We believe it is unlikely that the federal government will retreat from partnering as its preferred approach for optimizing public resources and for taking advantage of various skills both within and outside of the public sector. *Red Book III* outlines the Liberal strategy for using partnership arrangements to address local issues, such as the decaying municipal infrastructure and shortages of affordable housing for low-income Canadians.[35] One of the most important challenges will continue to be how best to structure effective accountability arrangements in the context of partnerships so that the key expectations of those involved can be met *and* reasonable approaches are in place to deal with problems as they arise.

On another front, Treasury Board has just announced major pay increases for senior managers in an effort to attract new people with the requisite skills to deal with e-government, partnering, and other aspects of the New Public Management.[36] Public servants can expect to be evaluated on their ability to manage in a more businesslike public sector environment; their skills and aptitude for partnering and for working collaboratively, more generally; their willingness to take on reasonable risks; and their service orientation.

The decentralization and devolution of responsibilities in the public sphere are also likely to continue, as demands for more local service increases. In the case of First Nations, for example, new self-government arrangements raise complex questions about how best to divide responsibilities and to design appropriate accountability frameworks that respect local autonomy. Such arrangements will continue to raise concerns about the extent to which the minister can reasonably be held to account for activities well beyond his or her control.

Although the Prime Minister's application to overhaul his web site was rejected recently (!),[37] the 'Government On-Line' program highlighted in *Red Book III* is expected to remain a priority in order to enhance public access to government services via the Internet and to improve ways of communicating with citizens. Service to the public will also likely continue to be an important public service value. And significant questions about the appropriate use of technology in this regard will require increased attention.

CONCLUSION

The impact of partnering, service to the public, shifting responsibility strategies, and information technology on the way we are governed is likely to be more pronounced as these trends become accepted as part of general practice. Government is just beginning to recognize that they may be deep and enduring. The Treasury Board Secretariat and the CCMD, for example, are each involved in studies of partnership, horizontality, and service to the public that focus, in part, on the challenges of managing ASD, accountability, and performance evaluation and reporting. A recent report of the Standing Committee on Public Accounts indicates that Parliament and the Auditor-General are also concerned about accountability and managing risks, and the adequacy and availability of information.[38] And as we have already noted, public servants at all levels feel they need guidance on how accountability and responsibility apply to them in this new environment.

NOTES

1 See, for example, Donald Savoie, 'Public Administration: A Profession Looking For a Home', in Laurent Dobunzinskis, Michael Howlett, and David Laycock, eds, *Policy Studies in Canada: The State of the Art* (Toronto: University of Toronto Press, 1996), 125-46.
2 See Canada, *Public Service 2000: The Renewal of the Public Service of Canada* (Ottawa: Supply and Services Canada, 1990).

3 See Gilles Paquet and Robert Shepherd, 'The Program Review Process: A Deconstruction', in Gene Swimmer, ed., *How Ottawa Spends 1996-97: Life Under the Knife* (Ottawa: Carleton University Press, 1996), 39-72.

4 The issues examined in this chapter have been addressed by the authors in consulting projects for several federal departments and agencies, including the Treasury Board Secretariat (TBS), the Canadian Centre for Management Development (CCMD), the Canadian International Development Agency (CIDA), the Department of Foreign Affairs and International Trade (DFAIT), the Canadian Food Inspection Agency (CFIA), the Department of Fisheries and Oceans (F&O), Indian and Northern Affairs Canada (INAC), and the Pest Management Regulatory Agency (PMRA).

5 In this chapter, we are using the terms 'general public' and 'citizen' to refer to all Canadians—whether they use a particular government program or service or not—who have established rights and obligations as Canadians. We use the term 'client' to refer to those who use the professional services of specialists in the public sector for such things as legal advice, accounting, program advice and secretariat services, and advocacy. We use the term 'customer' to refer to those who purchase goods or services from the public sector (e.g., passports, printing services, publications, or materiel). For further discussion of the distinctions, see Henry Mintzberg, 'Managing Government, Governing Management', *Harvard Business Review* 74, 3 (May-June 1996): 75-83.

6 'Representing' refers to the process by which the electorate is represented in Parliament through the electoral process. It also refers to the fact that interest and lobby groups are permitted and often encouraged to make their interests and concerns known to any one or all of Parliament, the cabinet and ministers, and the public service. See A. Paul Pross, *Group Politics and Public Policy* (Toronto: Oxford University Press, 1986), for a discussion of the role of interest and lobby groups in Canadian politics. 'Representative' refers to the role of these elements of the machinery of government in reflecting the breadth and depth of Canadian society. Kenneth Kernaghan and David Siegel summarize the literature on representative Canadian institutions, specifically representative bureaucracy, in *Public Administration in Canada: A Text,* 4th ed. (Toronto: Nelson, 1999), 575-95.

7 The Social Union Framework (Feb. 1999) outlines the principles to which Canadian federal, provincial, and territorial governments are committed in the areas of health, citizen mobility, and social programs. See web site: www.hc-sc.gc.ca/english/archives/releases/1999

8 It is our purpose to give an overview of the variety and complexity of federal partnerships, and the difficulties facing them. For a more thorough discussion see Jim Armstrong and Donald Lenihan, *From Controlling to Collaborating: When Governments Want to Be Partners* (Toronto:

IPAC, 1999). See also Kenneth Kernaghan, Brian Marson, and Sanford Borins, *The New Public Organization* (Toronto: IPAC, 2000), 179-206. Note that contracting-out (*client-contractor partnerships* in Armstrong and Lenihan, 13-14) has been excluded from our understanding of partnering because it does not involve the sharing of power and decision-making or, in most cases, joint risk-taking. Consultation (*consultative partnerships* in Kernaghan et al., 179-85, 190-1) has also been excluded, because we consider it to be a separate process, and one that is essential to successful partnering, service to the public, e-government, and other new public management strategies.

9   Support for partnering as an option for policy and program development and for service delivery was given in *Public Service 2000: The Renewal of the Public Service of Canada*, 41. In 1993-4, as part of Program Review, departments and agencies were asked to determine what programs or activities should or could be provided using partnerships or divested completely. The 1996 Annual Report of the President of Treasury Board to Parliament, *Getting Government Right: Government for Canadians* (Ottawa: Public Works Government Services Canada, 1996), indicated that partnerships within government and with outside parties are here to stay. And three consecutive *Annual Reports* to the Prime Minister on the state of the public service by Jocelyne Bourgon, then Clerk of the Privy Council, revealed a commitment at the highest levels to partnering as a predominant government strategy (Fourth Report, Feb. 1997; Fifth Report, Mar. 1998; and Sixth Report, Dec. 1998).

10 See John Tait, *A Strong Foundation: Report of the Task Force on Public Service Values and Ethics* (Ottawa: CCMD, 2000), especially 33-5, on horizontality.

11 Team Canada Inc, *Business Plan 1999-2002*, and *The Business Plan at a Glance 1999-2002* (Ottawa: Government of Canada, 1999). More information about TCI and its services is available at web site: www.exportsource.gc.ca

12 See web site: www.international.gc.ca/public/2_0_main/

13 The Sussex Circle, *National Capital Commission: Enhancing Relations* (Ottawa, Oct. 2000).

14 For the characteristics of an effective accountability relationship in the context of the new public management see Walter Baker and Anne Perkins, 'Clarifying and Valuing Accountability', *The Canadian Executive* 1 (Winter 2001): 24-27.

15 *Public Service 2000: The Renewal of the Public Service of Canada*, 51-61. Client-oriented service has been an integral part of the Total Quality Management (TQM) and Service Quality (SQ) movements in the private sector since the 1980s. Some federal departments considered adopting TQM/SQ in response to the PS 2000 client service challenge (e.g., Health and Welfare Canada; see Walter Baker, *Toward Strengthened Client*

and Stakeholder Involvement, report prepared for the Health and Welfare Canada Task Force on Service to the Public, July 1991). An overview of the key approaches to client service in the private sector and the government of Canada is given in Kenneth Kernaghan et al., *The New Public Organization*, 132-43.

16 Bruce Rawson (Chair), *Service to the Public Task Force* (Ottawa: Public Service 2000, Oct. 1990).

17 See Anne Perkins, 'The Quality Services Initiative Strategy for Client Satisfaction', *Canadian Government Executive* 3, 3 (1997): 18-21. Quality Services is now part of the Service and Innovation Sector at the Treasury Board Secretariat.

18 For more information on Service Canada, see Canada, *Service Canada Strategic Business Plan* (Ottawa: Treasury Board Secretariat, Dec. 1999), and the Service Canada web site: www.servicecanada.gc.ca

19 John Tait, *A Strong Foundation*, 32-3.

20 See Canada, *First Progress Report on La Relève: A Commitment to Action* (Ottawa: PCO, 1998), 42-3.

21 The GTS Katie case involved the hiring of a foreign freighter to transport National Defence armaments and vehicles from Yugoslavia after completion of a United Nations peacekeeping mission. The shipping company had defaulted on its debts and was unable to pay its docking fees in Canada. Therefore, it remained outside Canadian waters until the shipping company could resolve the situation.

22 We have drawn on the typology of decentralization set out by Pollitt and Bouckaert with some modifications. See *Public Management Reform: A Comparative Analysis* (New York: Oxford University Press, 2000), 83-6.

23 Michael Prince, 'Banishing Bureaucracy or Hatching a Hybrid?: The Canadian Food Inspection Agency and the Politics of Reinventing Government', *Governance*, 13, 2 (Apr. 2000), 215-32.

24 See Donald Savoie, *Thatcher, Reagan, Mulroney: In Search of a New Bureaucracy* (Toronto: University of Toronto Press, 1994), especially chap. 4.

25 Canada, 'Notes for an Address by André Lafond, Deputy-Director of Investigation and Research, Competition Bureau to the Canadian Bar Association, Competition Law Section' (Ottawa: Industry Canada, Sept. 1997). Note that all orders of government have also used partnerships to support private industry—for example, the Beaufort Sea and Hibernia natural resource projects, and, more recently, the hi-tech information and medical research industries.

26 See web site: www.tbs-sct.gc.ca/cmo_mfc/

27 See Canada, 'Using Technology Wisely and Well: Today's Key to Tomorrow's Strong Canada', Notes for an address by Mel Cappe, Clerk of the Privy Council and Secretary to Cabinet, at the Professional

Development Forum, Technology in Government Week (Ottawa: Privy Council Office, Oct. 1999).
28 Speech from the Throne (Ottawa: Oct. 1999).
29 See Canada, *Connection, Community, Content: The Challenge of the Information Highway*, Final Report of the Information Highway Advisory Council (Ottawa: Minister of Supply and Services, 1995).
30 KPMG and the Sussex Circle, *Technology and the Voting Process* (Ottawa: KPMG, Nov. 2000). An abstract of this report is available on the Elections Canada web site: www.elections.ca
31 Susan Phillips, 'How Ottawa Blends: Shifting Government Relationships with Interest Groups', in Frances Abele, ed., *How Ottawa Spends 1991-92: The Politics of Fragmentation* (Ottawa: Carleton University Press, 1991), 211.
32 See Canada, *Competencies in the Public Service* (Ottawa: Public Service Commission, 1999).
33 Recent surveys of citizens on the topic of citizen engagement indicate that when they were asked whether they had leanings toward liberalism or conservatism, almost 40 per cent responded that they had leanings neither one way or the other. 'Citizens want a middle way in the management of their programs and services that is not politically or ideologically-driven.' Findings of a national citizen survey presented by Frank Graves, President, Ekos Research Associates Inc., at the Institute of Public Administration of Canada Annual Conference, Ottawa, Ontario, 30 Aug. 2000,
34 CBC Radio Interview with Mr. David Pratt, MP for Gloucester-Carleton, 25 Jan. 2001.
35 Liberal Party of Canada, *Opportunity for All: The Liberal Plan for the Future of Canada* (Ottawa: Liberal Party of Canada, 2000), 26.
36 Kathryn May, 'Top Bureaucrats to Earn up to $310,000', *The Ottawa Citizen*, 11 Jan. 2001, A3.
37 Chris Cobb, 'Overhaul of PM's Website Rejected', *The Ottawa Citizen*, 13 Jan. 2001, A1-A2.
38 See Canada, 'Involving Others in Governing: Accountability at Risk', Thirteenth Report of the Standing Committee on Public Accounts, Tabled 8 June, 2000. In its response, Treasury Board Secretariat indicated that it is working with departments to provide information about ASD initiatives as an integral part of their performance reports; The Treasury Board Secretariat response can be found on web site: www.tbs-sct.gc.ca/Pubs_pol. For an indication of CCMD interest in horizontality, search for horizontal management and partnership on web site: www.ccmd-ccg.gc.ca

5

Aiming for the Middle: Challenges to Federal Income Maintenance Policy

GERARD W. BOYCHUK

The 2000 federal election provides an excellent opportunity to take stock of the evolution of income maintenance policy during the last Liberal mandate and to assess its likely future. Across western industrialized countries, the role of income maintenance has shifted from that of a buffer against market forces toward that of a facilitator of market adjustment. Recent developments in Canada have taken place within this broad framework.[1] However, the specific changes to income maintenance in Canada have also been shaped by additional factors, such as the operation of federal-provincial relations, the shifting politics of budgetary restraint and surplus, and electoral imperatives. As a result of these forces, the thrust of federal income maintenance policy over the Liberals' second mandate was to reorient federal policy toward the middle class.[2]

In examining these issues, the chapter provides a retrospective on governance in this policy area over the past five years, a brief consideration of the role of income maintenance in the election campaign as well as directions policy might take in the new Liberal mandate, and an overview of the impacts of this shift and the outstanding policy challenges that the government will continue to face. These challenges stem from the paradoxical effects of the shift in income maintenance. While federal income maintenance programs are now on more solid political footing, social protection for the lowest-income individuals and families in Canada has been weakening—with significantly differential gender effects. Pressures may mount as this balance is challenged by economic downturns in the future.

THE LIBERALS, 1997-2000: A RETROSPECTIVE

This section presents an overview of the broad patterns of development in federal income maintenance over the 1997-2000 period, followed by a more detailed examination of developments within individual program areas. Put broadly, over this period, '[t]he federal government has clearly been retreating from social activism and de-emphasizing poverty mitigation as a major goal of social policy.'[3] Employment Insurance (EI) premium reductions have provided tax relief primarily to middle-income earners, while eligibility restrictions for the most vulnerable in the labour force (which were tightened considerably in 1996) have not been relaxed. Secondly, there has been a shift away from federal transfers to the provinces for needs-tested social assistance in favour of direct federally-provided income-tested child benefits under the Canada Child Tax Benefit (CCTB) and the associated National Child Benefit (NCB). These income-tested benefits reach an ever-expanding portion of the middle class and are increasingly framed by the federal government as a mechanism of middle-income tax relief.

This policy reorientation has not been part of an overarching vision or strategy. The political pressures pushing federal policy toward support of the middle class have been varied. The government was reluctant to reduce EI premiums, because they were generating huge surpluses, but it eventually had to relent in the face of demands for premium reductions from the provinces and the opposition. The shift in the Canada Health and Social Transfer (CHST) toward health care rather than social assistance is the result of a consensus covering the provinces as well as the public on the importance of preserving universal health care—a program with strong middle-class appeal. Similar pressure to preserve or expand the federal role in social assistance has been relatively limited in comparison. Finally, the federal focus on child benefits is a function of intergovernmental dynamics, with the federal government focussing on child benefits as an opportunity to reassert its visibility in this policy area *vis-à-vis* the provinces, while politically framing the program as a *children's* benefit to minimize the risks of attacks from the right.

While these pressures have been varied, together they have driven the re-orientation of federal income maintenance policy toward the middle class. As well, this reorientation was a deliberate electoral strategy. The shift by the federal Liberals over the 1997-2000 term was motivated by a recognition—similar to that of American Democrats—that their electoral fortunes had come to 'depend on whether they can rediscover the hopes and dreams of the middle class.'[4] The Liberal campaign strategy in 2000 echoed the 1992 Clinton campaign strategy 'to use "middle-class" as a prefix for every policy initiative it proposed.'[5]

Employment Insurance

The orientation of EI has shifted toward the middle class in two ways: by increasingly restricting eligibility for benefits to those with strong attachment to the labour force, and, secondly, by channelling the EI surplus toward premium reductions while portraying these reductions primarily as a measure of tax relief for middle-income earners.

The repercussions of the 1996 reforms dominated EI policy through the Liberals' second term. The reforms had the effect of restricting benefits for those with vulnerable positions in the labour force— especially part-time workers and new entrants into the labour market (see Appendix). Since 1996, EI has tightened eligibility, and fewer people have received benefits relative to the total number of unemployed— most notably, fewer women and youth.[6] These reforms, combined with brightening economic conditions, made the EI program a federal cash cow, generating an annual surplus of over $7 billion a year in

1997 and 1998 and an accumulated surplus of $33.2 billion by the end of 2000.[7]

When the federal deficit was erased, the dilemma confronting the Liberals was how to allocate the EI surplus: to general budgetary relief, a re-expansion of coverage and benefits, or a reduction in premiums. Accelerated premium reductions were not favoured by the Liberals initially, but the pressures in this direction were considerable and the government relented. As the 2000 election loomed, premium reductions became the rallying point around which Liberals' defended their EI record. As a result of the reductions, EI premiums are estimated to be $6.4 billion less per year now than they would have been if the 1994 rates had been kept in effect.[8] The 2000 budget projected a further $6.9 billion in premium reductions over the next three years.[9]

Until recently, the Liberals were resistant to expanding benefits and relaxing eligibility requirements. The sole EI benefit expansion of the Liberals' second mandate relaxed parental leave, doubling the maximum benefit duration from six months to one year, lowering the entrance requirements from 700 to 600 hours of insurable work, and allowing parents to earn up to $200 per month in addition to benefits.[10] All together the estimated cost of these changes was $900 million per year. While significant, the cost of such expansion was considerably less than additional EI premium reductions, which, according to the 2000 Budget, were slated to reach $1.8 billion in 2002–3 alone.[11]

The Canada Health Transfer and the Canada Child Tax Relief Benefit

Federal transfers to the provinces for needs-tested social assistance have now, through a series of changes, been essentially transformed into tax relief for low- and middle-income families. Federal contributions have been shifting away from transfers to the provinces toward direct transfers to families, away from programs including adults toward programs specifically earmarked for children, and away from programs targeted to the poor toward those that include significant benefits for middle-income families.

The growing federal focus on the health care component of the CHST is indicative of a major shift in which the CHST is now seen as a transfer primarily for health care. Hobson and St Hillaire compellingly argue that 'the CHST does not embody *any* federal contribution toward provincial welfare expenditures.'[12] When the Liberals shifted federal transfers to the provinces from their previous basis under Established Program Financing (EPF) and the Canada Assistance Plan (CAP) to the CHST, 'CAP somehow vanished along the way.' Noël argues that the federal equal-per-capita rule for the CHST (announced in early 1999) 'implied that the federal government had simply left the social assistance field, the least popular and least rewarding of its previous responsibilities.'[13]

A more charitable—though not more compelling—interpretation is that 'the welfare component of the CHST remain[s] well below what [it was] prior to the period of expenditure restraint in the mid-1990s.'[14] Using Hobson and St Hilaire's calculations of notional federal cash transfers for social assistance, and adjusting for inflation, federal funding for social assistance is now $3 billion a year less than it was in the last year of CAP's existence. Cumulatively, the federal government will have reduced transfers for social assistance by nearly $12 billion from the inception of the CHST in 1996 to the end of the 2000 fiscal year (see Figure 5.1).

The federal government now portrays itself as contributing to non-contributory income maintenance primarily through the CCTB and its low-income supplement, the NCB.[15] The latter is described in the 2001 Throne Speech as 'the cornerstone of our collective efforts to provide children with a better start' and 'the single most important social program to be introduced in this country since Medicare in the 1960s.'[16] It has also been heralded in some quarters of the social policy community as a highly successful response to the issue of child poverty.[17]

However, 'even with projected funding increases ... the NCB by no means replaces previous federal contributions to social programs under CAP.'[18] Since the inception of the NCB in mid-1998, federal savings in social assistance transfers can be reasonably estimated to be around $6 billion as of March 2001. In contrast, increased federal expenditures under the NCB over the same period total $1.7 billion. The February 2000 budget announced increases to the CCTB of $2.5 billion per year by 2004 with the increases being roughly split between low-income and middle-income families.[19] Thus, the federal government by the end of 2004 will have reinvested roughly $6 billion in income-tested benefits to low-income families. However, cumulative savings on federal transfers for social assistance from mid-1998 will be roughly

Figure 5.1

Notational Federal Cash Transfers for Social Assistance, Health, and PSE (1995–2003)

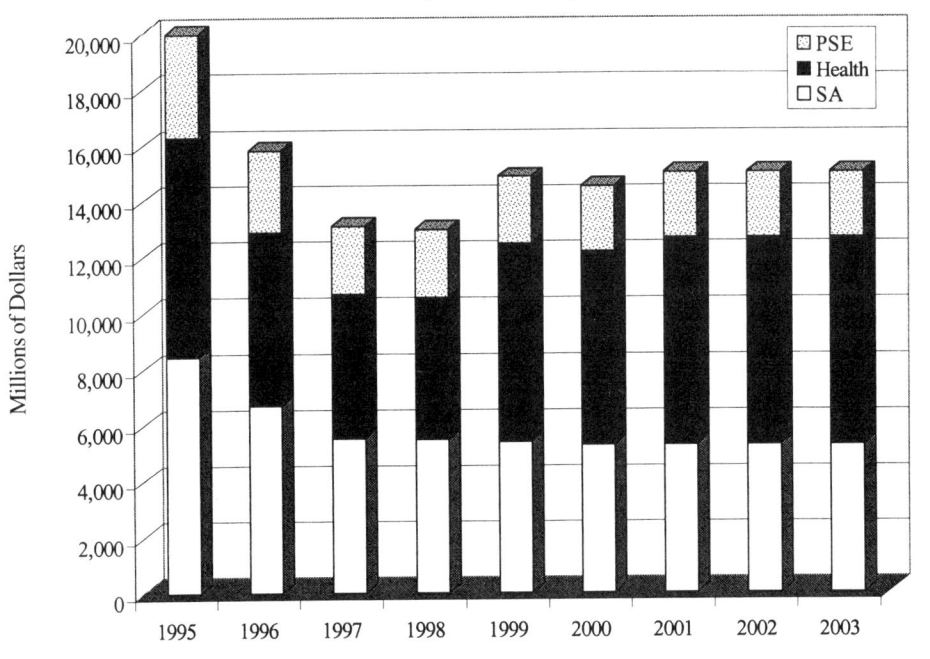

Source: Paul Hobson and France St Hilaire, 'The Evolution of Federal-Provincial Fiscal Arrangements', 176.

$16 billion by the end of 2004.[20] From an alternative perspective, the federal government spent $5.2 billion in 1995 on the CCTB and $7.8 billion under CAP, for a total expenditure of $13 billion on all non-contributory income maintenance benefits for children. Under the proposed schedule of CCTB expansion, total expenditures in 2004 will be $9 billion—$4 billion per year less in 2004 than they were in 1995, without considering inflation. Of the total of $9 billion, $6 billion is estimated to be aimed at low-income families.[21] Even this figure is $2 billion less per year than in the last year of transfers under CAP—again, not accounting for inflation.

There has also been a recent and quite dramatic shift in federal rhetoric regarding income-tested child benefits. When the NCB was introduced, the rhetoric spoke of investing in a stronger society through improving benefits for low-income families, while reducing disincentives to work. The program was portrayed as benefiting 'Canada's neediest children'—even if the characterization was misleading.[22] The CCTB has been portrayed more recently in budget speeches primarily as a measure of *tax relief* aimed not only at low-income but also significantly at middle-income Canadians. Given that the CCTB, for example, reaches two-children families with incomes of up to $82,000, this is more than just empty rhetoric (see Figure 5.2).

These changes represent a shift from programs such as means-tested social assistance designed to cushion the shock of economic dislocation to programs such as income-tested family benefits designed to encourage labour market flexibility. The changes also have been

Figure 5.2

Canada Child Tax Benefit

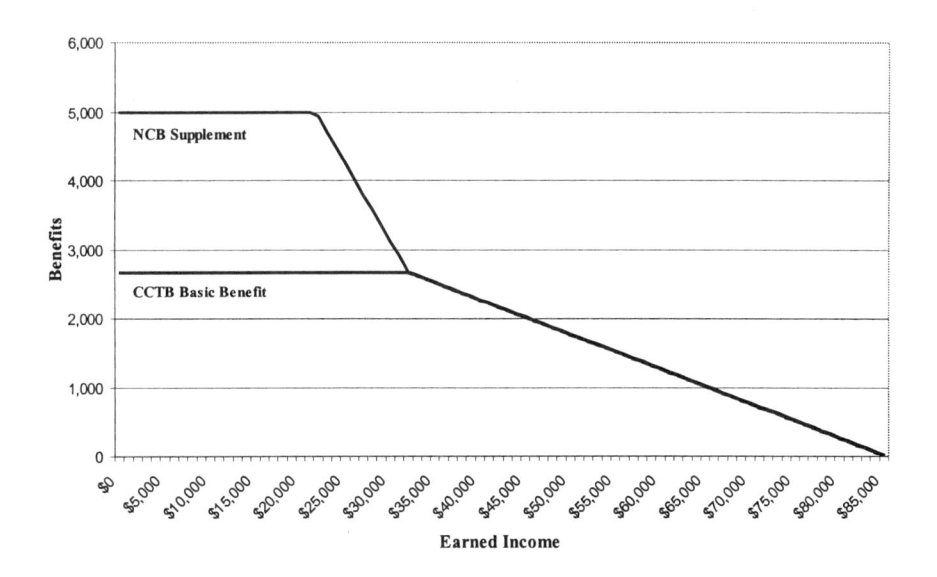

Source: Canada Customs and Revenue Agency, 'Changes to the Canada Child Tax Benefit (CCTB) for July 2001.' Web site: www.ccra-adrc.gc.ca/benefits/eco_statement-e.html

part of a deliberate strategy of focussing aid on families with dependents in order to encourage able-bodied persons without dependents into the labour market. At the same time, the shift toward health care rather than social assistance, and the extension of child benefits further and further into the field of income distribution (while rhetorically spinning these benefits as tax relief) appear to be a response to more ephemeral political considerations clearly evident in the recent federal election—the need to forge an electoral appeal to the middle class.

THE NEW MANDATE

Federal income maintenance programs as currently configured exhibit a strong middle-class bias—which is not surprising considering that the electoral support of this segment of the population, especially in central Canada, was the main prize in the 2000 federal election. The notable lack of discussion of income maintenance issues in the federal election campaign is suggestive of the political dynamics that make shifts in the current policy direction unlikely.

EI and the 2000 Federal Election

In income maintenance as well as other policy areas, 'the Liberals fought the key battles in th[e] campaign before Chrétien shuffled through the autumn leaves to ask Governor-General Adrienne Clarkson to put an early end to Canada's 36th Parliament.'[23] The electoral battle over EI was largely conducted in the opening days of the fall sitting of Parliament. The Canadian Alliance focussed its attack on the government almost solely on the issue of taxes, including EI premiums. However, the Liberals, having already responded to pressures to accelerate EI premium reductions, left the Canadian Alliance with little chance to score political gains on this front. Alliance references to 'job-killing premiums' only provided opportunities for the Human Resources Minister to repeatedly trumpet Liberal-led premium reductions.

The Bloc Québécois adopted a broader approach with a combined focus on the budget surplus and EI cutbacks. Every single day of the fall sitting the Liberals faced questions from the Bloc regarding the EI eligibility of seasonal workers, with the Bloc hammering the potent (if incorrect) point that two-thirds of working people in Canada were not eligible for EI. The Bloc's strategy gained further momentum as it increasingly linked the two lines of attack—claiming that the government's budgetary surplus was, at least in part, the result of changes to EI coverage and should be applied to the unemployment 'emergency'. This refrain was echoed by both NDP and Progressive Conservative members—especially those from Atlantic Canada. The Liberal defence consisted of pointing to the increase in jobs under the Liberal tenure as well as reduced EI premiums—neither of which stemmed the tide of questions regarding EI eligibility.

In response, the Liberals announced an EI expansion in late September. The changes removed the 'intensity rule', which had decreased benefits by 1 per cent of earnings for every 20 weeks of benefits claimed in the previous five years up to a maximum benefit reduction from 55 per cent of earnings to 50 per cent of earnings. The symbolism of this rule had generated a strong public backlash when it was announced in 1996, even though its actual effects were quite limited.[24] The proposed reforms left the most important of the 1996 provisions (including the hours-based system and its various eligibility thresholds) firmly in place.[25] Despite this, the proposals were announced amid gripping new reports of bitter political infighting in the Liberal cabinet and caucus, in which the Prime Minister championed the interests of seasonal workers and Atlantic Canadians and ultimately emerged victorious.[26] As an electoral ploy to forestall Bloc gains in Quebec and NDP/Progressive Conservative gains in Atlantic Canada, the proposals represented a clear aberration, although not a significant one, from the direction policy had been developing over the Liberal mandate. Estimated to cost $500 million a year, the proposed expansion paled relative to the simultaneously-announced premium reductions (from $2.40 to $2.25 per $100 insurable earnings), which totalled $1.2 billion.

The NCB and CHST

As with EI, the Liberals' main strategic moves with respect to the NCB and the CHST were taken before the election writs were dropped. Paul Martin's economic statement and budget update, presented just days before Parliament was dissolved, announced further increases to the CCTB, which accelerated the changes announced in the February budget.[27] The focus was on the NCB—the element of the system most clearly oriented toward low-income families. According to the February budget, it was expected that after an increase to the supplement of $200 effective July 2001, this element of the system would increase only through indexation.[28] However, the October economic statement announced that NCB benefits would be increased by an additional $100 for the first child effective July 2001. After this announcement, and perhaps because of it, non-contributory income maintenance programs were a non-issue in the federal election campaign. With the exception of the NDP commitment to doubling benefits under the CCTB, there was little focus on the issue of income-tested family benefits either in the party platforms or the election itself.[29]

In stark contrast, the CHST received considerable attention both before and during the election campaign—albeit solely in regard to its health care component. In preparation for the election, the Liberals announced that a CHST top-up deal had been negotiated with the provinces in early September. The deal would restore cash transfers under the CHST to their 1994 levels and would inject $23.4 billion into federal transfers for health care over five years.[30] Even so, health care still stole the social policy show in the election, despite the fact that there appeared to unanimous support among the parties for the conditions of the Canada Health Act and unanimous commitment to increase health care funding. Illustrative of the general transformation in the rhetoric surrounding the CHST, elements of the transfer other than health received virtually no attention.

The Aftermath

As income maintenance policy issues played a very minor role in the 2000 election, we cannot speak of a clear policy mandate in this area. The post-election landscape does, however, appear to be marked by features that may be significant in the future evolution of federal income maintenance policy. Especially toward the end of their last mandate, the Liberals appeared to feel considerably constrained by the electoral threat from the right posed by the Canadian Alliance. Now that these fears have been dispelled, there may be room for the Liberals to engage in more innovative social policy. However, at the same time, the parties that pushed for expansion in income maintenance programs in the last Parliament (the NDP, the Bloc, and, to a lesser degree, the Progressive Conservatives) have all lost significant numbers of seats. The political push for new social policy initiatives will have to come from within the

Liberal caucus itself. Even if there is some expansion in program spending, there appears to be little reason to expect a significant shift in the orientation of income maintenance policy.

The Liberals will certainly reintroduce their proposed EI amendments in 2001. However, as argued above, the proposed expansion under this legislation was relatively minor, even if it was important symbolically. With the considerable expansion of the Quebec and Atlantic contingents of the Liberal caucus and the addition of personalities such as Brian Tobin to Cabinet, there will likely be greater pressure toward more significant program expansion, or, at least, stronger resistance to any future program retraction. In light of the combination of these factors and the favourable current budgetary conditions, expansions to the EI program are not out of the question.

The portrayal by the Canadian Alliance and several provincial premiers of EI premiums as a tax on jobs pushed the Liberals to adopt a premium-cutting strategy—in part to undermine the electoral appeal of the Alliance. This constellation of pressures is unlikely to abate in the short term, and any EI expansions will likely be undertaken within the framework of current premium levels. At the same time, further premium reductions may no longer be in the cards. The Liberals were never very enthusiastic about reducing EI premiums. Pressure from the Canadian Alliance and concerns that the EI surplus would be an election issue were important factors pushing the government to cut premiums. With both concerns behind them, it is much less clear that the Liberals will continue on this tack. Rather, what seems more likely is that the Liberals will reintroduce reforms that remove premium rate-setting from the ambit of the Employment Insurance Commission and shift the EI mandate in a more permanent fashion toward 'forward-looking sustainability'—a euphemism for erasing the EI surplus from the books.[31] Taking these considerations together, it may well be that the EI program will stabilize in a somewhat expanded form under current premium levels.

The election had no impact on the social assistance component of the CHST. The federal role in social assistance is tenuous and it is difficult to foresee circumstances under which it would or could be reinvigorated. The federal government is already committed to further strengthening its role in income maintenance through the direct provision of income-tested child benefits. Future enrichments to the CHST will likely be notionally targeted by the federal government to health care or, possibly, considering the commitment in the 2001 Throne speech to promoting innovation and research, to post-secondary education.[32] Considering the focus on health care by all parties, it is unlikely that any party would be able to effectively criticize targeted enrichments or to argue that they ought to be channelled toward needs-based income maintenance. This situation appears unlikely to change: '[T]he federal government believes that it has brought closure to the whole debate concerning its role in funding social programs nationally. With budgetary surpluses now a reality, the federal government seems little inclined to ... restore non-health-related social transfers to the provinces. ... Rather, it seems more intent on developing new and highly visible federal initiatives.'[33]

The political construction of the CCTB first as a children's benefit and now as tax relief to middle-income families with children has been effective in muting criticism of the program from both the right and the left. With the re-election of the Liberals, the evolution of the CCTB will likely progress pretty much according to script. However, when the federal government reaches its target benefit (slated for 2004 though possibly occurring earlier), a sharply declining proportion of future enrichments of the program will likely be targeted to those at the lowest end of the income distribution.[34] After this point, expansions of the program will probably focus on increasing the proportion of all families receiving benefits (by lowering taxback rates and pushing income cutoffs higher into the income distribution) and increasing the proportion of beneficiary families who receive the maximum benefit.

To the degree that the impetus for income maintenance policy reform and innovation will have to come from within the Liberal party under reinvigorated central leadership, there may be little reason for social policy advocates to be optimistic. Shortly after the election, in the face of provincial resistance, opposition attacks, negative editorial commentary, resistance from business-affiliated organizations, and charges that the Liberals had campaigned on the basis of a hidden agenda, Chrétien swiftly and firmly disavowed media reports that the federal government was considering a move toward a guaranteed annual income.[35] Expected to emerge as a major focus in the Throne Speech in 2001, the proposal has dropped off the political radar screen. The incident reveals the range of forces aligned against expansion of policies targeted primarily toward low-income individuals and families as well as the extreme caution the Liberals appear likely to exercise in the area of social policy. The 2001 Throne Speech restated the government's commitment to the more modest aim of continuing to raise and to support benefits under the NCB existing initiatives to 'test innovations' in provincial income maintenance programs for single parents.[36]

Developments thus far provide little evidence to challenge Osberg's relatively dismal prediction for federal social policy: 'On balance there would seem to be more likelihood than not that the federal role in social policy will continue to shrink. ... The rhetoric of social union may continue, but not the reality—at least for those under 65. The direct impacts will clearly be felt primarily by the poor, who are a minority of society, with very little political influence, and among senior policymakers there may well be a diminished sense that this matters much.'[37]

OUTSTANDING CHALLENGES

The increasing orientation of federal income maintenance policy toward the middle class has had the ironic effect of placing federal programs on a more solid political footing while simultaneously weakening social protection for the lowest-income individuals and families in Canada. Over the course of the late 1990s, the traditional pillars of the Canadian social safety system—unemployment insurance and social assistance—have been pulling further away from one another, leaving a growing gap between the two as eligibility for both programs has become increasingly restricted.[38]

For those eligible for social assistance, the NCB agreement ostensibly ensured that no family would be worse off under the new set of arrangements. However, according to some observers there are initial indications that some provinces may be moving to reduce overall benefit packages: 'Recent announcements of cuts to social assistance in Ontario and Nova Scotia would appear to violate the federal-provincial agreement that no child would be "worse off"'.[39] Across provinces, the evidence is mixed. In Newfoundland and New Brunswick, total (federal and provincial) benefits for social assistance families in 1999 were significantly higher than they were prior to the inception of the

NCB, as these are the two provinces that did not institute a clawback of increased federal benefits. However, in five provinces total benefit income was lower for families with children on social assistance in 1999 than it was in 1997—primarily because of inflation. There are no indications yet that this erosion of benefits is taking place at an accelerated pace in the wake of the NCB agreement. At the same time, there are strong reasons to suspect that the NCB will contribute to undermining the political sustainability of provincial social assistance programs in the future.[40]

Both the electoral politics and the dynamics of federal-provincial relations that drove the reorientation of income maintenance now appear to have largely played themselves out, and the primary challenge the government will face will likely be pressures generated by a future economic downturn. The current configuration of programs, which has emerged during a period marked by the lowest rates of unemployment in twenty years, remains to be tested when the unemployment situation worsens—as it inevitably will. The challenge will be twofold—fiscal and political. The expanded CCTB will be more sensitive to economic fluctuations than the fixed per capita federal contributions to social assistance that existed under the CHST. This will generate at least some fiscal pressure on federal policy in future periods of elevated unemployment.

Secondly, significant political tensions will likely emerge between demands for adequate levels of protection for low-income families and demands for the maintenance of benefits to middle-income earners. Universal income maintenance programs in Canada may well be dead; however, the political imperatives that underpinned them are not. Even though they provide benefits well up the income scale, programs that are close to universal (such as the CCTB, which reaches 80 per cent of Canadian children) are impervious to many of the most potent arguments against universality, including the argument that 'wealthy bankers' wives shouldn't get family benefits.'[41] The pressures to preserve these children's benefits in the face of an economic downturn will be considerable.

This is not to argue that universal programs offer the best strategy to improve the level of social protection offered to low-income Canadians, or, obversely, that targeted programs necessarily undermine that protection. All other things being equal, universal programs probably do offer better protection than targeted programs. However, in almost all cases the other things are not equal, and as a result, the 'political theory of universality' suffers from a number of serious shortcomings. The theory overstates the political sustainability of universal programs, and cannot, for example, explain the fact that universal family allowances in Canada were the target of cutbacks and dismantling earlier than more targeted programs—a failure that has been characterized as a 'serious challenge to the political theory of universality.'[42] From a policy perspective, the theory fails to adequately recognize the degree to which the relative effectiveness of targeted programs in providing adequate benefits to those most in need must be sacrificed in order to gain the political strength of more broadly-based programs. It also largely ignores the complex interactions between multiple programs at multiple levels of government; these interactions have important implications for the political sustainability of targeted versus universal programs.[43] Finally, the political calculation of this model (which is based on a distinction between the poor and the non-poor) is too simplistic; it neglects other important bases of political support for and resistance to various social programs. For example, a primary element of the political strength of the CCTB relative to social assistance is not that it reaches a wider range of the income distribution but that its benefits are directed specifically toward children and offer high visibility to the federal government for their contribution. Recent changes to income maintenance programs have likely undermined the base of political support for provincial social assistance programs, not because social assistance programs are now more targeted, but because these changes strongly defined the main policy challenge as those people who deliberately choose welfare over work.[44]

From a feminist perspective, the pattern of differential gender impact evident in the recent reorientation of income maintenance programs will be depressingly familiar and follows the pattern aptly noted by Bashevkin: 'Gender, class and minority status may prove central to understanding welfare state resilience in some areas (... health care ...) compared with its vulnerability in other sectors—notably social assistance.'[45] Regarding EI, it was recognized immediately that the primary impacts of the 1996 reforms were on women and youth.[46] Despite this, the most recent proposals to re-liberalize EI focus primarily on relaxing restrictions that 'affect men more than women.'[47] Even if there is a considerable expansion in EI eligibility or benefits, it is unlikely to undo the changes that have primarily disadvantaged women and youth. The federal abnegation of a significant role in social assistance in favour of expanding directly-provided income-tested benefits to low- and middle-income families has contributed to the increased vulnerability of programs that primarily provide aid to the lowest-income families, the large majority of which are headed by women. The rhetorical shift that decoupled the well-being of children from the well-being of the mothers of those children divorces single mothers as recipients of social assistance from their role as mothers of families in need—a role that historically has underpinned the limited political sustainability of such programs.[48] Bashevkin's analysis of the political landscape in the wake of the 1993 Liberal victory led to the conclusion that 'the particular consequences of policy retrenchment for less affluent interests, including lone-mother households on social assistance or part-time women workers ... were unlikely to create serious difficulties for a majority government in Canada.'[49] This analysis appears applicable to the current political context.

CONCLUSIONS

The broad trajectory of income maintenance policy over the Liberals' last term was marked by an increasing orientation toward the middle class, with negative effects on women. This orientation appears unlikely to change soon. Future EI expansions are unlikely to be targeted to those with more vulnerable employment, such as part-time workers and new labour market entrants—the very groups hurt by the reforms of 1996. Increases such as those proposed in the fall of 2000, which ease eligibility or extend benefits for those already well protected under the program, will simply reinforce the reorientation of the program. In social assistance and income-tested family benefits, pressures on the system in a future economic downturn may simply solidify support for the more broadly-based income-tested children's benefits while placing greater pressure on targeted needs-tested programs—reinforcing the reorientation of the system that has occurred thus far.

However, this path of development is not preordained. The federal election outcome has shifted some of the forces at play in shaping future directions in income maintenance policy, and alternative paths of development may have opened up. However, a significant shift in the direction of Canadian income maintenance policy does not appear very likely. Paradoxically, income maintenance programs in Canada are now on a stronger political footing, even as they appear likely to weaken social protection for the most vulnerable individuals and families in Canada. How this new policy configuration will stand up to the pressures of a future economic downturn remains to be seen. This challenge will, inevitably, arise.

Appendix
Impact of 1996 EI Reform on Coverage

The two major components of the 1996 changes in EI eligibility were a shift in mid-1996 to requiring 26 weeks of work for new entrants and re-entrants, and the subsequent shift to an hours-based system effective January 1997. The hours-based system opened up eligibility for part-time workers, who previously had to work at least 15 hours a week to have the week count as insurable.

Assuming that people work the same number of hours per week for the whole year, the changes actually restricted eligibility in significant ways (see Figure 5.3). For workers in areas with average unemployment levels, the change to an hours-based system only extended benefits to those working 14 hours per week (from the former minimum of 15 hours), at the same time as it increased the number of weeks to eligibility for all persons working less than 35 hours a week. In some cases (e.g., persons working 15 hours a week), weeks to eligibility in areas of average unemployment more than doubled. Eligibility was extended to part-time workers in high unemployment regions working 8-15 hours per week, who previously could not qualify. However, for all workers in high unemployment regions working from 15 to 35 hours a week, weeks to eligibility would be increased—again, more than doubling in some cases. Entrants and re-entrants working part-time (less than 23 hours per week) were in most cases now ineligible for benefits. For all new entrants and re-entrants working up to 45 hours a week, weeks to eligibility would be greater than prior to

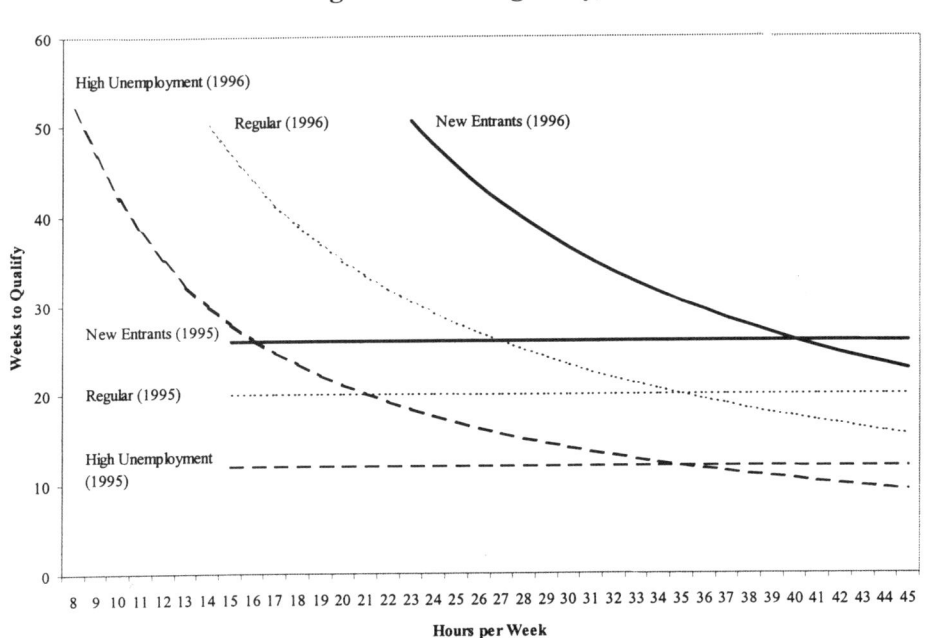

Figure 5.3
Changes in UI/EI Eligibility, 1996-7

Notes: Straight lines indicate weeks to eligibility under the weeks-based system prior to the 1996 reforms. Curved lines are weeks to eligibility under the hours-based reforms. Where the curved line is above the associated straight line, eligibility is more difficult under the new hours-based system. Where the curved line is below the associated straight line, eligibility is easier under the new hours-based system. Where the two lines intersect, ease of eligibility between the two systems is equal.

Source: Author's calculations.

the mid-1996 changes. At the same time, first-dollar-coverage would mean that all workers would begin to pay premiums, including those who could not hope to work the minimum hours required for eligibility.

NOTES

I would like to thank Angela McCallum for her research assistance, and the University of Waterloo for providing financial support. I would also like to thank the other contributors to this volume for their comments and Leslie Pal for his probing, constructive, and also extremely expeditious comments. Any errors of fact or interpretation remain mine.

1   For broader overviews of these shifts, see Denis Saint-Martin, 'De L'Etat-providence a l'Etat d'investissement social: Un noveau paradigme pour *enfant-er* l'économie du savoir?' in Leslie A. Pal, ed., *How Ottawa Spends 2000-2001: Past Imperfect, Future Tense* (Toronto: Oxford University Press, 2000), 33-57, and James J. Rice and Michael J. Prince, *Changing Politics of Canadian Social Policy* (Toronto: University of Toronto Press, 2000), esp. 141-3.
2   The 'middle class' is an amorphous concept. Rather than attempt to define it precisely, I will outline the broad contours of what I intend the term to suggest. In using the term middle income or middle class, I am referring to families and individuals whose income is nearly average (80% or greater) for that specific family type. In addition, I am referring to families with income earners who have some substantial attachment to the labour force. When referring to low-income families and individuals, I refer to families and individuals with incomes below one-half of the average income (the Statistics Canada Low Income Measure). The inevitable impression of these terms does not fundamentally undermine my argument that federal spending for income maintenance has shifted away from those with low or below-average incomes toward those with near-average or above-average incomes.
3   Lars Osberg, 'Poverty Trends and the Canadian "Social Union"', in Harvey Lazar, ed., *Canada: The State of the Federation 1999-2000, Toward a Mission Statement for Fiscal Federalism* (Kingston: Institute of Intergovernmental Relations, 2000), 218.
4   Stanley Greenberg, *Middle Class Dreams: The Politics and Power of the New American Majority,* rev. ed. (New Haven: Yale University Press, 1996).
5   Richard Iton, *Solidarity Blues: Race, Culture, and the American Left* (Chapel Hill: University of North Carolina Press, 2000), 169.
6   For an overview, see Tom McIntosh and Gerard W. Boychuk, 'Dis-Covered: EI, Social Assistance and the Growing Gap in Income Support for Unemployed Canadians', in Tom McIntosh, ed., *Federalism, Democracy and Labour Market Policy in Canada* (Kingston: Institute of Intergovernmental Relations, 2000). See also Human Resources Development Canada, *1998 Employment Insurance Monitoring and Assessment Report.* See web site: www.hrdc-drhc.gc.ca/ei/employ/sp121898/sum.shtml
7   Calculated from EI revenue and expenditure figures in Finance Canada, *Budget Plan 2000* (Ottawa: Public Works and Government Services Canada, 2000).

8. Human Resources Development Canada, News Release 00-66, 28 September 2000. See web site: www.hrdc-drhc.gc.ca/common/news/insur/00-66.shtml
9. Finance Canada, *Budget Plan 2000,* 20.
10. Speech from the Throne to Open the Second Session of the 36th Parliament of Canada (Ottawa: 12 Oct. 1999.)
11. Finance Canada, *Budget Plan 2000,* 22.
12. Paul Hobson and France St Hillaire, 'The Evolution of Federal-Provincial Fiscal Arrangements: Putting Humpty Together Again', in Harvey Lazar, ed., *Canada: The State of the Federation,* 175. Prior to the CHST, which rolled federal transfers for all social programs into one large per capita transfer, the federal government made transfers to the provinces under two programs, EPF and CAP. EPF was an equal per capita block fund for health and post-secondary education, while CAP was a transfer for social assistance that matched the funds spent by an individual province dollar for dollar. For an overview, see Hobson and St Hillaire, 'The Evolution of Federal-Provincial Fiscal Arrangements', 159-88.
13. Alain Noël, 'Without Quebec: Collaborative Federalism with a Footnote', in Tom McIntosh, ed., *Policy Challenges to the Social Union* (Regina: Canadian Plains Research Centre, 2001), forthcoming.
14. Hobson and St Hillaire, 'The Evolution of Federal-Provincial Fiscal Arrangements', 184.
15. The Canada Child Tax Benefit is the basic income-tested child tax benefit and has been in existence since 1978. The National Child Benefit is a low-income supplement and was implemented effective July 1998. Together with the range of provincial child tax benefits and other 'reinvestment strategies', the entire system is referred to as the National Child Benefit System. See the National Child Benefit web site at www.socialunion.gc.ca/ncb/ncb_e19.html
16. Speech from the Throne to Open the First Session of the 37th Parliament of Canada (Ottawa, 30 Jan. 2001).
17. For two examples of the many dissenting views, see Gerard W. Boychuk, 'SUFA, the Child Benefit, and Social Assistance', *Policy Options/Options politiques* 21, 3 (Apr. 2000): 46-7, and Richard Shillington, 'Two Casualties of the Child Tax Benefit: Truth and the Poor', *Policy Options/Options politiques* 21, 9 (Nov. 2000): 62-7.
18. Hobson and St Hillaire, 'The Evolution of Federal-Provincial Fiscal Relations', 180.
19. Finance Canada, *Budget 2000*, 89, 134.
20. These calculations are based on the last year of CAP transfers. Cumulative savings from the inception of the CHST in 1996 to 2004 will be $21.5 billion.
21. Finance Canada, *Budget 2000*, 219.
22. Shillington, 'Two Casualties', 65.

23 James Travers, 'An Ugly Outcome to an Unseemly Campaign', *The Toronto Star*, 25 Nov. 2000, B2.
24 'In reality, the provision has meant an average decrease in benefits of about $5.50 per week—enough to infuriate Atlantic Canadians but not enough to change seasonal work patterns.' Joan Bryden, 'PM Faces Fight to Restore EI Benefits: Cabinet Split over Bid to Woo Atlantic Voters', *The Ottawa Citizen On-Line,* 20 Sept. 2000.
25 A less visible but very important aspect of the proposed changes was the transfer of authority for the setting of premiums from the Employment Insurance Commission to Cabinet, which is discussed later in the chapter.
26 See Bryden, 'PM Faces Fight to Restore EI Benefits.'
27 Finance Canada, *Economic Statement and Budget Update 2000.* See web site: www.fin.gc.ca/ec2000/ecch1e.htm
28 Finance Canada, *Budget Plan 2000,*136.
29 New Democratic Party, *The NDP Commitment to Canadians* (2000), 11.
30 'Health Care to Get $23.4b Infusion', *The National Post*, 12 Sept. 2000, A1.
31 The HRDC backgrounder notes, 'Last fall, the House of Commons Finance Committee concluded that the rate setting process as currently set out in the *EI Act* is flawed. It requires looking back to take into consideration the level of past surpluses of revenues relative to program cost, when in fact there are no past surpluses sitting in a separate account. The Finance Committee states that: "EI rates should be set on the basis of the level of revenues needed to cover program cost over a business cycle looking forward and not taking into account the level of cumulative surplus or deficit, nor any interest associated with that cumulative position." HRDC, *Background Information on Employment Insurance*, 28 September 2000. See web site: www.hrdc-drhc.gc.ca/common/news/insur/00-66.shmtl
32 Speech from the Throne, 2001.
33 Hobson and St Hillaire, 'The Evolution of Federal-Provinical Fiscal Relations', 183.
34 At this point, income-tested federal benefits will have nominally replaced provincial social assistance benefits, so that provinces will not be required to reinvest clawed-back benefits. The ability of provinces to capture federal benefit increases above this amount will likely provide a significant disincentive to further increases to maximum benefits. See Boychuk, 'SUFA, the Child Benefit, and Social Assistance', 47.
35 Joan Bryden, 'PM Denies Income Plan on Agenda', *The Ottawa Citizen On-line,* 13 Dec. 2000.
36 Speech from the Throne, 2001.
37 Lars Osberg, 'Poverty Trends', 224.
38 See McIntosh and Boychuk, 'Dis-Covered', for an overview of these dynamics.
39 Richard Shillington, 'Two Casualties'.

40 See Gerard W. Boychuk, 'Social Union, Social Assistance', in Tom McIntosh, ed., *Policy Challenges to the Social Union.*
41 Linda McQuaig, quoted in Rice and Prince, *Changing Politics of Canadian Social Policy*, 174.
42 Rice and Prince, *Changing Politics of Canadian Social Policy*, 181.
43 For example, the potential for the broadly-based federal CCTB system to undermine the generosity of provincial social assistance programs is outlined in Boychuk, 'Social Union, Social Assistance'.
44 See, for example, Boychuk, 'SUFA, the Child Benefit and Social Assistance', and Boychuk, 'Social Union, Social Assistance'.
45 Sylvia Bashevkin, 'Social Policy During the Early Clinton and Chrétien Years', *Canadian Journal of Political Science* 33, 1 (Mar. 2000): 19.
46 Human Resources Development Canada, *1998 Employment Insurance Monitoring and Assessment Report*. As discussed in the Appendix, the likelihood of these effects should have been evident at the inception of these program changes.
47 Human Resources Development Canada, *1997 Employment Insurance Monitoring and Assessment Report*, chap. 2. See web site: www.hrdc-drhc.gc.ca/ei/employ/sp102198/chap2.shtml
48 This argument is outline more fully in Boychuk, 'Social Union, Social Assistance'.
49 Bashevkin, 'Social Policy During the Early Clinton and Chrétien Years', 33.

6

From Charity to Clarity: Reinventing Federal Government–Voluntary Sector Relationships

SUSAN D. PHILLIPS

In these times of leaner government and more collaborative governance, which involve the cooperation of multiple actors both within and outside the state in the design and delivery of public policy, the voluntary sector is often the silent and junior partner. Voluntary organizations provide a wide variety of public services either on contract or in partnership with government agencies. They often act in the absence of government. They also play an essential role in promoting active citizenship, because they rely upon voluntary participation of citizens in organizational governance and programming. By establishing networks of trust based on interpersonal interaction, they build social capital, and by giving voice to a diversity of communities, they help to create a more vibrant democracy. In spite of these contributions by the voluntary sector, historically the federal government's relationship with the sector has been more akin to charity than genuine partnership: government departments selectively handed out money to voluntary organizations to undertake certain projects or deliver programs that served departmental interests, and, with varying degrees of inclusiveness, they invited chosen 'stakeholder' groups to consult on policy issues.

Over its three terms, the Chrétien government has transformed its stance and policies toward the voluntary sector. For most of their first term, the Liberals followed the pattern set by the Conservatives before them: they slashed funding to a wide variety of voluntary organizations and ignored or even denigrated those who spoke out against government policy. The Liberals made an abrupt turnaround in the 1997 electoral campaign when, in Red Book II, they recognized the importance of the voluntary sector by declaring that it 'constitutes the third pillar of Canadian society and its economy' (the others being government and business), and committed a Liberal government to building capacity in the sector and a stronger relationship with it. Their second term followed through on this election promise by developing a framework policy known as the Voluntary Sector Initiative (VSI), committing almost $95 million over five years to it, and establishing a complex array of 'Joint Tables', which are unprecedented experiments in collaboration, to elaborate its details. The VSI is a multifaceted strategy that includes these initiatives: support for an 'accord' that will clarify and guide the establishment of a stronger relationship; research and information-gathering about the sector; capacity-building through skills and technology development; regulatory reform in the sector; and promotion of volunteerism during 2001, the International Year of Volunteers, and beyond. Although significant expenditures are involved, the VSI is less about programming that it is about building relationships.

The third Liberal mandate brings the test of implementation to this promise. In this implementation phase, the VSI has moved out of the limelight—receiving no mention in either Red Book III or the 2001 Speech from the Throne—and into the hard slogging of deciding upon and enacting program details.[1] Although the VSI has a strong presence within the government bureaucracy, the relative lack of public visibility raises the possibility that the old adage, 'out of sight, out of mind', may prevail. In particular, there is concern that Ottawa will implement only the easy parts of the strategy, while avoiding issues that it finds more contentious but that are nevertheless crucial for the future of the sector and its relationship to the federal government.

The success of the VSI will depend not only on its actual strategy, but on the process and structure through which it is implemented and on its ability to bridge two distinctive cultures. The chapter assesses each of these aspects—strategy, process and machinery, and culture—and concludes by speculating on the lessons learned from the VSI for collaborative governance more generally. It is helpful to begin by considering why the federal government is suddenly interested in a better relationship with the voluntary sector.

HOW THE VOLUNTARY SECTOR GOT DISCOVERED

Canadians have a strong tradition of volunteerism and civic participation. The 1997 National Survey of Giving, Volunteering and Participating indicated that 7.5 million Canadians annually volunteer a total of 1.1 billion hours through nonprofit organizations.[2] The result is a strong, vibrant, and diverse voluntary sector that consists of 78,000 organizations registered as charities with the Canada Customs and Revenue Agency (CCRA), about another 100,000 associations (such as advocacy, environmental, self-help, and women's groups) that do not qualify for charitable status, and an unsubstantiated number of more informal grassroots groups.[3] The range of activities in which the sector is engaged is enormous. It serves Canadians from womb to tomb, and its work involves both direct service delivery and public policy advocacy. Although the contribution of the sector to the economy is often overlooked, it, too, is significant. More than 570,000 people are employed by voluntary organizations, excluding hospitals and universities, and the voluntary hours contributed translate into the equivalent of more than a half-million full-time jobs.[4] It is important to note that, although it includes many large, sophisticated organizations with professional staff, the bulk of the sector consists of small organizations: 80 per cent of charities have annual revenues of less than $250,000 and 50 per cent, less than $50,000; 60 per cent have one paid employee or none.[5] The other interesting fact about the voluntary sector is that the public trusts it more than it does government or business. A 1998 Ekos survey showed that 89 per cent of respondents had moderate to high confidence in non-profit and voluntary organizations, while only 57 per cent had similar confidence in government and 76 per cent in private corporations.[6]

The reliance of governments on voluntary organizations to deliver human services and build communities predates the creation of the welfare state and has continued during welfare state retrenchment. Long before Confederation, the churches provided virtually all welfare and education services. The Canadian government first began a direct relationship with the voluntary sector in the early 1900s, when small grants were given to a few charitable organizations, such as the Canadian Lung Association and the Victorian Order of Nurses, to buy supplies and provide services to vulnerable populations that governments could not reach.[7] The relationship expanded considerably in the 1940s, when the federal government recognized the potential of voluntary organizations in nation-building and in constructing a distinctively Canadian citizenship.[8] The Citizenship Training Program, housed in the federal Department of Secretary of State, began funding voluntary organizations with the explicit goal of encouraging collective action as a training ground for good, loyal citizens.[9] In the late 1960s, indirect financial assistance to voluntary organizations began to be provided, first through a system of income tax deductions, and later through credits to taxpayers who made donations to recognized charities. So began a national system of registration and regulation of charities, now administered by the CCRA.[10] In the 1970s, operational funding to voluntary organizations engaged in promoting particular aspects of Canadian identity, such as official language minority associations and multicultural organizations, was expanded and institutionalized in the programs of Secretary of State.[11] Throughout the 1970s and early 1980s, voluntary organizations continued unobtrusively with their work, and the number of organizations grew rapidly.[12]

Things began to change for the worse in 1984, under the Mulroney government, when a succession of cuts was made to the core funding of a wide range of voluntary organizations. The motivation behind these cuts was partly financial—a desire to control the deficit—but not only financial, as evidenced by the fact that one year the money saved from voluntary organizations was used to pay for subsidies to industrial milk, rather than to reduce the deficit.[13] The Mulroney government also attacked the credibility of many voluntary organizations, particularly those critical of the government's social policy cutbacks, and questioned whether they, in fact, represented those whom they claimed to represent.[14]

The first term of the Chrétien government did not deviate much from the Mulroney pattern, but simply made funding cuts deeper and faster. An internal task force of Assistant Deputy Ministers (ADMs) set out a policy that only those organizations that directly supported the priorities and policies of departments should be funded, and most of this funding would take the form of project funding rather than core funding. The low point for the sector's relationship with the federal government was 1995-6, when the future direction of deep and continuing cuts articulated in the Program Review became fully evident, and it appeared that there was little interest in hearing from voluntary organizations on policy issues, unless they agreed with the government.

From this point, interest in building a more constructive relationship between the federal government and the voluntary sector developed along two parallel tracks, which merged in 1999. Until the mid-1990s, the voluntary sector in Canada had had no strong national leadership. Most of its 'national' organizations were structured according to subsector or service area, and there was no umbrella organization that spoke for the sector as a whole. A number of sector leaders came together to create such leadership, if not an actual organization. The Voluntary Sector Roundtable (VSR) emerged as a 'coalition of coalitions', whose twelve members represented the broad diversity of the sector, and which today remains unincorporated.[15] The VSR identified a number of priorities, including increasing charitable tax incentives and enhancing accountability, and received multi-year funding from the J.W. McConnell Family Foundation to pursue them. In the 1996 and 1997 federal budgets, lobbying efforts by the VSR proved successful in obtaining improved tax credits for charitable donations.

In order to be proactive in ensuring the sector's accountability and thus in maintaining its high level of public trust, the VSR set up an independent panel of experts, chaired by Ed Broadbent (former leader of the federal NDP), to conduct research, consult broadly, and make recommendations on improving accountability in the sector. The [Broadbent] Panel on Accountability and Governance in the Voluntary Sector saw in its mandate an opportunity not only to consider better self-regulation, but also to examine the sector's relationship with governments, particularly the federal government, which holds considerable regulatory powers through the tax system, and which seemed to be set on a path of imposing heavy-handed regulation on the sector. The Panel's February 1999 report made over 40 recommendations aimed at both the voluntary sector and governments.[16]

At this same time, an important shift in thinking was beginning to occur within the federal government. In preparation for the 1997 election, the Liberal party produced Red Book II, which made a commitment to increase the capacity of the voluntary sector to contribute to Canadian life. Why the change of direction? There were several reasons. The first was that a few key individuals in the Prime Minister's Office (PMO) and the Privy Council Office (PCO) had a deep appreciation of the sector's role not only in service delivery, but in democracy, and identified a link between the sector and the government's desire to engage Canadians. Second, the Chrétien government had also come to realize that it could not govern and deliver services on its own: that in an era of smaller government, it needed the voluntary sector as a partner more than ever. As the Prime Minister said at an international conference of volunteer managers in Edmonton in August 1998, 'After decades of thinking otherwise, we have had to come to terms—squarely and honestly—with the truth. That governments don't have the wisdom or the resources to do everything.'[17] Third, the federal government knew that it had lost visibility and credibility with Canadians—the provinces get much more credit for the services that most directly touch people's lives, and transfers and tax credits have rendered the federal government's indirect funding role in these services virtually invisible. Trust in government could be rebuilt, it was argued, by creating more social capital, and this is a distinctive contribution of the voluntary sector. The Canadian government was not alone in such thinking, in that most other developed democracies had also discovered the importance of the voluntary sector in the late 1990s. In particular, the Liberals have been able to look to the Blair government's 'Third Way' and its variety of measures to build stronger relations with the sector.[18] The particular Canadian twist on building a partnership with the voluntary sector is that that relationship can be used to support national unity. When relationships with the provinces are rocky, the federal government can maintain a direct connection with citizens and communities through support for voluntary action.

Following its re-election in 1997, the Liberal government began to work through an interdepartmental committee to examine how to give substance to the vague Red Book II promises. As with many interdepartmental mechanisms, the committee made slow progress. A Voluntary Sector Task Force with full-time staff was created and housed in the PCO—a location that gave it considerable stature—to assist and advance this effort. The Task Force's recommendations to cabinet for fulfilling the Red Book II promises, which drew upon the recently released final report of the Broadbent Panel, went forward in early 1999. At this critical point, ministers became directly involved with voluntary sector leaders when the ministers of Health, Human Resources Development Canada (HRDC), and Revenue hosted a working dinner attended by 10 other ministers and 20 representatives of the voluntary sector. Politicians' affinity with the voluntary sector should not be under-estimated, because most were active in a variety of civic organizations and service clubs before getting elected, and for the most part they have remained strong supporters of the VSI.

The sector's demands to be a full partner in the process of rebuilding a relationship and a realization that internal government mechanisms could not move the process forward on their own led to the establishment of a novel experiment in government–voluntary sector collaboration. In March 1999, three Joint Tables consisting of about 14 members each with equal representation from both sides and jointly co-chaired were created and charged with making proposals for building the relationship, strengthening capacity, and improving the regulatory framework respectively. Although the Tables had to finish their work by the end of August, the joint process was an enormous success, and the Tables' combined report, entitled *Working Together*, produced a set of recommendations that quite closely reflected those of the Broadbent Panel. For the next nine months, however, the joint process was suspended as government officials prepared the Memorandum to Cabinet (MC), ministers deliberated on it, and Treasury Board submissions were approved.[19] This cloak of silence caused considerable irritation in the sector, because the shift from the openness of the Joint Tables to the confidentiality of the executive policy process seemed abrupt and more extreme than in similar situations involving the private sector. It also produced fears that key recommendations would be lost. The first signal that the federal government would follow through came in the October 1999 Speech from the Throne, which committed Ottawa to enter into a framework agreement or accord with the voluntary sector and to provide support for the celebration of the International Year of Volunteers in 2001 and for an ongoing national volunteerism initiative. Funding allocations did not appear to follow in the February 2000 budget, however, which made no explicit reference to a voluntary sector initiative, although sector leaders were assured that the funds had been 'booked'.[20] On budget day, the Prime Minister gave a strong indication that action and funding would follow, thus subverting criticism from the sector, by announcing the creation of a Reference Group of eight ministers, chaired by Lucienne Robillard, President of the Treasury Board, to provide strategic leadership to the initiative. In early June 2000, Robillard officially announced the Voluntary Sector Initiative, with its twin objectives: to 'increase the capacity of the voluntary sector to meet the demands that Canadian society places on it', and to 'improve the Government's policies, programs and services to Canadians, leading to increased public confidence.'[21]

STRATEGY OF THE VOLUNTARY SECTOR INITIATIVE

The VSI's commitment of $94.6 million over five years beginning in 2000-1, most of which will be spent in the first three years, flows directly from the recommendations of the 1999 Joint Tables. The commitment holds a number of surprises, however, in what it identifies as priorities and what it excludes. The VSI is not simply an updated version of the abandoned Secretary of State programs. The model is not to provide core funding to individual organizations, but to finance the development of capacity-building processes and provide resources that will benefit the sector as a whole. The VSI sets out a general strategy and funding allocations for its main components, but the details are to be worked out by six Joint Tables, using the model of the 1999 experience.

As Table 6.1 shows, almost a third—$28.5 million—of the VSI budget goes to short-term programs to support the voluntary sector's involvement in departmental policy development. This allocation is one of the big surprises of the VSI. It was not a recommendation of *Working Together*, but emerged as a result of the confidential deliberations within government. There are two contrasting views as to why government, acting alone, decided to devote so much of the Initiative's funding to departmentally-based projects. The first is that, if the federal government is really going to work with the voluntary sector more effectively, this ultimately has to happen at the departmental level, and

Table 6.1
Activities and Allocations of the Voluntary Sector Initiative

Activity	Allocation ($ millions)
Involving voluntary organizations in the development of departmental policies and programs	$28.5
Strengthening the capacity of the voluntary sector	$24.9
Development of an accord and related relationship building mechanisms	$11.1
Enhancing the use of technology	$10.0
National Volunteerism Initiative and Celebration of IYV	$9.9
Regulatory reform	$8.6
Communications Strategy	$1.6
Study of federal funding policies	$1.0

this funding will allow departments to develop better practices. The second view is that this is the classic log-roll—a way to pacify and get the buy-in of departments that were not that keen on the proposed Initiative. Whatever the initial motive, the practical purpose of this funding, as encouraged by the voluntary sector, is to transfer as much of this money as possible to the voluntary sector, and to make it 'stick'. Projects undertaken by organizations will help them build greater capacity for policy development and engagement with government, and not simply let departments spend on their own projects or consultations. The first round of proposals was a highly mixed bag that reflected both vague criteria and the differing levels of sophistication among various departments and regional offices in engaging voluntary organizations.[22] It was thus apparent that the opportunities for voluntary organizations to benefit from this funding would be erratic and arbitrary. In order to improve this component of the VSI, one of the Joint Tables has undertaken the task of developing clearer criteria and open, transparent solicitation and review processes for approving departmental proposals, which will better meet the goals of enabling voluntary organizations to engage more effectively with the federal government.

Capacity building, the next largest allocation, includes a variety of measures, such as promoting skills development in the sector, expanding research, promoting awareness of the sector and its contributions, providing policy internships and academic fellowships, institutionalizing (on a three-year basis) the National Survey on Giving, Volunteering and Participating, and initiating a Satellite Account on voluntary activity within Statistics Canada's System of National Accounts, which will document the scope of economic activity and the contribution of the sector. Here, too, the VSI deviated unexpectedly from the original recommendations of the *Working Together* report. In preparing the MC, government officials asked the 1999 Joint Tables to identify among their many recommendations some 'quick hits'—things that could be done in a short time period that would show that progress was being made. Although these achievements would be immediately gratifying, they were never seen by the voluntary sector participants to be the real substance of the VSI. Yet many of these, such as the fellowships and the research agenda, now appear as core activities and the basis for budget allocations. In addition, the current process involves different people from the 1999 tables, not all of whom think that the original priorities should be maintained in the VSI. Consequently, the Joint Table dealing with capacity matters has had to refocus its work plan somewhat to ensure that important issues can be addressed under a funding framework designed to support mainly short-term objectives.

The establishment of an 'accord' between the government and the sector that sets out the expectations, mutual responsibilities, and good practices of their relationship, and the development of other (as yet undefined) initiatives, will receive $11.1 million. Of this amount, $2 million supports a much-needed coordinating secretariat within the sector and $2.4 million allows the Voluntary Sector Task Force to manage activities within government. Almost $10 million will be spent on a national initiative to promote volunteerism and celebrate 2001 as the International Year of Volunteers. In many respects, both of these are of higher priority to government than they are to the voluntary sector. Although both were part of the *Working Together* recommendations, they became elevated as priorities during the executive approval process because they are relatively 'quick hits'—things that can be done in a short period of time to show that progress is being made—and thus received substantial funding. Another $10 million is dedicated to enhancing the voluntary sector's capacity to use information technology, particularly to develop online tools, in a manner that is intended to complement the work of Industry Canada's VolNet Program over the past two years in connecting small organizations to the Internet. Regulatory reform involves review of the regulations and practices that the CCRA administers under the *Income Tax Act*. Finally, $1 million is allocated to an internal study of federal funding policies and practices related to the sector, and $1.6 million is devoted to a communications strategy.

The VSI is unquestionably an important step toward building a stronger government–voluntary sector relationship and it provides more money than ever before for capacity-building for the sector as a whole. There are several significant gaps in the Initiative, however, where the federal government has shied away from the major institutional and regulatory reforms articulated as top priorities by the Broadbent Panel or by the *Working Together* report.

The two issues that are of critical importance to virtually all voluntary organizations—advocacy and funding—but that are politically sensitive to ministers, have both been deliberately sidestepped by the VSI. As noted in the *Working Together* report, advocacy, as a form of free speech, can be considered an essential, constructive part of democracy and a benefit not only to the members and clients of voluntary organizations, but to the general public as well.[23] Yet, in spite of their recognition of the importance of the voluntary sector in service delivery, some departments still see its uninvited engagement in public policy advocacy as somewhat illegitimate. Advocacy by registered charities is unduly restricted (limited to 10 per cent of an organization's total resources annually), and the rules seem to be applied inconsistently, so that big charities, particularly universities, hospitals, and the large health charities are able to get away with much more than small organizations can.[24] In contrast to the charities, private corporations are virtually unfettered in their advocacy activities and can write off the costs as an expense of doing business, in effect enjoying a kind of public subsidy. The 1999 Joint Table, highlighting the unfairness of the restrictions on public policy advocacy, recommended considerable liberalization, with the caveat that advocacy activities should not become the dominant work of charities.

Like advocacy, government funding of voluntary organizations has been detrimentally affected by the public sector restructuring of the past decade. The result has been that voluntary organizations face a triple whammy. First, they have seen their government funding cut substantially and core funding withdrawn in favour of short-term project funding, leaving them with fewer resources and less ability to undertake long-term planning. Second, as governments cut or withdrew from the provision of many services, client demand for services provided by voluntary organizations increased. Third, because the entire sector is facing the same funding dilemma, there is increased competition in fundraising, so that it is more difficult to diversify funding sources. From the sector's perspective, the issues are not simply or even primarily *levels* of funding, but the need for stable, multi-year funding commitments in order to facilitate planning, recognition of the costs of administration and evaluation that are associated with projects and contracts, and consistency of practices across government departments.

The political directive given to the VSI is that neither advocacy nor funding is on the table for a full, joint review at this time. It provides only an internal government review of funding practices and a less visible review of policies surrounding advocacy, and sector-only working groups on both. The benefit of the VSI is that it is largely process-driven and flexible. Therefore, there is a possibility that the strategy will evolve to encompass a more serious and extensive joint engagement of these vitally important issues.

The other issues omitted by the VSI may seem more arcane and distant to the grassroots members of the sector, but they are nevertheless vital aspects of capacity-building. The first deals with the basis for determining charitable registration, and therefore which kinds of organizations are able to issue tax deductible receipts as incentives for giving. In making this determination, Canada, like other common law countries, relies on the English 1601 Statute of Elizabeth and the subsequent Pemsel case of the 1890s. The beauty—and the limitation—of the common law is that it remains as current as the last judicial interpretation. With regular judicial review, the common law could be highly flexible and adaptive to changing societal values and conditions, but in the absence of regular review, it risks getting out of step with contemporary society. The problems in Canada are twofold. First, the agency responsible for making decisions on charitable status is the Charities Directorate of the CCRA, which, as part of a tax agency, naturally has a primary and compelling duty to uphold the integrity of the tax system, and generally takes a conservative approach to permitting tax expenditures. Thus the CCRA has been criticized as being quite narrow in its interpretation of the common law in considering applications for charitable registration. This administrative restrictiveness is compounded by the fact that the appeal route for an organization that has been denied charitable status is to the Federal Court of Appeal, and this route is prohibitively expensive for most small organizations. Consequently, the Federal Court has heard only about 20 appeals of denial of charitable status over the past 30 years, and the Supreme Court only one.[25] The overall result has been that the interpretation of charitable status is more restrictive in Canada than in most common law countries. For example, in Canada, unlike Britain or the United States, organizations that promote racial harmony, environmental protection, volunteerism, and patriotism are not considered charitable and thus cannot use the tax system to help build communities of support.

The primary barrier to a review of the definition of charitable status and how it might be expanded is the Department of Finance, which fears that if more organizations are allowed to issue tax receipts, there will be a significant cost to the public purse. In addition, Cabinet perceives little political payoff in opening a controversial debate over charitable status.[26] The potential for political heat is probably less than imagined, however, because there are a number of obvious ways in which the policy could be relaxed in order to make Canada comparable to other developed countries.[27] The charitable sector is generally supportive of an expansion of the definition. The VSI has a mandate to assess the cost of a more expansive interpretation of charitable registration and to review the appeals process, but there seems little real interest on the part of the federal government in reviewing the definition of charity, even though this is a fundamental component of capacity-building.

Although the VSI has proposed some minor regulatory reform, institutional reform of the regulator itself has been quite timid. Constitutionally, jurisdiction over charities is a provincial matter, but most provinces (including Quebec, which administers its own tax and charitable registration system) do little to regulate or support the good governance of voluntary organizations. The federal government is involved, and indeed has become the *de facto* regulator, because organizations register as charities under the federal Income Tax Act, and in turn must file annual financial reports (called T3010s) and comply with certain restrictions on their conduct. The criticism is that the tax collector is not a suitable institution for regulating charitable organizations or for promoting good self-governance.[28] A strong case was made by the Broadbent Panel, by many charity lawyers, and by sector leaders themselves that a new institution, modelled loosely after the Charity Commission of England and Wales, should be created to replace the CCRA's role in the sector, and considerable work has already been done on institutional design.[29] The VSI has made a commitment not to implement institutional reform, but only to undertake further study of institutional models and conduct a targeted dialogue with the voluntary sector. Although this response is decidedly weak, given the extensive discussion that has already taken place on the subject, a stronger commitment to actually implement institutional reform may emerge from the Joint Tables.

In spite of these shortcomings, the VSI is a positive first step in building capacity in the sector and better relationships with the federal government. In many respects, the strategy itself is the most malleable aspect of the Initiative. Because the VSI sets up a collaborative process for the implementation of its strategy, there is a possibility that some of the issues currently left aside may become more central. There is a danger that the entire Initiative will suffer a significant loss of credibility, however, if the federal government is not sufficiently flexible and responsive in dealing with issues that emerge as central to the voluntary sector partners or to the participants in the extensive consultations that are planned as part of the process. The VSI will also need to be fleet-footed in another way: it must respect and respond to provincial and municipal initiatives in relationship-building. When the federal government began its efforts to build a stronger relationship with the sector in 1997, there was little serious activity at the provincial level to do the same, although the relationship is just as important provincially, if not more so. Over the past two years, however, many provinces and municipalities have taken some innovative steps toward better relations, including the development of proposals for accord-like agreements in Newfoundland, Quebec, British Columbia, Winnipeg, and the new merged city of Ottawa. These initiatives do not in any way pre-empt or diminish the importance of the VSI, but the federal government will need to ensure that, in its consultations and relations with provincial governments, it is sensitive to the implications of local developments.

PROCESS AND MACHINERY

The difference between governing in a unilateral, hierarchical manner and a collaborative, horizontal one is that the processes for governing take on new significance in the latter. Collaborative processes often require new institutional arrangements in order to work. For the VSI, both short- and longer-term issues of process and machinery are important. In the short term, during the actual development and implementation of the strategy, mechanisms for joint government–voluntary sector decision-making have been created by emulating the successful experiment of the 1999 Joint Tables. In the longer term, the question of machinery will focus on coordinating good practices related to the sector across government departments, and on providing mechanisms for obtaining input about and reporting publicly on their effects. This latter issue has received little attention so far.

Responsibility for determining specific priorities and projects under the VSI and for overseeing their implementation is assigned to six Joint Tables, and the coordination of common aspects of their work is managed by a Joint Coordinating Committee (JCC). This is a massive voluntary effort: both the public servants and the voluntary sector representatives have taken on the responsibilities of table participation in addition to their full-time jobs, receiving no stipends for their efforts. Each Joint Table consists of 14 to 16 members, half of whom are selected by the federal government and half by the voluntary sector, and each Table is co-chaired by a senior federal public servant and a representative of the voluntary sector (usually at the Executive Director level).[30] In order to ensure continuity of individuals' knowledge and experience with the Tables, both sides have agreed to a no substitution rule, so that if a member does not attend a meeting, an alternative cannot take his or her place. A prime factor in making it all work is simply time for full participation, particularly for the public servants, for whom this process may be lost in a multitude of other tasks. Whereas the voluntary sector leaders are also unquestionably very busy, they realize that this is probably their only shot at working out a better relationship in a systematic, collaborative way.

As Figure 6.1 illustrates, the six Tables map onto the main tasks of the VSI:

- The Joint Accord Table is responsible for developing a framework agreement between the federal government and the voluntary sector that establishes the principles, mutual undertakings, and good practices of a better relationship, and for leading an extensive consultation with both the sector and government departments.
- The Capacity Joint Table is charged with developing specific proposals for research, information sharing, and the development of human resource and other skills.
- The Regulatory Joint Table is mandated to make recommendations for regulatory reform starting in four priority areas: increasing transparency of the charitable registration process; examining intermediate sanctions for non-compliance with Income Tax Act regulations by registered charities (the only sanction at present is de-registration); reviewing the appeals process; and exploring options for the institution that registers and regulates charities.
- The National Volunteerism Initiative is responsible for developing programs that promote volunteer effort and increase the ability of the voluntary sector to provide beneficial experiences for volunteers.
- The Information Management-Information Technology (IM-IT) Table is given the task of supporting and expanding Internet use and enhancing the interactive tools available to voluntary organizations.
- The Awareness Table is intended to help raise public awareness about the voluntary sector and its contributions.

In addition to the six Tables, there are a number of working groups that deal with either more specialized tasks or ones that are not joint in nature, but allow important issues, including advocacy and funding, to be discussed within government and by the sector (See Figure 6.1).

Each of the Tables functions with considerable autonomy.[31] The JCC appears to be the kingpin in the organizational chart, with responsibility for general stewardship of the process and for coordination of cross-cutting activities such as communications and consultation strategies. It is not intended to impose its preferences regarding substantive issues on the individual tables, however. In part because the JCC has no overlap of membership with the other tables, it lacks intimate knowledge of the discussions of the other tables. The result is that the JCC has struggled to define a role for itself and has tended to focus on coordination, getting mired in detail, to the detriment of its vital stewardship function.

The position of the Tables in the broader governance structure poses its own set of problems related to leadership and accountability. As shown in Figure 6.2, the intra-governmental structure is a fundamental challenge to those who would institute collaborative governance. How does one coordinate actions and provide leadership across departments in a government structure still largely dominated by departmental silos and intra-departmental boutiques? On the government side, the Joint Table members report to interdepartmental working groups that initially reported to an ADM Steering Committee involving officials from 23 departments and agencies. Because the Steering Committee was large and attracted only spotty participation from many of its ADMs, a core group has been refashioned as an Executive Committee to provide more hands-on direction and guidance for ministers. It remains to be seen whether this Executive Committee can provide effective leadership and coordination of the Initiative within the public service. A related issue is that the Tables, as joint ventures, cannot themselves be directly accountable to either the ADM or the voluntary sector executive committee; rather their individual members are accountable to their respective sides. For the government members, the impact of traditional lines of accountability means that on occasion they need to stop the Table process to get approval to proceed from the ADM committee or from ministers. How accountability works for the voluntary sector members is necessarily ill-defined, since there is no grand umbrella organization governing the sector to which their Steering Committee reports.[32] Thus the accountability of the Steering

162 HOW OTTAWA SPENDS

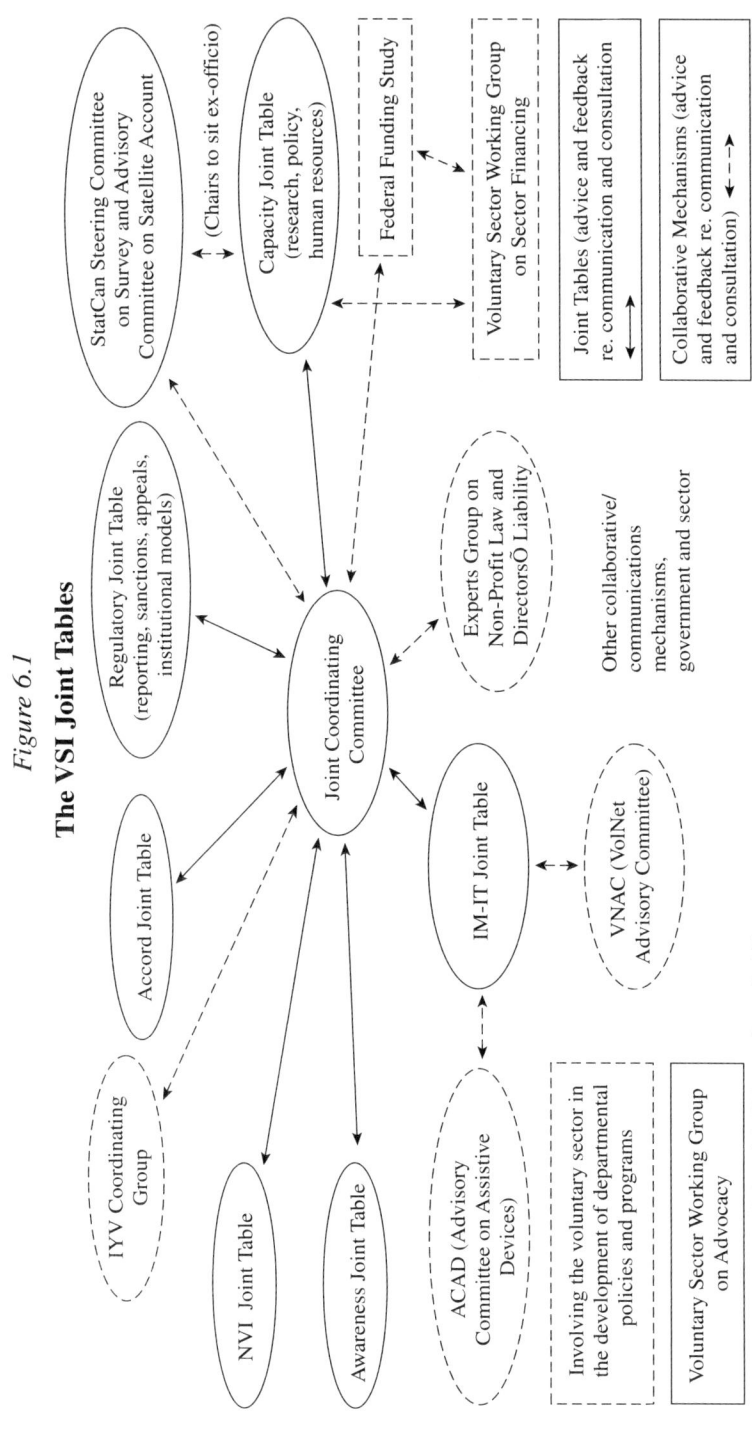

Figure 6.1
The VSI Joint Tables

Source: Reprinted by permission of the Voluntary Sector Task Force.

FEDERAL-VOLUNTARY SECTOR 163

Figure 6.2
Managing the VSI within Government

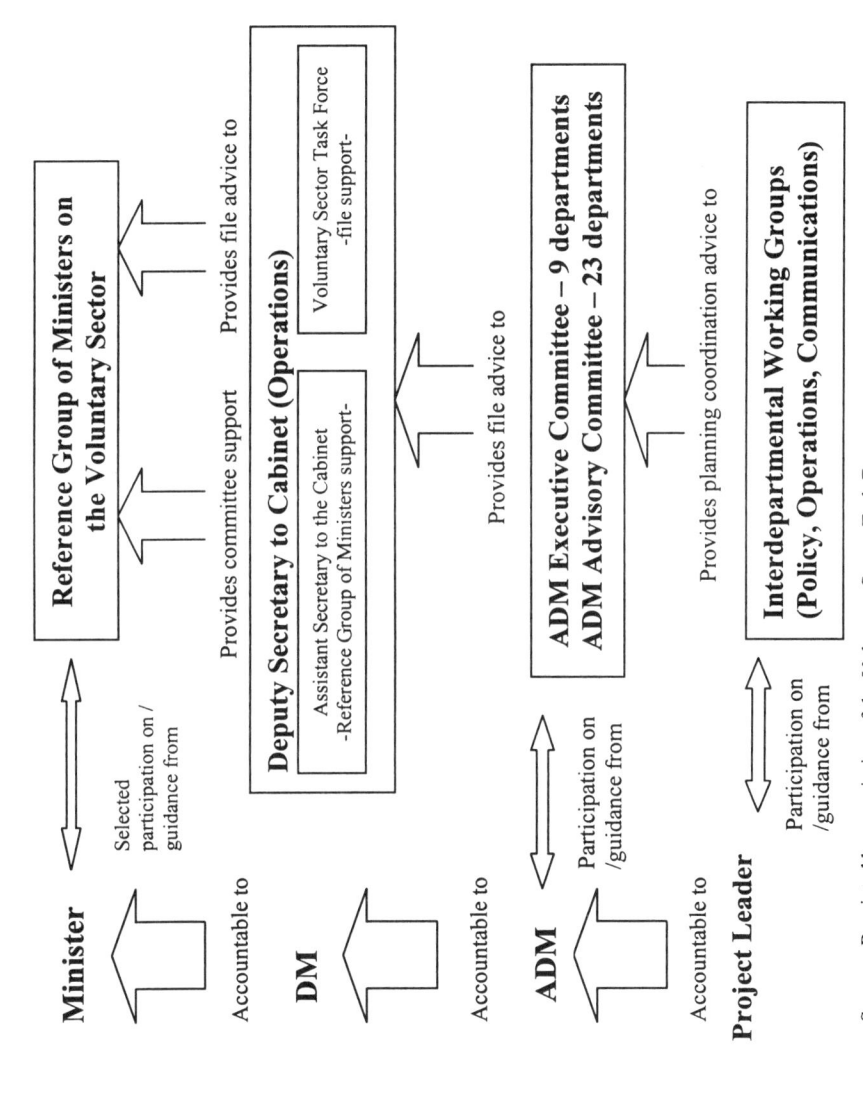

```
Minister  <--Selected participation on/guidance from-->  [Reference Group of Ministers on the Voluntary Sector]
  ↑                                                                ↑                    ↑
Accountable to                                              Provides committee support   Provides file advice to
  |                                                                |                    |
DM        <--                                              [Deputy Secretary to Cabinet (Operations)
                                                            Assistant Secretary to the Cabinet
                                                            -Reference Group of Ministers support-]
                                                           [Voluntary Sector Task Force
                                                            -file support-]
  ↑                                                                ↑
Accountable to                                              Provides file advice to
  |                                                                |
ADM       <--Participation on/guidance from-->  [ADM Executive Committee – 9 departments
                                                 ADM Advisory Committee – 23 departments]
  ↑                                                                ↑
Accountable to                                              Provides planning coordination advice to
  |                                                                |
Project Leader  <--Participation on/guidance from-->  [Interdepartmental Working Groups
                                                       (Policy, Operations, Communications)]
```

Source: Reprinted by permission of the Voluntary Sector Task Force.

Group derives from its credibility with the sector, and its influence over Table members relies primarily on moral suasion, since there are few sanctions or rewards that can be deployed (See Figure 6.2).

The governance structure also reveals the challenge of providing the political leadership necessary to steer a horizontal initiative in an era when power has become centralized in the PM and the PMO, and in which the number of the cabinet committees, whose job had been to coordinate and make tradeoffs at the political level, has been significantly reduced. The innovation of a 'Reference Group' of senior ministers has signalled the importance of the Initiative and helped to steer decisions through the many departments affected by it. The pilot is proving successful and is benefiting from the strong personal interest that Minister Robillard has taken in the Initiative. The tricky issues will be to ensure that the Reference Group continues to meet regularly with voluntary sector leaders and to ensure that expectations of the timing of deliverables are realistic, because the joint process will take longer to implement the VSI than politicians had at first imagined.

Perhaps the most cumbersome aspect of accountability in the entire VSI process is that the funding instruments that are available to support the participation of voluntary organizations in collaborations of this nature are ill-suited to true partnership. Governments have only two instruments through which they can fund third parties to do projects or participate in collaboration: grants and contributions.[33] Grants are transfers for which pre-determined eligibility or entitlement requirements have been met and that are not subject to an audit. Contributions are conditional transfers for a specified project as established by an agreement between a funding department and the recipient, and are subject to reporting, accounting, and auditing. As laid out in Treasury Board policy and reinforced by departmental requirements, the terms and conditions of contributions require that a proposal describing intended outcomes and deliverables be approved, that the work be completed in a fixed period, that periodic reporting on progress be made, and that payments be issued in instalments. In reality, almost all funding to voluntary organizations flows as contribution agreements, as does funding for the voluntary sector's Secretariat to the VSI. Even though the idea and role of the Secretariat had been regarded by government from the outset as a key component of the Joint Table process, the host voluntary organization, the Coalition of National Voluntary Organizations (NVO), nevertheless had to go through the standard requirement of submitting a proposal for its creation, complete with identification of outcomes and deliverables. The irony in trying to specify these at the beginning of the Joint Table process is that a primary objective of that process is to define the intended outcomes and deliverables. Due to the stringency currently employed in reviewing such proposals, it took over six months to get the contribution agreement signed and money flowing to the Secretariat. In the meantime, the work of the Joint Tables and the Secretariat had to proceed, so the host voluntary organization paid for its operation while waiting for receipt of the agreed federal funding. To do so, the NVO had to take out a bank loan, and one month almost did not make its own payroll. The rigidity of the contribution agreement as a funding instrument for the Secretariat is as frustrating to government officials as it is to the voluntary sector, and both the VSI government funding study and a recently formed HRDC working group are examining the possibility of developing a new kind of 'investment' or 'partnership' instrument. This would be a valuable contribution to making accountability more appropriately elastic, but no less effective, in the emerging forms of collaborative governance.

Many of the components of the VSI, such as funding for research and support for capacity-building, will be funded and implemented in the relatively short period of three to five years. The development of an accord, however, represents a change in governmental practices over the long term. Government departments will need to determine whether their practices meet the standards of conduct developed under an accord; practices must be made consistent across departments and must be monitored; and a review mechanism must be established to keep the accord 'evergreen' by regularly reviewing, reporting upon, and improving practices. The experience of other countries with similar framework agreements points to the necessity of creating a centrally placed administrative unit that has sufficient credibility and political clout to get the attention and compliance of departments. The natural home of such a unit would be a central agency, probably the PCO, where the Voluntary Sector Task Force has been given a temporary home. However, the PCO would be uneasy housing an interdepartmental coordinating unit, given its role in supporting the Prime Minister. But there is no obvious alternative. A home in a line department would diminish the unit's ability to influence others, and there are few plausible alternative models, since similar coordinating units, such as Status of Women Canada, have been allowed—indeed, encouraged— to atrophy during the Chrétien years. The dilemma is that horizontal governance cannot run entirely on informal, interdepartmental committees, but will require more institutionalized means of bridging, coordinating, and compelling. Although the federal government has embraced the horizontal nature of governing, it has not yet figured out the structural underpinnings to make it work as a permanent rather than a temporary form.

BRIDGING CULTURAL DIFFERENCES

The essence of collaborative governance is trust. For collaboration to work, it is important that the machinery established not simply reproduce the usual ways in which the partners work in their own organizations, but that it facilitate the creation of an appropriate climate in which trust can be built and true partnership can occur. The VSI Joint Table process brings together two very different cultures, as outlined in Table 6.2. Although many of the government officials at the Joint Tables are themselves board members of voluntary organizations and active volunteers, they live in a different organizational reality within the federal government. The fundamental differences between the partners are threefold. First, government is a hierarchy, while the voluntary sector operates as a flat network. The hierarchy of government provides relatively clear roles and responsibilities and a deference to authority, particularly to the minister, that from the outside may appear reverential at times. Information flows through official, hierarchical channels in an organized fashion, and confidentiality is often the norm. Adherence to standard operating procedure tends to take precedence over process. Second, the differences in financial, human, and technological resources are enormous. Third, the centrality of the VSI to the work of each partner is quite different. Perhaps it would be unfair to say that the VSI process is peripheral for most of the senior government officials at the Tables, but they do have many conflicting demands on their time and less control over it, and will experience fewer organizational and personal rewards for making the Joint Table process work. Although the voluntary sector members must also continue to run their organizations during this process, the VSI is a central

Table 6.2
Comparing Cultures: General Characteristics of the Voluntary Sector and the Federal Government

Characteristics of the voluntary sector and its leadership role in the VSI	Characteristics of the federal government and its leadership role in the VSI
national leadership circle is small, familiar, collegial	leadership circle is familiar and collegial at the very top, but much less connected beneath it
professional	professional
influence based on credibility	influence based on authority
flat, diverse network	large, contained hierarchy
open, broad sharing of information	closed, confidentiality respected, information moves mainly through vertical channels
thin, lack of capacity	well-resourced, strong capacity
multiple cleavages, including service/policy area, organizational size, geography, language, and culture	main cleavages are geography and language
focus on process	focus on procedure
atomized, held together by shared values	atomized, held together by political authority
VSI is central	VSI is peripheral

focus of their work, since the opportunity it represents may not come around again (see Table 6.2).

These differences have several implications. Sector members of the Tables hold their positions and exercise their influence partly by virtue of the credibility of the organizations they represent, but partly also by virtue of their personal credibility. They will need to convince the thousands of voluntary organizations that are not at the Tables that the VSI is a good idea, since they have no authority to impose conformity. Most of the voluntary sector Table members are used to being frugal and getting things done on a shoestring, and they recognize that the bulk of the sector has even fewer resources than their own organizations. Therefore, perceptions of how money is spent, and how much of it is spent, matters. So, too, does process, particularly in ensuring that a broad diversity of the sector can participate in meaningful ways in discussions about the implementation of the VSI.

Although the cultural differences across the voluntary and public sectors are significant, they are not necessarily impediments to the process. After all, the Table members from both sides are professionals; they share similar goals (notwithstanding, as noted above, that government has placed some constraints on the agenda) and they are willing to take chances in realizing these goals. Indeed, a first-time observer at many of the Tables would be hard pressed to identify who is from government and who represents the voluntary sector, because the style is not one of negotiation, but genuine dialogue. Differences in sectoral culture do present four potential problems, however. The first has to do with differing needs and expectations regarding information-sharing and confidentiality: whereas the government can comfortably control information until the end of the process, because neither MPs nor the public are clamouring to know details immediately, the voluntary sector members are under pressure to keep their boards and other organizations continually informed in the vital interest of being able to maintain their credibility and bring the rest of the sector along with the VSI. They need to get information out and obtain feedback in a timely manner. It thus has to be clear what information can be shared, and when. But care needs to be taken that the provision of information does not appear to set positions prematurely. It is also likely that public servants will feel compelled to withhold certain information from voluntary sector members if it is part of a response to or directive from ministers. The process becomes most sensitive when the recommendations emanating from the Tables move forward for cabinet approval, because the secrecy of this process is normally guarded carefully by officials. The Reference Group of Ministers has already demonstrated considerable flexibility, however, through its willingness to hear a joint presentation from the accord Table.

A second, related risk derives from the government's capacity to marshal information through commissioned reports. Although this information is valuable when shared in the Joint Table process, extensive contracting of consultants and reports risks intimidating the voluntary sector members and creating a sense that they must do the same. A third risk is that the process will be overpowered by the communications industry. The VSI will sponsor the biggest consultation with the voluntary sector that government has ever undertaken, and there is no question that a good communications plan is vital, but the risk is that communication of the strategy's content will take primacy over the content itself. The final concern is simply time—that Table members, particularly the government members, who may be sidetracked by other departmental issues, remain fully engaged as the initial glow of the collaboration wanes.

The biggest challenge for the voluntary sector members of the Tables does not arise from differences in culture with their government counterparts, however. As professionals for the most part representing fairly large organizations, the two are quite similar. The more significant differences are between the voluntary sector leadership at the Tables and those outside the Toronto/Ottawa circle, particularly those representing small groups and those working at the grassroots. To those in some parts of the country, especially in Quebec and in small centres, factors such as how the sector is viewed, the issues it faces, and the relevance of any relationship with the federal government appear quite different from the way they appear to those at the Tables. For many cash-strapped organizations, it could appear ludicrous to spend so much money on process—or on anything other than programming. Given these differences within the sector, the voluntary sector members of the Tables have a different stake in the process than do their government counterparts, and in many respects they have more at stake. It will be imperative for them to show members of the sector how the VSI money is spent and what difference it is likely to make. If they cannot sell the rest of the sector on the value of the VSI and their contribution to it, not only their personal credibility but their efforts over the past five years to knit the sector together may be in peril. Thus the engagement process cannot be run as a standard government operation in consultation, but needs to be sensitive to the unique roles and responsibilities of the voluntary sector Table members.

CONCLUSION: GOVERNING BY RELATIONSHIP-BUILDING

The VSI is an important development in the future of governance, not only because it, at last, recognizes the unique role played by the voluntary sector in service delivery and in democracy, but because it marks the beginning of a shift from governing by programming to governing by relationship-building. Admittedly, the federal government has long thought of the importance of building relationships with the private sector, with other countries in international affairs, and with provincial governments, where the autonomy of the other players is generally accepted. In most other areas, however, the federal government has tended to think in terms of 'constituencies' and the 'stakeholders' of its programs. The challenge was to convince them of the value of the program, or to quell their opposition, or perhaps to consult them about program design. But the establishment of long-term relationships based on shared expectations and mutual undertakings that are negotiated and codified in a framework agreement is a radical departure from dealing with stakeholders. The primary responsibilities of government in relationship-building are to provide an environment that enables the partner to fulfill its potential, to ensure that government commitments on particular standards of conduct can be met by relevant departments, and to facilitate ongoing collaboration by providing means for reviewing and improving the relationship. A shift from traditional programming, which focusses on hierarchy, accountability, and funding within a single department, to relationship-building, which involves collaboration, coordination, responsiveness, and flexible accountability, cannot be expected to occur in a flash. It requires a change both in attitudes and in governing machinery.

The VSI is an enormously positive step toward better relationships and a more constructive environment. It is relationship-building on a grand scale—government-wide and sector-wide. Over the next few years, we can expect to see similar framework agreements and extensive relationship-building at the departmental level. Although the VSI represents a sea change from the first Liberal mandate with respect to the federal government's view of the voluntary sector, there is still a certain reluctance to take some of the critical steps that would demonstrate full acceptance of the autonomy of the sector. The unwillingness to participate in a joint review of policies concerning advocacy, funding regimes, and modernization of the sector's access to the tax system is a holdover from thinking of voluntary organizations merely as stakeholders of government programs.

As the first big experiment in relationship-building, the VSI offers several lessons for collaborative governance in general. The emerging forms of collaborative, horizontal governance and relationship-building require both mechanisms for working jointly with partners and machinery for coordinating horizontally within government. The strength of the VSI is in the Joint Table process, which creates the closest thing to true partnership with the federal government that the voluntary sector has experienced. Its weakness is a product of the difficulty of creating and maintaining effective means of coordination across departments. This remains an unresolved problem in other policy areas as well. Not only are the coordinating structures not well developed, but there are few incentives and rewards for public servants to give priority to the management of and participation in horizontal issues. Relationship-building with the sector, particularly through the development of a framework agreement that binds both sides, at least morally, to certain standards of good practice, reveals the need to rethink and retool the central agency machinery in order to create an administrative unit that can appropriately coordinate departments, and monitor and report on adherence to the responsibilities assumed. The VSI also shows that collaborative governance requires more elastic accountability, new funding instruments, and fewer restrictions on confidentiality—a hard sell at the very time that accountability has become more routinized and rigid in the wake of the HRDC scandal (in which department officials were accused of mismanagement of millions of dollars worth of program funds). Finally, the VSI is a good reminder that a relationship involves other players, who, while interdependent, are also autonomous, and who come with differing cultures, resources, and political imperatives. In this case, the task of engaging and bringing along the enormous diversity of the voluntary sector in the VSI is perhaps the key challenge to making the Initiative work, and will require some of the most innovative thinking of all.

NOTES

1 Given that funding had already been committed to the VSI, it is not surprising that it did not appear in either document. It could be seen as a sign of the maturing nature of the federal government's relationship with

the voluntary sector that in a number of places in which the Speech from the Throne talks about the government's working with its partners, the voluntary sector is explicitly mentioned alongside the private sector.

2 Although the number of individuals volunteering had increased from a decade earlier, the number of volunteer hours decreased. See Canadian Centre for Philanthropy, Kahanoff Non-Profit Sector Research Initiative, Volunteer Canada, Canadian Heritage, Health Canada, Human Resources Development Canada, and Statistics Canada, *Caring Canadians, Involved Canadians: Highlights from the 1997 National Survey on Giving, Volunteering and Participating* (Ottawa: Ministry of Industry, 1998), 27.

3 The term 'voluntary' is used throughout this chapter because it is the only one of several adjectives—'nonprofit', 'nongovernmental' and 'third' are others—that does not describe the sector as a residual of (that is, as other than) something else. The term 'voluntary' does not imply that every organization in the sector uses volunteers in its program delivery, but all do so in their governance. For a discussion of the terms used to describe the sector, see [Broadbent] Panel on Accountability and Governance in the Voluntary Sector, *Building on Strength: Improving Governance and Accountability in Canada's Voluntary Sector* (Ottawa: Voluntary Sector Roundtable, 1999), 13. For a discussion of the nature of the sector in Canada, see Michael Hall and Keith G. Banting, 'The Nonprofit Sector in Canada: An Introduction', in Keith G. Banting, ed., *The Nonprofit Sector in Canada: Roles and Relationships* (Montreal and Kingston: McGill-Queen's University Press, 2000), 4-17.

4 Voluntary Sector Task Force, Privy Council Office, 'Partnering with the Voluntary Sector for the Benefit of Canadians', Presentation to the meeting of the Joint Tables, 23 Nov. 2000.

5 D.W. Sharpe, *A Portrait of Canada's Charities* (Toronto: Canadian Centre for Philanthropy, 1994), 16.

6 For a discussion of the Ekos study, see Frank L. Graves 'Rethinking Government as if People Mattered: From "Reaganomics" to "Humanonics"', in Leslie A. Pal, ed. *How Ottawa Spends 1999-2000: Shape Shifting: Canadian Governance Toward the 21st Century* (Toronto: Oxford University Press, 1999), 37-73.

7 Government of Canada/Voluntary Sector, *Working Together: Report of the Joint Tables* (Ottawa: Privy Council Office and Voluntary Sector Roundtable, 1999), 19.

8 Jane Jenson and Susan D. Phillips, 'Regime Shift: New Citizenship Practices in Canada', *International Journal of Canadian Studies* 14 (1996): 115-80.

9 Leslie A. Pal, *Interests of State: The Politics of Language, Multiculturalism and Feminism in Canada* (Montreal and Kingston: McGill-Queen's University Press, 1993), 75-6.

10 For a discussion of this history, see Law Reform Commission of Ontario, *Report on the Law of Charities* (Toronto: Law Reform Commission, 1996), 249-85.
11 See Susan D. Phillips, 'How Ottawa Blends: Shifting Government Relations with Interest Groups', in Frances Abele, ed., *How Ottawa Spends 1991-92: The Politics of Fragmentation* (Ottawa: Carleton University Press, 1991), 183-227.
12 Law Reform Commission of Ontario, *Report*, chap. 5.
13 Phillips, 'How Ottawa Blends', 183.
14 Probably the most strained relationships during the Mulroney years were with the women's movement; see Sylvia Bashevkin, 'Losing Common Ground: Feminists, Conservatives and Public Policy in Canada During the Mulroney Years', *Canadian Journal of Political Science* 29, 2 (1996): 211-42.
15 Patrick Johnston, 'Strengthening Voluntary Sector/Government Relations in Canada', Paper presented to the Independent Sector 2000 Annual Conference Pre-Session, Washington DC, Oct. 2000.
16 Of those recommendations directed at the federal government, four were key: capacity building; developing mechanisms to build a stronger relationship; reviewing the policy that determines which organizations can be officially registered as charities; and creating a new institution to replace the CCRA as the primary regulator of charities.
17 Quoted in Johnston, 'Strengthening Voluntary Sector/Government Relations in Canada', 9.
18 For a discussion of international experience, see Susan D. Phillips, 'Voluntary Sector–Government Relationships in Transition: Learning from International Experience for the Canadian Context', in Kathy Brock and Keith G. Banting, eds, *The Nonprofit Sector in Canada* (Montreal and Kingston: McGill-Queen's University Press, forthcoming).
19 The 1999 process of cabinet approval was unique in one respect. It is common practice that a brief providing 'Advice to Cabinet' written by federal officials be attached to a Memorandum to Cabinet (MC), and this was the case with the recommendations of the Joint Tables. What is unusual is that voluntary sector members were granted the opportunity to provide a parallel brief offering their own advice, and although it was not officially attached to the MC, it was circulated simultaneously. During this process, federal officials told their voluntary sector counterparts that the cabinet discussion had been positive and that the recommendations approved by Cabinet were based on the proposals that had been jointly prepared by the Tables, but these officials were unable to provide any further detail. See Johnston, 'Strengthening Voluntary Sector/Government Relations in Canada.'
20 See Johnston, 'Strengthening Voluntary Sector/Government Relations in Canada'. The initiative probably was not mentioned in the 2000 budget

because the focus was on tax cuts and the Finance Minister wanted to downplay the spending aspects of the budget. In the aftermath of the HRDC scandal, there was little interest in being seen to give out money to third parties that have considerable discretion to make decisions.

21 Ironically, the statement of purpose does not say if the intent is to increase public confidence in the sector, in government, or in both. Voluntary Sector Task Force, Privy Council Office, *Partnering for the Benefit of Canadians: Government of Canada–Voluntary Sector Initiative* (Ottawa, 9 June 2000), 1.

22 In developing the criteria, the federal government consulted with the voluntary sector, and, while the criteria may have seemed appropriate at the time, more problems than anticipated arose in the implementation phase.

23 Government of Canada–Voluntary Sector Initiative, *Working Together*, 50.

24 See Richard Bridge, *The Law of Advocacy by Charitable Organization: The Case for Change* (Vancouver: Institute for Media, Policy and Civil Society, 2000).

25 In the case of the Vancouver Society of Immigrant and Visible Minority Women, the Supreme Court denied registration to an association whose aim is to help immigrant and visible minority women integrate into society by providing vocational counselling and job skills training and by engaging in incidental advocacy activities. Its decision was based on the reasoning that providing educational and training assistance to immigrants could not be viewed as 'other purposes beneficial to community', because not all immigrants, particularly those who came in as skilled independents under the point system, are in need of such assistance. By its decision, the Court not only showed its narrow view of the common law, but demonstrated that it has no intention of taking the lead role in reforming the law. It openly invited Parliament to undertake such reform, however. See Wolfe D. Goodman, 'A Personal View of the *Vancouver Society* Decision', *The Philanthropist/lePhilanthrope* 15, 2 (2000): 20-2; David Stevens, 'Vancouver Society of Immigrant and Visible Minority Women v. M.N.R.', *The Philanthropist/lePhilanthrope* 15, 2 (2000): 4-13; and Kernaghan Webb, *Cinderella's Slippers? The Role of Charitable Tax Status in Financing Canadian Interest Groups* (Vancouver: SFU-UBC Centre for the Study of Government and Business, 2000), 70-5.

26 For some politicians and senior bureaucrats, the main concern is whether public money should be spent on advocacy activities, by allowing organizations that engage in extensive advocacy to register as charities and issue tax receipts, and by allowing registered organizations to spend publicly donated (tax receipted) money on advocacy. They are unlikely to move on the issue until they are convinced that there is a consensus within the voluntary sector and among the Canadian public, or until the

implications of the Vancouver Society case become politically embarrassing.

27 A core set of 'public benefit' purposes have been outlined in detail by Drache and Boyle that would make Canada's approach to charitable registration roughly equivalent to that of the USA or the UK. See Arthur B.C. Drache with Frances K. Boyle, *Charities, Public Benefit and the Canadian Income Tax System: A Proposal for Reform* (Toronto: Kahanoff Non-Profit Sector Research Initiative, 1998). Although voluntary organizations already registered as charities might be expected to oppose further expansion, because it would increase competition for fundraising, the Broadbent Panel observed, on the basis of its extensive consultations with the sector, that there is strong support for an extension of the policy of charitable registration.

28 Drache lays out clearly the problems associated with the CCRA as the regulatory agency. Within the CCRA there is a clash between the predominant culture (which sees its function as the collection of taxes and the enforcement of compliance) and that of the Charities Directorate (which provides advice to charities encouraging compliance). Yet, advice about good governance and compliance, not mere enforcement, is exactly what most small organizations need. For most ambitious public servants, the Charities Directorate is only a temporary stepping stone in career advancement, and thus there is a lack of training, knowledge, and institutional memory about the voluntary sector within the regulatory agency. This lack of training and stretched resources means that the average waiting time for an organization applying for charitable status to receive notice of the Directorate's decision is seven to fifteen months. Arthur B.C. Drache with W. Laird Hunter, *A Canadian Charity Tribunal: A Proposal for Implementation* (Toronto: Kahanoff Non-Profit Sector Research Initiative, 2000); see also Panel on Accountability and Governance, *Building on Strength*, 56-7.

29 Drache with Hunter, *A Canadian Charity Tribunal*; Government of Canada–Voluntary Sector Initiative, *Working Together*, 54-7.

30 The selection process reflects the level of interest in this Initiative within the voluntary sector. To ensure that representation from the sector is broad and diverse, the VSR established an independent selection committee, which received self-nominations for membership in the Tables. Almost 1,500 nominations were received for 65 positions. Government members of the Tables were selected by a steering committee of ADMs.

31 The resources to support the work of each Table rests with a government department, primarily with HRDC, Heritage, or the CCRA. How each Table is supported by government and the authority of the Tables to contract varies considerably, depending on how the relevant department developed the Treasury Board submission for its component of the funding.

32 The Voluntary Sector Steering Group consists of the members of the VSR and the voluntary sector co-chairs of the Tables.
33 A third instrument is the contract, but because it is used in more limited, clearly defined circumstances to deliver an identified service or project to government, it is not discussed in this context. It poses many of the same problems as a contribution agreement.

7

Citizenship by Instalments: Federal Policies for Canadians with Disabilities

MICHAEL J. PRINCE

In modern disability politics, citizenship is the chief term of discourse and the central aim of policy reform. Disability groups are seeking to alter the language of their policy community and that of the wider Canadian society as well in order to achieve equality of status through full citizenship. The purpose of this chapter is to examine federal government activities that are defining, strengthening, or limiting citizenship for Canadians with disabilities. What reforms did the Liberals undertake in their last mandate? What policy challenges remain?

For people with disabilities in Canada, the story of citizenship is not the conventional liberal-democractic narrative recounting the continual and steady extension of rights and responsibilities over many decades or centuries.[1] The struggle for the status of full citizenship for people with disabilities began relatively recently, and it has been struggle characterized by rhetoric, setbacks, and frequent delays, a few major successes, and many marginal gains. For Canadians with disabilities, the promise of inclusion and equal status has meant citizenship by instalments.

Within contemporary Canadian politics, five elements of citizenship are especially relevant to an understanding of disability policy. These are the discourse of citizenship, legal and equality rights, democratic and political rights, fiscal and social entitlements, and economic integration.[2] Each element is a sphere of policy action with a particular blend of ideas, programs, institutions, and connections with the other elements. Each element has a formative period of development, which, in the case of Canadians with disabilities, clusters around the last 10 to 20 years. At the same time that governments were downsizing the state, disability groups were asserting their claims for inclusion in the public domain. These contradictory agendas help to explain why, for disability groups, the movement toward full citizenship has been partial, slow, and incomplete.

CITIZENSHIP AS DISCOURSE

Citizenship is a bundle of rights, duties, programs, and entitlements. It is also a bundle of reasonings, declarations, promises, and expectations.[3] The discursive element of citizenship is a highly noteworthy focus of interest and action in disability policy. Governments are reviewing and reorienting conceptions of disability, the place of people with disabilities in Canadian society, and the role of public institutions and programs. Everyday language, terminology in legislation, and the conceptual underpinnings of disability policy receive considerable attention from disability advocates, their organizations, and government decision-makers. Disability offices issue guidelines to educate the public and the media about avoiding the use of inappropriate, obsolete, and inaccurate terms about people with disabilities, and using instead terms that are current, respectful, and descriptive. Legislative reviews and reforms have thus modernized the language as well as the law concerning Canadians with disabilities. Such measures represent a reordering of the symbolic fabric of citizenship, and disability groups regard them as important gestures that express what kind of nation we wish to be.

In the last 20 years, federal, provincial, intergovernmental, and disability community documents have adopted citizenship as the central organizing principle and benchmark in policy advocacy, analysis, and agreements.[4] The notion of citizenship presented in these documents recognizes disability experiences, and at times acknowledges the interplay of disability with age, culture, and gender. These documents share a belief that, for people with disabilities, the principle of citizenship is inadequately realized in Canadian society, the economy, and public policy. Following two years of collaboration and consultations, federal, provincial, and territorial ministers responsible for social services released, in late 1998, a policy framework to guide governmental action in the field of disabilities. *In Unison: A Canadian Approach to Disability Issues*, is the first substantial consensus among governments, not including the government of Quebec, on a national vision for disability policy. The theme of this shared vision is that persons with disabilities should participate as full citizens in all aspects of Canadian society.[5]

This vision rests on the values of equality, inclusion, and independence as well as on the principles of rights and responsibilities, empowerment, and participation. These values and principles of full citizenship are to be implemented through three interrelated 'building blocks' of disability policy: services and supports for daily living; education, training, and employment; and income security programs.

The goal is that the notion of citizenship, as the overarching idea for this vision, will mobilize all sectors to facilitate the full and equal participation of persons with disabilities, and to make all domains of Canadian society as inclusive as possible. The policy direction agreed to by governments is to amend and adopt policies that promote access to generic programs and services. Chart 7.1, which comes from *In Unison*, shows the essential changes in the approach to disability issues adopted by governments.

These proposed changes represent the promise of a shift in the paradigm for disability policy. At present, disability policy is in varying states of amendment and transformation both within and across jurisdictions in Canada. The most significant advance in policy to date has been a new emphasis on the employability of working-age persons with disabilities. This is linked to the intention to change the way Canadian with disabilities are portrayed, so that they will be seen as independent participants endowed with skills and experiences. The most challenging policy reforms will concern making benefits and services more

Chart 7.1

Shifting Approaches to Disability Issues

Old	New
Recipients	Participants
Passive income support	Active measures to promote employment in addition to providing necessary income support
Dependence	Independence
Government responsibility	Shared responsibility
Labelled as 'unemployable'	Identification of work skills
Disincentives to leave income support	Incentives to seek employment and volunteer opportunities
Insufficient employment supports	Opportunities to develop skills and experience
Program-centred approach	Person-centred approach
Insufficient portability of benefits and services	Portable benefits and services
Multiple access requirements	Integrated access requirements

Source: *In Unison: A Canadian Approach to Disability Issues,* 1998.

portable, and making program delivery more holistic and person-centred.

CITIZENSHIP AS LEGAL AND EQUALITY RIGHTS

Civil or legal rights are called the first generation of citizenship rights in that they were the first ones to receive recognition by governments. Their acceptance preceded by many decades the widespread acceptance of political rights and social entitlements.[6] For Canadians with disabilities, however, legal rights continue to be debated and developed, even as we enter the twenty-first century. This ongoing struggle for the definition and interpretation of basic civil rights in judicial forums is contributing to a 'legalization' of citizenship,[7] a process in Canadian politics not unique to people with disabilities, but one especially central to their struggle for full membership.

Criminal Justice Reforms

After the government, in consultation with the disability community, reviewed federal legislation related to disability, an omnibus bill was passed in 1992 amending several laws, including the Access to Information Act, the Criminal Code, and the Privacy Act. Gaps remained, and new issues emerged through the 1990s, many dealing with the criminal justice system. The disability community's agenda of amendments to the Criminal Code and the Canada Evidence Act was presented to the Department of Justice during consultations over the 1993–1996 period and, in 1996, to the Federal Task Force on Disability. The aim of these amendments was to ensure that law-making and the administration of justice took into account the concerns of people with disabilities, by accommodating and better integrating them within the criminal justice system. A change to the Criminal Code in 1994 added 'the consideration of an aggravated offense when the crime is motivated by the vulnerability of the victim as a result of his/her disability.'[8] Further amendments made to the Criminal Code and the Canada Evidence Act in 1998 improved the access of people with disabilities to criminal and civil proceedings and other justice services under federal jurisdiction.

Human Rights

The role of the Canadian Human Rights Commission (CHRC) is to promote equality of opportunity and, according to the Canadian Human Rights Act, to protect individuals from discrimination based on several grounds, including disability. In addition, the Commission has the mandate to correct disadvantageous conditions of employment experienced by people with disabilities, as well as by other designated groups, under the Employment Equity Act, 1996, which covers federally regulated private sector companies as well as federal Crown corporations, departments, and agencies. Separate from the CHRC is the Canadian Human Rights Tribunal, a quasi-judicial body that conducts public hearings and renders decisions.

After many years of lobbying by the disability community, the Canadian Human Rights Act was amended in 1998; a 'duty to accommodate' was added to ensure 'that federal employers and service providers are supportive of, and accessible to, persons with disabilities.'[9] The Canadian Human Rights Tribunal has since reported an increase in the number of disability cases it is handling. As the Tribunal explains,

'In the fall of 1999, the Supreme Court changed the legal test for an employer's defence of *bona fide* occupational requirements. In brief, the Court eliminated the distinction between direct and adverse effect discrimination. The past jurisprudence, which eliminated most disability cases going to Tribunal, is no longer defining these cases. New case law must be developed.'[10]

From April 1999 to June 2000, an independent panel established by the Minister of Justice conducted a review of the Canadian Human Rights Act, the first comprehensive review of the law since its passage in 1977. The review afforded an opportunity to assess whether present human rights protections, at the federal level, are sufficient to defend the rights of Canadians with disabilities. It was of particular interest to the disability community that the panel was asked to determine whether the Act should be amended to prohibit discrimination based on the results of genetic testing, to prohibit discrimination on the grounds of social condition, and to add certain social and economic rights to the Act.

The Act defines disability as any previous or existing mental or physical disability. To make the law clearer, the Council of Canadians with Disabilities pushed for the addition of perceived disability and a predisposition to having a disability to the definition. The panel agreed, in part, recommending that the definition of disability in the Act be expanded to include 'the predisposition to being disabled'.

On the question as to whether social condition, that is, patterns of socio-economic disadvantage, should be a prohibited ground for discrimination, the panel noted that such factors as low income and lack of education are barriers associated with groups characterized by other grounds, such as race, sex, and disability. Discrimination based on factors related to an impoverished social and economic status might be challenged on these existing grounds, but the panel reported that, in fact, such cases are rarely successful. The panel therefore recommended that social condition be added to the prohibited grounds for discrimination listed in the Act, but that the prohibition be limited so that it protects socially and economically disadvantaged groups, such as Canadians with severe and prolonged disabilities, and that certain government programs be exempted.[11]

The review panel also considered the issue of adding social and economic rights, which are recognized in international agreements to which Canada is a signatory, to the Act. 'Canadians with disabilities are not tangential to this debate,' the Canadian Association of Independent Living Centres stated in a submission to the panel.[12] In the light of a number of concerns that were raised, the panel decided not to recommend the inclusion of social and economic rights in the Act at that time. The panel did recommend, however, that the CHRC 'should have the duty to monitor and report to Parliament and the United Nations Human Rights Committee on the federal government's compliance with international human rights treaties, included in its legislation.'[13]

This important report, released in June 2000, did not receive a full response by the Liberal government or examination by Parliament before the November 2000 election. Reform proposals for federal human rights policy will surely be the focus of considerable debate during the third Chrétien government, between social liberals and other progressives on one side and social conservatives on the other.

Equality Rights: The Charter and the Court Challenges Program of Canada

Under section 15 of the Charter, people with disabilities are specifically included and guaranteed a set of equality rights. Section 15(1) states, 'Every individual is equal before and under the law and has the right to the equal protection and equal benefit of the law without discrimination and, in particular, without discrimination based on race, national or ethnic origin, religion, sex, age or mental and physical disability.' The section expresses four kinds of equality (equality before, equality under, equal protection, and equal benefit), which should be reflected in the administration and enforcement of law, in the substance of legislation, and in procedurally fair provision of benefits, be they regulations, transfer payments, or public services.

The Court Challenges Program of Canada, in operation from the late 1970s and then terminated in 1992 as part of the Mulroney government's restraint plan, was reinstated by the Chrétien Liberals in 1994. The Program intends to clarify constitutional rights and freedoms, and to enable equality-seeking and minority language groups and individuals to pursue their legal and constitutional rights through the courts. Funded at $2.75 million a year by the Department of Heritage Canada through a contribution agreement, which runs from 1998 to 2003, the Program is administered by a non-profit agency working at arm's length from the government. With respect to equality rights, the Program only funds cases that involve a challenge to a federal law, policy, or practice, that raise equality arguments, and that are test cases dealing with a problem or raising an argument not already decided by the courts. Such test cases have 'the potential to stop discrimination or improve the way the law works for members of a disadvantaged group or groups in Canada.'[14]

People with disabilities are eligible for funding, as individuals or as groups, as a *party* directly affected by a case or as an *intervener* who wishes to raise constitutional arguments not raised by others in a case. Since the Program's reinstatement, disability issues have been a prominent feature of the equality rights applications and the case funding decisions.[15] Results of litigation for rights and against discrimination are mixed. In cases involving a range of institutions as diverse as a local school board, the federal correctional services, and provincial health care services, the Supreme Court of Canada has held that employers have a duty, under section 15, to make reasonable accommodations to the needs of a person with a mental or physical disability.[16] The accommodations, however, may often be narrowly interpreted and only slowly implemented.

CITIZENSHIP AS POLITICAL RIGHTS

Public membership in the community and popular participation in it are central rights of political citizenship. This side of citizenship includes the right to vote, to stand for and hold elected office, and to participate in political and governmental processes, and these rights are supported by the fundamental freedoms of expression, association, and assembly. These rights and freedoms find institutional expression through the electoral system, parliamentary and other forms of government operative in Canada, and interest groups.

The right to vote and to access the electoral system
For many people with disabilities, the right to vote or to have guaranteed access to the electoral system did not exist until the last decade. Remarking on the tardiness of the federal government's fulfilment of its guarantee of full political rights to people with disabilities, Fraser Valentine and Jill Vickers note, 'It was only in 1991, after the disability rights movement challenged the *Canada Elections Act* in the courts

and won, that people with mental disabilities gained the federal franchise. For people with physical disabilities, full access to the franchise was guaranteed only in 1992 when the architectural accessibility of polling stations became mandatory.'[17]

In fact, the process of securing full access to the right to vote continues. Further amendments were made to the federal electoral law and to administrative practices in 1993, 1996, and 2000. In brief, major reforms of particular interest to people with disabilities include special ballots allowing Canadians to vote by mail, or in person, at the office of their returning officer; guaranteed access to Government of Canada buildings with polling stations; and the provision of mobile polling stations at institutions where persons with disabilities reside. For a candidate with a disability, permitted personal expenses now include expenses directly related to that disability.[18] A reform introduced in 1993, that the special needs of voters be identified in the enumeration process, has been eclipsed as a result of the replacement of the enumeration of voters door-to-door with the mail-out of voters' cards. It is uncertain whether this change has had an adverse affect on the ability of people with disabilities to vote. The historically low turnout rate for the 2000 federal election appears to offer no comforting evidence.

The right to organize, to advocate, and to participate
Ottawa's funding of disability organizations since the 1970s reflects the belief that it is in the public interest to support the formation, maintenance, and active participation in the policy process of organizations representing traditionally disadvantaged groups. When the Disabled Persons Participation Program was established in 1985 within the then Department of the Secretary of State, this funding increased and gained greater visibility.[19] Funding peaked in the early 1990s, then declined in both absolute and real terms during the first Chrétien mandate and into the second. Funding to disability groups was frozen for one year at 1996-7 levels, and was destined to expire as of 1998-9.

Strong lobbying by disability interests, together with an improving fiscal situation for the federal government, led in 1998 to the creation of the Social Development Partnerships (SDP) program. The SDP 'supports activities of the social non-profit sector in line with Human Resources Development Canada's (HRDC) mandate. These activities identify, develop and promote nationally significant best practices and models of service delivery and build community structural capacity to meet the social development needs and aspirations of populations who are or may be at risk.'[20] Funding is directed at four areas: social development, disability issues, community inclusion for people with intellectual disabilities, and the voluntary sector.

In his October 2000 report, the Auditor General critically reviewed the SDP program, which is to be formally evaluated by HRDC probably in the 2001-2 fiscal year. Throughout the HRDC grants and contributions crisis in 2000, and in the Auditor General's review as well, one overlooked point was that federal funding to disability organizations is well below the level of support given 10 years ago. While disability groups are not vilified by Ottawa as special interest groups, it can be argued that they are under-funded relative to their needs, their past levels of support, and the citizenship rhetoric used to showcase the SDP program. It is to be hoped that the HRDC evaluation will take heed of management issues as well as the Liberal government's promise to help the disability community increase its policy and program development capacity and its participation as a partner in working toward the goal of full citizenship.[21]

CITIZENSHIP AS ACCESS TO SOCIAL AND FISCAL BENEFITS

Government transfers and tax benefits are a defining part of modern citizenship for virtually all Canadians. For people with disabilities, fiscal and social benefits are especially critical means for overcoming obstacles to the achievement of membership and participation in Canadian society.

Income Security Programs
At the federal level, there are three major income programs related to disability. These are the Canada Pension Plan Disability Benefit (CPPDB), veterans' disability benefits, and the sickness benefit under the Employment Insurance (EI) program (see Table 7.1).

These programs share the objective of offering income protection against the risks of sickness, disability, or death. The CPPDB and the EI Sickness Benefit are social insurance programs based on previous employment and contributions, and provide incentives for claimants to return to work, an objective that has received greater policy and administrative attention in recent years. The veterans' disability benefits have the distinctive purpose of offering veterans societal recognition and financial reparations. Given these eligibility criteria, all three programs involve some form of medical assessment of the disability or sickness. Citizenship, therefore, is not the entrée to these income benefits, although the administration of the programs does emphasize the rights and responsibilities of claimants, and includes mechanisms for the review and appeal of decisions.

Canada Pension Plan Disability Benefits
In the mid-1990s, CPP disability benefits came under critical scrutiny by the Auditor General of Canada, because of the sharp rise in benefit

Table 7.1
Main Federal Income Security Programs Related to Disabilty

Program and origin	Basic objectives	Policy technique	Planned expenditures 2000-1 ($ millions)
Canada Pension Plan Disability Benefits, 1970[a]	• Income protection • Work incentives	Social insurance	2,874
Veterans' Disability Pensions, 1919	• Societal recognition • Income support	Compensation	1,177
Employment Insurance Sickness Benefits, 1971	• Income protection • Work incentives	Social insurance	539

a   While the Canada Pension Plan came into effect in January 1966, disability benefits did not become payable until 1970, in part to phase in the implementation of this major new social program and in part in response to some governmental concerns over the complexity and cost pressures associated with offering disability benefits.

Source: *Main Estimates, 2000-2001.*

payments and in the number of beneficiaries. From 1985-7 to 1995-6, CPP disability benefits more than tripled, from $841 million to close to $3 billion, and the number of recipients rose from 155,000 to 300,000. In an audit of the CPPDB program published in September 1996, the Auditor General's staff concluded that 'improvements need to be made in management practices related to the eligibility of Disability benefits. Moreover, CPP management does not have complete and relevant data that would enable it to manage eligibility with due regard to economy.' The auditors argued that significant savings could come from improving the administration of CPP Disability without causing any prejudice to applicants who meet the eligibility criteria of the Plan, and made several recommendations to that end.[22]

In February 1997, Finance Minister Paul Martin announced an intergovernmental consensus on reforming the CPP.[23] Reforms to disability benefits went beyond the Auditor General's proposal of clearer objectives, improved data systems, and tighter administration, to include actual retrenchment of disability payments under the CPP. (The changes affect only people under age 65 as of 31 December 1997 and those not in receipt of a CPP disability benefit.)

Before the 1998 reforms, eligibility for the disability benefit depended on a person's having worked and contributed to the Plan in two of the previous three or five of the previous 10 years. The new regime requires a person to have worked and contributed in four of the previous six years, thus strengthening the test of attachment to the labour force. People already receiving early retirement benefits are ineligible for a disability benefit. The earnings-related portion of disability benefits, which was based on an average of three years' maximum pensionable earnings, is now calculated on the basis of the previous five years. The rationale is that this is in line with most private pension plans. The way CPP retirement pensions are calculated for disability beneficiaries was also squeezed, the intended effect being to modestly reduce the average pension amount persons with disabilities receive from CPP when they reach age 65.

The legislation requires that disability claims be more rigorously assessed. Recipients will be more frequently reassessed than before in order to determine if they still have a severe and prolonged disability, and the procedures for the appeal of program decisions are more rigorous. During 1999-2000, for example, HRDC did about 10,000 reassessments of disability claims, and as a result of this initiative expects to achieve savings of $91 million over the 1998-9 to 2000-1 period.[24]

Veterans Affairs Disability Pension Program
Each year Veterans Affairs Canada (VAC) receives about 14,000 new applications for disability pensions and pays out about $1.1 billion. The number of disability pension clients has been steady at around 152,000 in recent years, slightly more clients than a decade ago because of the aging client base and the fallout from the Gulf War and peacekeeping operations of the 1990s. In recent years, VAC has successfully reduced the time required for clients to receive a decision on their disability pension applications from an average of 18 months to under five months. In 2001-2, as part of its commitment to enhance the quality of life for clients and to improve service delivery, VAC is beginning to implement improvements to the Table of Disabilities and Medical Guidelines.[25]

While many federal social programs were restrained or cut back in recent times, veterans' transfers have been increased periodically, and on a number of occasions the eligible clientele has been expanded. Just before the 2000 election call, Bill C-41, the omnibus veterans' benefits legislation, passed. It extended various benefits, including disability pensions, to a number of groups that previously had little or no access to pensions for service-related disability.[26] Furthermore, amendments to the Pension Act will provide disability pension benefits to Canadian Forces members and still-serving RCMP members disabled by service-related injuries incurred in Canada. Previously, Canadian Forces members only received a VAC pension if the disability arose out of service on a foreign deployment, and RCMP members only received a disability pension upon discharge or retirement. These amendments remove some contemporary gaps and inequities in coverage for sick and injured Canadian Forces and RCMP personnel.

Employment Insurance Sickness Benefits
Introduced in 1971 as part of the major reform of the then 30-year-old Unemployment Insurance program, sickness benefits have grown since 1971 to become Ottawa's third largest disability income benefit program. Embedded within the much larger and controversial Employment Insurance (EI) system, sickness benefits account for about 5 per cent of income benefit expenditures in any given year. The sickness

benefit, by insuring against illness or injury that causes involuntary unemployment and wage loss, underscores the social policy role of EI.[27] As with the CPP and VAC disability benefits, a medical certificate is required informing program staff of the nature and expected length of the illness or injury. Within the EI system, sickness benefit claims represent about 10 per cent of new claims each year.[28]

The Unemployment Insurance program was substantially restructured by the Liberals in 1996 and renamed EI. Early evidence suggests that this has had little effect on the provision of sickness benefits. A comparison of claims and benefits under the last full year of UI (1995-6) with those in the first full year under EI (1997-8) identified a slight decline of 1.8 per cent in new sickness benefit claims, to 202,850. In addition, the average weekly benefit remained constant, at $253, as did the average duration of benefits, at 8.9 weeks. By gender, about 59 per cent of the new claimants are women and 41 per cent are men, a minor change from the past pattern.[29] This muted impact of the 1996 policy reform on sickness benefits is probably due to the fact that the focus of the reforms was to control the costs of the regular benefits. For special benefits, the entrance requirement, which had been expressed as 20 weeks of insurable employment, was now to be expressed as 700 hours, which equates to the previous threshold (20 weeks x 35 hours per week). Consequently, expenditures on regular EI benefits have declined over the past five years while spending on sickness and other special benefits has increased, in the case of sickness benefits by 27 per cent since 1996-7.

The Tax System and Disabilities
The federal tax system has several major disability-related programs, some dealing with income support and tax relief, and others promoting independent community living, education, employment, family support, and caregiving. The 1997-2000 Liberal government brought down three budgets and one mini-budget, and these plans introduced 17 fiscal measures related to disability policy, offering tax relief or addressing economic and social objectives.

The October 2000 mini-budget was anything but petite from the perspective of disability policy. It provided more than twice the amount of new tax spending for people with disabilities than the February 2000 budget did.[30] The budget and mini-budget of 2000 combined prom-

Table 7.2

Primary Federal Disability-Related Tax Measures and Projected Revenue Impacts, 2001

Tax Measures	$ Millions
• Attendant Care Expense Deduction	Less than 5
• Caregiver Tax Credit	125
• Disability Tax Credit	285
• Infirm Dependant Credit	7
• Medical Expense Tax Credit	430
• Medical Expense Supplement for Earners	40

Source: Government of Canada, *Tax Expenditures and Evaluations, 2000* (Ottawa: Finance Canada, 2000). This report captured the February 2000 budget but not the October 2000 mini-budget. Estimates for the Caregiver Tax Credit and Disability Tax Credit reflect changes in the mini-budget.

ised, over the next five years, an estimated $655 million in added tax assistance for Canadians with disabilities and their caregivers. This builds on the further tax assistance announced in the 1998 and 1999 federal budgets, generating a total of $1.6 billion in additional tax assistance for people with disabilities by 2004-5 arising from the second Liberal mandate.

The federal government uses six primary measures of disability-related tax support in the personal income tax system. Table 7.2 outlines the tax expenditures related to these measures, along with their projected federal revenue impact for 2001.

The amount of revenues foregone as a result of these tax expenditures has expanded, as has the number of recipients.[31] For the Disability Tax Credit, the number of beneficiaries had grown from 65,000 in 1985 to over 500,000 by 2000, reflecting a growing client group and expanded eligibility over this time. Changes have also expanded the range of professional and occupational groups empowered to determine the degree and nature of disabilities.

Tax assistance for persons with disabilities, however, is a mixed blessing. On one hand, tax supports serve the social welfare function of recognizing human needs and influencing the income, goods, and services available to persons with disabilities and their families. On the other hand, the increasing use of the tax system to deliver disability benefits makes the system more complex, and ultimately more confusing and less accessible. Tax relief is a relatively straightforward policy instrument for the federal government to select in regard to disability issues, though it is not necessarily the most beneficial reform for individuals and families. For national disability groups, tax-related benefits are not always a high priority. Such budgetary measures place these groups in the awkward position of having to decide whether to loudly oppose, publicly support, or just quietly accept these incremental reforms.[32]

CITIZENSHIP AS ECONOMIC INTEGRATION

In our present age, citizenship is associated with employment and productivity, which implies an essentially market-oriented concept of belonging. This suggests a move away from a state-centred understanding of citizenship, which stresses legal and political status, toward an emphasis on partnerships with the private and voluntary sectors to promote the employability of persons with disabilities.

This investment view of social policy—employment as a building block for achieving full citizenship—is strongly apparent in government documents on disability issues. Attentiveness to employment is understandable in light of changing ideas about disability, and the fact that the unemployment rate among Canadians with disabilities is about double the national average. Research suggests that if barriers are removed, more than half of working-age persons with disabilities could enter paid employment.[33]

Three federal employment-related initiatives define the Liberals' disability policy agenda and record: the Employability Assistance for People with Disabilities (EAPD), the Employment Benefits and Support Measures (EBSM), funded under the EI program, and the Opportunities Fund for People with Disabilities.[34] All three have the goal of reducing barriers to the participation of Canadians with disabilities in workplaces and thereby promoting financial independence, by providing a range of measures in conjunction with other stakeholders. Where they differ, as Table 7.3 shows, is in the size of their budgets, in their clientele focus, in their program governance, and in their delivery arrangements.

The EAPD has two parts: an umbrella multilateral agreement and a series of bilateral administrative agreements that are negotiated within it. The multilateral framework enunciates five principles: the direct support of employability; a focus on individual needs and participation; flexibility in program design and delivery; accountability for implementation; and coordination of programs and services related to people with disabilities. The EAPD has a strong focus on employability and labour market activities.[35] The Quebec government did not endorse the multilateral framework, although its officials observed the proceedings and undertook bilateral negotiations, securing a cost-shared arrangement with the federal government. Funding for the EAPD is through equal contributions from the province/territory and the federal government in each year of the agreements. The bilateral agreements operate for five years, April 1998 to March 2003, with an annual ceiling of $193 million of federal funds.

Employment Benefit and Support Measures (EBSM) receive funding under Part II of the Employment Insurance Act. EI Part II program spending for 2000-1 is planned to be nearly $2.2 billion. Employment benefits, for which most of these expenditures are allocated, include targeted wage subsidies, earnings supplements, self-employment assistance, job creation partnerships, and skills loans and grants. Support measures are shorter-term interventions, often of a few days or weeks in duration, and include employment assistance services such as counselling, labour market partnerships, and research and innovation activities. Benefits and measures are delivered through the Labour Market Development Agreements in a co-management arrangement between governments, or solely by the provincial or territorial government.

People with disabilities are one of the four groups designated under the Employment Equity Act to be monitored for participation in the EBSM as claimants. From a national average of 2 per cent in 1995-6, the participation rate for persons with disabilities in EBSM increased to

Table 7.3
Major Federal Employment-Related Programs for People with Disabilities

Program and origin	Policy features	Planned expenditures 2000-1 ($ millions)
Employability Assistance for People with Disabilities, 1997	• Cost-shared intergovernmental agreements for five years • Delivered by provincial and local agencies	195
Employment Benefits and Support Measures, 1980s	• For people with disabilities eligible for Employment Insurance • Delivered usually by provincial or local partners under Labour Market Development Agreements	75[a]
Opportunities Fund, 1997	• For people with disabilities ineligible for Employment Insurance • Disability organizations involved in design and delivery • Administered through HRDC offices	33

a   Estimate by author based on the participation reate of self-identified peole with disablilties during 1997-8, as reported in *1998 Employment Insurance Monitoring*.

Source: Human Resources Development Canada, *Main Estimates 2000-2001, Part III*.

3.6 per cent in 1997-8. This compares with participation rates for the other designated groups of 4 per cent for Aboriginal peoples and for visible minorities and 42 per cent for women, in 1997-8.[36]

The 1997 federal budget introduced the Opportunities Fund (OF) as a three-year $90 million initiative, to help people with disabilities integrate into the workforce. The OF supports a range of employment-related activities, and offers some forms of financial assistance, for people with disabilities not eligible for EI benefits and measures. A preliminary evaluation of the OF found varied results in working with third-party delivery organizations and in improving the employability of participants. Work is needed to improve collection of client information and to leverage resources from other assistance programs. HRDC's management response to the evaluation highlights 'a strong involvement of persons with disabilities and organizations representing persons with disabilities in providing leadership in the implementation of this program at the national level. This offers an innovative way of bringing sensitivity to a program established to meet the employment needs of persons with disabilities by involving them in the design and delivery.'[37] The 2000 budget extended the program, committing $33 million for 2000-1, $37 million for 2001-2, and $32 million for 2002-3. HRDC has said that it expects the program to help almost 3,200 Canadians with disabilities each year improve their employability, and that of those, more than 1,300 will find employment each year.[38]

During the third mandate of the Liberals it is important to evaluate more fully the participatory governance, cost effectiveness, and outcomes of the OF. It is equally important to consider systematically the interactions among these employment programs.

CONCLUSION: BEYOND INSTALMENTS?

In 1998, Prime Minister Chrétien accepted on behalf of Canada the Franklin Delano Roosevelt International Disability Award, which is presented by the United Nations. In his acceptance speech, the Prime Minister spoke of the national partnership of organizations and governments committed to the proposition that people with disabilities have a basic right, as citizens, to enjoy and access any opportunity that life has to offer. Chrétien went on to note that Canadians with disabilities are active and vocal partners in this societal project:

> And believe me, the disability community has not been shy about letting my government know when it is not happy with what we are doing. But our disagreements have been about means, not ends; about the pace of change; about the availability of resources.

> All Canadians have made sacrifices to restore the fiscal health of our nation. And today, I want to say to my partners—here in this room and beyond—that as Canada begins moving into a post-deficit era—as we make strategic investments that enhance opportunity for all—Canadians with disabilities will be included.
>
> As I accept this award on behalf of Canada, I realize that this is an opportunity to look in two directions. As we look to the past, we can savour the many achievements we have made as a nation to enable Canadians with disabilities to play a fuller role in our society. As we look to the future, it is with the knowledge that the full inclusion of Canadians with disabilities is a work in progress.
>
> A work that we must have the will to complete.

The Prime Minister concluded with a remark of the sort expected in a feel-good political speech, a remark that now, at the start of a third majority mandate, in a period of budget surpluses, takes on greater significance. He stated, 'Nothing would make me prouder than to be here again in five years—again in the company of my partners—to accept another FDR Award for what we will have accomplished since today.'[39]

In July 1999 the federal government released *Future Directions to Address Disability Issues for the Government of Canada: Working Together for Full Citizenship*. *Future Directions* sets out seven priorities for federal policy:[40]

- increasing public accountability and improving policy and program coherence on disability issues;
- building a comprehensive base of knowledge in disability issues;
- supporting the capacity of the disability community to participate in the policy process;
- addressing the acute needs of Aboriginal peoples with disabilities;
- improving access and removing barriers to disability supports and income programs through life transitions from school to work to the community;

- enhancing the employability of persons with disabilities, which includes promoting better access to information, technology and transportation; and,
- reducing injury and disability rates through prevention and health promotion.

This list is the agenda for disability policy-making in the Liberals' third mandate. For the Prime Minister, there is a fundamental question. Will the pace of change quicken, and will the scope of reform deepen, not to complete the work on inclusion, for major reform is never finished, but rather to substantially improve the status of people with disabilities? Only then will the vision of full citizenship truly begin to come into focus for Canadians with disabilities. This would indeed be a proud legacy.

NOTES

1 A similar point, of course, applies to women, Aboriginal peoples, and visible minorities, among others. See William Kaplan, ed., *Belonging:The Meaning and Future of Canadian Citizenship* (Montreal and Kingston: McGill-Queen's University Press, 1993); Alan C. Cairns et al., eds, *Citizenship, Diversity and Pluralism* (Montreal and Kingston: McGill-Queen's University Press, 1999); James J. Rice and Michael J. Prince, *Changing Politics of Canadian Social Policy* (Toronto: University of Toronto Press, 2000).

2 These five elements of citizenship are based on sections of the Canadian Charter of Rights and Freedoms as well as on other domains of public policy. The classification, while relatively wide in scope, is not intended to be exhaustive. Other elements, dealing, for example, with Aboriginal and treaty rights or reproductive rights, could be added in a fuller analysis.

3 Much more than the political right to speak in public places, citizenship as discourse is a set of cultural, rhetorical, and symbolic practices that *construct the notion of citizenship itself* and thus help to define membership in society.

4 Major reports include *Equal Citizenship for Canadians with Disabilities: The Will to Act*, Report of the Federal Task Force on Disability Issues (Ottawa, 1996); *Future Directions to Address Disability Issues for the Government of Canada: Working Together for Full Citizenship* (Ottawa: Human Resources Development Canada, July 1999); *Government of Canada Response to Reflecting Interdependence: Disability,*

Parliament, Government and Community, the Sixth Report of the Standing Committee on Human Resources Development and the Status of Persons with Disabilities (Ottawa: Human Resources Development Canada, Nov. 1999); and *A National Strategy for Persons with Disabilities: A Community Definition* (Ottawa: Council of Canadians with Disabilities, Nov. 1999), a document developed and endorsed by several community organizations.

5 'In Unison: A Canadian Approach to Disability Issues' (Oct. 1998), 1. See web site: www.socialunion.gc.ca

6 See, for example, T.H. Marshall, *Sociology at the Crossroads* (London: Heinemann, 1963); and Dawn Oliver and Derek Heater, *The Foundations of Citizenship* (London: Harvester Wheatsheaf, 1994).

7 Michael Mandel, *The Charter of Rights and the Legalization of Politics in Canada* (Toronto: Thompson Educational Publishing, 1992).

8 Human Resources Development Canada, 'The Government of Canada's Record on Disability'. See web site: www.hrdc-drhc.gc.ca/common/news/9821b4.html

9 *Future Directions*, sect. 4, 1.

10 Canadian Human Rights Tribunal, *2000-2001 Estimates, Part III* (Ottawa: Supply and Services Canada, 2000), 11.

11 Canadian Human Rights Act Review, *Promoting Equality* (Ottawa: Supply and Services Canada, 2000), chap. 17, 16. See web site: www.chareview.org

12 Quoted in *Promoting Equality*, chap. 17, 17.

13 *Promoting Equality,* chap. 17, 20.

14 The Court Challenges Program of Canada, 'Funding for Equality Rights Cases', 2. See web site: www.ccppcj.ca/e/i-fundequality.html

15 Over the October 1994 to March 2000 period, litigation on grounds of disability under section 15 represented 13.5 per cent of the funding, more than for issues of race, sex, and age, and second only to cases dealing with Aboriginal issues. Of the 25 cases funded for disability issues, eight were at the first instance in the court system, nine were at the level of appeal, and eight were at the Supreme Court of Canada. Overall, individuals and groups from the disability community received funding as a direct party in 16 of the cases and for interventions in the other nine cases. Court Challenges Program of Canada, *Annual Report 1999-2000* (Winnipeg: CCPC, 2000), 47-51.

16 See Peter W. Hogg, *Constitutional Law of Canada*, 2000 Student Edition (Toronto: Carswell, 2000), 1023-4 and 1039-40.

17 Fraser Valentine and Jill Vickers, '"From the Yoke of Paternalism and Charity": Citizenship and the Rights of Canadians with Disabilities', *International Journal of Canadian Studies* 14 (Fall 1996): 173.

18 For details see Election Canada on-line, General Information, Backgrounders: 'Accessibility of the Electoral System'. See web site:

www.elections.ca/content.asp
19 Michael J. Prince, 'Touching Us All: International Context, National Policies, and the Integration of Canadians with Disabilities', in Frances Abele, ed., *How Ottawa Spends 1992-93: The Politics of Competitiveness* (Ottawa: Carleton University Press, 1992), 217.
20 Office for Disability Issues, HRDC, 'Organizational Funding for National Disability Organizations', 1. See web site: www.hrdc-drhc.gc.ca/hrib.sdd-dds/odi/content/natOrgs.shtml
21 *Future Directions*. See also the *Report of the Auditor General of Canada, October 2000* (Ottawa: Supply and Services Canada), chap. 11.
22 Auditor General of Canada, *Annual Report* (Sept. 1996), chap. 17. See web site: www.oag-bvg.gc.ca/domino/reports.nsf/html/9617me.html
23 Finance Canada, Ottawa. See *Securing the Canada Pension Plan, Agreement on Proposed Changes to the CPP* (Feb. 1997). See web site: www.cpp-rpc.gc.ca
24 Human Resources Development Canada, *Estimates, Part III, 1999-2000*, 3-29.
25 For more detail on this portfolio, see Michael J. Prince, 'Battling for Remembrance: The Politics of Veterans Affairs Canada', in Leslie A. Pal, ed., *How Ottawa Spends 2000-2001: Past Imperfect, Future Tense* (Toronto: Oxford University Press, 2000), 131-59.
26 These groups include members of the Canadian Red Cross and St. John Ambulance who served as Overseas Welfare Workers, the Corps of Canadian Fire Fighters, pilots of Ferry Command who transported aircraft over the Atlantic, and the Newfoundland Overseas Forestry Unit. For details see Veterans Affairs Canada, 'Backgrounder: Bill C-41, Omnibus Veterans' Benefits Legislation'. See web site: www.vac-accgc.ca
27 On the origins of the sickness benefit, see Leslie A. Pal, *State, Class, and Bureaucracy: Canadian Unemployment Insurance and Public Policy* (Kingston and Montreal: McGill-Queen's University Press, 1988), 79-80.
28 The actual amount a person receives in sickness benefits is determined from the individual's average insured earnings in the previous 26 weeks, a basic benefit rate, the unemployment rate in the person's region, and other sources of income. Any money from employer group insurance for sickness or from CPP retirement income is deducted dollar for dollar from sickness benefits, while other sources of income, such as disability pensions and private sickness wage-loss insurance, do not affect the benefit amount. This information on Sickness Benefits comes from the Human Resources Development Canada web site: www.hrdc-drhc.gc.ca/insur/claimant/201017.shtml
29 See *1998 Employment Insurance Monitoring and Assessment Report* and *Annexes* (Ottawa: Canada Employment and Insurance Commission, Dec. 1998).

30 See Finance Canada, *Economic Statement and Budget Update 2000: Annex 1*, 'Spending, Tax Relief and Debt Reduction Since 1997' (Ottawa: Oct. 2000). See web site: www.fin.gc.ca/ec2000/ecale.html
31 The frequent use of the tax system as an instrument of policy is the product of a number of forces, including court decisions, sustained lobbying efforts by disability groups, the role of the Finance Department, and the active support of parliamentary committees. Furthermore, the shift to greater tax assistance seems affected by the shift toward care in the community and the privatization of responsibility for care. Placements in group homes for adults with moderate to severe disabilities, for example, are more difficult than ten or twenty years ago, when large facilities were de-institutionalized and other support programs were cut back. At least part of the pressure for tax assistance reflects this shift in responsibility for caregiving.
32 See Erin Anderssen, 'Disability Groups Berate Ottawa for Unfulfilled Promises for Help', *The Globe and Mail* [Toronto], 1 Mar. 1999, A1, A10.
33 Human Resources Development Canada, *Evaluation of the Opportunities Fund for People with Disabilities (Phase 1)*. See web site: www.hrdc-crhc.gc.ca/edd/OFPD.shtml
34 In several other policy areas, too, the federal government is taking steps to remove disincentives to work and remove barriers to employment for people with disabilities. Under changes to the CPP, disability benefit clientele can work on a volunteer basis without having their eligibility automatically reviewed. Clients who return to work can keep their benefits for a period of three months in order to facilitate the transition, and clients can retain their disability benefits while in school, college, or university. In tax policy, the Refundable Medical Expense Credit was introduced in 1997 for low-income working Canadians with disabilities to help defray medical costs. Other tax measures too, outlined earlier, support people with disabilities in their educational and working lives. Legislative and regulatory changes, such as those in the Canada Labour Code and a new Employment Equity Act in 1996, aim to advance the employment of people with disabilities.
35 Consequently, the following are not likely to be cost shared: medical treatment services, programs provided in sheltered workshops, and work activity programs not directly linked to meeting employability needs. Federal funding for previous VRDP programs inconsistent with EADP is to be phased out over a three-year period.
36 See *1998 Employment Insurance Monitoring*.
37 *Evaluation of the Opportunities Fund*.
38 Human Resources Development Canada, *2000-2001 Estimates, Part III*, 31.
39 The Right Hon. Jean Chrétien, Prime Minister of Canada, 'Accepting the Franklin Delano Roosevelt International Disability Award', Office of the Prime Minister. See web site: www.pm.gc.ca
40 *Future Directions*, sect. 6, 1.

8

The Case of Disappearing Targets: The Liberals and Gender Equality

SANDRA BURT
SONYA LYNN HARDMAN

In 1995 the Chrétien government committed itself to implementing gender-based analysis in policy development and evaluation. In the *Plan for Gender Equality,* the document created by Status of Women for the Fourth United Nations Conference in Beijing (1995), then Secretary of State for Status of Women, Sheila Finestone, promised to 'change the impact of government on the lives of women by including the perspectives of women.'[1] In this chapter, we evaluate the federal government's fulfillment of that 1995 promise. While we focus specifically on progress during the last year of the Chrétien government's second mandate (when it was still wrestling with the deficit) and its promises for the third mandate (offered in the Speech from the Throne as building a more inclusive Canada with a higher quality of life for all Canadians), we also take a long look backward, to see how gender-based analysis fits within the government's overall strategy of equality for women.

THE 'OLD' LIBERAL MANDATE:
THE TRUDEAU VISION OF EQUAL OPPORTUNITY

Historically, the most significant improvements in women's rights at the federal level in Canada have been made during periods of Liberal rule. The first of the post Second World War initiatives came in 1953, when the Liberal Minister of Labour, Milton Gregg, rose in the House of Commons to announce his government's intention to create a Women's Bureau within his department. This Bureau was the first federal administrative unit charged exclusively with analysing the status of Canadian women in the labour market. The Bureau focussed on the participation of Canadian women in the paid labour force, and, with a staff of only three in its early days, contributed to the development of the first equal pay (1956) and maternity leave legislation (1971), and published an annual summary of women's paid work.[2]

These early Liberal initiatives were not without their flaws. The first equal pay legislation, for example, limited equal pay to 'identical or substantially identical work' in federally-regulated businesses. Even then, there was a significant gap between the measures proposed by the women working within the Bureau and the government's plan of action. While the government was prepared, in those early days, to accept procedural equality for women (treating women and men alike when they were in similar situations), the Bureau was pressing for a modest version of substantive equality—treating women and men alike even when they are differently situated (that is, in different jobs but with similar levels of training and responsibility). Nevertheless, the early Liberal initiatives represented a significant step forward in the federal government's commitment to advancing women's equality.

In the 1970s the Liberals moved closer to accepting the principle of substantive equality for women. In 1970, the government tabled the *Report* of the Royal Commission on the Status of Women, and set about implementing some of the Commission's 167 recommendations.[3] The earliest reforms included affirmative action, stronger equal pay laws, some child care initiatives, and improved pensions for women. The Liberal government also put in place the policy machinery that was charged with advancing women's status. While there were always problems with this machinery, it did represent a public commitment by the Liberal government of Pierre Trudeau to work toward some measure of political and economic equality. Two units in this machinery have proved to have lasting significance, for they survived the budget cuts of the 1990s.

The first of these was the Women's Bureau. In the 1970s the Bureau was flourishing. In 1976 it was given some policy development responsibilities in addition to the information-gathering that was its chief responsibility in its earliest years, and in 1979 it was promoted to the status of a branch of the Department of Labour. It was also in the 1970s that the Bureau was specifically charged by the Liberals with monitoring federal programs on equal pay and affirmative action. It was to play a key role in assessing the measures taken by employers to improve women's opportunities in the paid labour force, and to maintain Canada's profile internationally on issues related to women and employment.

The second unit, set up in 1971, was Status of Women Canada, or what came to be known simply as 'Status'. Until 1976 the Co-ordinator of Status (who reported to the newly created Minister Responsible for the Status of Women) was located in the Privy Council Office (PCO). From this vantage point, the Co-ordinator chaired an Interdepartmental Committee on the Status of Women, which was intended to co-ordinate the federal government's response to the Royal Commission on the Status of Women.

From its inception, Status had difficulties carrying out its mandate of monitoring Cabinet's 1976 decision to require all federal departments 'to establish "integration mechanisms" to ensure that policy relating to the status of women was integrated into general departmental policy development.'[4] For, while departments were formally required to attach an 'impact on women' statement to all proposals, there was no compliance mechanism linked to the requirement. Since Status, like most other departments, had only limited access to cabinet proposals, it was not able to make gender impact recommendations at an early stage in the policy process. Finally, the department was poorly organized and small. In her comparison of women's policy machinery in Canada, Australia, and New Zealand, Marion Sawer concludes that Status was weak from the outset, because 'it was neither located within the chief co-ordinating agency nor, because of its free-standing character, did it have a powerful department behind it.'[5]

Nevertheless, its very existence was proof of the Liberal government's formal commitment to address the problem of women's economic inequality. Furthermore, it was surrounded by a women's policy machinery that stretched across several departments, all charged with improving the status of Canadian women. They were all part of a strategy for change that was popular among industrialized states in the post-war period—in part at least in response to the initiatives of the United Nations that culminated in the 1979 Convention on the Elimination of all Forms of Discrimination Against Women.

The policy instrument with the greatest impact on women's lives was the Women's Program in the Secretary of State (established in 1973), a Program that grew out of the federal government's involvement in International Women's Year (1972). The Program was successful in two ways. First, it contributed to the activism of grassroots women's groups that were busy, for example, setting up shelters for abused women, or employment referral services for immigrant women, in local communities. Secondly, it provided operating funds to feminist organizations, who were then able to lobby the federal government for policy changes. Because these community-based groups were not part of the government power structure, they could often propose and/or implement a much broader range of initiatives than was possible for bureaucrats. Even feminist bureaucrats (or femocrats, as they were labelled first in Australia), who might be committed to fundamental transformations in women's roles, were sometimes constrained by the federal government's equal rights agenda.

These Liberal measures introduced in the 1970s were part of a general strategy of improving all citizens' economic, legal, and social rights. But this strategy was steeped in the principles of equal opportunity, and like most western government programs for women in this period, it was designed to bring women into previously existing political and economic structures, without fundamentally altering any of those structures. In other words, women's 'interests' were constrained by overarching government policies. For the most part, the measures developed during the 'old' Liberal mandate only barely began to address issues such as affordable and accessible child care, male violence against women, and persistent traditional and patriarchal attitudes about women's roles and men's roles in society.

But in spite of the limits imposed by the equal opportunity model, the 1970s were marked by some significant improvements in women's lives.[6] The equal pay laws did result in some modest improvements in women's wages. Affirmative action language (if not legislation) ended the explicit segregation of jobs by gender (in both job advertisements and job descriptions), even though it had less impact on the gender segregation of the paid labour force. As well, there was just a hint that more sweeping changes might be possible. There was a growing commitment by the Liberal government to take into account women's special needs in the areas of health and personal safety. It was this commitment that led a growing number of women to hold 'on to their faith in government reform. What mediated their frustrations and sustained the optimism of many of these women was the apparent willingness of the government to integrate women into the policy-making processes of the state. For the first time, feminists felt their issues were represented in the "corridors of power"'.[7]

THE RISE OF NEOLIBERAL VALUES AND THE DECLINE IN THE VISIBILITY OF EQUALITY TARGETS

Weak as the Trudeau measures were, they nonetheless contributed to the development within government circles of a discourse of women's equality, based on the proposition that women should have the same rights, opportunities, and obligations as men in the public sphere of politics and paid work. That discourse was muted during the Conservative governments between 1984 and 1993. The transition was gradual, and often difficult to detect. It was less a case of rejecting equality rights for women, and more one of embedding them within a powerful economic agenda of globalization and technological development. With the rhetoric of neoliberalism came cutbacks in government expenditures, and specifically the reduction in the proportion of the budget devoted to improving women's economic status. Michael Prince makes a distinction between the restraints placed on social spending between 1984 and 1988, and the restructuring of the social role of government that began in 1987.[8] In the first phase of restraint, women's programs were kept on hold or cut back, and there were few legislative initiatives on status of women issues.

By 1987, the gender equality targets started to disappear. The most obvious manifestation of the transition could be seen in the Conservatives' approach to the successful Women's Program in the Secretary of State. By 1987, the Program's annual budget was $12.7 million—money that was used to sustain the operations of national women's groups, shelters for women, and special service groups. In 1990 the budget was reduced to $9 million, and funding guidelines were revised to include all women's groups, even those committed to a *reduction* in women's presence in the paid labour force and a return to more traditional family values. At the same time, the Conservatives dropped plans for improved child care funding, and instead raised the child care tax deduction ($5,000 per child). As well, in 1992 the universal family allowance payment was replaced by a selective child tax credit. Expenditure control was firmly in place, and it overshadowed if not eclipsed the principle of equal opportunity for all.

In 1993, the newly elected Liberals led by Jean Chrétien carried on with the politics of restructuring. For women, restructuring specifically meant a shift in 1995 away from special programs for women to the rhetoric of mainstreaming gender concerns, or the application of a 'gender lens' to all aspects of government policy. In Canada, the gender lens was labelled gender-based analysis (GBA). Despite this so-called lens, under the Liberals the federal government has continued the shift that originated in the 1980s, away from a focus on women's equality to a concern for the needs of children. This shift can be seen in the background papers prepared by the government in preparation for the creation of Human Resources Development Canada (HRDC), where the poverty faced by single-parent families (most of which are headed by women) was described as 'children's poverty'. This shift was apparent throughout the first two Liberal mandates, and has been carried into the third.[9] Until the 1980s, Canadian governments sought to alleviate child poverty by targeting the income levels of their parents. In the current rhetoric, child poverty is presented as a separate issue.

On the face of it, the movement to GBA in 1995 appeared to be an improvement over earlier gender initiatives. The fundamental premise of GBA is that women's experiences, knowledge, and needs will be taken into account in the development and implementation of policy as a matter of course. By 1995, GBA had been adopted as a strategy in a few other countries (notably the Nordic countries and New Zealand), and seemed to be working well. In the light of positive reports about the gender lens, in particular in Sweden and Norway, it had been promoted as a better strategy for change by some feminists in Canada, although they called it a feminist lens, and they included in their recommendations some specific guidelines for changing existing gender roles.[10] The concept of a feminist lens first appeared in a government document in 1993, in the Report of the Canadian Panel on Violence Against Women.

The optimism of early advocates of the gender lens was based in part on the perceived failure of the extensive women's policy machinery that had been put in place in the 1970s. For by the mid-1980s, policy analysts reviewing the federal government's record on advancing women's interests were expressing some reservations about the effectiveness of departments such as Status of Women.

Some of the critics suggested that public bureaucratic structures are inherently hierarchical and patriarchal, and offer little possibility for meaningful and fundamental policy initiatives that would address, among other issues, male violence, child care, and the power imbalance between women and men. They were concerned about both the *location* of the women's issues policy machinery, and the 'co-optation' of femocrats into the government's agenda. The dilemma facing women in the 1970s and the early 1980s was a common one for reformers in opposition to the status quo. If they became part of the state bureaucracy, working in reasonably well-paid jobs with some job security, there would be pressure to work within the government's understanding of women's needs. But if they opted out of the process, there would be no one within government to speak for women with a feminist voice.

In part, the failure of the women's policy machinery was attributed to the fact that the feminist agenda and the government's agenda were quite far apart. Suzanne Franzway et al., in their discussion of sexual violence, illustrate the difference between these two perspectives. Feminists see sexual violence as a specific manifestation of a general assertion of patriarchal power by men over women. The state has viewed sexual violence through the lens of the family, and as a result 'both rape law and social policy on child sexual abuse are shaped by the state's commitment to patriarchal familial relations.'[11] In the case of social policy, this commitment has resulted in a failure to consider, for example, the particular problems faced by women who are single parents. The replacement of universal family allowances with the child tax benefit has increased the financial pressure on these women to obtain paid employment, even when their children are very young. But the absence of a comprehensive child care strategy makes this option problematic. Some of the women working within the women's policy machinery have acknowledged the problems they faced in a hierarchical bureaucratic culture steeped in the public administration values of neutrality.[12] While neutrality is an attractive concept in some contexts, it fails to capture the reality of gender differences in opportunities and needs.

In light of these misgivings about the status of women's policy machinery, some women approved of the federal Liberals' decision to remove most of that machinery shortly after their election in 1993, and to initiate GBA in its stead. By the end of 1995, most of the network of women's policy advisory groups had been dismantled. Early in their first mandate, the Liberals removed the women's advisor from Health and Welfare, disbanded the Advisory Council on the Status of Women, removed most of the funding dollars from the Women's Program and relocated the Program within Status of Women Canada, and downgraded the cabinet position of the Minister Responsible for the Status of Women to the lower rank of Secretary of State Responsible for Status of Women.

GENDER-BASED ANALYSIS (GBA)

As the Liberals entered their second mandate, in 1997, the newly reorganized machinery of status of women included only Status of Women Canada, with a much reduced Women's Program within it, and the Women's Bureau in the newly established HRDC. The mandate of Status was to continue in its earlier role of representing Canada internationally on status of women issues; to maintain links with women's groups across the country, primarily through its Women's Program; and to co-ordinate GBA throughout the federal bureaucracy. The Bureau was given responsibility for GBA within HRDC, in addition to its historic role as a research unit within Labour Canada.

Like most of the major status of women initiatives from the federal government, GBA was partly a response to international pressure. The Platform of Action adopted by 189 countries attending the United Nations Fourth World Conference on Women in 1995 included a call for integrating gender perspectives in the development and implementation of policy. The intention was to 'ensure that before policy decisions are undertaken, an analysis of their impact on men and women is carried out.'[13] This process became known as GBA, or the gender lens. The delegates' decision at that UN Conference reflected their concern that the separate policy machineries set up in many countries to move status of women issues forward were often segregated from the mainstream of policy development. The intention was to institutionalize at the centre of policy-making the concept that policies have gender-specific impacts. But GBA is a loosely-defined tool of policy analysis. If the ultimate goal is women's equality, policy-makers need to articulate their vision of equality. Equality is a highly contested concept that could be so extensive as to include reforms in child care provisions and family law, or limited to improving opportunities for women to compete for jobs in the public sphere.

At its best, GBA gives public servants a tool for challenging the traditional bureaucratic adherence to the principle of neutrality. For it is a way of approaching policy development that specifically requires bureaucrats to take the differing social and economic realities of women and men into account. GBA recognizes that policies may affect women and men differently. It is grounded in the assumption that the attainment of gender equality may require gender-specific policies—that take into account women's and men's differing economic, social, and political circumstances. The Nordic Council of Ministers has described the philosophy of GBA this way: 'Equality between the sexes does not mean that men and women have to be similar. It means that the dissimilarity between men and women must not lead to inequality in terms of status or treatment in society.'[14] In theory, the adoption of GBA should make considerations of gender a central part of the policy cycle.

GBA has the potential to ensure that the positive and negative effects of policy choices on women and men are understood before policy decisions are made. It requires policy-makers to accept the principle of substantive equality; that is, that men and women may have different circumstances and needs, and that treating them alike does not necessarily result in equal outcomes. The key to good policy is asking the right questions, to reveal the differences in the socio-economic conditions of women's and men's lives, and thereby to anticipate both intended and unintended consequences of a particular policy option. For example, 'the use of a gender-based analysis ... will point to other factors such as women's concentration in the lower-paying "McJobs" and demonstrate how economic restructuring and any adjustment policies can have a differential impact on women given their current lower-wage, highly concentrated position in the workforce relative to men.'[15]

However, GBA does not always lead to policies that are better for women, for several reasons. First, the concept as it was first developed in Beijing does not take into account differences *among* as well as between women. For example, the employment and/or pension needs of Aboriginal women living in Saskatchewan may be very different from the needs of urban women of British origin. Secondly, the ideological context within which policies are generated figures largely in problem definition and policy development. If the policy context includes economic restructuring, balanced budgets, tax cuts, and globalization, and if these approaches generally disadvantage women, the application of GBA to specific policy initiatives will have only a very limited impact. Indeed, GBA may add the veneer of legitimacy to measures that clearly do not contribute to women's well-being. If GBA is applied in the middle of the policy cycle, after a policy direction has been set, it can have only a limited impact on the shape of policy.

Nevertheless, GBA has the potential to succeed where women-specific programs have not. It is intended to bring the particular needs of women and men into mainstream policy discussions, at an early stage of the policy cycle—the stage of policy development rather than policy evaluation. And it links countries together in an international project of achieving gender equality.

THE CANADIAN APPLICATION

The Canadian Concept of GBA

According to reviewers who have concluded that Canadian femocrats[16] had relatively little success when they were at their strongest in terms of numbers (1973 to 1995), it was the core bureaucratic culture of neutrality that presented the biggest obstacle to making policies that would be good for women. A former Director of the Women's Bureau, Linda Geller-Schwartz, writes that 'the idea that civil servants should adopt the role of internal lobbyists for women as a definable group was an anathema.'[17] So the adoption of GBA by the federal government was seen by many as a step forward, and as a vehicle for developing a gender perspective within government.

The federal government's 1995 submission to the Fourth United Nations World Conference on Women was the blueprint for this new vehicle. In *Setting the Stage for the Next Century*, the federal government set eight objectives for future action:

- implement GBA throughout federal departments and agencies;
- improve women's economic autonomy and well-being;
- improve women's physical and psychological well-being;
- reduce violence in society, particularly violence against women and children;
- promote gender equality in all aspects of Canada's cultural life;
- incorporate women's perspectives in governance;
- promote and support global gender equality;
- advance gender equality for employees of federal departments and agencies.[18]

The wording of that 1995 document was general enough to suggest several possible interpretations of GBA. Indeed, much of the effort of the bureaucrats charged with implementing GBA has been devoted to developing clear policy guidelines. In 1995 as well, the federal government adopted a five-year action plan to advance women's equality, with the overarching objective of implementing GBA. Status of Women Canada was given the responsibility of developing the process for GBA—acting as a central source of information for government departments, and providing them with the tools necessary for the application of GBA. The Women's Bureau had the specific responsibility of promoting GBA throughout its home department, HRDC. Both Status of Women and the Women's Bureau developed some more specific guidelines for action. These guidelines, which were published in 1996 and 1997 respectively, listed the different stages in the policy cycle, and called for the mainstreaming of gender concerns at every stage.[19]

However, it is not clear that the bureaucrats working in either agency have found a way to implement these guidelines in the policy-making process in Canada. They face three main obstacles. The first is the general Liberal strategy of economic restructuring and the downsizing of government. The second is their peripheral location within the bureaucratic structure in Ottawa. The third is the conceptual fuzziness of GBA, particularly with respect to its implementation. In 2001, the

Women's Bureau is still developing training modules for implementing GBA within HRDC, and Status of Women is still developing tools, training materials, and procedures for GBA throughout other government departments.

THE LIBERAL STRATEGY

With respect to achieving the goal of women's equality through the application of GBA, two dimensions of the Liberals' approach to public policy as they ended their second term in office and campaigned for their third term are important. The first of these is the Liberals' strengthened commitment to balancing the budget and managing costs, and their new commitment to reducing taxes. Gender equality does not fit well within this rhetoric of restructuring. In the 1999 Speech from the Throne, the Liberals targeted for action children and youth, the economy, health care, the environment, Aboriginal peoples, and Canada's place in the world.[20] The theme of the February 2000 Budget tabled by Finance Minister Paul Martin was 'better finances, better lives'. The tone of the document is optimistic. The deficit has been eliminated, the debt is disappearing, unemployment levels are down, and the economy is booming. It is time to spend money—on health care, education, and university-based research. And it is time to cut taxes, and increase the child tax benefit. Such a strategy fails to acknowledge the increasing feminization of poverty, the ongoing problem of inadequate child care, and the growing burden placed on women as home care providers for the sick and the elderly. It is hard to see the evidence of GBA in the rhetoric of better finances and better lives. Cutting taxes, for example, helps only those who are members of the paid labour force. Given that about 40 per cent of women who are single parents are not working for wages, they are doubly disadvantaged by a tax cut strategy. Not only do they not receive the benefit of lower taxes, but they also see reductions in social services and income support.

The Liberals' campaign promises in the fall of 2000 echo the priorities set out in the February budget. *Opportunity for All* promises 'greater prosperity and more opportunity for all Canadians'.[21] The document targets research, health, the environment, safe communities, Aboriginal peoples, children, and Canada's image abroad. But gender equality is not on the list. In the 2000 election platform, the Liberals promised to stay on the track of economic restructuring with a balanced budget, lower taxes, and lower interest rates. The Liberals promised that one-half of the budget surplus would go to 'social and economic investments'.[22] There was no indication in the campaign literature that gender will figure into the calculation of spending choices. Gender was a forgotten issue during the campaign, discussed only in the context of a lacklustre leaders' forum on women's issues. The omission of gender in the campaign was repeated in the new government's future plans as outlined in the 2001 Speech from the Throne.

The second important dimension of the Liberals' policy strategy at the beginning of their third mandate is their continued commitment to what has become known as new public management. The language of the new approach to public administration is the language of business. Core values include cost effectiveness, efficiency, and value. In the new public management approach, government departments are required to prepare accountability frameworks, to compare targets with performance; it is not clear how GBA fits within these frameworks. The Task Force reporting in 1996 on public service values and ethics made no reference to GBA in its report, but did reaffirm the values of excellence, professional competence, merit, objectivity, and impartiality in advice.[23] In its guidelines for policy-making, Status of Women identifies three factors necessary for GBA: 1) an awareness of one's own values, and those of the environment in which one works; 2) an understanding of how these values influence one's decision-making; and 3) a sensitivity to gender issues in general. It is hard to accommodate these two sets of guidelines within one approach to policy-making.

The Location of GBA
In addition to these background factors, the bureaucrats charged with implementing GBA have had to deal with the problems associated with their location within the federal government. From its inception, Status of Women has had internal, organizational problems, as well as the problems of visibility and effectiveness characteristic of all horizontal departments. Status functioned best when it had strong ministers with other significant portfolios. These ministers were able to use the leverage of their position withincabinet to advance the concerns of Status as well. When the cabinet position was downgraded to Secretary

of State (and Secretaries of State do not sit in cabinet), Status lost its position of privilege at the cabinet table.

In theory, the adoption of GBA should help Status increase its profile within government. For GBA is a lever for gaining access to other departments. However, the department continues to be plagued with small budgets, a small staff, and problems of organization. In March 1999, Status set up a GBA Directorate, with the specific tasks of developing GBA training programs and assisting departments in the creation of action plans that will integrate GBA into their work. The GBA Director chairs an Interdepartmental Committee on GBA, which brings together representatives from Justice, Health, Citizenship and Immigration, HRDC, Indian and Northern Affairs, Canadian Heritage, and the Canadian International Development Agency. In its 1999 Performance Report, Status stated that 'much work remains if we are to ensure the systematic application of GBA.'[24] In the new Estimates for 2000-1, the GBA directorate has been increased in size from one to three people, and its networking function has been reinforced. But the self-assessment in the 1999 Report suggests some clear limits to the work that these three people can accomplish. To date, the greatest success has been the establishing of research networks and working groups. Among its other projects, Status includes participation in United Nations activities, increasing public awareness of issues such as violence prevention, and identification of research gaps in areas of human rights.[25]

Even more illustrative of the significance of location is the story of the Women's Bureau, and its attempts to implement GBA. The Bureau began its life within the Ministry of Labour. When Labour was absorbed in 1993 into the new mega-department, HRDC, the Women's Bureau moved with it. The Bureau contributed to the federal government's submission to the Fourth International Conference on Women (Beijing), and has been part of the federal government's GBA initiative from the outset.

HRDC was itself an amalgamation of four formerly autonomous departments: Employment and Immigration, Welfare (from Health and Welfare), some aspects of Secretary of State, and Labour. The Women's Bureau began its life in HRDC working on four issues: work and family, women's participation in non-traditional occupations, older women and the paid labour force; and occupational health and safety. It was primarily a research unit, isolated from program development.

In addition, it administered a small annual grants program of $100,000. But toward the end of its first year in HRDC, the Bureau tried to become more active in policy development. GBA proved to be a vehicle for this transition. In 1995, when the Bureau published the *Gender-Based Analysis Guide and Backgrounder*, it adopted an internal policy focus. In an effort to improve its capacity to implement GBA, the Bureau made plans to reorganize internally.

At about the same time, HRDC was also rethinking its structure. When the four founding departments came together in HRDC, each brought with it its own strategic policy unit, and these reassembled as the new department's Strategic Policy Branch. The Women's Bureau stayed briefly in the Social Policy Directorate, and was situated there when it began to work on GBA. Its position within Social Policy was problematic, since its mandate was to implement GBA throughout HRDC. Its location within Social Policy was a poor fit, and senior Social Policy bureaucrats likened it to 'an unfamiliar and out-of-control appendage'.[26] In addition, there were several senior personnel changes, and each new Director-General of the Social Policy Directorate had a different view of the significance of gender. Physical location was a problem as well. The Women's Bureau was situated on a different floor from the rest of Social Policy. This made it difficult for Bureau members to stay in touch with their colleagues. All of these factors contributed to the invisibility of the Bureau, and of GBA.

In 1997, when the Bureau was moved from Social Policy to the Strategy and Co-ordination Directorate, it appeared that most of these problems would disappear. Members of the Bureau saw this move as an opportunity for it to become a more central player in policy development. At about the same time, the Bureau tried to raise its profile by preparing a document outlining its priorities and role within HRDC. *Setting the Stage for the Next Century* outlined a strategy for becoming more involved in policy development.[27] Even before it moved into the Strategic Policy Branch, the Bureau proposed what it called a hub-and-spoke model. A 'hub' of staff would remain within the Social Policy Directorate of the Strategic Policy Branch of HRDC, and 'spoke' staff would move to strategic locations within the other branches of the department. The hub would serve as the central focus for discussions of gender within HRDC, and would co-ordinate the GBA initiative. The spokes would develop links with relevant 'clients and partners', develop and maintain an extensive knowledge base concerning the activities of the particular branch where each was located, and work to ensure that GBA became an integral part of the policy development process within each branch. And all of this would be accomplished with only five spokes!

The Women's Bureau has always been under-staffed. When the hub-and-spoke model was first developed, the Bureau hoped that it could assign one person to each of the branches of policy within HRDC. But given the Bureau's small staff, each person assigned to the spokes was responsible for three or four areas. There had been no decision by the minister responsible for HRDC to increase the size of the Bureau to meet its new commitments, which were set out in the 1995 *Federal Plan for Gender Equality.*

When the hub-and-spoke model was first proposed by the Bureau, it was welcomed by the Director-General of Strategic Policy. But by the end of 1997 that support was dwindling, and it was becoming increasingly difficult for the Bureau staff to implement the GBA initiative. There are several explanations for this declining support. The Bureau itself was struggling to develop an implementation model. As recently as the middle of November 2000, it was still working on the specific guidelines for implementation—five years after it had begun the process! In addition, the Bureau was in a weak position within HRDC. When the Bureau first moved to HRDC, the senior position was reclassified from the level of Director-General to Director, and control over staffing and operational budgets was shifted to the Director-General of Social Policy. As a result, the Bureau's resources were pooled with those of the Social Policy Directorate generally, and it had to compete for money with other groups working on higher-profile social policy initiatives, such as those for seniors, children, and youth. In this competition, children and youth had been targeted as the priorities of the Liberal government. In their 2000 campaign platform, the Liberals reaffirmed these priorities. As a result of its weak position strategically within HRDC, the Bureau has heavily relied on the views of senior bureaucrats concerning the value of GBA. In the first two years of its relocation within the Strategic Policy Branch, it worked with a Director-General who supported the GBA initiative. As a result, the Bureau's Director was able to present the GBA initiative to the Deputy Minister of HRDC by the end of 1997. But only two years later, Strategic Policy had a new Director-General, and the Bureau was back in its earlier position of justifying the implementation of GBA within its own policy branch.

The Bureau's search for an effective strategy for implementing GBA continues today. In 1999, most of the people who had constructed the hub-and-spoke model left the Bureau. The new staff opted for a network model instead, and have focussed on training about 50 people from all branches within HRDC to serve as GBA advisors within their own working groups. The network model is now about one year old, and the Bureau is developing an evaluation framework.

Implementation of GBA

In spite of these problems associated with location, GBA has affected the way in which the Liberals have made policies. For example, the gender lens is now applied to some aspects of immigration policy, and during its second mandate the Liberal government began to take into account the fact that women are at greater risk of domestic violence. The most impressive changes have taken place in the Department of Justice and in Health Canada. Health Canada has set up five Centres of Excellence to carry out research on women's health. The Department of Justice uses GBA in policy development and program evaluation, and has integrated the language of gender difference into its operations. In addition, the Department of Indian and Northern Affairs created the position of Senior Policy Advisor on Women's Issues and Gender Equality.

The restructuring of employment insurance by the Liberals in 2000 provides another good example of the successes and failures of GBA. In 1994, the Liberals decided to change the eligibility criteria and the benefits for EI, in a bid to save $4.8 billion over two fiscal years (1995-7). The restructured EI did not work well for many women. Under the new rules, women needed 700 hours of work (or about 29 weeks) to qualify for pregnancy benefits, versus the 20 weeks required under the old rules. On average, women work fewer hours than men in the paid labour force. When the Liberals moved from a week-based to an hours-based qualifying formula, they made it particularly difficult for women to qualify for benefits. In its 1998 Employment and Monitoring Report, HRDC noted that the number of women who successfully claimed employment benefits dropped by 20 per cent, versus a drop of 16 per cent for men.[28] In their election platform, the Liberals committed themselves to extending maternity and parental benefits from six months to one year by 1 January 2001. But they did not address the qualification problems created in their earlier reforms.

These 1994 changes were implemented in spite of GBA. In its EI gender impact study, HRDC produced disaggregate employment data by sex. But it focussed on workers rather than jobs, and therefore failed to consider the reasons for, and the impact of, the gender segregation of the paid labour force (with women highly concentrated in the clerical, service, nursing, and teaching sectors). In addition, it failed to consider some of the structural barriers facing women as paid workers—notably the lack of affordable and accessible child care.[29] When the rhetoric of moving people off benefits is taken more seriously than the need for social programs, consideration of the structural barriers to employment is far removed from government discourse.

In 2000, in response to a new and improved GBA, the Liberal government removed some of the worst aspects of the reformed EI, at least as they relate to women. It reduced the number of insurable hours of work needed to qualify for benefits from 700 to 600 hours. Also, for the first time, parents will be able to work part-time while they claim some benefits. And the maximum maternity leave has been extended from 25 to 50 weeks.

At the same time there are some obvious examples of the absence of GBA at the policy-development stage of the policy cycle. One of the most serious is the replacement in 1995 of the Canada Assistance Plan (CAP) and Established Programs Financing with the Canada Health and Social Transfer (CHST). Although that change came early in the Liberal government's first term, its impact has persisted into the third term. At the time, women's groups like the National Action Committee on the Status of Women protested that the end of CAP would penalize women disproportionately. Sylvia Bashevkin notes that 'in quantitative terms, data show Canadian provinces as a group spent less per person on social assistance after 1995 than before. Data from the National Council of Welfare show an increase after 1995—the year the CHST was announced—in the already high percentage of young, single-mother led families living in poverty—from 83 per cent in 1995 to more than 91 per cent in subsequent years.'[30]

In their February 2000 Budget, the Liberals promised to put an additional $2.5 billion into the CHST. But this will do little to alleviate the specific problems faced by women heading single-parent families, particularly if they are stay-at-home mothers. Since 1996, provincial governments have found it easier to tie their social programs that are funded in part by the CHST to labour-force participation, arguing that self-sufficiency and independence should be the goal of all welfare recipients. But this argument is grounded in assumptions of gender neutrality, 'assuming that the labour market treats all individuals equally and that gender (as well as race and class) is not [an] important reason for unemployment or underemployment.'[31] The argument also fails to consider the consequences for children of moving their low-income mothers into the paid labour force, and undervalues mothers' unpaid work as caregivers in the home. A gender-based analysis of social policy would have taken into account the different impact of employment on men and women, and among women in different economic and social circumstances.

CONCLUSION

Most of the specialized policy machinery set up in the 1970s to give expression within government to women's interests has by now been dismantled. GBA reflects the new strategy of mainstreaming gender issues within all government departments. However, the strategy has several flaws. First, GBA has been assigned to two small units (within Status of Women and HRDC respectively) that do not have the resources necessary to carry out its implementation. Secondly, the government is still not clear about the meaning of women's equality. As a result, the nature of the policies that are most important for women's lives—employment insurance, employment strategies, child care, and welfare—suggests that the apparently inclusive strategy of GBA can sometimes be subordinated to strategies of economic restructuring and growth.

The success of GBA is dependent on the visibility of women's and men's concerns, and the success of the training modules that are currently being developed. Ironically, the cancellation of the status of women mechanisms within the federal government has contributed to the fragility of both of these projects. While there are some small signs of success, in particular in Health and Justice, it is not yet clear if this third mandate will be remembered by those concerned about gender equality for the growing invisibility of their concerns, or for the growing success of the mainstreaming strategy. The five-year limit for the implementation of GBA has passed, and fully developed implementation procedures are still not in place.

NOTES

1 Canada, Status of Women, *Setting the Stage for the Next Century: The Federal Plan for Gender Equality* (Ottawa: Status of Women, Aug. 1995).
2 For a longer history of the Bureau, see Catherine Briggs and Sandra Burt, 'The Canadian Women's Bureau: Leading the Fight for Justice and Fair Play', in Robert Hesketh, ed., *Canada: Confederation to Present* (Edmonton: Chinook Multimedia Inc., forthcoming).
3 In 1979 the Canadian Advisory Council on the Status of Women evaluated the federal government's implementation record, and concluded that of the 122 recommendations, 43 were implemented, 53 were partially implemented, 24 were not implemented, and 2 were no longer applicable. See Canada, Canadian Advisory Council on the Status of Women, *The Royal Commission Report: 10 Years Later* (Ottawa, Oct. 1979).
4 Marion Sawer, *Femocrats and Ecorats: Women's Policy Machinery in Australia, Canada and New Zealand* (Geneva: United Nations Research Institute for Social Development, 1996), 12.
5 Ibid.
6 These changes are discussed at greater length in Sandra Burt, 'The Changing Patterns of Public Policy', in Sandra Burt, Lorraine Code, and Lindsay Dorney, eds, *Changing Patterns: Women in Canada*, 2nd ed. (Toronto: McClelland and Stewart, 1993), 212-42.
7 Sue Findlay, 'Feminist Struggles with the Canadian State, 1966-1988', *Resources for Feminist Research* 17, 3 (Sept. 1988): 7.
8 Michael J. Prince, 'From Health and Welfare to Stealth and Farewell: Federal Social Policy 1980-2000', in Leslie Pal, ed., *How Ottawa Spends 1999-2000: Shape-Shifting: Canadian Governance Toward the 21st Century* (Toronto, Ont.: Oxford University Press, 1999),156-7.
9 See for example the 30 Jan. 2001 Speech from the Throne, where the Governor-General calls for the elimination of child poverty, but does not mention the poverty of their custodial parents, most of whom are women. See web site: www.sft-ddt.gc.ca/sftddt_e.htm
10 See for example the presentations made to the Standing Committee on Human Resources Development in Canada, House of Commons, *Minutes of Proceedings and Evidence of the Standing Committee on Human Resource Development*, Issue 60, 13 Dec. 1994, Halifax, Nova Scotia, 192-4.

11 Suzanne Franzway, Dianne Court, and R. W. Connell, *Staking a Claim: Feminism, Bureaucracy and the State* (Cambridge, UK: Polity Press, 1989), 106-7.
12 See, for example, Sue Findlay, 'Facing the State: The Politics of the Women's Movement Reconsidered', in Heather Jon Maroney and Meg Luxton, eds, *Feminism and Political Economy* (Toronto: Methuen, 1987); see also Canadian Centre for Management Development, *A Strong Foundation: Report of the Task Force on Public Service Values and Ethics* (Ottawa, 1999).
13 United Nations, *The Beijing Declaration and the Platform for Women* (New York: United Nations Department of Public Information, 1996).
14 Nordic Council of Ministers, *Gender Equality: The Nordic Model* (Copenhagen, 1995).
15 Canada, Human Resources Development Canada, Women's Bureau, 'Gender-Based Analysis'. See web site: www.HRDC-drhc.gc.ca
16 This term was first coined in Australia, and was used to describe women working within government bureaucracies who are committed to feminist principles.
17 Linda Geller-Schwartz, 'An Array of Agencies: Feminism and State Institutions in Canada', in Dorothy M. Stetson and Amy Mazur, eds, *Comparative State Feminism* (Newbury Park, California: Sage, 1995), 49.
18 Canada, Status of Women Canada, *Setting the Stage for the Next Century: The Federal Plan for Gender Equality* (Ottawa, Aug. 1995), 14-5.
19 Canada, Status of Women, *Gender-Based Analysis: A Guide for Policy-Making* (Ottawa: Status of Women, 1996), and Canada, Women's Bureau, *Gender-Based Analysis Guide* (Ottawa: Women's Bureau, March 1997).
20 Speech from the Throne to Open the Second Session of the 36th Parliament of Canada (Ottawa, 12 Oct. 1999).
21 Liberal Party of Canada, *Opportunity for All: The Liberal Plan for the Future of Canada* (Ottawa, 2000), 2.
22 Ibid., 3.
23 Canadian Centre for Management Development, *A Strong Foundation*, (Ottawa, Dec. 1996), 55.
24 Canada, Minister of Public Works and Government Services, *Status of Women Canada: Performance Report for the period ending March 31, 1999* (Ottawa, 1999), 1.
25 Ibid., 12.
26 The recent changes in the Bureau are explored in Sonya Lynn Hardman, 'Necessary Evils and Uncomfortable Bedfellows: Femocrats, the Women's Movement, and the Canadian State', unpublished MA Thesis, Dept. of Political Science, University of Waterloo, 1998.

27 Canada, Women's Bureau, *Setting the Stage for the Next Century* (Ottawa, 1995).
28 Canada, Human Resources Development Canada, Employment Insurance, ii, as cited by Joan Grace, 'The Politics of Policy Transformation in Canada: A Feminist-Institutional Analysis', paper presented at the Annual Meeting of the Canadian Political Science Association, University of Sherbrooke, June 1999, 14.
29 Ibid.
30 Sylvia Bashevkin, 'Road Testing the Third Way: Welfare Reform During the Clinton, Chrétien and Blair Years', paper presented at the International Political Science Association meetings, Quebec City, Aug. 2000, 15.
31 Maureen Baker, 'Poverty, Social Assistance and the Employability of Mothers: Restructuring Welfare States', paper presented at the International Political Science Association meetings, Quebec City, Aug. 2000, 14.

9

New Economy/Old Economy? Transforming Natural Resources Canada

G. BRUCE DOERN

MONICA GATTINGER

Natural Resources Canada (NRCan) was a product of the major 1993 reorganization of the federal government and, for much of the Chrétien Liberal government era, has been several steps removed from the political limelight. Recent concerns about high gasoline prices may end this relative obscurity, but even bursts in energy prices are unlikely to return NRCan to anything like its political halcyon days of the early 1980s. Then, as the Department of Energy Mines and Resources (EMR), it was the focal point for the highly interventionist Trudeau era National Energy Program (NEP). Nonetheless, NRCan's recent history reveals what may be a quieter but ultimately more important political-institutional struggle, namely its effort to reposition itself and the natural resource industries, perceived often to be the quintessence of the *old economy*, as a *new-economy* sector. The dual influence of the innovation policy paradigm on the one hand, and the sustainable development policy paradigm on the other, propelled this repositioning. The *old-economy* label evokes the image of a Canada that lives mainly and historically off its abundant resource endowment rather than its wits and knowledge. It suggests an economy in which the norm is the export of resources, with little or limited value-added production of related products within the Canadian economy. The *new economy* is quintessentially evoked by the Internet and biotechnology as the twin enabling technologies propelling a knowledge-based economy and redefining the boundaries of industrial sectors. It also suggests globalization, fast-flowing movements of financial capital, and free-trade-oriented policies internationally and domestically.

The purpose of this chapter is to examine the origins and evolution of NRCan in the Chrétien era and its effort to change the image and reality of these often simplistic but nonetheless politically important images of the Canadian economy. The old economy-new economy trade-offs are in particular examined in the context of the Liberals' embrace of both the innovation policy and sustainable development policy paradigms as vehicles to strengthen not only Canada's natural resource industries but to enhance NRCan's own influence in the Ottawa power structure. While the chapter is predominantly retrospective, casting an eye backward over the first two Liberal government mandates, it is also, in keeping with the theme of this year's edition of *How Ottawa Spends*, forward-looking. We estimate, where possible, the impact of the third Liberal government mandate on the future role of NRCan.

The analysis proceeds in three sections. First, we examine how the sustainable development and innovation paradigms are influencing both ministerial and departmental learning at NRCan, and how government-wide institutional politics are also driving NRCan's effort to reposition itself. In this section, we not only describe the original Liberal conception of the twin paradigms articulated in the first Red Book, but also discuss the extent to which these paradigms have continued and are likely to continue to guide policy-making in the Chrétien era. Second, we sketch out the current mandate of NRCan, linking it back to the origins of NRCan in the early 1990s, a restructuring that was, among other things, intended to create a more integrated natural resource department rather than a loose holding company of policy and sectoral fiefdoms for oil, gas, nuclear energy, mining, forestry, and the like. Given its current mandate and structure, we also consider the role NRCan is likely to play in future Liberal policy initiatives under the sustainable development and innovation policy rubrics. The third section then briefly highlights two contemporary issues in which the old-economy versus new-economy tensions and trade-offs come to the fore. The first case involves developments in mining and metals policy and the industry's transformation in the global economy. The second involves the Sustainable Development Technology Fund, which emerged out of the 2000 federal budget and created both opportunities for, and constraints on, NRCan. These cases also embrace resource, budgetary, regulatory, and capacity questions, all of which are likely to affect the ability of NRCan to realize its new ambitions. Conclusions then follow.

THE SUSTAINABLE DEVELOPMENT AND INNOVATION PARADIGMS: MINISTERIAL AND DEPARTMENTAL LEARNING

If Canadians have any clear image of NRCan and its predecessor EMR, it is probably of a department whose job it is to support the development of its economic constituency, namely, the mining and metals, energy (oil, gas, nuclear), and forestry industries.[1] This central image is still fundamental to understanding NRCan as an institution, because its support of resource industries is still at the heart of its mandate and its internal culture. But the analytical thrust of this chapter on NRCan is to examine how this core task has been influenced by the presence and pressure of the sustainable development and innovation policy paradigms in the last decade. For many observers, these are key aspects of how the new economy is defined.[2]

Our first task is to define these twin paradigms and to capture the ways in which they became a part of ministerial and departmental learning at NRCan. We will examine these issues under three headings: the Liberal Red Books and the manner in which policy ideas defined, captured, and communicated these paradigms; internal pressure from Environment Canada and Industry Canada, the main intra-governmental champions of these paradigms; and the influence of NRCan ministers in the Chrétien era.

The Red Book and Party Influences
The Liberal party's embrace of the sustainable development and innovation policy paradigms in its 1993 election platform (*Creating*

Opportunity: The Liberal Plan for Canada)[3] was both evidence of the growing prominence of these ideas in popular, scholarly, and policy-making circles, and a prophecy of the extent to which these concepts would penetrate national policy-making under a Liberal government. Although subsequent Liberal documents, including policy papers, budgets, and the party's second and third Red Books, also espoused the sustainable development and innovation policy paradigms, the Liberals' championing and definition of both of these ideas is most clearly visible in the party's first Red Book. The dedication of an entire chapter to each topic within the eight-chapter document is testament to the prominent place that these ideas had acquired on the party's policy agenda.

The chapter on innovation communicates the Liberal interpretation of the paradigm, as well as the party's views of the role of government in promoting innovation. The 1993 Red Book defines innovation as a process of continuous improvement through experimentation, and delineates the role of the private and the public sectors in that process. It is the market's task to innovate, and the state's task to create a supportive environment for innovation. 'Innovation means trying new things. In any human endeavour, improvements can come only by experimenting with new ways to solve old problems. Innovation depends on the use of ideas for the continuous improvement of products and services, and this has been the traditional and appropriate role of the private sector and the free enterprise system. ... It is the job of government not to protect entrepreneurs against all failure but rather to create the best economic conditions and institutions to allow entrepreneurs to get on with the job.'[4] The 1993 Red Book identified the supportive role of government with such measures as balanced fiscal and monetary policy, collaboration with the private sector to identify and capitalize on strategic opportunities, and supportive business framework policies in research and development (R&D), education and training, environmental regulation, taxation, and the like. To this end, *Creating Opportunity* made proposals along both sectoral and horizontal lines, through initiatives for small and medium-sized enterprises, the manufacturing sector, community and regional development, infrastructure development, and, of greatest relevance for NRCan, the natural resource sector.[5]

The Liberals characterized the relationship between the natural resource industries and innovation as one of necessity: because the sector faced 'severe pressure' from international competitors and environmentally-conscious consumers, innovation was crucial to its future prosperity. The 1993 Red Book promised to assist the natural resource industries by providing a supportive environment, encouraging investment, ensuring that Canada has qualified workers, settling Aboriginal land claims, resolving delays in regulatory processes, and addressing the difficulties posed by overlapping federal/provincial jurisdictions.

The 1993 Red Book's chapter on sustainable development confirmed the Liberals' adoption of the sustainable development paradigm, and explained the party's approach to sustainable development policy-making. The document defined sustainable development as the integration of economic and environmental objectives, and designated prevention as the underlying principle for Liberal policy-making in this field. The Red Book presented a Liberal conception of sustainable development congruent with its view that investment in social programs is supportive of economic policy. Sustainable development—the integration of economic with environmental goals—fits in the Liberal tradition of social investment as sound economic policy. Preventive environmental care is the foundation of the Liberal approach to sustainable development; it is a wise public investment like preventive social policies and preventive health care.[6] The chapter detailed Liberal plans to honour Canada's international environmental commitments, to encourage industry to practise sustainable development, to enhance public awareness of environmental issues, and to take a leadership position in international environmental policy-making.

Of course the pronouncement of election promises does not guarantee their fulfillment. Although the Liberals prepared a glowing progress report of their first three years in office,[7] others have been less complimentary about the extent to which the Liberals have followed through on the 1993 Red Book's sustainable development and innovation policy initiatives.[8] Nevertheless, *Creating Opportunity* elucidates the way the Liberal party has championed, defined, and communicated the sustainable development and implementation policy paradigms that have had such a profound impact on NRCan.

Following the release of *Creating Opportunity*, the twin policy paradigms continued to receive prominent billing by the Liberals. Their second Red Book (*Securing Our Future Together: Preparing Canada for the 21st Century*)[9], released in the run-up to the 1997 election, again showcased innovation and sustainable development. In *Securing Our Future Together*, the Liberals broadened their interpretation of the two paradigms. The party continued to define innovation as putting knowledge to productive use, but extended the locus of innovative activities to include innovation in social institutions. The Liberal definition of sustainable development was also broadened to include social considerations: sustainable development began to be defined as the integration of environmental, economic, and social goals.

The two paradigms were also evident in the 2000 federal election campaign. While the paradigms were not given top billing by all parties, virtually all election platforms highlighted the role of innovation in economic growth, the need for Canada to focus on new-economy sectors, and the importance of protecting the environment. The third Liberal Red Book (*Opportunity for All: The Liberal Plan for the Future of Canada*)[10] was no exception. Innovation figured prominently in the Liberals' goal of making Canada a 'smart country': 'Under a Liberal government, Canada will expand its considerable knowledge, innovation, and research capacity, and accelerate its leadership in the new-economy.'[11] To accelerate innovation, the Liberals pledged to double federal expenditures on R&D, maintain R&D tax credits, and work to commercialize discoveries made in government and university laboratories. The Liberals did not accord such a central role to sustainable development, tending instead to communicate a vision that bases environmental policy-making objectives on concerns for public health and safety. The party pledged to improve air and water quality, increase funding to research on the health effects of toxins, protect and expand Canada's system of national parks, continue to protect species at risk, and continue to act on climate change. Although *Opportunity for All* places less emphasis on the sustainable development paradigm than previous Red Books, as we discuss in the second section of this chapter, the importance it accords to climate change and to innovation is likely to afford NRCan an important role in the third Liberal government mandate.

Environment Canada and Industry Canada as Paradigm Champions

The paradigm of sustainable development emerged largely out of Environment Canada's advocacy and has gradually been endorsed at a government-wide level as a part of national policy.[12] In many senses, because it is a paradigm of prevention, it requires greater reliance on non-regulatory instruments of governance and depends upon the capabilities of a department such as Environment Canada to influence the policies and decisions of fellow departments at much earlier stages in the decision process than had previously been the case. This does not mean that sustainable development has been practised as such, but it has been institutionalized to some extent. A further element of institutionalization emerged in the implementation of the 1993 Red Book commitment to establish an environmental auditor reporting to Parliament. The Commissioner of the Environment and Sustainable Development was created as part of the Office of the Auditor General of Canada, with the role of scrutinizing and regularly reporting on the extent to which all departments were developing and implementing sustainable development strategies and other environmental measures. Again, this institutional presence does not guarantee changed behaviour, but it does exert pressure, simply because departments such as NRCan have to continuously report in a more public manner.[13]

The innovation policy paradigm also came onto the federal agenda to replace old-style industrial policy, with Industry Canada as its chief advocate.[14] In addition to launching the concept of innovation in the 1993 Red Book, the Chrétien government made it central to its main micro-economic policy paper *Building a More Innovative Economy*.[15] Evolving out of free trade, the globalization of production, the revolution in telecommunications, computers, and capital and financial mobility, the dominant view inherent in innovation policies was that liberalized markets were the best overall policies for governments to follow. But also central to this view was the notion of innovations being generated and fostered by an even larger *national system of innovation*. As de la Mothe has stressed, 'an "innovation system" approach allows us to move towards more accurate depictions of how knowledge actually leads to growth, underpins our economic and social union, and how institutions adapt to rapidly changing circumstances. This embraces the reality that no institution—firm, research lab or government agency—can "know it all" or "do it all."'[16] In this context, Industry Canada had also become far more inclined than it once was to see progressive environmental and sustainable development policy as a potential source, and indeed driver, of innovation.[17]

Some of the embrace of the new paradigms is also undoubtedly budget-related. All departments faced heavy cuts in the first half of the 1990s and hence needed to seek each other out in more cooperative ways than had been the norm in earlier eras. For example, a memorandum of understanding was reached on science and technology policies and resource strategies for sustainable development among several of the federal science-based natural resource departments.[18]

As a part of the federal government, NRCan was aware of both of these strands of thinking and within its own ranks it had officials who supported these ideas. But, given its core resource industry clientele, it was not at all clear exactly how it could respond to these ideas or embrace them and how quickly it could move. After all, in the test-case of climate change policies and global warming, it would appear that the core instinct urged on by energy business interests, and by Alberta and other key energy provinces, is to defend the oil and gas industry and to avoid or slow down precipitous post-Kyoto targets. This is still undoubtedly true, although in institutions such as the Climate Change Secretariat there is a new institutionalized link between NRCan and Environment Canada, and with business, NGOs, and provincial stakeholders.

But at another level, the NRCan response has been to try to combat the belief that too many parts of the rest of the federal government were beginning to lump its industries in with the new economy of Canada's natural resource-dominated past, rather than its new economy centred on knowledge and innovation. At the insistence of both its current minister and key parts of its resource industries, NRCan has sought to reassert that the natural resource industries have always been innovative (and global) and have always been underpinned by long-standing first-class earth sciences capacity. Furthermore, NRCan's own role in earth sciences constituted an additional basis for the department's positive response to the innovation policy mantra. It was quite possible and valid for it to argue that the historic science and technology role of its earth sciences branch had always been a crucial public good underpinning the ongoing modernization of Canada's oil, gas, mining, and forestry sectors. As a result, as we will see in the next section, NRCan's own presentation of its mandate and mission focusses on the innovation paradigm and, furthermore, links the department closely to sustainable development.[19]

NRCan Ministers in the Chrétien Era
We look next at NRCan's ministers in the Chrétien era to date. In 1993 Anne McLellan was named the Chrétien government's first NRCan minister. An Alberta-based politician and a lawyer, she arrived in the portfolio both new to elected office and devoid of any previous cabinet experience. As a new minister, she had limited knowledge of the key NRCan sectors but was personally very interested in the sustainable development issues that were part of the new NRCan statutory mandate. At the same time, as an Alberta politician, she had to move with great care and caution on the then looming climate change policy file, the file that many saw as the ultimate litmus test of the sustainable development commitment. Not only was this an intrinsically difficult file that was inherently cross-governmental in its complexity, it was also one with an enormous impact on the Alberta and Western Canadian oil and gas industry, whose production of hydro-carbon emissions was the target of any present and future climate change commitments. Any strong federal intervention to control and reduce such emissions through federal taxation, environmental policy, or other measures was easily portrayed in Alberta as 'another NEP', imposed again by an Ontario-dominated federal government. During McLellan's tenure the initial steps were taken toward the establishment of the Climate Change Secretariat, with its accompanying joint coordination with Environment Canada.[20] However, for the most part, she did not have the political power in Cabinet to advance very much of NRCan's agenda, and for much of this time, which also coincided with Program Review budget cuts, NRCan seemed to hunker down into a defensive mode of operation.

The second minister, Ralph Goodale, brought a broader set of experiences and skills to the NRCan portfolio. As a Saskatchewan-based minister, he brought a more diverse set of political contacts with energy and mining interests. He personally and frequently reminded his officials that sustainable development is part of the NRCan departmental *legislation*. Unusual for any minister, Goodale also personally wrote the vision statement of NRCan, which, as we will see in the following section, emphasizes the importance of sustainable development and innovation. Goodale also has other ministerial responsibilities that appear to have fed into his thinking about NRCan's sustainability and innovation mandates. He is the Interlocutor or lead minister in dealing with the Métis in federal Aboriginal policy. His role as a Saskatchewan minister and as minister whose mandate encompasses numerous remote mining and resource communities has led to initiatives from himself and from Cabinet regarding what innovation and sustainable economic development mean for such communities. And, very importantly, he has been the chair of the Cabinet Committee on the Economic Union, which means that he is fully involved in the larger debate about innovation policy, including the ideas and pressures on these fronts emanating from both Industry Canada and the Department of Finance.

In these forums, Goodale and senior NRCan officials were also becoming concerned with the degree to which Canada's natural resource sectors were being labelled as 'old-economy' and hence not garnering attention as a still crucial and very innovative part of the Canadian economy. To influence and change this perception, NRCan would have to be more active and aggressive in engaging the rest of the government, and being, and being *seen* to be, involved in shaping the new-economy agenda. As we have seen, this involved reasserting that innovation has always been part and parcel of the natural resource industries, and that the department's own earth sciences branch played a crucial role in innovative activity in the natural resource sector. And as we will see in the case study on the Sustainable Development Technology Fund, NRCan has sought to demonstrate its engagement in the new-economy agenda by playing a lead role in the Fund's implementation.

These ministerial dynamics are of course not easy to pinpoint and represent quite subtle day-to-day and month-to-month interactions. They are a part of a department's processes of adapting to change as it interprets, and learns from, its own industrial and socio-economic clientele. However, it also is a part of what we could cast as a kind of policy pincer movement, as both the sustainable development and innovation policy paradigms emerged on the federal scene in the last decade.

THE NRCan MANDATE AND STRUCTURE

The NRCan mandate flows from its vision and mission statements. In a rare move for a minister, Goodale personally wrote the department's vision statement:

> As we enter the millennium, Canada must become and remain the world's 'smartest' natural resources steward, developer, user and exporter—the most high tech, the most environmentally friendly, the most socially responsible, the most productive and competitive—leading the world as a living model of sustainable development.[21]

NRCan's mission is that it 'provides the knowledge and expertise for sustainable development and use of Canada's natural resources and the global competitiveness of the resource and related sectors for the well-being of present and future generations.'[22]

The content of these statements reflects NRCan's concerns and opportunities in its old economy-new economy nexus and demonstrates how the department believes the sustainable development and innovation policy paradigms will help it to deal with its circumstances. The NRCan mandate centres on its duty to develop national policies to strengthen the country's natural resources through strategies and practices for sustainable development and by fostering innovation. These core mandates are provided by statute.

With this mandate, NRCan is likely to play an important role in the new Liberal government's economic and environmental policy agendas. As previously discussed, the third Red Book contained commitments to act on climate change and to double federal R&D expenditures. With regard to the former, *Opportunity for All* outlined specific climate change commitments, including promoting increased energy efficiency, funding new energy technologies, increasing renewable energy use, and encouraging consumers to purchase more energy-efficient products. NRCan's joint coordination of the Climate Change Secretariat with Environment Canada and its statutory commitment to sustainable development is sure to translate into a meaningful role for the department in the third Liberal government mandate. That being said, this role may not be easy to play, as the department's traditional instinct may be to defend its energy business interests. As to the latter, *Opportunity for All* stated that R&D expenditures were to be directed to a number of key sectors, including 'natural resource management'. NRCan's knowledge and expertise in the management of natural resources, as well as the congruence between the department's core mandate and natural resource management R&D, are likely to assure it a prominent place in development and implementation of R&D programs in this sector. And, potentially of greater importance, the department could lever this involvement into greater political-bureaucratic influence in the ongoing evolution and shaping of the government's new-economy agenda.

As to NRCan's organizational features, given its history and internal culture, much of the policy development activity in the department deals with sectoral policy files. These are typically managed, as in other government departments, through a process in which sectors analyse, develop, and submit proposals to the deputy minister and through the Departmental Management Committee (DMC). The DMC is a key forum and focus of information exchange and makes decisions on departmental direction, policy, S&T and other key issues, departmental administration, and management. The department's sectoral policy-making approach is reflected in the responsibilities of the five assistant deputy ministers reporting to the Deputy Minister of Natural Resources (for the Canadian Forest Service, the Energy Sector, the Earth Sciences Sector, the Minerals and Metals Sector, and the Corporate Services Sector). Also reporting directly to the deputy minister are Directors General for the Strategic Planning and Co-ordination Branch, Legal Services, Communications, and Audit and Evaluation, and also the previously mentioned Climate Change Secretariat. NRCan's total planned spending for 2000-1 is $667.1 million and its activities employ a planned staff of 3,775 full-time equivalents.[23]

The minister and deputy minister must manage both a department and a 'portfolio'. The portfolio elements arise because other quasi-independent or arm's-length agencies report through the minister to Parliament or simply have special forms of legislative status. These portfolio agencies include Atomic Energy of Canada Ltd., the Canadian Nuclear Safety Commission, the National Energy Board, the Canada-Newfoundland Offshore Petroleum Board, the Canada-Nova Scotia Offshore Petroleum Board, the Emergency Supplies Allocation Board, and the Cape Breton Development Corporation (DEVCO).

For the *horizontal* policy files, NRCan employs an 'Office of Primary Interest' (OPI) model, which is quite different from that employed by many other federal departments. Under the OPI model the deputy minister has designated 'DMs as OPIs'. In this capacity, they champion and provide policy leadership and representation within the department on horizontal issues such as the Minister's Action Plan for Winning in the Knowledge-Based Economy (or the 'Forward Agenda'), S&T capacity, Sustainable Development, Aboriginal issues, rural issues, regulatory reform and risk management, and innovation.

The mandate and structure of NRCan must also be briefly traced back to the 1993 reorganization that led to NRCan's formation. In the overall 1993 federal reorganization plan, the federal government saw the creation of its new Department of Natural Resources as a structure that would bring three major economic sectors, mining, energy, and forestry, into one 'natural resources' organization. It also stressed the imperatives of international competitiveness and hence the imperative to 'manage the growing environment and trade issues in these sectors, which are increasingly influenced by public expectations, national and international.'[24] It was further suggested that new synergies would be created, which would also bring a 'natural resource perspective' to the government-wide agenda.[25] These potential horizontal payoffs were quickly counterbalanced in the reorganization rationale by the significant differences faced by each of the three sectors. The administrative and institutional aspects were also propelled by the need to achieve savings in overhead costs from the integration of the former EMR and Forestry Canada. Corporate services were cut back by 25 per cent and, important for our purposes in this chapter, its central policy group was reduced to a corporal's guard and the policy function resided mainly in the sector branches. Thus, at the very moment when a more integrated natural resources approach, anchored by the sustainable development and the innovation paradigms, was expected, the central policy capacity of NRCan was reduced.

TWO POLICY ISSUES:
OLD ECONOMY-NEW ECONOMY TRADE-OFFS

It will be useful to complement the more general analysis presented above by taking a closer look, in the context of NRCan's changing institutional role, at how it has faced two policy issues. The first of these concerns the mining and metals industry, and the period that we will discuss spans the last decade; the second concerns the $100 million Sustainable Development Technology Fund, which emerged from the 2000 Federal Budget, seemingly out of the blue. Space does not allow a full account of these issues, but a sketch of the key elements is instructive nonetheless.

The Mining Industry and the New NRCan

In the sound-bite politics of the new century, the mining sector in Canada often gets stuck with the old-economy label, by which is usually meant that it is not instinctively seen as an innovative sector. It is also often seen as 'old-economy' in contexts that attach that label to sectors perceived as laggards with respect to environmental or sustainable development. But in many ways the mining sector is more new-economy than most with respect to its global presence, export orientation, high wages, and high productivity (and its use of new technologies to increase productivity).[26] It is also new-economy with regard to the pressures on the industry to deal with the issues of sustainable development.

In the last 10 to 15 years, the Canadian mining industry has in many respects been turned on its head. This transformation was the result of policies, decisions, and forces only some of which NRCan can control. The principal transformation is that the Canadian mining industry has become a very large global player. While it has always been global as a major exporter of metals and minerals, now it is global in the more crucial and complete sense that Canadian mining and mineral companies are investing heavily abroad. And this foreign investment stimulates demand in other sectors in Canada that supply related equipment and services, including, quite starkly, the Canadian financial services sector, which finances these foreign-based initiatives.[27] Thus the contemporary Canadian mining 'sector' consists of much more than just domestic mining companies that export. Canadian firms are making careful and strategic choices about investment, enticed by other governments, including those of former Soviet Union states, who covet investment as a part of their now more market-oriented national development policies.

When one thinks of policies related to mining in an earlier but not so distant era, the array would include good (and bad) macro-economic and exchange rate policies by finance departments and central banks. These often produced sharp cycles of change that crucially affected mining production, inventories, export cycles, and investment patterns, such as the 1981-2 and 1991-2 recessions. It would also include federal taxation policy and the comparative tax policies (including particular provisions, such as flow-through shares and taxation) of other countries, which affect investment incentives. Furthermore, the array of traditional policies would have included those concerning strategic minerals that could and did restrict use and export, the policies in many developing countries of nationalizing foreign mining companies, and federal and provincial policies that periodically used state ownership for troubled mining and mineral companies (the establishment of DEVCO, for example). Finally, mining policies in the recent past included the early development of environmental regulation in the 1970s and 1980s, which gradually and increasingly prompted mining company owners and shareholders to believe that they no longer truly 'owned' their assets or property, because of the demand for multiple permits, licences, and permissions by provincial governments and the federal government.[28]

In this earlier era, NRCan (and EMR before it) felt and understood its core role to be to support the industry in much the same way that Industry Canada saw its role as supporting the auto industry or any of its other industrial sectors. But NRCan had to act on its supportive instincts in a practical way, knowing that mining was largely still a provincial field and that even in the federal domain NRCan did not command all or even close to all the policy levers.

To finesse its way through this changing mineral policy and industrial context, NRCan (and earlier EMR) became engaged in the 1992 to 1994-5 period in what became known as the Whitehorse Mining Initiative (WMI). The WMI ultimately centred on policy development processes and consultations with the federal and provincial mines ministers, but it also included a complex multi-stakeholder process that involved mining companies and their interest groups, national, provincial, and local NGOs, and Aboriginal peoples. The WMI process involved extensive discussion, the development of numerous studies on particular aspects of the changed and changing mineral and metals policy situation, and actual negotiations to produce some areas of consensus.

At the start of the twenty-first century, NRCan maintains two interlocked pictures of the Canadian mining industry, one as seen from Canada's perspective, and the other as seen (or so it is hoped) from other countries. As a new-economy player, NRCan sees the mining sector as a world-class, high-tech producer; a sector with higher than average wages and high measured productivity; a provider of considerable employment in remote regions of all provinces and territories; a vital producer of jobs and growth; a key vehicle for investment; and a supplier of mining investment in Canada and internationally.[29]

NRCan's complementary picture, the mining sector as seen from abroad, is of a sector that is present in 100 or more countries; is sought after to develop foreign economies; has access to deposits abroad as well as in Canada; provides increased trade for the Canadian mining equipment and service suppliers through foreign operations; and is welcomed by foreign governments and foreign companies.

In this brief account we have by no means done justice to all the changes in approach that have arisen from old economy-new economy trade-offs. For example, in 2000, NRCan's effort to privatize DEVCO received legislative approval and thus altered two decades of support for coal mining in Cape Breton through the vehicle of state enterprise.[30] However, the net effect of this overall transformation is that NRCan has to make, foster, encourage, and develop in the mining and metals sector in much more complex interactive ways. It has to deal more openly and directly with the sector as a socio-economic entity as the sustainable development and innovation paradigms thread their way into and out of a still very big and important industry for Canada.

The Sustainable Development Technology Fund (SDTF)
The SDTF emerged as one of a number of initiatives in Budget 2000 announced by Finance Minister Paul Martin. Each dealt with the environment and sustainable development and included initiatives such as an extension of the Climate Change Action Fund, the Green

Municipal Enabling Fund, the Green Infrastructure Fund, a Green Power Procurement initiative, and the Canadian Foundation for Climate and Atmospheric Science.

The $100 million SDTF was not an NRCan initiative, but rather originated in the Finance Department at the urging of Environment Canada, which advocated an *environmental* technologies fund. But NRCan's minister, Ralph Goodale, lobbied for NRCan to be given the lead role in implementing the SDTF, in part to demonstrate NRCan's engagement in government-wide initiatives, particularly regarding sustainable development and innovation. Additionally, as we discuss below, the key implementation challenge—and potential opportunity—was the positioning of the fund within Canada's national system of innovation, and the consequent shaping of the definition and meaning of the innovation policy paradigm. While NRCan's desire to take the lead in implementation is evidence of its efforts to position the department as a new-economy player, as we will see, the SDTF case is also an example of the trade-offs inherent in NRCan's old economy-new economy nexus. As we will discuss, government preferences for third-party funding arrangements on horizontal new-economy initiatives may pose a threat to NRCan's internal S&T and R&D capabilities.

Bill C-46 was tabled just before the 2000 election and specified two principal objectives for the Canada Foundation for Sustainable Development Technology (CFSDT). It is to fund 'projects to develop and demonstrate new technologies to promote sustainable development including technologies to address climate change and air quality issues.'[31] The focus was on the development and demonstration parts of the innovation continuum, and climate change and air quality were mentioned specifically. The other specified provision emanating from the Department of Finance was that the fund had to be administered by a 'third party' foundation, the aforementioned CFSDT. Such a third party or arm's-length mode of delivery had become the federal government's favoured device in the three previous budgets, beginning with the formation of the Canada Foundation for Innovation.[32] However, with each new example of this delivery mode, the key issue became one of supporting science and innovation inside government or outside in the private sector. And in almost every case external (third party-administered) S&T was winning the argument or was at least the favoured institutional mode.

NRCan was required to develop the implementation plan in consultation with the Minister of the Environment and the Minister of Industry. Bill C-46 died with the October 2000 federal election call. As a result, a non-legislative temporary foundation is being readied to allow the initiative to proceed. The key challenge is the positioning of the CFSDT within the national innovation system. This positioning challenge soon became known as the 'complementarity' issue, in that the fund had to complement, not duplicate, existing federal funding programs and activities related to innovation, technology advancement, and sustainable development. This array of initiatives, along with university and industrial research, was cast as Canada's *national innovation system* and hence ran headlong into defining exactly what this system was or was becoming.[33] Complementarity meant that several elements would arise analytically and practically. These included the operational characteristics of existing programs; issues of repayment and intellectual property; the types of technologies created; and the position of the fund on the so-called innovation spectrum (basic research, applied R&D, initial deployment, increased market penetration, etc.).

The federal array of technology programs and activities was already quite complex, and covered most if not all aspects of the innovation spectrum. Indeed, existing programs included NRCan's own CANMET Energy Technology Branch and the Program of Energy R&D (PERD), and, of course, directly or indirectly, the entire in-house science capacity of NRCan's own earth sciences sector. This sector was vulnerable to being traded-off, in that the larger choices were, as indicated, between internal and external modes of delivery. In addition to the third-party foundation, there would be project-by-project funding to the private sector, research centres, and other institutes, but no funding to the foundation itself. A levered funding regime (33 per cent from the foundation, the rest from applicants) is to be put in place to encourage public-private partnerships and alliances. The regime would also encourage ways to disseminate intellectual property and new technologies and the focus would be on challenges facing many companies within an industrial sector rather than on projects specific to one company.

Institutionally, the CFSDT will have mechanisms regarding the appointment of its board to ensure its independence, but at the same time the federal government wants to influence its overall work. The eventual legislation will shape this balance to some extent, but there will also be a funding agreement between the federal government and the CFSDT that will specify terms, conditions, and operations.

One cannot of course judge the efficacy of the new foundation or indeed of the other recent third-party model experiments. However, it does change the composition of resource and energy R&D. The CFSDT's initial $100 million may be followed, as happened with the CFI, by future additions. This sum compares favourably with the $90 million annual funding for non-nuclear energy S&T, of which $57 million is via the PERD program.

Both within NRCan and across the federal science-based departments and agencies (SBDAs), the fund has raised issues and choices regarding external versus internal S&T delivery and capacity. NRCan has a very mixed set of views about these developments, because the fund represents both opportunities and threats. The department wants to emphasize its sustainable development and innovation mandate. It wants to be engaged, and be seen to be engaged, in the agenda of the government as a whole, particularly as that agenda relates to the twin paradigms. However, for much of the 1997 to 2000 period its ADM for science chaired the government-wide process examining internal federal science capacity. This included the so-called 'rust-out' of federal laboratories that support crucial federal regulatory roles, and, more broadly, the need for strategies and practices to attract and retain first-class young scientists in the public sector.[34] While these issues are usually cast in terms of science for the regulatory system, they also include science in support of a longer-term *public goods* role, the quintessential example of which is NRCan's own earth sciences sector. For NRCan it also includes much more controversially the question of the extent to which it can also obtain R&D support for the nuclear industry and for Atomic Energy of Canada Ltd (AECL). The nuclear R&D demands include a request made by NRCan's minister for more than $400 million to replace the aging Chalk River research reactor in order to accommodate not only research on nuclear energy but also on new materials. AECL is also arguing that nuclear energy helps the climate change agenda, because it does not produce hydrocarbon emissions.[35]

Given the strong preference (in Finance and Industry Canada) for the third-party models, there is genuine concern within NRCan as to whether its own in-house science capacity will be supported through renewed direct investment after at least a decade of both budget cuts and benign neglect. Other federal SBDAs (including those dealing with health, the environment, and food regulation) have also been waiting in the federal budgetary queue and they may be able to make more politically saleable cases than can some areas of NRCan, such as earth sciences. Although the earth sciences role makes a range of important S&T contributions, it may simply be seen, albeit shortsightedly, as too general a public goods realm, with insufficient immediate or prospective innovation payoff.

The two case studies surveyed above are each quite different and involve vastly different time lines of gestation, the mining one long and evolving, and the SDTF, short, sharp, and even unexpected. But both involve NRCan in a process of thinking through and acting on the twin paradigms at the centre of their mandate.

CONCLUSIONS

This chapter has examined the origins and evolution of NRCan in the first two mandates of the Liberal government and its effort to shift the image and reality of its supposed *old-economy* domain to that of a *new-economy* player. We have examined this process mainly through a discussion of the Liberals' embrace of the innovation and sustainable development policy paradigms as vehicles both to enhance Canada's natural resource industries and to enhance NRCan's own influence in the Ottawa power structure. The latter ambition is also centred on NRCan's stated mandate of becoming a more integrated *natural resource* department rather than a holding company of resource sector fiefdoms.

The chapter has by no means done justice to the full NRCan mandate. This would require a much more complete discussion of its key policy and S&T realms, such as forestry and earth sciences, and particular areas of energy policy, such as oil and gas and nuclear energy. But the analysis does show how in the first two terms of the Liberal government the department has sought to embrace both the sustainable development paradigm and the innovation policy paradigm through the Red Book impetus, its own ministerial adoption of the concepts, and the internal pressure of Environment Canada and Industry Canada as in-house champions of the paradigms.

This does not mean that these paradigms leave a clear track of successful implementation. Ideas of this kind are complex and they interact in numerous ways. Moreover, they have to be interpreted through a departmental culture that still has, and should have, strong instincts to support its core industries, industries that still employ and will continue to employ many tens of thousands of Canadians.

Some of the ambivalence about the old economy-new economy world NRCan must deal with was revealed by the two case studies. Our brief look at the mining sector showed how in a very short period of time the Canadian mining and metals industry has changed markedly, as a result of both its own status as a more completely global industry and its need to engage with NRCan in complex socio-economic policy and consultation processes. At the same time, it genuinely needs NRCan's steady provision of earth science capacity. The SDTF case showed NRCan's need both to be engaged in sustainable development policy initiatives launched elsewhere and to support the national innovation system, even when this might occur, in reality, or partly, at its own expense. The SDTF case also showed that federal S&T policy, in the name of innovation, is increasingly dividing along political fault lines of internal versus third-party S&T support funding.

While our analysis has been mainly retrospective, we have tried, where possible, to assess the future prospects for NRCan in the third Liberal mandate. While high oil and gas prices may redirect the national spotlight toward NRCan, even in the absence of such a 'back to the future' scenario the Liberals' continued commitment to promoting innovation and combating climate change are likely to keep NRCan's bureaucratic and political-bureaucratic hands full. NRCan's experience to date suggests that the department will have more than enough to do as it struggles to follow the difficult twin paradigm policy star to which it has hitched its future.

NOTES

1 For historical background on the politics and economics of resource policy, see John N. McDougall, 'Natural Resources and National Politics: A Look at Three Canadian Resource Industries', in G. Bruce Doern, ed., *The Politics of Economic Policy* (Toronto: University of Toronto Press, 1985), 163-220, and F.J. Anderson, *Natural Resources in Canada* (Toronto: Methuen, 1985).

2 For discussion, see Glen Toner, 'Canada: From Early Frontrunner to Plodding Anchorman', in William M. Lafferty and James R. Meadowcroft, eds, *Implementing Sustainable Development: Strategies and Initiatives in High Consumption Societies* (Oxford: Oxford University Press, 2000), chap. 3; M. Hessing and M. Howlett, *Canadian Natural Resource and Environmental Policy* (Vancouver: University of British Columbia Press, 1997); W.T. Stanbury, *Environmental Groups and the International Conflict over the Forests of British Columbia, 1990 to 2000* (Vancouver: SFU-UBC Centre for the Study of Government and Business, 2000); and Thomas J. Courchene, ed., *Policy Frameworks for a Knowledge Economy* (Kingston: John Deutsch Institute, Queen's University, 1996).

3 Liberal Party of Canada, *Creating Opportunity: The Liberal Plan for Canada* (Ottawa, 1993).

4 Ibid., 43-4.

5 Red Book I identified five groups in the natural resource sector: forestry, mining, energy, agri-food, and fishing. This discussion focusses only on Liberal commitments to the first three of these groups, because the latter two do not reside in the NRCan portfolio.

6 Liberal Party, *Creating Opportunity*, 63.

7 Liberal Party of Canada, *A Record of Achievement: A Report on the Liberal Government's 36 Months in Office* (Ottawa, 1996).

8 See, for example, on sustainable development, Luc Juillet and Glen Toner, 'From Great Leaps to Baby Steps: Environment and Sustainable Development Policy Under the Liberals', in Gene Swimmer, ed., *How Ottawa Spends 1997-98: Seeing Red: A Liberal Report Card* (Ottawa: Carleton University Press, 1997):179-209. On innovation policy, see Gilles Paquet and Jeffrey Roy, 'Prosperity Through Networks: The Bottom-Up Strategy That Might Have Been', in Susan Phillips, ed., *How Ottawa Spends 1995-96: Mid-Life Crises* (Ottawa: Carleton University Press, 1995), 137-58.

9 Liberal Party of Canada, *Securing Our Future Together: Preparing Canada for the 21st Century* (Ottawa, 1997).

10 Liberal Party of Canada, *Opportunity for All: The Liberal Plan for the Future of Canada* (Ottawa, 2000).

11 Liberal Party, *Opportunity for All*, 3.

12 See Toner, 'Canada: From Early Front Runner.' See also G. Bruce Doern and Tom Conway, *The Greening of Canada* (University of Toronto Press, 1994) chap. 11.

13 See Natural Resources Canada, *Sustainable Development: From Commitment to Action* (Ottawa: Natural Resources Canada) and Canada, *2000-2001 Estimates: Natural Resources Canada (Part III)* (Ottawa: Public Works and Government Services, 2000), 39.

14 See G. Bruce Doern and Markus Sharaput, *Canadian Intellectual Property: The Politics of Innovating Institutions and Interests* (Toronto:

University of Toronto Press, 2000).
15 Industry Canada, *Building a More Innovative Economy* (Ottawa: Industry Canada, 1994).
16 John de la Mothe, 'Government Science and the Public Interest', in G. Bruce Doern and Ted Reed, eds, *Risky Business: Canada's Changing Science-Based Regulatory Regime* (Toronto: University of Toronto Press, 2000), p. 34.
17 Doern and Sharaput, *Canadian Intellectual Property*.
18 See Canada, *1996-97 Annual Report on the Memorandum of Understanding Among the Four Natural Resources Departments on Science and Technology for Sustainable Development* (Ottawa: Minister of Public Works and Government Services Canada, 1997).
19 See Canada, Natural Resources , *2000-2001 Estimates: Natural Resources Canada (Part III)*; Natural Resources Canada, *Playing It Smart: 'Natural Resources Sector for the 21st Century* (Ottawa: Natural Resources Canada, 1999); and Natural Resources Canada, *Innovation: The State of Canada's Forests 1998-99* (Ottawa: Natural Resources Canada, 1999).
20 The secretariat also works in cooperation with the provinces and stakeholders through the operation of several issue tables, and manages the Climate Change Action Fund (CCAF). See Canada, *2000-2001 Estimates: Natural Resources Canada (Part III)* (Ottawa: Public Works and Government Services, 2000), 11.
21 Canada, *2000-2001 Estimates: Natural Resources Canada (Part III)*, 1.
22 Ibid., 3.
23 Ibid., 13.
24 Natural Resources Canada, *Department of Natural Resources Proposals for Organizational Structure* (Ottawa: Natural Resources Canada, 14 July 1993), 16.
25 Ibid., 15.
26 See Natural Resources Canada, *Playing It Smart*.
27 See Canada, *2000-2001 Estimates: Natural Resources Canada (Part III)*, 12; Canadian Intergovernmental Working Group on the Mineral Industry, *Overview of Trends in Canadian Mineral Exploration* (Ottawa: Minister of Public Works and Government Services, 2000); Natural Resources Canada, *Canada's Global Position in Mining* (Ottawa: Natural Resources Canada, 1997).
28 For analyses of some of these policy successes and failures, see F.J. Anderson, *Natural Resources in Canada*; John McDougall, 'Natural Resources and National Politics'; and Michael Prince and G. Bruce Doern, *The Origins of Public Enterprise in the Canadian Mineral Sector* (Kingston: Centre for Resource Studies, Queen's University, 1985)
29 Natural Resources Canada, *Canadian Suppliers of Mining Goods and Services* (Ottawa: Natural Resources Canada, 2000).

30 See Canada, *Information on the Future Direction of the Cape Breton Development Corporation* (Ottawa, 28 Jan. 1999).
31 See web site: www.parl.gc.ca/36/2/parlbus/chambu...bills/government/C-46/C46-1/90124Ee.HTML
32 For a discussion of this matter, see G. Bruce Doern and Richard Lévesque, *NRC in the Innovation Policy Era: Changing Hierarchies, Networks and Markets* (Toronto: University of Toronto Press, forthcoming), chap. 8.
33 See Richard Lipsey and Ken Carlaw, *A Structuralist Assessment of Technology Policies: Taking Schumpeter Seriously on Policy* (Ottawa: Industry Canada [Working Paper No. 25], Oct. 1998).
34 See Council of Science and Technology Advisors, *Building Excellence in Science and Technology (BEST): The Federal Roles in Performing Science and Technology* (Ottawa: Industry Canada, 1999), and G. Bruce Doern and Ted Reed, eds, *Risky Business*.
35 For a discussion on this matter, see G. Bruce Doern, Arslan Dorman, and Robert Morrison, eds, *Canadian Nuclear Energy Policy: Changing Ideas, Institutions and Interests* (Toronto: University of Toronto Press, 2001).

10

Regional Development Policy: A Nexus of Policy and Politics

RODNEY HADDOW

Ottawa first began to address regional development during the early 1960s, as a natural extension of the much larger social and economic policy role that it accepted after 1945. This post-war government expansion had special characteristics in Canada. 'Place sensitivity' was already central to Canadians' political identities before the war. Ottawa's more active post-1945 role consequently had a 'nation-building' quality; it addressed regional sensitivities by providing 'income security, justified as a means of eliminating inter-regional disparities in benefits, related to the differential income sources of provincial governments.'[1] Regional development spending was designed to address these inequalities.

Since its inception, however, regional development has been controversial both as a *policy* instrument and in respect of the *political* incentives that support it. The current debate over regional development has taken these disputes to a new level. The emergence since

1993 of the Reform party, now the Canadian Alliance, and the Bloc Québécois as the main electoral alternatives to the governing Liberals has challenged the brokerage style of politics that previously prevailed in Canada. Issues that were once the subject of consensus between the major parties are now challenged by an opposition that strongly criticizes government intervention, the role of the federal government, and 'old style' patronage politics. In this context, political debates have become more pronounced. The policy arguments for and against regional development spending changed significantly during the 1990s. In the 2000 election campaign, regional development was more central to the electoral platforms and calculations of parties than at any time since at least the early 1970s.

This transformation of the contours of regional development policy, and its long-term implications, are the central themes of this chapter. Prime Minister Chrétien's Liberal administration made regional development policy for the Atlantic region a central plank of its victorious re-election strategy in November 2000. Neither in its 1993 nor its 1997 election campaigns had regional development been as prominent. This strategic choice revealed much about the more ideologically—and regionally—polarized politics that appeared to be crystallizing in Canada at the turn of the millennium.

The chapter first examines the policy and political considerations that motivated regional development spending between the 1960s and the early 1990s. It then reviews the evolution of these programs during these years, addressing (i) their administrative design, (ii) their policy objectives, and (iii) the federal-provincial relationships that they engendered. Using these same categories, the second section appraises the Chrétien Liberals' first term in office and the early part of its second, a period spanning from 1993 to mid-1998. The third section examines the two years preceding the November 2000 election, when the Liberals acquired a renewed interest in regional development.

THE HISTORICAL SETTING, 1961–1993

Partisan political considerations helped stimulate regional spending by governments in Canada. Brokerage parties historically have predominated in Canada's political party system. The main ones—the Liberals and the Progressive Conservatives—had few long-term ideological commitments, instead seeking to build electoral coalitions that cut across enough of the nation's regional, linguistic, and religious divides to ensure election victories. In the mid-1950s the Conservatives, long relegated to the opposition benches in Ottawa, elected John Diefenbaker as their leader. In the 1957 and 1958 elections he overtook the previously-hegemonic Liberals in the western and Atlantic provinces. Diefenbaker promised to address these regions' unique economic and social development needs. The creation of an Agricultural and Rural Development Act (ARDA) and an Atlantic Development Board (ADB) were the main steps taken to achieve this. For their part, the opposition Liberals overhauled their party program in 1960, promising to outdo the Tories in addressing the needs of the outlying regions. After returning to office, they expanded the remit of ARDA and the ADB.[2] Thereafter, from the 1960s to the early 1990s, each party remained firmly committed to regional development programs, although many changes in program design and funding occurred during these years.

Yet the original regional development measures were not justified exclusively on the grounds of political expediency; they also reflected new policy ideas. By the late 1950s, the then-predominant Keynesian economic theory was subject to increasingly critical scrutiny. Keynesianism relied on macro-economic tools—fiscal and monetary policies—to stabilize aggregate demand at levels high enough to sustain full employment. It did not address questions of supply, and had little to say about the role that structural and regional imbalances might play in inhibiting the spread of economic prosperity from prosperous to poorer regions. It seemed clear to many observers, as Canada entered a recession during these years, that such barriers existed, and that to rectify them government would have to act to improve the supply of capital and skilled labour in economically lagging areas. These ideas helped motivate the Diefenbaker initiatives; their influence was well entrenched when the Liberals returned to power.[3] While Keynesian macro-economic policies would continue to be relied upon to maximize income and employment at the national level, supply-side interventions such as regional development and manpower training would supplement this wherever structural impediments prevented macro-economic policy from having its desired effect.

This broad political and policy framework endured for the next three decades, but during this period regional development nevertheless was subject to repeated changes, in the direction of policy, in the administrative tools used to deliver it, and in the federal-provincial relationships that it encouraged. In terms of policy objectives and administrative design, regional spending made use of a number of quite distinct models. During the 1960s, several poorly-co-ordinated initiatives were taken to support regional development. In addition to ARDA and the ADB, an Area Development Agency (ADA) was inaugurated shortly after the Liberals returned to power in 1963, and a Fund for Rural Economic Development (FRED) commenced in 1966. These initiatives had two main goals: to raise the standard of living in poor rural areas of Canada (via ARDA and FRED) and, above all, to stimulate economic development, especially in Atlantic Canada (via the ADA and the ADB).[4] During the last half of the 1960s, the budget of the ADB, which operated only in Atlantic Canada, exceeded that of the other three initiatives combined; regional development therefore largely focussed on Atlantic Canada. It also had a strong 'social' flavour, giving priority to short-term employment in deprived communities, rather than maximizing long-term region-wide growth[5] (see Table 10.1).

The Department of Regional Economic Expansion (DREE), created in 1969, was intended to integrate these pre-existing federal initiatives.[6] It was replaced by a Department of Regional and Industrial Expansion (DRIE) in 1982. DRIE brought together regional development and industrial development programs, the latter mainly relevant to central Canada. But several complaints—one administrative and three relating to policy—plagued DREE and DRIE. The administrative issue had to do with the degree of centralization of these departments. When they were relatively centralized (as DREE was from 1969 to 1974, and as DRIE was with respect to policy formulation), it was objected that federal initiatives were too inflexible to address the needs of distinctive regions. When it was decentralized (DREE between 1974 and 1982), concerns were raised about apparent arbitrariness in program application and about the ability of regional officials to exercise influence in Ottawa. DREE and DRIE never seemed to get the centralization-decentralization balance right.[7]

A key policy change that followed DREE's creation was that the rural and social focuses of 1960s development policy persisted, but were now supplemented by measures that concentrated on stimulating growth in the most promising, usually urban and industrial, parts of

Table 10.1
Regional Development Policy in Canada
Chronology of Important Events

1960: Passage of the Agricultural and Rural Development Act (ARDA).
1962: Creation of Atlantic Development Board (ADB).
1963: Area Development Agency (ADA) launched.
1966: Fund for Rural Economic Development (FRED) commences.
1969: Department of Regional Economic Expansion (DREE) integrates most existing regional development measures.
1974: First General Development Agreements (GDAs) signed with the provinces.
1982: Department of Regional Industrial Expansion (DRIE) replaces DREE; merges regional development programs with industrial policy measures.
1984: First Economic and Regional Development Agreements (ERDAs) are signed with the provinces; these replace the GDAs.
1987: Except in Quebec, regional development programs are separated from industrial policy programs and assigned to region-specific agencies: Atlantic Canada Opportunities Agency (ACOA), Western Diversification (WD), Federal Economic Development Initiative in Northern Ontario (FedNor), and Enterprise Cape Breton Corporation (ECBC).
1991: Creation of the Federal Office of Regional Development-Quebec (FORD-Q).
1994: First Cooperation Agreements are signed with the provinces; these replace the ERDAs.
1996: ACOA, WD, and FORD-Q are re-attached to the Industry Minister's portfolio, but remain organizationally separate from his department.
1998: FORD-Q is renamed Canada Economic Development for Quebec Regions (CED).
2000: Atlantic Investment Partnership (AIP) is announced.

the target regions. DREE and DRIE devoted a substantial part of their budgets to stimulating manufacturing, often by using grants and loans to attract large outside investors.[8] These firms often did not survive once public financial support was terminated. Moreover, this now highly-fragmented policy seemed to many observers to be ad hoc and directionless. There was no evident 'plan' or 'strategy' underlying the plethora of rural and urban/industrial programs.[9]

DREE's creation was also accompanied by a substantial extension in the regional reach of these measures. Once largely concentrated in Atlantic Canada, regional development spending now covered most of the country. A crucial shift in the political context that the Trudeau Liberals faced in the early 1970s accounted for this. The party faced heightened political challenges from Quebec, where the sovereigntist Parti Québécois won seats in a provincial election for the first time in 1970, and where the October Crisis kidnappings and murder occurred. It also had problems in the western provinces, which became increasingly dissatisfied with the Liberals throughout the decade. Initially, it was planned that at least 80 per cent of DREE's budget would be spent in Atlantic Canada and eastern Quebec. But in the wake of the 1970 October Crisis, the city of Montreal was designated as eligible for DREE's major industrial assistance program, and between 1970 and 1975 Quebec's share of DREE spending rose from 12 per cent to 39 per cent. A couple of years later the West's share also began to rise. Whereas 53 per cent of DREE's budget was spent in Atlantic Canada in 1970-1, this share fell to 36 per cent by 1980-1.[10] This did not change significantly during DRIE's existence. Atlantic Canadian observers complained that this broadening of regional development spending deflected it from its original purpose of assisting growth in poorer regions, and added unnecessarily to costs. (Indeed, western development spending was justified by Ottawa as an attempt to diversify that region's economy, not as a bid to stimulate economic growth.)

The third policy concern pertained to money. Regional development spending increased during the early 1970s, as its geographic focus expanded, but it was restricted later in that decade, when Ottawa began to experience chronic deficits. More cuts were made in the late 1980s and early 1990s. During much of the period after 1976, the most disadvantaged regions received a declining share of a shrinking pie.

Yet another reorganization was undertaken in 1987. DRIE's regional development responsibilities were transferred to separate agencies for each region—the Atlantic Canada Opportunities Agency (ACOA), Western Diversification (WD), and a Federal Economic Development Initiative in Northern Ontario (FedNor). Enterprise Cape Breton Corporation (ECBC) also was launched; its president would be a vice-president of ACOA. ACOA and WD each would have a minister in the federal cabinet. ECBC would report through ACOA's minister, and FedNor through the Industry Minister. Regional development spending in Quebec continued temporarily to be administered by Industry Canada, under an agreement with the Quebec government. But in 1991, a separate Federal Office of Regional Development-Quebec (FORD-Q) was established, also with its own cabinet minister. Its name was changed to Canada Economic Development for Quebec Regions (CED) in 1998.

The creation of separate agencies had an impact on program administration. The 'decentralization' option had won out; funds could now be expended in a manner that was more responsive to regional needs. Giving each of the agencies its own minister also provided them with a strong voice at the cabinet table. But it is less clear that the policy content overseen by these new instruments changed noticeably. When funding businesses, the new agencies were expected to concentrate more resources on locally based small and middle-sized enterprises (SMEs), and to move away from offering large loans and grants to big firms from outside their regions. But such firms continued to receive significant assistance from the agencies during the early 1990s. Regional development spending also continued to finance projects that related to a variety of objectives, ranging from rural development and fostering entrepreneurship in disadvantaged communities to projects designed to foster growth in more promising urban areas and in advanced technology sectors.[11] Moreover, Ottawa continued to distribute its regional development funds across Canada, including urban and relatively prosperous parts of western Quebec and the West (see Table 10.2).

Ottawa's involvement in regional development also spawned a complex range of federal-provincial relationships. During the 1960s, its regional development interventions were regarded critically by provinces, especially Quebec. Even the Atlantic provinces complained that

Table 10.2

**Program Spending, Regional Development Agencies
1988/89-2000/01
current (1992) dollars (,000)**

Agency Fiscal Year	Atlantic Canada Opportunities Agency	Enterprise Cape Breton Corporation	Canada Economic Development for Quebec Regions	Western Economic Diversification Canada
2000-1	288.6	9.2	230.0	167.4
1999-2000	253.4	9.5	284.5	176.5
1998-9	295.3	7.7	314.9	288.8
1997-8	287.1	8.1	275.5	237.8
1996-7	335.2	10.6	348.6	341.7
1995-6	356.2	16.8	452.4	434.0
1994-5	368.2	10.2	428.5	443.3
1993-4	311.6	9.6	227.6	278.0
1992-3	334.0	10.5	191.6	301.3
1989-90	414.5	11.9	NA	322.9

Note:
Between 1991 and 1998, Canada Economic Development for Quebec Regions (CED) was known as the Federal Office for Regional Development-Quebec (FORD-Q). In 1989-90, Quebec regional development spending was disbursed by the Industry Department. Separate Estimates were not submitted to Parliament for this spending. Spending estimates for the Federal Regional Development Initiative for Northern Ontario (FedNor) are included with those of the Department of Industry; they are not reported separately, and are therefore not included in this table.

Source: Canada. Department of Finance *Estimates, Part 1* (for each agency), 1989-90 to 2000-1.

Ottawa failed to consult them about program changes or to coordinate its initiatives with theirs. In 1974 Ottawa signed bilateral General Development Agreements (GDAs) with each province whenever the governments committed themselves to devoting specific sums of money to agreed-upon objectives. These were usually defined through subsidiary agreements, or 'subsidiaries', which typically focussed on an individual industry. GDAs were replaced with Economic and Regional Development Agreements (ERDAs) ten years later,[12] and by cooperation agreements in 1994. While the agreements improved relations with the provinces, problems remained. Many initiatives taken by each level of government were outside the purview of the agreements, and therefore were not coordinated with the other jurisdiction. This was true, for instance, of more than half of federal and provincial spending in Nova Scotia during the early 1990s. Provinces often continued to pursue development priorities that were very different from Ottawa's.[13] The subsidiary agreements also reflected the extreme heterogeneity, and the lack of strategic vision, in development spending in general.[14] Many subsidiaries were defined so broadly that a wide range of initiatives could be taken by officials under their authority.

LIBERAL REGIONAL DEVELOPMENT POLICY, 1993-8

The 1993 election was a watershed in Canadian political history. The Bloc Québécois (BQ) and the Reform party emerged as the most prominent challengers to the Liberals during that campaign and the Progressive Conservatives were nearly annihilated. Since Confederation the party system had been anchored by the Liberals and the Tories, who shared a brokerage orientation that muted ideological differences between them. In the post-1993 era, by contrast, the governing Liberals faced significant challenges from a right-of-centre party with origins in western Canada but seeking nation-wide support, and from a sovereigntist party in Quebec. The result was a more ideologically- and regionally-polarized politics. Reform and its successor, the Canadian Alliance, were raised to Official Opposition status in the 1997 and 2000 elections; these also confirmed the BQ as a major political force in Quebec. This had a visible impact on debates about regional development. While a broad consensus in favour of regional development prevailed between the Liberals and the Tories from the 1960s to 1993, it was now challenged by Reform and the Alliance.

Reflecting the views of the provincial Parti Québécois, the BQ, too, has challenged federal involvement in this policy field.

The Partisan Debate: The Liberals' 1993 Red Book criticized regional development spending for focussing too much on 'direct investment and incentives to attract new businesses to slower-growth areas', and on expanding 'physical capital in the form of plant, machinery, and equipment.' The Liberals proposed to continue regional development, but to concentrate on 'infrastructure, including tourism; commercial application of research and development through local institutions; and specific aid to small business.'[15] The Red Book also stressed three approaches to economic policy: working cooperatively with the private sector, supporting small and medium-sized firms, and stimulating innovation and high-technology growth. The technology theme was particularly prominent, and reflected the strong interest of Paul Martin, who co-authored the Red Book and hoped to become the Industry Minister if the Liberals won the election. (In the event, of course, he was assigned to the finance portfolio instead).[16] The Liberals' 1997 election platform ('Red Book II') said nothing about regional development. But the innovation and technology themes were again prominent,[17] and still dominated the Liberals' thinking about how to do regional development differently.

Preston Manning's Reform party, by contrast, wished to abandon the regional development tradition. Several months before the 1993 election, Manning released his party's detailed proposals for program cuts. Programs slated for elimination included the regional development agencies, the disappearance of which would account for $800 million of the $18.6 billion in proposed savings. 'Giving companies money to locate or continue operating in depressed areas', Manning suggested, 'does not stimulate economic revitalization.' More broadly, the Reform party was committed to reducing the role of government in the economy, and to relying on the private marketplace and lower taxation levels to stimulate job creation and growth. Reform's critique of regional development was repeated during the 1997 campaign.[18] With this proposal, Reform broke the political consensus in favour of regional development. The BQ did the same, arguing that this was a field of exclusively provincial jurisdiction. The Conservatives temporarily abandoned their support for regional development during the 1997 election, when leader Jean Charest proposed that all of the agencies except for ACOA be eliminated. This position was not maintained under Joe Clark's leadership.[19] The NDP continued to support regional development spending.

After the 1993 election, Reform used its standing as the major Parliamentary alternative to the Liberals in English Canada to press its argument. It highlighted the evidence of political meddling that has plagued regional development from its inception. Better to rely on the free market, Reformers argued, than to waste money on patronage-based and wasteful government spending. In January 1995 Reform MPs alleged that WD was allocating inordinate amounts of money in the Winnipeg riding of Lloyd Axworthy, WD's minister. CTV journalists claimed to have uncovered evidence that David Dingwall, the minister responsible for ACOA, pressured his officials to lend money to his friends.[20] ACOA also attracted negative publicity because of changes in its leadership. Mary Gusella, who had been appointed by the Mulroney Conservative government, was removed as ACOA president in 1995, after being praised by Peter O'Brien, a Nova Scotia business spokesman, for trying to de-politicize ACOA's grants and loans programs. When her replacement, Norman Spector, resigned in April 1996, it was widely rumoured that he had been pressured by Dingwall and by Liberal MPs in the region to finance projects that they favoured. Spector had publicly vowed that he would eliminate patronage from ACOA's business.[21]

The most damaging criticism, however, came from presumably politically neutral or bipartisan sources. In 1995, Auditor-General Denis Desautels criticized the development agencies for providing inadequate information on the impact of projects, making it difficult to assess whether they had met their objectives, and exaggerating the quantity and quality of jobs created by them. FORD-Q, he argued, had violated its own rules in assisting some projects, and only one-third of WD's projects had met their objectives. Optimistic assessments of the number of jobs created by its loans and grants are now typically among the highlights of the agencies' Performance Reports, annual documents that attempt to demonstrate that they are fulfilling their objectives.[22] These projections were now being called into question by a highly credible critic. The Senate Banking Committee went even further than the Auditor-General, proposing that the regional agencies be eliminated.[23]

Those who are sceptical about regional development also often allude to comparative data on levels of economic prosperity (measured by Gross Domestic Product per capita; see Table 10.3) and of unemployment (see Table 10.4) across Canada. If regional development has worked, they argue, why has it not reduced the disparity between Canada's poorer provinces, above all those in Atlantic Canada, and the affluent provinces? In fact, as Table 10.3 indicates, the Atlantic provinces have gradually improved their relative GDP per capita levels since regional development spending began in the early 1960s. In the Maritimes, at least, most of the improvement has occurred since the early 1980s. But as Table 10.4 demonstrates, there is much less evidence of a convergence between Atlantic Canada's chronically high unemployment rates and the national rate.

Data such as these must be treated cautiously. Relative economic well-being within Atlantic Canada may have improved in recent years as the result of circumstances that have little to do with regional development spending, and may decline in the absence of these circumstances. These may include the size and scope of other assistance offered to the region by Ottawa, recent economic stimuli in the energy sectors in Nova Scotia and Newfoundland and in the call centre industry in New Brunswick, and a short-term boost to P.E.I.'s economy when a fixed link was built between it and the mainland. Unemployment figures also can vary widely as the result of short-term considerations. Even if there was no evidence of regional convergence in income, moreover, one could not conclude that regional development spending had failed: it might be that the Atlantic region, poorly endowed with resources and distant from large markets, would have gotten poorer, in relative terms, without these measures. Long-time students of regional development, such as Donald Savoie, have therefore suggested that aggregate economic data such as these should not be the main criteria used to measure whether regional policies have succeeded.[24] Nevertheless, for many observers the continued relative poverty of Canada's most disadvantaged provinces can be expected to represent *prima facie* evidence of regional development's failure.

The Policy Debate: Reform's opposition to regional development echoed the views of many policy specialists about the appropriate economic role of government. The principle that private markets are best left to allocate investment resources on their own, with only limited government oversight, now appears to be the mainstream view

Table 10.3

Provincial Gross Domestic Product Per Capita Relative to the Canadian Average (per cent)
(first year of decade, and most recent available year)

	1961	1971	1981	1991	1997
Newfoundland	50.2	56.0	58.0	65.0	68.3
P.E.I	49.4	51.5	56.8	63.7	75.9
Nova Scotia	65.3	67.6	61.4	78.6	75.8
New Brunswick	60.2	64.3	60.6	75.6	79.2
Quebec	90.6	90.1	86.0	91.5	88.4
Ontario	120.2	117.8	102.7	109.6	107.7
Manitoba	90.1	89.1	87.4	85.7	90.4
Saskatchewan	78.0	83.3	103.0	80.8	97.7
Alberta	108.7	107.0	157.2	115.1	125.7
British Columbia	111.4	106.0	112.7	105.3	98.4

Note:
This table indicates what each province's GDP level per capita was in relation to the national average for the specified years. For instance, if a province had a score of '90', its GDP per capita would be 90 per cent of that for Canada as a whole.

Source: Statistics Canada, *Canada Year Book, 1994* (Ottawa: Statistics Canada, 1993), 614; updated with data from Statistics Canada, *Canada Year Book, 1999* (Ottawa: Statistics Canada, 1998), 85, 320.

Table 10.4
Provincial Unemployment Rates
Relative to the National Average (per cent)
(first year of decade, and most recent available year)

	1961	1971	1981	1991	2000
Newfoundland	275	135	186	179	246
P.E.I.	—	—	150	163	176
Nova Scotia	114	113	134	117	134
New Brunswick	148	98	154	123	147
Quebec	130	118	137	116	124
Ontario	77	87	87	93	84
Manitoba	70	92	79	85	72
Saskatchewan	58	56	61	72	76
Alberta	66	92	50	80	74
British Columbia	120	116	88	96	106

Note:
This table indicates what each province's unemployment rate was in relation to the national average level for the specified years. For instance, if a province has a score of '175', this would indicate that its unemployment rate was 1.75 times the rate for Canada as a whole.

Source: Donald Savoie, *Regional Economic Development*, 2nd ed. (Toronto: University of Toronto Press, 1992), 193; updated with data from Statistics Canada, *Canada Year Book, 1994* (Ottawa: Statistics Canada, 1993), 617, and Statistics Canada, 'Canadian Statistics: Labour force, employed and unemployed'. Web site: www.statcan.ca/.../ish/Pgdb/People/Labour/labor07.a.ht (consulted on 1 February 2001).

among economists. Internationally, it is championed by the Organization of Economic Cooperation and Development (OECD) and the International Monetary Fund (IMF). From this perspective, government intervention in the economy distorts the price signals that allocate capital in properly-functioning markets, resulting in reduced output and employment. By using tax revenues to finance investment in low-growth areas, government diverts capital from its most efficient possible use to purposes that the market has itself defined as sub-optimal. These views have acquired a stronger following since the broad post-war expansion of government's role began to reverse in the late 1970s and 1980s, in a context of slower economic growth and increasingly competitive international markets. In Canada they are reflected in publications by the C.D. Howe Institute and the Fraser Institute. Specific criticisms of regional development spending that start from this position have been made by prominent academic business and economics professors, such as Richard Lipsey and Fred Lazar. The Business Council on National Issues (BCNI), the main interest group representing big business views in Canada, also advocates ending regional development. Even within Atlantic Canada, the region most dependent on development spending, the erstwhile consensus in favour of regional development disappeared during the 1990s. The Atlantic Institute for Market Studies (AIMS), a business-funded advocacy body, demanded the elimination of these measures. But the Atlantic Provinces Economic Council (APEC), the traditional voice of Atlantic business, continued to support them.[25]

Advocates of a continuing government role in regional development have therefore been on the defensive. But during the early 1990s, perspectives that might justify a degree of government involvement in disadvantaged regions began to receive attention from a broader public. The economist Paul Krugman argued that a case can sometimes be made in favour of support for firms in new, technologically-advanced sectors of the economy. If these are properly chosen, and the timing and assistance appropriate, domestic producers might acquire an enduring advantage over foreign competitors. Other writers, usually not economists, endorsed a government role with fewer qualifications. Robert Reich, for example, recommended a greater public commitment to skills training, and Lester Thurow favoured industrial policies with few of Krugman's reservations.[26] The views of Reich and Krugman, in particular, helped persuade Paul Martin, when he co-authored the 1993 Red Book, that government should stimulate high-technology development.[27]

Other literature that became increasingly popular in the 1990s added a specifically regional dimension to this argument. Michael Porter used the term 'clusters' to refer to geographically and sectorally proximate firms; these, he argued, were the most likely venues for successful innovation. The 'Regional Innovation Systems' (RIS) literature similarly stresses the extent to which innovation in high-value-added sectors depends on the presence of stimulative networks among contiguous firms, universities and other research institutions, suppliers and customers, sources of financing, etc.[28] The free market alone may not secure prosperity for a particular locale or region if it does not possess these qualities. Public policy can increase a region's innovation potential. '[O]ne of the key developmental roles of the state', two RIS scholars argue, 'is to create the conditions ... whereby firms, intermediate associations, and public agencies can engage in a self-organized process of interactive learning.'[29]

These justifications for regional development spending differ significantly from those used three decades earlier. The latter responded to then-dominant Keynesianism by suggesting that supply-side interventions were needed if poorer regions were to benefit fully from Keynesian policy. This approach often justified interventions that were undertaken in defiance of market conditions, on the assumption that these could be rectified. Emerging at a time when market-oriented assumptions have largely displaced Keynesian ones in policy circles, the newer arguments instead argue that government's role should be facilitative, fostering private-sector activities that already exist, but that may not flourish unassisted. These activities are more likely to be in high-technology and innovative economic sectors, not in the rural and resource-based ones favoured by many regional development measures since the 1960s.

The Liberals' Policy Record, 1993-8: These ideas affected Liberal regional development policy. But policy was also moulded by another factor that the Chrétien administration confronted immediately after coming to power—a $42 billion deficit. Eliminating this quickly became the Liberals' top priority, especially when Finance Minister Paul Martin decided to tackle the deficit firmly in his February 1995 budget. Yet the deficit did not have an immediate impact. On the contrary, as Table 10.2 shows, federal regional development spending rose significantly between 1993-4 and 1995-6 for most of these agencies. This reversed a steep decline in spending that had occurred under the Tories between the first full fiscal year of the agencies' operation (1989-90) and 1993-4, and during the longer-term stagnation of spending since 1976. The increases were particularly important for the Quebec, western Canada, and Cape Breton agencies, whose budgets nearly doubled in real dollar terms. A significant part of this increase was due to the Liberals' infrastructure program, which had been a prominent commitment in the 1993 Red Book. But the 1995 cuts entirely reversed this pattern by 1997-8, even as infrastructure spending continued to be included in agency budgets. These three agencies now saw their allocations cut by about half; ACOA also lost all of the gains that had accrued to it since 1993. Adjusted for inflation, spending in all of these agencies except FORD-Q was now below 1993 levels; all four had smaller budgets than in 1989.

Despite the cuts, the new government committed itself to several significant departures in regional development policy. Five were particularly important: (1) a greater focus on SMEs, rather than the large outside employers who had often received assistance in the past; (2) a shift from grants to loans in assisting firms; (3) greater use of partnerships with private-sector actors; (4) an increased focus on stimulating advanced technology and research and development; and (5) a more strategic focus for federal spending. Overall, these implied focussing federal efforts— previously fragmented among a disparate array of rural and urban, resource- and manufacturing-sector, and 'social' and economic objectives—on industries and firms that were likely to contribute to long-term economic growth. Each theme echoed the 1993 Red Book: the first reflected its small business focus; the second and third, its preference for initiatives that are consistent with market forces and support existing private-sector capacities; and the fourth, its 'high technology' emphasis. The final element reflected its promise to spend development funds more efficiently.

However, it is not clear that the Liberals improved significantly the effectiveness of regional development spending. The SME focus, for instance, was not invented by the Chrétien government; it emerged in February 1988, when the development agencies' core lending program was relaunched by the Mulroney Conservative administration. This emphasis was increased when the agencies' budgets were cut in

1989.[30] In the mid-1990s, the Liberals nevertheless announced that they were amplifying this small-business focus, and turning away from encouraging outside firms to relocate to poorer provinces.[31]

The shift from grants to loans for firms receiving assistance, designed to focus resources on more market-ready and self-reliant firms, has proceeded at a different pace in different regions. In the relatively prosperous western provinces, WD was already largely restricting itself to low-interest loans by 1992; it took the additional step of abandoning direct lending altogether in 1995, transferring this responsibility to private banks.[32] In the much poorer Atlantic provinces grants were a major part of ACOA's business assistance program until the 1995 budget cuts; ACOA then moved entirely to loans, but continued to administer them directly. FORD-Q also abandoned grants at that time, and together with FedNor followed WD's lead by reaching agreements with private banks to deliver these loans. However, Cape Breton's ECBC, serving the most economically disadvantaged region covered by any of the agencies, continued to dispense grants after the 1995 budget.[33]

Private-sector partnerships and high-technology growth have been much-repeated themes in the agencies' *Estimates* and press releases since the mid-1990s. Most projects funded under federal-provincial cooperation agreements now require a private-sector sponsor. The agencies also sought private-sector assistance in 'identifying and supporting growth opportunities'.[34] When FORD-Q launched a fund to assist new high-technology firms in 1997, it was to be delivered by private financial institutions. WD had begun a similar program two years earlier.[35] Other examples of the greater focus on high technology during these years included a joint project of FedNor and the Royal Bank to extend the availability of high-speed data services, a similar high-technology initiative in Quebec, and funding for private-sector technology development in Atlantic Canada.[36]

Nonetheless, it is hard to determine whether the changes really answered the oft-repeated criticisms of regional development. Agency officials claim that many problems uncovered in internal program reviews or by the Auditor-General have been solved. But the evidence for this is largely anecdotal; the government's *Estimates* do not permit one to ascertain whether spending patterns have altered significantly; internal performance reviews by regional agencies are conducted sporadically and are often not published; and, as we have seen, agency job creation projections are widely disputed. While WD has moved entirely from grants to bank-delivered loans, moreover, the rate of loan default under this new regime is very high.[37] The only safe conclusion that can be drawn at this point is that the Liberals did introduce changes in regional spending between 1993 and 1998 to realize the 1993 Red Book commitments. But it remains unclear whether the new agenda has improved the economic value of these programs.

Administrative Reform: In January 1996, the Liberals partly reversed the previous administration's 1987 decision to devolve regional development programs to region-specific agencies. The three largest agencies—ACOA, FORD-Q, and WD—were reattached to the Industry Department, and would answer to its minister, John Manley. They would continue to exist as discrete entities, but would no longer be represented in the cabinet. Instead, more junior secretaries of state (who are not cabinet ministers) would, under Manley's oversight, assume responsibility for them. ECBC continued to be overseen by the ACOA president. FedNor remained attached to the Industry Department.[38]

This change was intended to accomplish two things. Manley announced that it signified that '[p]ork barrel is not in'. The cabinet ministers previously attached to agencies—Dingwall in Atlantic Canada, Axworthy in the West, and Martin in Quebec—had been accused of meddling in their business; by eliminating the role of these ministries, and assigning only junior ministers to the agencies, the government attempted to alleviate this concern. The change also promised to accelerate the agencies' emphasis on high-technology sectors. This focus was already well established at Industry Canada, and was championed by Manley, who declared that '[w]e're looking to help build regional economies that are able to respond to the challenges of global competition and changing economic circumstances.'[39]

But the administrative reform was not universally endorsed. Peter O'Brien, a Nova Scotia business spokesman, was supportive. But Donald Savoie, intellectual author of the regional agencies in 1987, had envisaged that through them the poorer regions would have a strong political voice in cabinet; he vehemently opposed the change. Savoie argues that Industry Canada, focussed on encouraging 'high end' industrial development far more likely to succeed in Central

Canada, consistently has been hostile to regional development agencies.[40]

Federal-Provincial Friction: The fifth of the Liberal regional development priorities identified above—a more strategic approach to programming—was especially relevant to the Cooperation Agreements that it signs with provinces. Ottawa hoped to replace the unfocussed interjurisdictional arrangements of the past, which included many unrelated subsidiary agreements, with more integrated ones that concentrated on a few carefully selected sectors. In the mid-1990s, consequently, the subsidiaries were abolished; agreements would now concentrate on broad targets.

This new approach was superimposed on a federal-provincial setting that was already complex and that varied considerably across the country. Even in Atlantic Canada relations with Ottawa were imperfect. Frank McKenna, New Brunswick's premier between 1987 and 1997, allegedly attached little value to ACOA.[41] Nova Scotia officials often complained that ACOA made program changes without consulting them, and that federal priorities often were at cross-purposes with theirs; but in this jurisdiction, at least, Ottawa's more strategic approach after 1996 nevertheless did help the province focus some of its own initiatives.[42] In Ontario, the main complaint now is that it is alone in not benefiting from a federal development agency, other than lightly-funded FedNor for its north. The Ontario government complains that FedNor initiatives are often launched without consulting it.[43] In general, during the 1990s Ontario governments became increasingly aggressive in questioning a range of federal spending initiatives, including regional development, that are a net drain on Ontario taxpayers.[44]

The most difficult intergovernmental relationship for Ottawa, however, has been with Quebec. Many FORD-Q and CED initiatives during the 1990s paralleled those of the Quebec government. They included greater regionalization of administration, and the use of private-sector consultative bodies. Yet since the return of the Parti Québécois to power in 1994, these have been met with consistent provincial demands that Ottawa transfer all responsibility for regional development to the province. The two governments were unable to sign a Cooperation Agreement when their ERDA expired in December 1994. Thereafter, they proceeded on separate, though often parallel, courses. The province barred individuals appointed to federally-sponsored community bodies from sitting on their provincial counterparts. Announcements by one government of a special initiative for a depressed Quebec region—such as the Gaspé—are frequently matched by a similar declaration from the other.[45]

During the Liberals' first five years in power, some elements of the landscape of regional development policy remained unchanged. The perception remained widespread that regional development was used by the federal government for narrowly political purposes; yet this charge was now made in a political climate in which the old consensus in favour of regional development had disappeared. There were other changes. With the old intellectual justifications for regional programs losing their credibility, the Liberals now defended them in terms of a new policy paradigm. Yet it is difficult to discern whether the consequent reforms improved the impact of regional spending. Some had been at least partly launched before the Liberals came to power; the impact of others was variable or difficult to measure, in part because there is little independent evaluative data, and because the agencies' own evaluations are widely considered to be inaccurate. Organizational reforms designed to expedite change have themselves been criticized as regressive steps and efforts to create a more strategic approach to federal-provincial relations were caught up in pre-existing jurisdictional tensions.

THE CONTEMPORARY CONJUNCTURE: POLITICS AND POLICY

In the 1997 election, the Liberals won 22 fewer seats than in 1993; the losses were heaviest in Atlantic Canada, where their standing fell from 31 to 11 of the region's 32 seats. Major cuts in transfer payments to the region, especially Employment Insurance, were widely judged to have contributed to this result. In mid-1998 the Liberals began to reconsider their regional development initiatives as part of preliminary planning for the next campaign. Frank McKenna, now retired from the New Brunswick premiership, endorsed a proposal that the government concentrate on stimulating high-technology sectors. While this theme had been stressed by the Liberals since 1993, its impact on regional development spending so far was unclear, as we have seen. Andy Scott, Solicitor General and MP for a New Brunswick riding, promoted it vigorously.[46] It also influenced a committee of the Liberals' Atlantic caucus, which in 1999 was asked to address the region's policy needs. In an interim report, the committee suggested that ACOA be replaced by a full-scale department, to be represented at cabinet, and given a much-expanded budget. This was resisted by Industry Minister Manley and Finance Minister Martin, and was dropped from the final version of the Committee's report, released in November. The latter nevertheless repeated the high-technology theme, identifying seven sectors as appropriate focuses of additional government support.[47]

In June 2000, Prime Minister Chrétien announced an 'Atlantic Investment Partnership' (AIP), which committed $700 million over five years (with about $285 million in new money) to a variety of purposes, including support for high-technology sectors.[48] The views of the Atlantic Liberal caucus were one source of this initiative, but not the only one. In preparing for the next election, the Liberals also had to address a crisis at Human Resources Development Canada (HRDC). When a new Employment Insurance system was created in 1995 that reduced benefits for many claimants, Ottawa created a Transitional Jobs Fund to provide short-term job opportunities for people affected by the changes in high-unemployment areas. It was later extended, under the title of the Canada Jobs Fund. The Fund granted money to business persons in constituencies that experienced high unemployment rates. MPs played an important role in identifying potential recipients. Complaints that funds were used for patronage purposes by Liberal politicians became widespread after June 1999. Friends of the Prime Minister allegedly benefited unfairly from the Fund in his Saint-Maurice constituency. An internal audit concluded that the Fund was not managed adequately.[49] The issue became a major embarrassment for the government. Consequently, one week before Chrétien announced the AIP, the Jobs Fund was cancelled by HRDC minister Jane Stewart. Its $110 million budget was transferred to the five regional development agencies.[50] ACOA's share of this sum—about $150 million over five years—later was directed toward the AIP. Introducing the AIP so quickly after terminating the Jobs Fund could have been expected to help reduce a public perception that the Liberals were using job creation and development funds largely for patronage purposes that had little economic value. By focussing on the 'new economy', prized by everyone, the AIP was less vulnerable to this critique.

How much of a change does the AIP represent in the content of regional development programming? It should be recalled that it has no bearing on measures administered by any agency other than ACOA; it also leaves unchanged many pre-existing ACOA programs. These continue to reflect the heterogeneity of purposes that has characterized regional programs since the 1970s. The AIP was promoted as breaking with this pattern by concentrating on initiatives with a significant potential long-term impact in high-technology industries. While it does hold some promise of moving in this direction, there are also some limitations.

Two of the AIP's main components clearly have a high-technology focus. The Atlantic Innovation Fund (AIF), allocated $300 million over five years, will promote 'new economy clusters which are emerging in sectors such as information technologies, bio-technology, medical services and technologies, and ocean industries.' It will finance collaborative research among Atlantic Canada's universities and research institutions, which are expected to identify new technologies and applications relevant to the region's industry. Another $110 million will be used to enhance the National Research Council's (NRC) research centres in the region, and to forge links with private-sector partners.[51] Using the vocabulary of 'clusters', 'networks', and 'innovation', documents released by the government to explain the AIP owe a clear debt to the Porter and Regional Innovation System literature described earlier.

But some of the heterogeneity typical of earlier regional development spending is still evident: the AIP includes a 'Partnership for Community Economic Development', expected to cost $135 million over five years, which provides 'a clear demonstration of the Government's continued commitment to the rural populations of Atlantic Canada.' It will support local economic planning and finance small business in rural communities.[52] Other features of the Partnership also suggest a need for caution in assessing its potential success. Its budget is small in relation to the enormous task of attempting to build a robust high-technology economy in Atlantic Canada. Moreover, the program elements described above have been characterized by many observers as vague and ambiguous. Officials within ACOA apparently have had some difficulty deciding what to do with the AIF component. The region's universities created an elaborate procedure for vetting proposals to set up research and teaching programs to fulfil its objectives. ACOA officials, charged with evaluating these and other proposals to receive funds, are said to be 'looking for good ideas' about what to do. These officials had been working on their own ideas about how to stimulate innovation in the region before the AIP was announced; they have been left scrambling to respond to the sudden infusion of new money. There is also widespread concern about the Atlantic region's capacity to 'absorb' the funds effectively. Universities and research institutes may have trouble finding enough research designs that could credibly be expected to promote high-technology growth in the region. And the regional economy, which currently has a very modest mass of high-technology activity,[53] will have trouble using the results of this research when they materialize.

While one might have to wait some time to assess the AIP's success as policy, the results of the 27 November 2000 election permit an evaluation of its political value. Along with other efforts to mollify Atlantic Canadians, such as a promise to restore some EI benefits, the AIP helped the Liberals restore some of their previous support in the Atlantic region. They won 19 seats there, which helped assure them a third successive majority government.

The market-oriented critique of regional development policy by the Reform party and the Canadian Alliance has affected the Liberals in a number of areas. For instance, the Liberals' significant tax cuts in their two 2000 budgets reflected, in part, a desire to curtail the potential appeal of the Alliance's commitment to even deeper tax reductions. In the regional development field, however, this impact has been less straightforward. The AIP was announced shortly before the 2000 ballot in the face of persistent criticism of these measures from the Alliance and many business interests; and it was justified by the 'new economy' arguments that the Liberals have used since 1993 to deflect this critique. On the other hand, the largesse was not extended to the other regional agencies. A task force of the western Liberal caucus was created in 1999 to help prepare the party for the next election. Its February 2000 report echoed the Atlantic caucus report in proposing more regional development spending in the west. But David Anderson, a prominent western cabinet minister, opposed the recommendation, and it was not acted upon.[54] Spending data for four of the agencies, reported in Table 10.2, demonstrate that their fortunes diverged significantly after regional development hit its low point, in the wake of the 1995 cuts, in the 1997-8 fiscal year. In inflation-adjusted dollars,

ACOA's budget was stable during this period; indeed, the incremental funds needed to finance the AIP (not reported in Table 10.2) will add another $60 million to its budget. ECBC's budget also increased by almost $1 million. By contrast, CED, the Quebec agency, saw its budget reduced by $55 million, and WD's fell by $70 million. When ACOA's budget increased in the spring 2000 budget (along with FedNor's), while WD's and CEQ's fell, commentators were quick to detect an electoral strategy: blocked by the Alliance and the BQ in the West and Quebec, the Liberals were concentrating their efforts on attracting voters in Atlantic Canada, and using FedNor's budget to shore up support in Ontario.[55]

This recent shift was not the first time that regional distribution of spending has responded in part to electoral incentives. Governments used regional development spending to broker specific regional blocks in the 1960s (to increase the Tories' appeal in Atlantic Canada and the rural west) and the 1970s (to shore up Liberal support in Quebec and the West). While the Alliance has challenged 'old style' brokerage politics in Canada, that style continues to flourish in this policy sector. Indeed, from an Atlantic (and, perhaps, Quebec or Northern Ontario) perspective, the Alliance's opposition to regional spending can itself be seen in traditionally brokerage terms. Relatively prosperous, westerners may be ambivalent about receiving such benefits and reluctant to pay the taxes to support them. In any case, the political debate about regional development is now part of a partisan dynamic in Canada that is becoming even more fractious, both ideologically and regionally, than it has been historically.

Policy ideas—the second dynamic traced throughout this chapter— also affected recent developments in this field in a way that reflects the contemporary conjuncture. The AIP was shaped by the 'new economy' thinking that has influenced the Liberals. By attempting to use government to stimulate high-technology growth in Canada's poorest region, the Liberals are submitting this thinking to a very severe test, one that much of the scholarly literature on clusters and regional innovation would predict is likely to fail: proximity to existing stocks of financial and human capital and to markets is, in this literature, a crucial determinant of innovation; using government to foster these factors when they are not otherwise present is, at the very least, a risky enterprise.

The Liberals, moreover, have not alleviated three problems that have persisted since regional development's emergence four decades ago: (1) How should regional development be organized, on the one hand, to apply coherently and consistently across the country and have influence within the federal cabinet and, on the other hand, to respond to regional needs (the administrative problem of centralization and decentralization)? (2) What should policy seek to promote—the survival of communities, often rural and in economic decline, or the most economically promising sectors, often located in the most prosperous cities—in what balance and with what degree of integration around explicit strategic goals (the policy problem of focus and program fragmentation)? (3) How should federal-provincial tensions, ubiquitous, but more visible in some regions than others, be addressed? Here too political and policy concerns are intimately interconnected. To be seen to be building either a 'remote, bureaucratic monolith' or 'checkerboard federalism'; 'abandoning rural communities' or not fostering long-term growth; 'capitulating to' or 'running roughshod over' the provinces: these are unpalatable options. These tensions, like the policy and political incentives that give rise to them, are therefore unlikely to disappear soon as powerful forces shaping regional development policy in Canada.

NOTES

1. Jane Jenson, 'The Roots of Canada's Permeable Fordism', *Canadian Journal of Political Science* 23, 4 (1990): 681.
2. James Bickerton, *Nova Scotia, Ottawa, and the Politics of Regional Development* (Toronto: University of Toronto Press, 1990): 154-67.
3. Robert Campbell, *Grand Illusions* (Peterborough: Broadview Press, 1987), 130-6; Anthony Careless, *Initiative and Response* (Montreal: McGill-Queen's University Press, 1977), 36-42.
4. Careless, *Initiative and Response*, 47.
5. Bickerton, *Nova Scotia*, 180, 182-7.
6. R. Harley McGee, *Getting it Right* (Montreal: McGill-Queen's University Press, 1992), xxv-xxvi.
7. Donald Savoie, *Regional Economic Development*, 2nd ed. (Toronto: University of Toronto Press, 1992), 34-6, 54-8, 109-10.
8. Bickerton, *Nova Scotia*, 213.
9. Savoie, *Regional Economic Development*, 111-12, 114, 116.
10. Bickerton, *Nova Scotia*, 216-17, 223, 275.

11 Savoie, *Regional Economic Development*, 207-8.
12 Ibid., 54-5, 88-9.
13 Rodney Haddow, 'Economic Development Policy: In Search of a Strategy', in P. Clancy, J. Bickerton, R. Haddow, and I. Stewart, eds, *The Savage Years* (Halifax: Formac, 2000), 105.
14 Savoie, *Regional Economic Development*, 274-8.
15 Liberal Party of Canada, *Creating Opportunity: The Liberal Plan for Canada* (Ottawa, 1993), 59.
16 Edward Greenspon and Anthony Wilson-Smith, *Double Vision* (Toronto: Doubleday, 1996), 43-4.
17 Liberal Party of Canada, *Securing Our Future Together* (Ottawa, 1997), 37-41.
18 John Schreiner, 'Forgo Business Grants to Cut Deficits: Manning', *The Financial Post*, 14 Apr. 1993, 3; 'Pre-election Fever Hits Ottawa', *The Financial Post*, 28/30 Dec. 1996, 10.
19 Neville Nankivell, 'Charest's Gutsy Gamble May Pay Off', *The Financial Post*, 20 Mar. 1997, 19; John Lovinc, 'Mr. Middle of the Road', *The National Post*, 26 Oct. 2000, A15.
20 Brian Underhill, 'Put Wasteful ACOA to Rest, Reform Critic Says', *The Chronicle-Herald* [Halifax], 6 Sept. 1995, A1; 'Liberal Minister Favours Winnipeg for Federal Development Money', *Canadian Press Newswire*, 27 Jan. 1995; Andrew Mitrovica, 'Patronage by Former Public Works Minister David Dingwall', *Media* 3, 2 (1996): 19.
21 Tom McDougall, 'ACOA President's Days Numbered—Source', *The Chronicle-Herald* [Halifax], 24 Apr. 1995, C8; Brian Underhill, 'Spector Quits ACOA Post', *The Chronicle-Herald* [Halifax], 22 June 1996, A3.
22 For a summary list of such claims by one agency see Department of Finance, *Estimates, Canada Economic Development for Quebec Regions: Performance Report for the Period Ending March 31, 1999* (Ottawa: 1999), 15-45.
23 'Job Creation Claims Questioned by Auditor-General Report', *The Financial Post*, 22 Nov. 1995, 5; 'Federal Lending Agencies Defend Independence Against Senate Committee's Call for Merging', *The Financial Post*, 6/8 Apr. 1996, 14.
24 Donald Savoie, *Regional Economic Development*, chap. 12.
25 'Lessons in Knowledge Industries' [book review], *The Financial Post*, 11 Apr. 1996, 15; 'Report Lambastes Regional Incentives', *The Financial Post*, 16 Jan. 1997, 13; 'Finance Minister Martin Says Business Must Do More to Boost Canada in the New Economy', *Canadian Press Newswire*, Apr. 2000; 'ACOA Job Claims Bunk', *Canadian Press Newswire*, 31 Oct. 1996; Fred McMahon, 'Chrétien's Atlantic Tech-sector Destruction Program', *The National Post*, 5 July 2000, C15; Elizabeth Beale, 'Atlantic Facts', *The National Post*, 25 Aug. 2000, A17.

26 Paul Krugman, *Peddling Prosperity* (New York: W.W. Norton, 1994), chaps. 9-10; Robert Reich, *The Work of Nations* (New York: Vintage Books, 1992), part 4; Lester Thurow, *Head to Head* (New York: Morrow, 1992), esp. 290-8.
27 Greenspon and Wilson-Smith, *Double Vision*, 43.
28 Michael Porter, *The Competitive Advantage of Nations* (New York: Free Press, 1990); Phillip Cooke and Kevin Morgan, *The Associational Economy* (Oxford: Oxford University Press, 1998), chap.1.
29 Cooke and Morgan, *The Associational Economy*, 23.
30 Department of Finance, *1989-90 Estimates, Part III, Atlantic Canada Opportunities Agency*, 7, 10.
31 Dominique Fromont, 'La priorité devrait aller à la survie des entreprises', *Les Affaires*, 13 April 1996, B8; 'Study of Failed Federal Mega-Projects Pins Blame on Bureaucrats', *Canadian Press Newswire*, 4 Sept. 1995.
32 Anonymous, 'Investing in Ideas', *BC Business*, Sept. 1992, 5; Larry Johnsrude, 'Fund Quits Loans', *The Calgary Herald*, 1 Mar. 1995, D1.
33 'ACOA Grants Become Loans', *Canadian Press Newswire*, 7 Feb. 1995; Alain Duhamel, 'Paul Martin veut amener les banques à soutenir le développement des PMEs', *Les Affaires*, 2 Sept. 1995, 7; Doug Saunders, 'How Ottawa's Millions Fail Cape Breton', *The Globe and Mail* [Toronto], 19 Aug. 1995, A5.
34 Department of Finance, *1995-96 Estimates, Part III, Atlantic Canada Opportunities Agency*, 17.
35 Pierre Théroux, 'Les institutions financières multiplient les ententes avec des organismes gouvernementaux', *Les Affaires*, 23 Aug. 1997, 25; John Schiener, 'BDBC Establishes $25 Million Loan Fund in West', *The Financial Post*, 11 Nov. 1995, 12.
36 Michelle Naval, 'Bell Expands Data Services in Northern Ontario', *Computer Dealer News*, 2 Nov. 1998, 47; Pierre Théroux, 'Des milliards de dollars investis par les sociétés publiques de financement', *Les Affaires*, 23 Aug. 1997, 24; Department of Finance, *1997-98 Estimates, Part III, Atlantic Canada Opportunities Agency*, 8.
37 Peter O'Neill, 'Costs for Programs Intended to Aid the West', *The Vancouver Sun*, 17 Feb. 2000, A1.
38 Bonnie McKenna, 'Three Agencies Go to One Minister', *The Globe and Mail* [Toronto], 26 Jan. 1996, B7.
39 Ibid.
40 'Regional Development Shifts Back to Ottawa', *Daily Commercial News*, 5 Feb. 1996, A16; Donald Savoie, *Regional Economic Development*, 213-14.
41 Donald Savoie, 'Looking for Jobs on the East Coast', *Policy Options/Options politiques* 17, 6 (July/Aug. 1996): 83.
42 Haddow, 'Economic Development Policy', 103-4.

43 Savoie, *Regional Economic Development*, 153; David Crane, 'How Ontario's Getting Short-changed', *The Toronto Star*, 17 Mar. 1996, D2.
44 Thomas Courchene and Colin Telmer, *From Heartland to North American Region State* (Toronto: Centre for Public Management, University of Toronto, 1998), 223-37.
45 Jean-Pierre Langlois, 'La décentralisation a repris des couleurs ces dernièrs années', *Les Affaires*, 15 Apr. 1995, B-3; Jean-Paul Gagné, 'Ottawa et Québec ne renouvelleront pas l'entente auxilière Canada-Québec', *Les Affaires*, 2 Nov. 1999, 9.
46 Campbell Morrison, 'Atlantic Politicians Focus on Jobs, Jobs, Jobs', *The Hill Times*, 6 July 1998.
47 Brian Underhill, 'Replace ACOA, Report Says', *The Chronicle-Herald* [Halifax], 30 Sept. 1999, A6; Underhill, 'Grits Hope to Catch the Wave', 9 Nov. 1999, A11.
48 'Ottawa to Spend $700 Million on High Tech Economy in Atlantic Canada', *Canadian Press Newswire*, 29 June 2000.
49 Daniel Leblanc, 'New Allegations of Patronage Levelled Against Chrétien', *The Globe and Mail* [Toronto], 11 June 1999, A4; Andrew McIntosh, 'Hotels in PM's Riding Get $3 Million More in Federal Help', *The National Post*, 15 June 1999, A1-A2; John Geddes, 'Saving Ms. Stewart', *Maclean's*, 14 February 2000, 14.
50 Andrew McIntosh, '"It's Over", Stewart Says: Bedevilled Jobs Fund Shut', *The National Post*, 23 June 2000, A1.
51 ACOA, 'Atlantic Investment Partnership' (*Press Release*, 29 June 2000), 1-2.
52 Ibid., 2.
53 See, for instance, Frances Anderson, *An Overview of Statistical Indicators of Regional Innovation in Canada: A Provincial Comparison* (Ottawa: Statistics Canada, 1998).
54 Mike Scandiffio, 'Grit Study Wants More Money in West', *The Hill Times* [Ottawa], 21 February 2000, 1, 9.
55 Andrew McIntosh and Robert Fife, 'Economic Development Spending Rises in Maritimes, Ontario: Increases Seen as Liberal Election Strategy', *The National Post*, 1 March 2000, A7.

11

A Delicate Dance: The Courts and the Chrétien Government

RAINER KNOPFF

Ottawa spends—and must thus first acquire—symbolic as well as financial resources. The symbolic variety includes legal resources embodied in laws and court decisions.[1] Indeed, court decisions loom ever larger in the symbolic calculus. From 1867 to 1982, Canada's constitutional evolution involved the replacement of a nineteenth-century 'system of checks and balances at least as extensive as the American constitution of the same era' with one of dominant political executives, checked primarily by their interaction with each other in the arena of executive federalism.[2] Courts played an important political and policy role during this period, but nothing like the role they play today. Since 1982, with the advent of the Charter of Rights, judges and political executives have danced a regular *pas de deux* at the centre of Canada's political stage.

The dance is subtle and complex, with both sides acting in highly strategic ways. Governments act strategically to acquire and spend legal resources, always attempting to strengthen their hand against other governments or partisan foes. Courts are just as strategic, pursuing their own interests and agendas. This chapter seeks to illuminate the strategic dialectic between the two institutions. It is a dance that sometimes finds its partners drawn into a warm and approving embrace, and at other times sees them stepping more gingerly, at arm's length. The chapter begins with an overview of court-government interaction during the first two Chrétien mandates (1993-2000). The bulk of the chapter then undertakes two detailed case studies of the strategic interplay between the federal government and the courts.

OTTAWA AND THE COURTS, 1993-2000

Judges were thoroughly involved in many of the political issues that dominated the public agenda from 1993 to 2000. Perhaps the most prominent example is the Supreme Court's opinion in the 1998 *Secession Reference*,[3] an opinion solicited by Ottawa itself through the reference procedure. (The reference procedure, which is unconstitutional in such countries as the United States and Australia, allows the Canadian government to refer issues directly to their highest court of appeal rather than waiting for ordinary litigants to bring them up through the judicial hierarchy.) The *Secession Reference* is the latest in a string of judgments—dating back to the 1981 *Patriation Case*—that have been pivotal in Canada's continuing mega-constitutional politics of national unity. In a bold and expansive opinion—one that reads more like a political and philosophical treatise than a legal judgment[4]— the Court created an obligation on the part of the rest of Canada to negotiate with Quebec after a clear affirmative answer to a clear referendum question on secession (thereby splitting the difference between the two extremes). 'Leading decision' is too mild a term for this judgment. Commentators agree that it is a judicial bombshell, and predict widespread and lingering fallout for constitutional politics and jurisprudence.

Courts also had an important impact on women's issues during the Chrétien mandates, even though the Supreme Court was relatively restrained on these issues.[5] In *Thibaudeau*,[6] the Court upheld a law that taxed custody payments in the hands of the recipient (usually the mother), while deducting them from the taxable income of the payer (usually the father). Although the government technically 'won' this case, it was persuaded by the controversy it generated to change the law.

Perhaps more dramatically, the government and the court engaged in a running feud about the rules governing sexual assault trials. The government wanted clear legal rules that would benefit the alleged victim in sexual assault cases, while the Court's majority, in the name of a fair trial, insisted on virtually unfettered discretion for trial judges. In a series of cases beginning shortly before the Chrétien government came to power, the Court invalidated restrictions on judicial discretion. Parliament had limited the ability of defence counsel to explore a complainant's sexual activity with third parties, but in *Seaboyer*[7] the Court struck down that limit. *O'Connor*[8] similarly nullified legislation restricting access to a complainant's therapeutic records, and *Carosella*[9] prevented sexual assault centres from destroying those records. Judicial discretion triumphed even over common law rules disallowing drunkenness as a defence in cases of sexual assault; in *Daviault*,[10] the Court insisted that extreme drunkenness could get an otherwise guilty party off the hook. In the majority's view, judicial discretion, not categorical rules, should determine whether to admit the kind of evidence or defences at stake in these cases.

The government resisted these rulings with various degrees of effectiveness. Since the drunkenness defence in *Daviault* was a court-created common law rule, the government could simply override it with new legislation—and that is what it did.[11] It was more difficult to reverse the constitutionally based decisions about a complainant's sexual conduct and therapeutic records in *Seaboyer* and *O'Connor*. Using the section 33 notwithstanding clause to reinstate the invalidated legislation was, for reasons explored below, not an attractive option for the Chrétien government. The government thus sought less dramatic ways of resisting the full impact of the Court's rulings. With respect to *O'Connor*, for example, it exploited a disagreement among the judges. A dissenting minority, led by Justice L'Heureux-Dubé, had suggested stricter rules for the disclosure of therapeutic records than the majority was prepared to accept.[12] The government enacted new legislation mimicking this minority opinion. Not surprisingly, the new law was also challenged, and some lower courts, finding it incompatible with the judgment of the *O'Connor* majority, struck it down.[13] In *Mills*,[14] however, a somewhat differently constituted Supreme Court[15] upheld the legislative implementation of the *O'Connor* dissent.

The sexual assault cases reflected the entanglement of women's issues with the law-and-order dimension of the contemporary policy agenda. The same two themes—with federal-provincial tensions added to the mix—were involved in the *Firearms Reference*.[16] Enacted partly in response to Marc Lepine's tragic 1989 massacre of 14 women in Montreal, the Firearms Act extended gun registration to hunting rifles and shotguns. The law was unpopular in the West, the North, and rural areas in other parts of Canada. Several Western provinces indicated that they would not enforce the law,[17] and Alberta referred the question of its constitutionality to its Court of Appeal. In a split decision, that Court upheld the law.[18] Alberta, with the support of five other provinces and both territories, appealed to the Supreme Court, which also upheld the law. The Court's unanimous, unsigned, and unusually short opinion signalled the judges' acute awareness of the level of controversy involved. In marked contrast to their similarly unanimous and unsigned (but much longer) opinion in the *Secession Reference*, the judges took a highly technical and legalistic approach to the gun-control issue, eschewing all broad questions of policy wisdom and effectiveness in favour of narrow jurisdictional analysis. It was not for them, they insisted, to pronounce on the wisdom of Ottawa's initiative; they were concerned only with whether Ottawa had the federal jurisdiction to enact the law.[19]

Law and order was also at issue in the highly controversial 1996 *Feeney* case.[20] As in the sexual assault cases, the Court in *Feeney* was very solicitous of the rights of the accused. Police officers, on the trail of a murder suspect, had pushed open an unlocked door to discover the sleeping suspect covered in the victim's blood. The Court insisted on excluding the evidence because the police had not acquired a judicial warrant before entering the building.[21] The *Feeney* ruling triggered public outrage, and the federal government intervened with new legislation that more or less codified the court's judgment.[22]

Aboriginal communities have posed some of the most vexing policy issues in recent years, and again the courts have been centrally involved. As Peter McCormick has written, '[T]he new realities of Aboriginal politics in Canada have the Supreme Court's fingerprints all over them.'[23] Three of the most important decisions during our period were *Delgamuukw*[24] in 1997 and the two *Marshall* decisions of 1999. *Delgamuukw* held, among other things, that oral tradition and testimony was to be given substantial weight in determining the scope and nature of constitutionally protected Aboriginal rights. The first *Marshall* decision relied on an alleged oral understanding to read a right to fish for a 'moderate livelihood' into a 1761 Nova Scotia treaty that did not mention fishing.[25] Moreover, '[a]lthough the immediate case dealt with a Mi'qmaq man catching eels out of season, the decision was couched in more sweeping terms, to such an extent that it was invoked not just for hunting and fishing but for natural resources as well, and not just on the east coast but right across the country.'[26] In the second *Marshall* decision—which arose out of an intervener's request to rehear the case—the Court tried to stem this tide of rising expectations, indicating that the ruling was limited to fish and to the Nova Scotia treaty.[27] Aboriginals across Canada continue to make more sweeping claims based on the earlier *Marshall* decision, however. Meanwhile, the East Coast fishery, to which the decision does apply, was disrupted by violence between natives fishing out of season and non-native fishermen who deplored racially based rights over a scarce resource. The result has been new spending by Ottawa, which 'tried to buy peace by appropriating $160 million to buy up the licences of white fishermen and purchase boats and nets for Indian fishermen in their place.'[28]

Like Aboriginals, gays and lesbians have been very active in the courtroom. At the beginning of our period, the Supreme Court was ambiguously restrained on gay rights issues. In *Mossop* (1993),[29] the Court upheld a federal public-service regulation providing bereavement leave to heterosexual but not to homosexual partners. In *Egan* (1995),[30] the Court unanimously found homosexuals to be a protected minority under section 15 of the Charter, but nevertheless voted 5-4 to uphold a federal law restricting spousal retirement benefits to heterosexual couples. By the end of our period, however, the *Egan* minority had become part of a dominant majority, and the Court clearly reversed course. In *Vriend*,[31] the full Court, over the partial and limited dissent of only one judge, rewrote Alberta's Human Rights Act to include sexual orientation among its list of prohibited grounds of discrimination. In *M. v. H.*,[32] 8 of 9 judges struck down an Ontario law that, by defining 'spouse' in opposite-sex terms, provided various legal protections and family law remedies only to heterosexual couples.

Although *Vriend* and *M. v. H.* concerned provincial laws, they had a substantial impact on federal politics and policy. *M. v. H.* raised widespread fears that the full-scale legalization of same-sex marriage might be in the offing. As a result Parliament quickly passed a resolution stating 'that marriage is and should remain the union of one man and one woman to the exclusion of all others, and that Parliament will take all necessary steps ... to preserve this definition of marriage.'[33] This did not mean that the government was opposed to extending 'spousal' status and benefits to homosexual couples. Far from it. Even before the Supreme Court had ruled in *M. v. H.*, Ottawa had chosen not to appeal *Rosenberg*,[34] a judgment of the Ontario Court of Appeal striking down a provision in the Income Tax Act that defined 'spouse' in opposite-sex terms. Nor did Ottawa intervene on the similar issues in *M. v. H*. In 2000, moreover, the Chrétien government enacted Bill C-23, The Modernization of Benefits and Obligations Act.[35] This act amended 68 federal laws to extend the status of 'common law' couples to homosexual partners. Opponents of same-sex marriage, including many within the Liberal caucus, managed to add a clause to the bill that paralleled the earlier motion defining formal marriage in opposite-sex terms.[36] But since Bill C-23 also erased all but the most symbolic of distinctions between formal marriage and the common-law status, the restriction of formal marriage to heterosexual partners was seen as a hollow victory by many traditionalists. Clearly, C-23 generated substantial controversy, even within the Liberal caucus, and the government thus used the preceding string of court decisions as rhetorical cover for its initiative. Again and again in the parliamentary debates on C-23, the government emphasized that it really had no choice, that the new law was required by the constitution, as read by its official custodians—the courts.[37]

As we have seen, the government did not acquiesce quite as tamely in the Court's sexual assault jurisprudence. Nor did it so easily accept 1999 judgments in *Sharpe v. the Queen*,[38] which struck down a Criminal Code provision making it a crime to possess child pornography.

The government may have declined to appeal *Rosenberg*, but it very quickly appealed *Sharpe*, expressing its vigorous opposition to the ruling, and its conviction that the Supreme Court of Canada would ultimately uphold the law (as, in large part, it did). Like the *Daviault* judgment, *Sharpe* triggered a wave of public outrage, and the government sided with the public against the judgment. However, it did not go nearly as far as recommended by the opposition, which wanted the government to use section 33 of the Charter to override the trial decision and/or to speed up the judicial process by referring the issues directly to the Supreme Court. As we shall see below, the government's response to *Sharpe* is explained at least in part by electoral calculations.

This brief overview of judicial involvement in public life from 1993 to 2000 is by no means exhaustive. The courts were also major players in the politics of family relations,[39] fetal rights,[40] euthanasia,[41] and election spending limits,[42] among many other issues. The foregoing suffices, however, to show just how thoroughly judges are embroiled in many of the most contentious issues on the political agenda. It also highlights the wide variety of choices open to both judges and governments in their interactions with each other. Governments must, among other things, choose whether to invite judicial involvement through the reference mechanism; whether to appeal a 'loss' in the lower courts; whether and how to oppose a decision they dislike, including in some instances whether to employ the section 33 override; and whether to embrace enthusiastically or merely consent to be 'forced' by a decision they like. For their part, courts must make such decisions as whether to undertake policy innovation or duck the substantive policy issues; whether to stick with precedents or abandon them; whether to give victory clearly to one side or split the difference; and whether to retreat from particularly contentious decisions or go ahead with them, knowing they might have to back down in the face of consistent government opposition. Strictly jurisprudential considerations are no better at explaining the varying judicial answers to such questions than the overt rhetoric of politicians is at explaining their choices. In both cases, careful analysis of the surface justification often discloses deeper strategic moves. To more fully illuminate the complex court-government two-step, the chapter now looks more closely at two cases: the *Secession Reference* and *Sharpe* (the child pornography case).

THE SECESSION REFERENCE

In its 1995 secession referendum, Quebec claimed the right to bypass the Canadian constitution and leave Canada unilaterally. Legal separation, the province insisted, did not require a constitutional amendment involving the consent of other Canadian legislatures; a unilateral declaration of independence (UDI) would do. Anti-separatists urged Ottawa to formally challenge this view through a reference to the Supreme Court, but the government initially refused. Opposing calculations lay at the heart of this disagreement. The proposed reference reflected the so-called 'tough love' or 'Plan B' approach to the unity question. Plan B held that law-abiding Quebecers would reject the separatist option if they clearly understood the revolutionary illegality involved, and thus the likelihood that the Rest of Canada (ROC) would not cooperate in the process of disengagement. Proponents of the opposite strategy—known as Plan A—feared a nationalistic backlash to the tough love approach. It was too risky, in this view, to emphasize that separatists could achieve their goals only through the very constitutional order they wished to escape. Prime Minister Chrétien clearly embraced Plan A, insisting that 'the central issue in the months ahead is whether or not the citizens of Quebec want to stay in Canada, and that we should not allow ourselves to be side-tracked into a discussion of how separation might occur.'[43] There would be no reference as part of the referendum campaign.

While the government could refuse to bring a reference directly to the Supreme Court, it could not prevent Plan B enthusiasts from launching proceedings in the lower courts. Both Guy Bertrand, a Quebec City lawyer and former Péquiste, and Stephen Scott, a McGill constitutional lawyer, filed legal challenges to the constitutionality of Quebec's actions. (Bertrand filed in his own name, while Scott did so on behalf of Dr. Roopnarine Singh and others.) Consistent with its Plan A inclinations, the Chrétien government refused to intervene in support of either *Bertrand* or *Singh*. Plan A also inspired promises made by Chrétien late in the campaign to counteract the unexpected rise of the separatist option in the polls. Although Chrétien had initially resisted offering constitutional reforms to Quebec, he now promised Quebec precisely the 'distinct society' recognition he had opposed in the Meech Lake Accord. He similarly promised to restore a Quebec veto over constitutional amendments affecting the province.

As it turned out, Plan A did not work nearly as well as expected. Although the No side won the referendum on 30 October 1995, it did so only by a whisker—50.58 per cent to 49.42 per cent. Shocked, the Chrétien government began to reconsider its options. Plan A was clearly not abandoned, but Plan B was just as clearly brought into play.

On the Plan A side, Chrétien made good on his late-stage campaign promises, passing a parliamentary motion recognizing Quebec as a distinct society and a law making Ottawa's consent to constitutional amendments conditional on the support of the five major regions of the country, including Quebec. On the Plan B side, Ottawa finally embraced the legal route and sought a judicial declaration that UDI was unconstitutional. Having disdained the *Bertrand* and *Singh* cases during the campaign, it now intervened—successfully—to oppose a post-referendum motion by the Quebec government to dismiss both cases.[44] Ottawa was not content, however, to allow the *Bertrand* and *Singh* cases to run their course, especially because Quebec, rejecting the legitimacy of Canadian courts' deciding her fate, refused to participate in a hearing on the merits and would not appeal a loss to the Supreme Court.[45] In order to ensure an early and authoritative legal determination of the UDI issue—precisely what it had been determined to avoid during the referendum campaign—Ottawa now referred the issue to the Supreme Court.

The Chrétien government had clearly reoriented its strategy, and the Supreme Court was central to its plans. Quebecers were to be disabused of any lingering notions about the legality of UDI, and the Supreme Court was to deliver the message. True, because Quebec refused to participate in the proceedings, the Chrétien government appointed a stand-in—known as an *amicus curiae*, or friend of the court—to argue the other side, but it clearly expected the *amicus* to lose.

While the Supreme Court is a regular dance partner for the government, it is not easily led. The Court is a powerful choreographer in its own right, designing moves in light of its own considerations and imperatives. In particular, the Court must constantly take care not to erode its own legitimacy in the overall structure of governmental institutions. In order to be publicly influential, the Court must retain its legitimacy with both of its major audiences: governments and the public at large. In this case, the radical polarization within its governmental audience—i.e., between Quebec and the ROC's other governments—put the Court in a particularly ticklish situation. On the one hand, as a branch of the government of Canada, a branch whose authority depends above all on the legitimacy of the Canadian constitution, the Court could hardly support Quebec's rejection of the relevance of that constitution. As Andrée Lajoie has said, although 'the Court is fond of applying the "living tree" metaphor to the constitution ... it cannot saw off the branch on which it is sitting.'[46] In this sense, the Chrétien government's confidence in support from the Court was not misplaced. On the other hand, keenly aware of the fragility of its authority in Quebec, the Court could not easily countenance the full-scale attack on its legitimacy already undertaken by Quebec, and certain to be intensified by a clear (and expected) defeat of the province in the reference. In David Schneiderman's words, the Court 'was in trouble.'[47] No doubt the institutional imperative to overcome its own troubles overlapped with the natural human desire to find a statesmanlike way out of the troubles of the wider polity.

If the Court was in trouble, 'it managed to save itself.'[48] It did so by finding a way to calm rather than agitate the troubled political waters. This is not the first time the Court has showed itself to be a master of political choreography. In order to fully appreciate the Court's accomplishments in the *Secession Reference*, it is helpful to briefly review the 1981 *Patriation Case*, which confronted an earlier generation of Supreme Court judges with a similar dilemma, and from which the Secession Reference Court learned important strategic lessons.

Like the *Secession Reference*, the *Patriation Case* involved severely polarized governmental positions. On one side, the Trudeau government (in which Jean Chrétien was then Justice Minister) insisted that it had the legal authority to patriate the constitution unilaterally (i.e., without provincial consent). On the other side, the so-called 'gang of eight' provinces maintained that provincial consent was legally required. If the Court sided clearly with Ottawa, the new constitutional dispensation—including the Charter of Rights and Freedoms—would begin its life with a severe legitimacy crisis among provincial governments. The Court's own legitimacy would be similarly under attack for acting as midwife to a bastard constitution, and its ability to enforce that constitution would be diminished. The crisis of legitimacy ultimately experienced by the Charter of Rights in Quebec, the only government that did not in the end consent to the patriation package, might well have been a more general phenomenon. In particular, Quebec might not have been the only province to make regular use of the section 33 override. Siding clearly with the provinces, on the other hand, might well have killed a popular package of constitutional amendments, and deprived the Court of the appealing prospect of Charter jurisprudence. The Court resolved its dilemma by splitting the difference between the two contending positions. Ottawa, it said, had the *legal* right to proceed unilaterally, but if it did so it would be infringing a profoundly important *conventional* rule that required 'substantial provincial consent' for such amendments. By giving important legal resources to both sides, this decision induced a new round of negotiations that ended with all Canadian governments but Quebec agreeing to a revised patriation package.

The strategically *political* character of this judgment is revealed by the incoherence of its jurisprudence.[49] In order to split the difference, the Court could not treat the convention of provincial consent as legally binding. Had it done so, Ottawa would have lost completely. Thus, the Court accepted Ottawa's claim that conventions were *political* entities that could not be enforced by judges. But if convention is not law, and hence not legally enforceable, what business does a court of law have defining it? The answer, of course, is that unless the Court did so, the provinces would have lost completely. In short, the Court's political goal—a complete victory to neither side—could be achieved only through the jurisprudentially suspect tactic of judicially defining what is not *law*.

The incoherence was compounded by the fact that the Court adopted a version of convention—*substantial* provincial consent—suggested by only one of the participating governments (Saskatchewan). The other seven members of the 'gang of eight' insisted that the convention required *unanimous* provincial consent. But how can just one of the relevant political actors determine a convention that, by the Court's own account, emerges out of political *agreement* among relevant actors? Here again, political calculation supplies the most plausible explanation: the Court, obviously anticipating the prospect of some continued provincial resistance (on the part of Quebec, at least), did not want the popular patriation package to fail on that account. As Peter Russell has argued, the *Patriation Case* has all the marks of 'bold statescraft' on the Court's part, a statescraft that comes to light precisely through an appreciation of its 'questionable jurisprudence'.[50]

Questionable jurisprudence is similarly the clue to political calculation in the *Secession Reference*. Here, too, the Court split the difference between the contending positions. As Ottawa had anticipated, the Court emphasized the clear unconstitutionality of a UDI. A legal separation could be accomplished only by way of the amending procedures of the very constitution Quebec wished to escape. Such an amendment would require the consent of Ottawa and provincial governments. Round one to the federal government. But the Court did not stop there. While Ottawa had gotten 'what it wanted', it also got 'much more than it bargained for.'[51] The Court declared a constitutional obligation on the part of the ROC to negotiate separation in good faith after a referendum in which Quebeckers clearly answered yes to a clear question on secession. Round two to Quebec.

But where had the constitutional obligation to negotiate come from? Like the convention of '*substantial* provincial consent' in the *Patriation Case*, the duty to negotiate was a surprising development. It was more surprising, in fact, than substantial consent had been. Substantial consent had been suggested to the Court by at least one of the participants in the *Patriation Case*, while none of the participants in the *Secession Reference* had proposed the duty to negotiate. This duty, said Peter Hogg, was a 'stunningly new' addition to the constitutional law of Canada, one that ran counter to all relevant secession precedents, such as the attempted secession of the southern American states in 1861, of Nova Scotia in 1868, and of Western Australia in 1934.[52] 'If the Supreme Court's new rule had applied to these earlier precedents,' wrote Hogg, 'presumably the Confederacy, Nova Scotia, and Western Australia would have become new nation states.'[53] Instead, despite the support of the local majorities for each of these secession movements, they were successfully defeated by national governments that clearly felt no duty to negotiate. The Court deduced the obligation to negotiate not from any specific constitutional provisions but from the constitution's four underlying principles: democracy, federalism, constitutionalism and the rule of law, and respect for minorities. As José Woehrling points out, however, these principles 'are present today in every democratic, liberal, and federal constitutional system in the world.'[54] Moreover, in Hogg's words, these 'vague principles ... hardly seem sufficient to require a federal government to negotiate the dismemberment of the country that it was elected to protect.'[55] John D. Whyte could also discern no obvious constitutional source for the obligation to negotiate. The Court, he concluded, pulled it 'out of rarefied air'.[56]

In addition, the various components of the duty to negotiate are themselves too vague to be easily considered rules of law. The Court gave no guidance, for example, about what either a clear majority or a clear question would look like. Was 50 per cent plus one a sufficiently clear majority, as Quebec insisted, or was a more substantial majority required, as Ottawa contended? Was Quebec right in arguing that the questions posed in the 1980 and 1995 referenda were perfectly clear, or were the critics right in considering them tendentiously ambiguous? The determination of such questions, the Court said, must be left to the political process. The conditions for the duty to negotiate, in other words, would be neither legally defined nor subject to legal enforcement. In which case, mused Hogg, 'it is not entirely clear' why the duty to negotiate 'is a legal rule' at all.[57] But, of course, this is not the first time we have seen the Court undertaking to define and underline non-law.

As in the *Patriation Case*, this questionable jurisprudence was essential to what most commentators consider the 'bold statescraft' of the *Secession Reference*. The Court understood full well that it 'could not decide entirely in favour of Ottawa ... unless it was ready to provoke Quebeckers into outright secession.'[58] So, following the *Patriation Case* precedent, it sought a way to divide 'the pie in two'.[59] The rather unlawlike duty to negotiate was Quebec's half. As in the earlier case, the Court had, in effect, awarded 'legality to Ottawa and legitimacy to Quebec.'[60] And, once again, the newly apportioned legal resources helped, at least for a time, to calm the political waters. Quebec, which had been poised to reject the judgment—indeed, to use it to whip up secessionist sentiment in the province—now embraced the decision as underlining its own long-term position that the ROC would indeed come to the table after a successful referendum on separation.[61] On the other hand, Ottawa took comfort in the fact that the duty to negotiate depended on a clear answer to a clear question, concepts it claimed a role in clarifying. The decision left plenty to argue about, but it contained attractive legal resources for the various players, who rushed to claim them.[62] The Court's own legitimacy was no longer at stake, and, for a time at least, the extreme claims leading up to the decision were moderated. As Robert Young has said, the judgment 'tossed the extremists out of court, and tilted the political playing field on both sides toward moderation and civility rather than polarization.'[63]

In sum, while the Chrétien government had tried to lead the dance in bringing a reference case to the Supreme Court, it should have known from past experience that the Court would be a stubborn partner that would impose steps and directions of its own.

THE CHILD PORNOGRAPHY LITIGATION

Whereas the *Secession Reference* provides a good example of the strategic interaction of courts and governments in the arena of intergovernmental relations, the child pornography litigation shows how the courts and the Charter figure in the legislative and electoral arenas of party politics.

The public outrage sparked by the January 1999 trial decision in *Sharpe*,[64] a British Columbia case, led the Reform party to introduce the following motion in the House of Commons on February 2:

> That the government should take legislative measures to reinstate the law that was struck down by a recent decision of the Court of British Columbia regarding the possession of child pornography, even if that entails invoking section 33 of the Constitution Act, 1982 (the notwithstanding clause).[65]

Roughly 70 members of the Liberal caucus had previously written to the government to similar effect:

> We ask that the government not wait for the appeal of the BC decision to be heard but immediately act in the defence of Canada's children. The undersigned Liberal members of parliament recommend that strong new child pornography legislation be introduced as soon as the House resumes. We ask also that we consider the use of the notwithstanding clause or other equivalent effective measures to send a clear message that the charter of rights will never again be used to defend the sexual abuse of Canada's children.[66]

Although both statements contemplate the possibility of using section 33 of the Charter to override the court, neither insists on the override, and they are ambiguous about just when it might be brought into play. These issues were central in the debate on the Reform party motion, with the Liberals rejecting pressure to employ the override in the near term.

Not that the Liberals were any less vociferous in their criticism of the child pornography decision. John Bryden, Liberal member for Wentworth-Burlington, called it an 'abominable decision',[67] while Tom Wappel, member for Scarborough Southwest, referred to it as 'boneheaded'[68] and based on 'rubbish thinking'.[69] Most Liberals were not this extreme in their rhetoric, but all agreed with Reg Alcock, member for Winnipeg South, that the BC court had 'ruled in error and ... that ruling should be overturned as quickly as possible.'[70]

The Liberals, however, wanted the ruling overturned by higher courts of appeal, not by the section 33 override. The normal legal process should be allowed to run its course, they argued, not only because this gave proper respect to the judicial process, but also because an ongoing 'dialogue' between the courts and the legislature might improve the law. The trial judge was certainly wrong, but that did not mean that the legislation was perfect. As Tom Wappel put it, 'The judge has rendered a decision based on rubbish thinking, but that does not render this law inviolate.'[71] Legislators, said Ethel Blondin-Andrew, Secretary of State for Children and Youth, 'have a duty to be as smart and as skillful as we can in crafting laws to protect our children. We must use every resource available to us to protect the human rights of children. One of those resources, a very valuable resource, is the appeal court.' 'With an appeal court ruling on this important issue we will all be better placed to craft better laws to protect our children.'[72] Liberal member Paul deVillers (Simcoe North) argued that 'the courts can help us by determining how [the goal of protecting children] can be achieved with the least disruption to other fundamental freedoms. There must be a dialogue between Parliament and the courts.'[73] Peter Adams, parliamentary secretary to the leader of the government in the House of Commons, approvingly paraphrased a constituent who suggested that 'the child pornography law is flawed and it should be left to the Supreme Court to comment on it and then for parliament to amend it in the light of intelligent, informed, judicial discussion.'[74] The Minister of Justice, Anne McLellan, did not think the law was flawed—she was confident that it would pass constitutional muster as it stood—but conceded that 'in the unlikely event that the Supreme Court were to make a finding with which the government did not agree, we would then explore the possibility of legislative reform.'[75]

In response, the Reform party asked why continuing dialogue through the appeal process was incompatible with the immediate use of section 33. Reformer Jim Abbott insisted that this was not 'an either/or' situation: 'The appeal can proceed. We can do both, and that is what Canadians want.'[76] The appeal process should continue and new legislation (if necessary) should be enacted. In the meantime, however, the trial judge's invalidation of the existing law threatened children, and the override was needed to protect them until the legal niceties could be sorted out. Indeed, Reformers pointed out that a section 33 override could be enacted for less than the five-year maximum set out in the Charter. Parliament could enact the clause for whatever shorter period it thought was needed to conclude the appeal process and legislative revisions.

The Liberals' response to this position was twofold. First, they argued that the override was inappropriate at this early stage because it would unnecessarily concede the unconstitutionality of the law. As Paul deVillers put it, '[I]nvoking section 33 of the Charter implies that we think that the action taken is not reasonable in a free and democratic society. Is this really what we wish to do?'[77] Attorney General John Maloney did not think so. 'To invoke the notwithstanding clause at this time', he said, 'would weaken our case, a case where we feel we are constitutionally strong.'[78] If the government truly believed that the law was constitutional, it should intervene strongly in favour of that position in the appeal process, as it had in fact immediately done. Only if the Supreme Court, at the end of the appeal process, also found the law unconstitutional could section 33 be considered.

Second, the Liberals insisted that the trial judge's ruling did not place children at risk. Justice Shaw sat on the Supreme Court of British Columbia, which despite its name is not the highest court in the province (the Court of Appeal is); the Supreme Court is an intermediate-level court (known as Queen's Bench in some provinces). The decision of a judge of this court binds neither other judges of the same court nor judges in other provinces, to say nothing of higher-level courts. In this case, Justice Shaw's decision bound only the lower 'provincial courts', and only in British Columbia. Everywhere else it was business as usual. And even in the BC provincial courts, cases were being temporarily adjourned, not dismissed, pending the outcome of the appeal process.

Reformers offered rebuttals for both of these Liberal claims. They strongly denied that employing section 33 amounted to an admission of unconstitutionality. The section was not, as the Liberals maintained, a 'nuclear bomb' to be used only to resurrect an obviously unconstitutional law—once a determination of unconstitutionality had been made by the Charter's ultimate oracle, the Supreme Court—but a perfectly legitimate way for legislatures to disagree with courts about the proper meaning of the constitution. In this view, courts did not have a monopoly on constitutional interpretation; legislators had every right to come to their own conclusions about the meaning of the Charter and to express their disagreements with judges by means of the section 33 override.

As for the contention that Justice Shaw's decision led only to adjournments in provincial-court cases in British Columbia, Reformers replied that this was bad enough, that it amounted to an undesirable weakening of law enforcement. Justice delayed, in effect, is justice denied. They also pointed out that those accused under the law would now inevitably elect trial by the crippled provincial courts. Finally, Reformers worried about the persuasive effect Justice Shaw's reasoning might have on other courts in other jurisdictions if Parliament did not send the clear signal of a section 33 override.

Into this debate about whether to invoke the notwithstanding clause or let the legal process run its normal course, Peter MacKay, a prominent Progressive Conservative member, injected an intermediate position. Agreeing with Reform that the normal appeal process was too slow, he nevertheless worried about section 33. Why not refer the question immediately to the Supreme Court, he asked. This would speed things up without involving the 'nuclear bomb' of section 33.[79] Reformer Gary Lunn embraced this suggestion, but, again, did not find it to be incompatible with the override: 'We should expedite [the legal process] in every way we can', including a reference case, 'but we must invoke the notwithstanding clause today, immediately, to protect the children of British Columbia.'[80] The Liberals, however, did not embrace the reference alternative, preferring to stick with the normal route of appeal, though they constantly emphasized their early intervention in that process and their pressure for expedited hearings.

Reports of the demise of Parliament notwithstanding, no one who reads this debate can fail to be impressed by its subtlety and sophistication. There is real point and counterpoint here, with speakers producing serious and cogent responses to the arguments of their opponents. One often has the sense that the debaters are learning from each other and coming to a richer understanding of the issues. Equally impressive, however, is the obvious partisan constraint on the debate. With some minor exceptions, all members of each party stuck to fairly consistent party lines. The Liberals in particular sang in unison from the same hymn book. It is difficult, however, to believe that all of the many Liberals who wrote to their government demanding quick action, including perhaps the use of the notwithstanding clause, wanted to await the end of the normal appeal process before invoking that clause. Nor can one easily believe that none of them was attracted by the Conservatives' suggestion of a reference case. In fact, when the debate was over, four Liberals broke ranks and voted in favour of the Reform motion;[81] in the absence of party discipline many more would surely have done the same. But party discipline had clearly been imposed, and for strategic reasons not apparent on the surface of the debate.

To appreciate the partisan calculations that likely informed the Chrétien government's position in this debate, one needs only fast-forward to the 2000 election. Prime Minister Chrétien repeatedly characterized the election campaign as a battle about values, and he made it clear that Liberal values were embodied in the Charter of Rights. On 28 October 2000, for example, in a speech to the 50th Congress of Liberal International, Chrétien explained that 'we are very proud of some of the values that my party, the Liberal Party of Canada, has put forward', and provided a list of laws and policies exemplifying those values. Prominent in that list was the Charter of Rights. The Charter, said Chrétien,

> is considered around the world as one of the most modern and encompassing the values that need to be protected in society and we have to keep working on that because we never know when there will not be a force who will come and appeal to the dark side that exists in human beings.[82]

In other words, the values of the Liberal party, as represented by the Charter, were essential to keeping the 'dark side' of human nature in check. 'Liberals', Chrétien continued, 'always appeal to the good side in people, to generosity, to the value of sharing, to understanding, to trust....'[83]

Two days later, in Barrie, Ontario, Chrétien again praised the Charter and accused the Canadian Alliance (the successor to the now defunct Reform party) of wanting to destroy it. His evidence? The Alliance's support for the section 33 override. The notwithstanding clause, said Chrétien, is 'a nice way to destroy the Charter of Rights.'[84] In this context, Chrétien again emphasized that he, as a Liberal, never appealed 'to the dark side of people'.[85] To advocate the use of section 33, in short, was to be an enemy of the Charter and thus a representative of 'the dark side.' Chrétien never quite closed the logical circle by explicitly accusing the Alliance of being on the 'dark side'. Indeed, when asked whether this was his meaning, he retreated into calculated ambiguity: 'I don't say that. It's for you to pass judgment.'[86] But Chrétien himself did not have to connect the dots for the picture he was drawing to be perfectly clear: in the election's battle of values, the Alliance represented the forces of darkness because of its support for the section 33 override. In his speech to the Liberal International, Chrétien had used the Second World War as his prime example of the battle between Liberalism and the 'dark side'.[87] Again, he never drew an explicit connection between fascism and the Alliance, but the implication was too obvious for others to miss. When Stockwell Day tried to deny that his party was on 'the dark side', a *Toronto Star* columnist asked his readers to 'Imagine Heinrich Himmler ... living in Canada. How do you think he'll vote?'[88]

The 'dark side' component of Chrétien's election strategy provides a plausible explanation for his government's reluctance to use section 33 to override the trial court in the child pornography case. Certainly it would have been impossible to use the Alliance's support for section 33 as evidence of its dark agenda to destroy the Charter if the Liberals themselves had invoked the override. The Liberals had long portrayed the Alliance's predecessor, the Reform party, as an extremist, illiberal, and racist party. This had been a successful rhetorical move for the Liberals in the past, especially in seat-rich Ontario, and its extension into the 2000 election was entirely predictable. There is every reason to think, therefore, that the Liberals would be careful to husband—indeed, to increase—any rhetorical resources they had on this front. While particular Charter decisions are sometimes quite unpopular—*Daviault*, *Feeney*, and the lower-court judgments in *Sharpe* being examples—the Charter in the abstract is highly popular.[89] Being able to present oneself as the party of the Charter, and one's main opposition as its enemy, is thus a significant rhetorical resource. The Liberals could employ this strategy, of course, only if they themselves never invoked the override.

Never mind that section 33—allegedly so hostile to the Charter—is itself part of the Charter. Or that Jean Chrétien himself was central to the negotiations that led to this section. Or even that Chrétien was solely responsible for the fact that the federal government has the right to invoke section 33—something the provinces that wanted the section never demanded. Or that, when the partisan shoe was on the other foot, Chrétien had disagreed with Brian Mulroney's famous statement that the override made the Charter 'not worth the paper it's written on'.[90] The opportunity to vilify the Alliance's advocacy of the notwithstanding clause was an opportunity too valuable to be foregone. No matter how unpopular the child pornography decision was, the Chrétien government was not about to squander its long-term rhetorical advantage by invoking the override.

The same electoral calculations likely explain the government's refusal to consider Peter Mackay's suggestion of a reference case to speed things up in the child pornography litigation. As the *Secession Reference* shows, speeding up the legal process can indeed be a cogent justification for referring a case directly to the Supreme Court. But that case also highlighted the political calculations underlying the decision whether or not to refer. In the child pornography case, an immediate reference to the Supreme Court would increase the chance of a decision prior to the next election, while allowing the normal appeal process to drag on would diminish that prospect. A pre-election decision was by far the riskier course for the Liberals. If the Supreme Court upheld the existing law, all would be well, and the Liberals could claim vindication for their legal strategy. If the Supreme Court struck the law down, however, the Liberals would face a dilemma. The pressure to use the override would be renewed, presumably even by some of the Liberal backbenchers who had originally pressured their government to act quickly. John Bryden, for example, had expressed his belief 'that every member in the House would support invoking the notwithstanding clause if by the rarest of chance [*sic*] the appeal court upheld this abominable decision.'[91] Similarly, Tom Wappel argued that if the Supreme Court upheld the lower court, 'no matter how fast I hurried I would probably still not be the first person to call for the invocation of section 33 of the Constitution.'[92] If it wished to maintain its electoral resource, however, the government could no more use section 33 after a Supreme Court decision than it could earlier. Indeed, having argued that the use of section 33 conceded unconstitutionality—hence, presumably, hostility to the Charter—it would be even less likely to use it. In this respect, it is noteworthy that neither the Justice Minister nor any other member of cabinet reiterated the pro-override arguments of backbenchers Bryden and Wappel. They preferred to muse about legislative amendments in the case of a Supreme Court invalidation of the law. Nevertheless, the government might have to quell a section 33 movement, and doing so in the run up to an election—especially if this was likely to reveal division within the Liberal ranks—would not have seemed an inviting prospect. Far better to try to avoid an early Supreme Court decision and hope that the election would be held first. True, the government had to call for expedited hearings in the lower courts in order to satisfy the call for quick and decisive action, but there was every reason to avoid too much expediting, and thus to reject a reference case.

 Calculations of partisan electoral advantage were not the only political reasons for the government to steer clear of the section 33 override. As Ted Morton has pointed out, the government benefits in another way from the widespread perception that the courts have a monopoly on constitutional interpretation and that legislative backtalk, in the form of the notwithstanding clause, is illegitimate.[93] In particular, this perception allows governments to shield themselves from blame for controversial policies by claiming that the constitution, as interpreted by the courts, requires those policies. We have seen that this is how the Chrétien government defended the legislative extension of common-law status to same-sex couples. The claim that court decisions require legislative innovation, of course, would dissolve if section 33 were considered a legitimate way for legislatures to disagree with courts.

Conserving this rhetorical resource thus depends on portraying section 33 as an illegitimate 'nuclear bomb.'

In the case of the *Secession Reference*, the Supreme Court met the lead of the Chrétien government with its own choreography. There is reason to think that the Court's response to *Sharpe* was similarly calculated. Strategic considerations likely affected the very timing of the decision's release. The Court heard *Sharpe* in January 2000 and decided it a full year later, which is two to three times the normal gestation period. It has plausibly been speculated that the Court took so long in order to avoid releasing its judgment before or during the 2000 election, when the decision, whatever it was, would have been dragged into the partisan fray.[94] When the judgment finally came down in late January 2001, it was clear that the Supreme Court had taken careful note of the widespread support for the law. Given that all federal parties and all of the country's governments were united in their support of the law, it would have taken a very bold Supreme Court to uphold the lower courts' invalidation of it. Instead, three of the Supreme Court's judges voted to uphold the law in its entirety and the other six claimed to do so in most respects. Emphasizing that the law was basically sound, the six-judge majority established what they considered two minor exceptions, both covering self-produced material created exclusively for personal and private use. The first exempted expressive material such as personal journals, while the second exempted the visual self-recording of consensual sexual activity, as long as the activity was otherwise lawful (e.g., the sexual encounters of a married teen-age couple). As some commentators pointed out, rewriting the law by adding the two exceptions was still an act of judicial activism, not unlike the activism seen in *Vriend*. For the most part, however, this was hardly noticed in the collective sigh of relief that followed the Court's careful endorsement of the law's essence. The Court had gotten itself off the hook, and, given the majority's rewriting of the law, it had done so without completely caving in to public pressure. As Andrew Coyne observed, 'so dazzled was the audience' by the Court's 'political footwork' that the judgment 'left both sides of the debate convinced they had won, trimming federal child pornography legislation of its worst excesses even as the headlines read "High court upholds child porn ban".' Convinced that a judgment purporting to protect free speech would actually harm it in the long run, Coyne concluded that '[a]s in the secession reference, political legitimacy has once again been bought at the expense of logical coherence.'[95]

CONCLUSION

The judiciary has been the Chrétien government's regular dance partner throughout its first two mandates. Sometimes, as in the issue of same-sex relationships, the government has drawn the judges into a close embrace, using the judgment in *M. v. H.* to deflect criticism of policy innovations it supported. At other times, as in *Daviault* (the drunkenness-defence case), it pushed its judicial partner away, rejecting and reversing a courtroom policy innovation. Sometimes, as in the *Secession Reference*, the government invited the Supreme Court onto the dance floor, but got a less compliant partner than it bargained for. At other times, as in *Sharpe* (child pornography) or *O'Connor* (sexual assault trials), judges forced a reluctant governmental partner onto the floor, and, after some pushing and jostling, a compromise of sorts ensued. In many cases, judicial intervention changed government policy, but sometimes, as in *Thibaudeau*, the government ended up abandoning a policy it had successfully defended in court. Always, the partners in this *pas de deux* acted strategically, playing not only to each other, but also to an audience composed of legislatures, parties, and public opinion.

In the November 2000 elections, the Chrétien government won a third straight majority in the House of Commons. As its third mandate began, the Supreme Court was again making headlines. Soon after the election, for example, the Supreme Court decided *Little Sisters*,[96] upholding customs legislation that censored obscenity at the border, while criticizing the high-handed and discriminatory manner in which customs officials applied this legislation to homosexual materials. In mid-January 2001, the Court upheld Robert Latimer's conviction for killing his disabled daughter, thus placing the difficult issue of euthanasia back onto the political agenda.[97] A week later, the Court delivered its long delayed judgment in *Sharpe*. Politics is unpredictable, and so it is difficult to foresee the precise controversies that will bring the federal government and the courts onto the dance floor during Chrétien's third mandate. As *Sharpe* demonstrates, an unexpected trial court decision can quickly convulse the body politic. And as the *Secession Reference* shows, whether or not to launch a reference case is a decision subject to changing strategic calculations. However, no one can gainsay the increasing tendency of the courts to become embroiled in many of our most contentious public issues, or for courts and governments to treat each other strategically. The delicate dance will continue.

NOTES

The author wishes to thank the Donner Canadian Foundation for its financial support and Dennis Baker for his valuable research assistance.

1. Peter Russell, 'The Supreme Court and Federal-Provincial Relations: The Political Use of Legal Resources', *Canadian Public Policy* 11, 2 (June 1985): 161-70.
2. Tom Flanagan, 'Canada's Three Constitutions: Protecting, Overturning and Reversing the Status Quo', in Patrick James, Donald E. Abelson, and Michael Lusztig, eds, *The Myth of the Sacred: The Charter, the Courts and the Politics of the Constitution in Canada* (Montreal: McGill-Queen's University Press, forthcoming).
3. *Reference re: Secession of Quebec* [1998] 2 S.C.R. 217.
4. David Schneiderman, 'Introduction', in David Schneiderman, ed., *The Quebec Decision: Perspectives on the Supreme Court Ruling on Secession* (Toronto: James Lorimer & Company Ltd., 1999), 1-13. The decision was written by the Court to be readable by an audience beyond legal elites (see Sean Fine, 'Behind the Scenes as History Was Made', *The Globe and Mail* [Toronto], 6 Feb. 1999, 4).
5. Peter McCormick, *Supreme at Last: The Evolution of the Supreme Court of Canada* (Toronto: James Lorimer and Company Ltd., 2000), 162.
6. *Thibaudeau v. Canada* [1995] 2 S.C.R. 627.
7. *R. v. Seaboyer* [1991] 2 S.C.R. 577.
8. *R. v. O'Connor* [1995] 4 S.C.R. 411.
9. *R. v. Carosella* [1997] 1 S.C.R. 80.
10. *R. v. Daviault* [1994] 3 S.C.R. 63.
11. Canada, An Act to Amend the Criminal Code (Self-Intoxication) (Bill C-72, 1995). Granted Royal Assent on 13 July 1995.
12. *O'Connor* [1995] 4 S.C.R. 411, at 444-515.
13. *R. v. Mills* [1997] 56 Alta. L.R. (3d) 277, 301 (QB) (Belzil J.).
14. *R. v. Mills* [1999] 3 S.C.R. 668 (SCC).
15. On the central issue of the production of records in the possession of third parties, the *O'Connor* majority consisted of Lamer, Sopinka, Cory, Iacobucci, and Major. The minority in *O'Connor*, who preferred a higher standard for production, consisted of L'Heureux-Dubé, McLachlin, La

Forest, and Gonthier. By the time of *Mills*, the court had added Binnie and Bastarache to replace Sopinka and Cory. The two new members joined with the remaining *O'Connor* dissenters (L'Heureux-Dubé, McLachlin, and Gonthier) to form the *Mills* majority. Both Iacobucci and Major switched from the *O'Connor* majority to the *Mills* majority, presumably as a result of their explicit reliance on the 'dialogue' theory of court-government interaction. Chief Justice Lamer is the only member of the *O'Connor* majority to dissent in *Mills*.

16 *Reference re: Firearms Act (Can.)* [2000] 1 S.C.R. 783.
17 Don Thomas, 'Provinces Urged to Enforce Law on Gun Control', *The Edmonton Journal*, 16 June 2000, B9. See also Leslie A. Pal, 'Gun Control in the United States and Canada' (paper presented to the annual meeting of the Canadian Political Science Association, 1999), 20-7.
18 (1998) 65 Alta. L.R. (3d) 1.
19 *Reference re: Firearms*, 791.
20 *R. v. Feeney* [1997] 2 S.C.R. 13.
21 Ibid., 70-1.
22 Canada, An Act to amend the Criminal Code and the Interpretation Act (powers to arrest and enter dwellings) (Bill C-16, 1997). Granted Royal Assent on 18 December 1997.
23 McCormick, *Supreme at Last*, 160.
24 *Delgamuukw v. British Columbia* [1997] 3 S.C.R. 1010.
25 *R. v. Marshall* [1999] 3 S.C.R. 456 (Marshall no. 1).
26 McCormick, *Supreme at Last*, 160.
27 *R. v. Marshall* [1999] 3 S.C.R. 533 (Marshall no. 2).
28 Tom Flanagan, 'Are Aboriginals Canadian?', *Cité Libre* 28, 4 (Fall 2000): 60-6.
29 *Canada (Attorney General) v. Mossop* [1993] 1 S.C.R. 544.
30 *Egan v. Canada* [1995] 2 S.C.R. 513.
31 *Vriend v. Alberta* [1998] 1 S.C.R. 493.
32 *M. v. H.* [1999] 2 S.C.R. 3.
33 Canada, House of Commons, Debates, vol. 135, no. 240 (8 June 1999), 16068-9.
34 *Rosenberg v. Canada (Attorney General)* 158 D.L.R. (4th) 664.
35 Canada, An Act to modernize the Statutes of Canada in relation to benefits and obligations (Bill C-23, 2000). Granted Royal Assent on 29 June 2000.
36 Canada, The Standing Committee on Justice and Human Rights, Second Report, 23 Mar. 2000.
37 Canada, House of Commons, Debates, vol. 136, no. 49 (15 Feb. 2000); vol. 136, no. 53 (21 Feb. 2000); vol. 136, no. 82 (10 Apr. 2000).
38 *R. v. Sharpe* (1999) 22 C.R. (5th) 129; [1999] BCCA 416 (CA).
39 See *Bracklow v. Bracklow* [1999] 1 S.C.R. 420.

40 See *Winnipeg Child and Family Services (Northwest Area) v. G. (D.F.)* [1997] 3 S.C.R. 925 and *Dobson (Litigation Guardian of) v. Dobson* [1999] 2 S.C.R. 753.
41 See *Rodriguez v. British Columbia (Attorney General)* [1993] 3 S.C.R. 519.
42 See *Libman v. Quebec* [1997] 3 S.C.R. 569 and *Attorney General of Canada v. Harper* [11/10/00] (SCC).
43 Warren J. Newman, *The Quebec Secession Reference: The Rule of Law and the Position of the Attorney General of Canada* (Toronto: York University Press, 1999), 8.
44 Ibid., 10-22.
45 Ibid., 27-31.
46 Andrée Lajoie, 'The Double and Inextricable Role of the Supreme Court of Canada', *Canada Watch* 7, 1–2 (Jan.-Feb., 1999), 14.
47 Schneiderman, 'Introduction', 1.
48 Ibid.
49 Rainer Knopff, 'Legal Theory and the Patriation Debate', *Queen's Law Journal* 7: 1 (1981); Peter Russell, 'Bold Statescraft, Questionable Jurisprudence', in Keith Banting and Richard Simeon, eds, *And No One Cheered: Federalism, Democracy and the Constitution Act* (Toronto: Methuen, 1983), 210–38.
50 Russell, 'Bold Statescraft', 234.
51 Schneiderman, 'Introduction', 8.
52 Peter Hogg, 'The Duty to Negotiate', *Canada Watch* 7, 1–2 (Jan.-Feb. 1999): 33-5.
53 Ibid., 34.
54 José Woehrling, 'Unexpected Consequences of Constitutional First Principles', *Canada Watch* 7, 1–2 (Jan.-Feb. 1999): 18-19.
55 Hogg, 'The Duty to Negotiate', 34.
56 John D. Whyte, 'The Secession Reference and Constitutional Paradox', in Schneiderman, *The Quebec Decision*, 130-6.
57 Hogg, 'The Duty to Negotiate', 35.
58 Lajoie, 'The Double and Inextricable', 14.
59 Ibid., 15.
60 Ibid., 15.
61 Newman, *Quebec Secession Reference*, 77, note 7. See 'Ruling Legitimized Sovereignty Drive, PQ Leaders Say', *The Globe and Mail* [Toronto], 21 Aug. 1998, A7.
62 Chris Cobb, 'Native Groups Pleased with Court Ruling: Quebec Cree Leader Says Judgment Confirms Aboriginals' Equal Status', *The Ottawa Citizen,* 21 Aug. 1998, C5.
63 Robert Young, 'A Most Politic Judgment', in Schneiderman, ed., *The Quebec Decision*, 107-12. See also Monahan, 'The Public Policy Role of the Supreme Court of Canada', *National Journal of Constitutional Law* 11 (Nov. 1999): 67.

64 *R. v. Sharpe* (1999) 22 C.R. (5th) 129.
65 Canada, House of Commons, Debates, vol. 135, no. 172 (2 Feb 1999), 11246.
66 Ibid., 11263.
67 Ibid., 11254.
68 Ibid., 11306.
69 Ibid., 11303.
70 Ibid., 11295.
71 Ibid., 11303.
72 Ibid., 11264.
73 Ibid., 11273.
74 Ibid., 11278.
75 Ibid., 11267.
76 Ibid., 11272.
77 Ibid., 11273.
78 Canada, House of Commons, Debates, vol. 136, no. 9 (22 Oct. 99), 553.
79 Canada, House of Commons, Debates, vol. 135, no. 172 (2 Feb. 1999), 11257.
80 Ibid., 11262.
81 Ibid., 11312-13.
82 'What Chrétien Said', *The Globe and Mail* [Toronto], 31 Oct. 2000, A4.
83 Ibid.
84 Thomas Walkom, 'Chrétien's Charter Arguments Are Curious', *The Toronto Star*, 2 Nov. 2000, A6.
85 Ibid.
86 William Walker, 'PM Accuses Day of Threat to Rights', *The Toronto Star*, 31 Oct. 2000, A1.
87 'What Chrétien Said', A4
88 Joey Slinger, 'Bring Day Your Bigots, Racists, Your Sexist Masses', *The Toronto Star*, 2 Nov. 2000, A2.
89 Joseph F. Fletcher and Paul Howe, 'Public Opinion and the Courts', *Choices* (IRPP) 6: 3 (May 2000).
90 Walkon, 'Chrétien's Charter Arguments', A6.
91 Canada, House of Commons, Debates, vol. 135, no. 172 (2 Feb. 1999), 11254.
92 Ibid., 11306.
93 Ted Morton, 'Chrétien and the Charter', *The National Post*, 6 Nov. 2000, A16.
94 'Analysts Speculate Judges May Be Holding Back Pornography Ruling for Political Reasons', *The National Post*, 15 Nov. 2000, A11.
95 Andrew Coyne, 'Free Speech and the Kiddie Porn Case', *The National Post*, 5 Feb. 2001, A15.
96 *Little Sisters Book and Art Emporium v. Canada (Minister of Justice)* 2000 SCC 69.
97 *R. v. Latimer* 2001 SCC 1.

APPENDIX A

CANADIAN POLITICAL FACTS AND TRENDS

Canadian Political Facts and Trends presents a snapshot of key political developments between January 2000 and March 2001, particularly those events that are related to chapters in this year's edition. It was compiled and written by Rachel Laforest.

2000

6 January: New CRTC regulations for the Canadian Broadcasting Corporation will lead to the elimination of the showing of blockbuster films, the reduction of professional sports coverage, and the expansion of regional content and children's and arts programming.

13 January: The Supreme Court of Canada concludes that the Prince Edward Island government had violated section 23 of the Charter of Rights and Freedoms when it refused to build a French language school in the city of Summerside.

18 January: Industry Minister John Manley announces that the federal government is committed to negotiate individual aid packages for the six National Hockey League clubs based in Canadian cities. The federal government reverses itself three days later.

19 January: An audit report is made public revealing that accounting practices at Human Resources Development Canada (HRDC) are seriously lacking, with projects approved without adequate paper work and money handed out with little follow-up.

25 January: The Supreme Court of Canada rules that provincial regulators can freely communicate confidential investigative information across provincial and national borders.

26 January: The federal government offers $100 million to the Royal Bank of Canada, the Canadian Imperial Bank of Commerce, and the Bank of Nova Scotia in order to keep them as partners in the Canadian Student Loans Program.

27 January: Minister of Health Allan Rock presents his new plan to save Canada's health care system.

The United Alternative holds its convention over the weekend.

30 January: The federal government authorizes the acquisition of Canada Trust by the Toronto-Dominion Bank.

1 February: The merchant mariners win $50 million in federal compensation, ending a 55-year battle for recognition.

4 February: Provincial premiers rally to request a complete restoration of social and health transfers to their 1994 level.

11 February: Justice Minister Anne McLellan introduces an omnibus Bill (The Modernization of Benefits and Obligations Act) that will amend 68 federal statutes to extend benefits and obligations to same-sex couples on the same basis as common-law, opposite-sex couples.

17 February: Transport Minister David Collenette proposes a new policy framework for restructuring airline legislation, granting Air Canada two years with the market to itself under government supervision. The new legislation restores old powers to the Canadian Transportation Agency.

21 February: HRDC releases lists of grants and contributions.

28 February: The federal budget is tabled.

15 March: The House of Commons passes Bill C-20, known as the Clarity bill.

The Ontario court dismisses Conrad Black's claim against the Prime Minister.

27 March: The Reform party officially becomes the Canadian Reform Conservative Alliance, or Canadian Alliance for short, and takes over as the official Opposition.

2001

13 June: Finance Minister Paul Martin introduces new legislation for financial services.

29 June: The Clarity Act, which sets rules for the next Quebec referendum by requiring a clear question and a clear majority of Yes votes before secession negotiations can begin, becomes law.

29 June: Prime Minister Jean Chrétien announces the creation of a $700-million Atlantic investment fund to support universities, colleges, research labs, and high-tech firms in the region.

5 September: An internal audit states that Human Resources Development Canada (HRDC) is improving the way it handles grants programs.

5 September: International Co-operation Minister Maria Minna unveils a five-year plan to focus Canadian aid on health, education, and children.

11 September: The federal government and the provinces agree on a formula for health care funding that gives the provinces an additional $23.4 billion for health and social programs over the next five years to support agreements by first ministers on Health Renewal and Early Childhood Development.

11 September: Former Ontario premier Bob Rae agrees to act as mediator between Mi'kmaq fishermen from the Burnt Church First Nation and the Department of Fisheries and Oceans (DFO) over control of the lobster fishery in Miramichi Bay, New Brunswick.

12 September: Federal fisheries officers seize four native fishing boats off New Brunswick's Burnt Church reserve and arrest 14 people, including the band's chief.

12 September: Canada follows the lead of the European Union by lifting political sanctions against Austria on the grounds that it no longer fears Vienna would adopt policies that infringe on human rights.

12 September: Justice Minister Anne McLellan announces increased funding for legal aid.

19 September: Members of the Burnt Church band begin working with federal fisheries officers, following a deal brokered by mediator Bob Rae.

20 September: Quebec Superior Court rules that Canada's major tobacco companies must meet a December 23 deadline to put larger and more graphic warnings on cigarette packages.

21 September: The deal between the Mi'kmaq fishermen and DFO falls apart. The Department gives defiant Mi'kmaq fishermen from the Burnt Church reserve 24 hours to pull their traps out of Miramichi Bay or face arrest.

21 September: The Senate passes into law a generous pension plan for MPs.

28 September: Pierre Elliott Trudeau, former prime minister of Canada, dies.

28 September: The federal government announces it will enhance Employment Insurance benefits for women and seasonal workers.

4 October: The World Trade Organization rules that Canada has until 19 February 2001 to terminate the Auto Pact because the Pact violates several international trade rules.

5 October: Heritage Minister Sheila Copps announces the creation of a new cultural fund that will provide $50 million a year for the production and promotion of feature films.

6 October: Natural Resources Minister Ralph Goodale and Environment Minister David Anderson announce a $500-million plan to combat global warming and eliminate 65 megatonnes of greenhouse gases annually by the year 2012.

6 October: Defence Minister Art Eggleton announces an increase in defence spending of $42 million over the next three years to help pay for the increase in the size of the military reserves and to provide new equipment for reserve units.

11 October: Mr. Justice John Brockenshire of the Ontario Superior Court rules that the federal government is liable for breaching a fiduciary trust with veterans by knowingly withholding interest payments from the veterans' disability pension cheques.

11 October: The federal government limits the capacity of the Employment Insurance Commission to set EI premiums.

13 October: Canadian and American negotiators agree on the Ozone Annex to the Canada-U.S. Air Quality Agreement, which will require a 50 per cent reduction in nitrogen oxide emissions from fossil-fuel power plants in southern Ontario.

17 October: Auditor-General Denis Desautels issues his final report, which includes strong criticisms of HRDC.

17 October: In a cabinet shuffle, Prime Minister Jean Chrétien appoints Brian Tobin as the new industry minister, John Manley takes over as foreign affairs minister, and Ron Duhamel becomes veterans' affairs minister and Secretary of State for Western Diversification and the Francophonie.

18 October: Finance Minister Paul Martin delivers an economic statement.

19 October: Auditor-General Denis Desautels cannot answer questions about his annual report before the House Public Accounts Committee because all the Liberal members of that committee fail to show up to form a quorum.

20 October: Federal Natural Resources Minister Ralph Goodale orders a public review of the effects of oil and gas exploration off the coast of Cape Breton.

22 October: Prime Minister Jean Chrétien calls a federal election for November 27.

23 October: The Court of Queen's Bench in Calgary grants a request to suspend various sections of the Elections Act that would limit third-party spending to $150,000 nationally or $3,000 in any single constituency.

25 October: The Progressive Conservatives release their election platform, which includes a five-year, $56-billion tax-cut plan weighted toward the lower middle class and those who earn money from investments.

1 November: The Liberals launch their party's election platform by stressing investments in the 'information economy', reiterating the party's plans to inject new money into health care, and highlighting their October tax cuts.

7 November: A confidential policy background document of the Canadian Alliance is leaked to the press.

8 November: The five leaders of the main political parties face off in the first of their televised debates.

10 November: The Supreme Court of Canada temporarily rules to limit electoral expenses of interest groups or third parties.

12 November: The Canadian Alliance threatens legal action against the Liberal Party of Canada, claiming its health care ads are false and defamatory.

14 November: Liberal Leader Jean Chrétien admits that his government is partly responsible for the growth of private health-care facilities in Canada.

18 November: Prime Minister Jean Chrétien says his political opponents are beneath contempt for accusing him of improperly lobbying a bank president on behalf of a constituent.

19 November: A Canadian Alliance candidate, Betty Granger, resigns over her comments about an 'Asian invasion' of Canada.

21 November: The Prime Minister's Ethics Counsellor, Howard Wilson, rules that it is entirely appropriate for a prime minister to call a Crown-owned bank on behalf of a constituent, with the exception of members of quasi-judicial bodies such as the Canadian Radio-television and Telecommunications Commission.

27 November: The Liberal party is elected with 172 seats. The Canadian Alliance wins 67, the Bloc Québécois 38, the New Democrats 13, and the Conservatives 12.

8 December: DFO releases a status report that suggests that current catch levels will reduce the spawning stock to the size it was just before the cod moratorium was imposed in September 1993.

13 December: Finance Minister Paul Martin announces that there will be no February 2001 budget.

15 December: Canada signs two United Nations protocols to curb illegal immigration and a treaty to curb international crime.

19 December: Finance Minister Paul Martin announces a moratorium on debt payments to Canada from some of the world's poorest countries.

21 December: A report, produced by the new Performance Tracking Directorate at HRDC, shows a marked improvement in management of approved projects and in record keeping.

10 January: The federal government approves a 8.7 per cent pay raise for high-ranking civil servants and creates a new top rank of bureaucrat with a potential annual salary of more than $300,000.

11 January: Premier of Quebec, Lucien Bouchard, announces that he is quitting politics.

26 January: The Supreme Court of Canada upholds a law criminalizing the possession of child pornography with some exceptions to protect private works of the imagination or photographic depictions of oneself.

29 January: The Department of Foreign Affairs and International Trade formally asks the Russian government to waive the usual immunity for one of its diplomats, accused of killing one woman and seriously injuring another while impaired.

29 January: Peter Milliken is elected Speaker of the House of Commons.

30 January: Adrienne Clarkson, Governor-General of Canada, delivers the Speech from the Throne to launch the new parliament.

2 February: Environment Minister David Anderson proposes a law to protect endangered species.

5 February: A new Office of Critical Infrastructure Protection and Emergency is created to protect key elements of the country's communications, transportation, safety, and utilities networks from civil emergencies, natural disasters, or deliberate attacks.

7 February: The federal government tables its financial services reforms, which are aimed at making banks, insurance companies, and credit unions more competitive in Canada and abroad.

9 February: Opposition MPs demand that any new ethics rules for cabinet ministers be debated by Parliament, not set by the Prime Minister.

19 February: The RCMP announce that they will not investigate allegations that Prime Minister Jean Chrétien intervened improperly to secure a government loan for a friend.

19 February: Environment Minister David Anderson commits $120 million to improve air quality.

12 March: In the Alberta election, the Conservatives win with 74 seats; the Liberals elect 7, and the NDP 2.

15 March: The Liberals introduce the Criminal Law Amendment Act, which includes provisions to prevent the circulation of child pornography on the Internet.

27 March: The Ethics Counsellor Wilson releases 11 documents he says demonstrate conclusively that Mr. Chrétien had disposed of his interest in the golf club and was not in a conflict of interest when he lobbied a federal bank on behalf of the adjacent hotel.

APPENDIX B

FISCAL FACTS AND TRENDS

This appendix presents an overview of the federal government's fiscal position, and includes certain major economic policy indicators for 1990-2000, as well as some international comparisons.

Facts and trends are presented for federal revenue sources, federal expenditures by ministry and by type of payment, the government's share of the economy, interest and inflation rates, Canadian balance of payments in total and with the United States in particular, and other national economic growth indicators. In addition, international comparisons on real growth, unemployment, inflation, and productivity are reported for Canada, the United States, Japan, Germany, and the United Kingdom.

The figures and time series are updated each year, providing readers with an ongoing current record of major budgetary and economic variables.

Table B.1
Federal Revenue by Source
1990-1 to 1999-2000

As a Percentage of Total

Fiscal Year	Personal Tax [a]	Corporate Tax	Indirect Taxes [b]	Other Revenue [c]	Total Revenue	Annual Change
1990-1	58.9	9.8	21.9	9.4	100.0	5.0
1991-2	62.8	7.7	20.6	8.9	100.0	2.2
1992-3	63.0	6.0	21.7	9.4	100.0	-1.4
1993-4	60.1	8.1	23.0	8.8	100.0	-3.7
1994-5	61.0	9.4	22.0	7.6	100.0	6.3
1995-6	60.4	12.2	20.4	7.0	100.0	5.7
1996-7	59.0	12.1	20.7	8.3	100.0	8.1
1997-8	58.5	14.7	20.1	6.7	100.0	8.7
1998-9	59.0	13.9	20.2	7.0	100.0	1.6
1999-00	59.1	14.0	19.8	7.1	100.0	6.4

Revenue by Source is on a net basis.

a   Employment Insurance contributions are included in the total.
b   Consists of total excise taxes and duties.
c   Consists of non-tax and other tax revenues.

Source: Department of Finance, *Fiscal Reference Tables*, September 2000, Table 3.

Figure B.1
Sources of Federal Revenue as a Percentage of Total, 1998-9

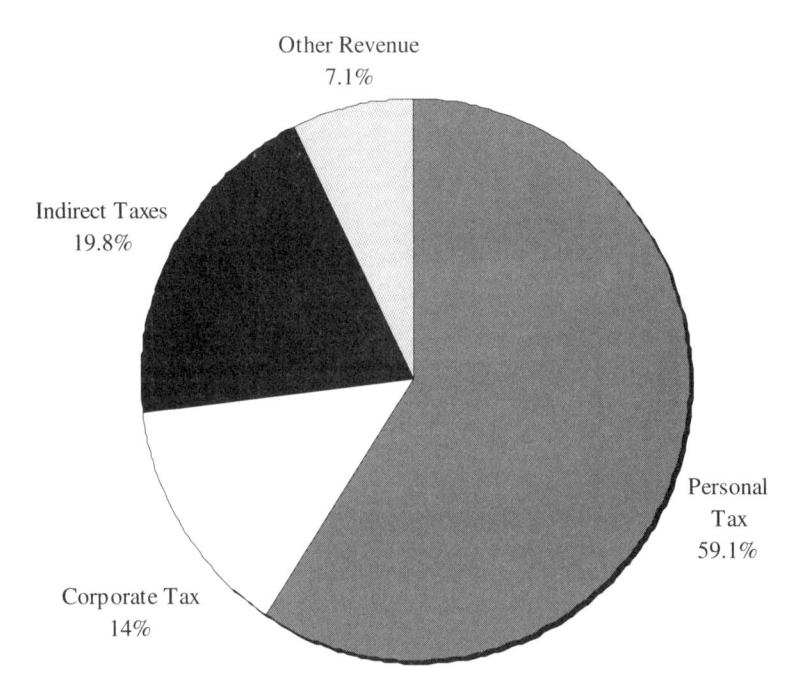

Other Revenue
7.1%

Indirect Taxes
19.8%

Corporate Tax
14%

Personal Tax
59.1%

Source: Department of Finance, *Fiscal Reference Tables*, September 2000, Table 3.

Figure B.2
Federal Expenditures by Ministry
2001-2 Estimates

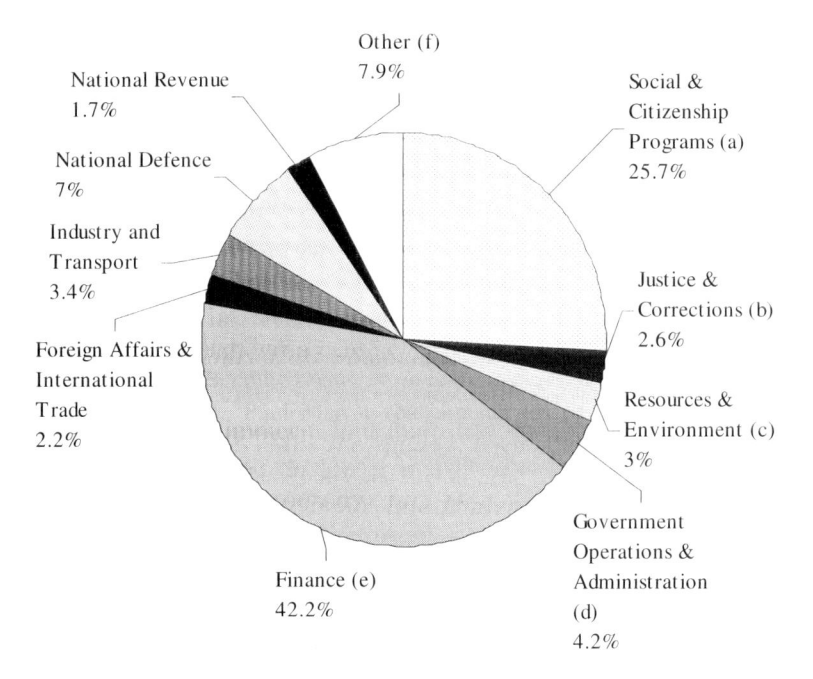

- Other (f) 7.9%
- National Revenue 1.7%
- National Defence 7%
- Industry and Transport 3.4%
- Foreign Affairs & International Trade 2.2%
- Finance (e) 42.2%
- Government Operations & Administration (d) 4.2%
- Resources & Environment (c) 3%
- Justice & Corrections (b) 2.6%
- Social & Citizenship Programs (a) 25.7%

(a) Social and Citizenship programs include departmental spending from Canadian Heritage, Citizenship and Immigration, Human Resources Development, Veterans Affairs, Health, and Indian Affairs and Northern Development.
(b) Justice and Corrections includes spending from the Department of Justice and the Solicitor General.
(c) Resources and Environment includes departmental spending from Agriculture and Agri-Food, Environment, Fisheries and Oceans, and Natural Resources.
(d) Government Operations and Administration spending includes that from Public Works and Government Services, the Governor General, Parliament, the Privy Council, and Treasury Board.
(e) Finance expenditures include, but are not limited to, spending on public interest charges and many major social transfers to the provinces.
(f) Other includes the consolidated specified purposes account (Employment Insurance).

Source: Department of Finance, *Main Estimates, Budgetary Main Estimates by Standard Object of Expenditure*, Part II, 2000-2002, 1-24 to 1-20.

Figure B.3
Federal Expenditures by Type of Payment
1996-7 to 2002-3

[Line chart. Y-axis: Billions of Dollars (current), 0 to 60. X-axis: Fiscal Year, 96-97 to 02-03(e). Series shown: Other Program Spending (d), Public Debt Charges, Social Transfers to Persons (a), Social Transfers to Governments (b), Defence, Other Transfers to Governments (c).]

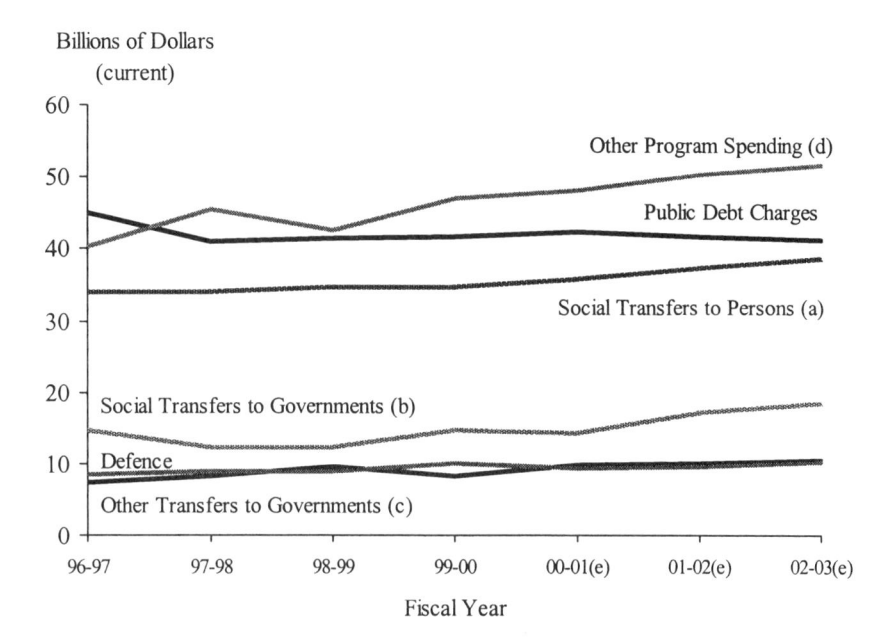

(a) Includes elderly benefits and Employment Insurance benefits.
(b) Consists of the Canada Health and Social Transfer (CHST). Prior to the CHST, two separate social transfers existed: Established Programs Financing for health and post-secondary education expenditures, and the Canada Assistance Plan for welfare and welfare services. The CHST figures include cash transfers to the provinces, and do not include the value of the tax point transfer.
(c) Includes fiscal equalization and transfers to Territories, Alternative Payments for Standing Programs, and "other" fiscal transfers.
(d) Includes all other federal non-defence operating and capital expenditures.
(e) Figures for these years are budgetary estimates.
(f) Includes program spending and public debt charges. It is not a summation of the reported program categories.

Source: Department of Finance, *Economic Statement and Budget Update 2000*, Table 4.6; Main Estimates, Part I, 2001-2002; *Public Accounts of Canada*, Vol. I, External Expenditures by Type, various years.

Figure B.4
Federal Revenue, Program Spending, and Deficit/Surplus as Percentages of Gross Domestic Product 1992-3 to 2002-3

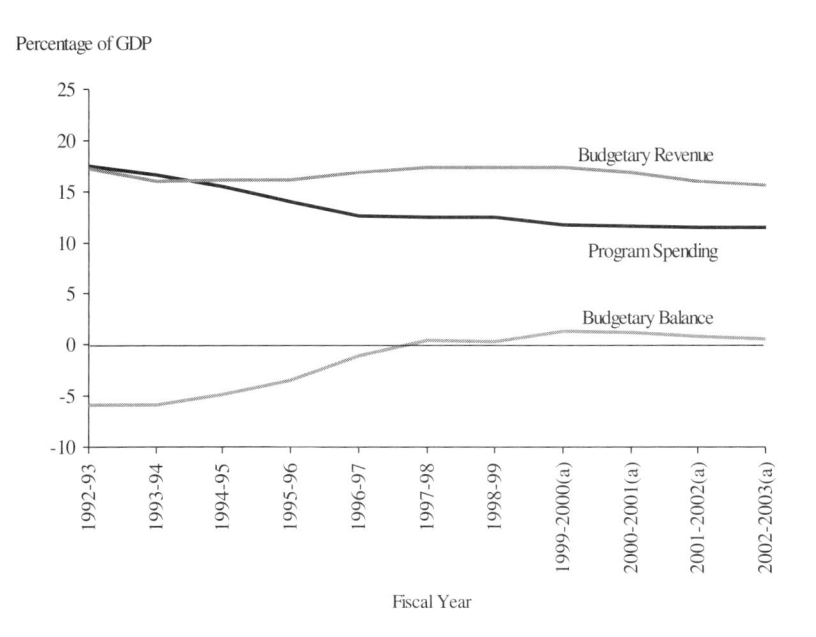

(a) Figures for these years are estimates.

Notes:
Budgetary revenue and program spending are based upon fiscal years, while GDP is based on the calendar year. Revenues, program spending, and the deficit are on a net basis. Program spending does not include public interest charges. GDP is nominal GDP.

Beginning in 1997-98, the budgetary deficit trend line changes to indicate a budgetary surplus as a percentage of the GDP.

Source: Department of Finance, *Fiscal Reference Tables*, September 2000, Table 2; Department of Finance, *Economic Statement and Budget Update 2000*, 18 October 2000, Table 1.4.

Table B.2
Federal Deficit/Surplus
1992-3 to 2002-3

Billions of Dollars (current)

Fiscal Year	Budgetary Revenue	Total Expenditures	Budgetary Deficit/ Surplus	As % of GDP
1992-3	120.4	161.4	-41.0	5.9
1993-4	116.0	158.0	-42.0	5.8
1994-5	123.3	160.8	-37.5	4.9
1995-6	130.3	158.9	-28.6	3.5
1996-7	140.9	149.8	-8.9	1.1
1997-8	153.2	149.7	3.5	0.3
1998-9	155.7	152.8	2.9	0.3
1999-00[a]	165.7	153.4	12.3	1.3
2000-1[a]	173.7	161.9	11.8	1.2
2001-2[a]	174.5	166.3	8.2	0.8
2002-3[a]	178.4	170.8	7.6	0.6

a Figures for these years are estimates.

Note:
While revenue, expenditures, and deficit categories refer to fiscal years, nominal GDP is based upon a calendar year. Total expenditures include program spending and public debt charges.

Source: Department of Finance, *Fiscal Reference Tables,* September 2000, Tables 1 and 2; Department of Finance, *Economic Statement and Budget Update 2000*, 18 October 2000, Table 1.4.

Figure B.5
Federal Revenue, Expenditures, and the Deficit/Surplus 1993-4 to 2002-3

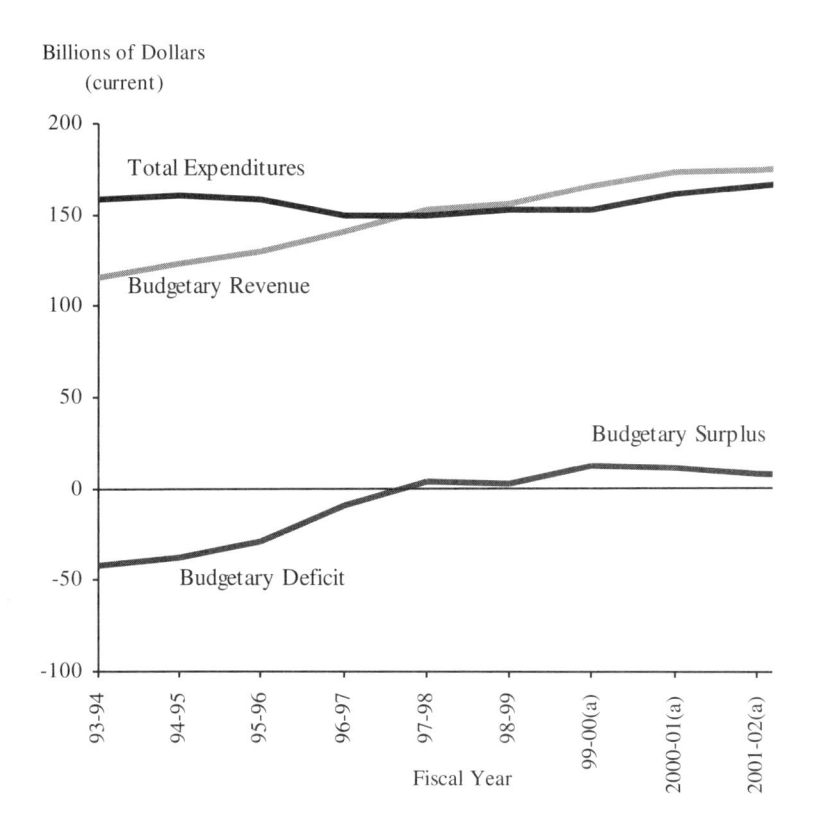

(a) Figures for these years are estimates.

Note:
Expenditures include program spending and public interest charges on the debt.

Source: Department of Finance, *Fiscal Reference Tables*, September 2000, Tables 1 and 2; Department of Finance, *Economic Statement and Budget Update 2000*, 18 October 2000, Table 1.4; *Public Accounts of Canada*, Statement of Revenues and Expenditures, various years.

FISCAL FACTS AND TRENDS 321

Figure B.6
**Growth in Real GDP
1991-2000**

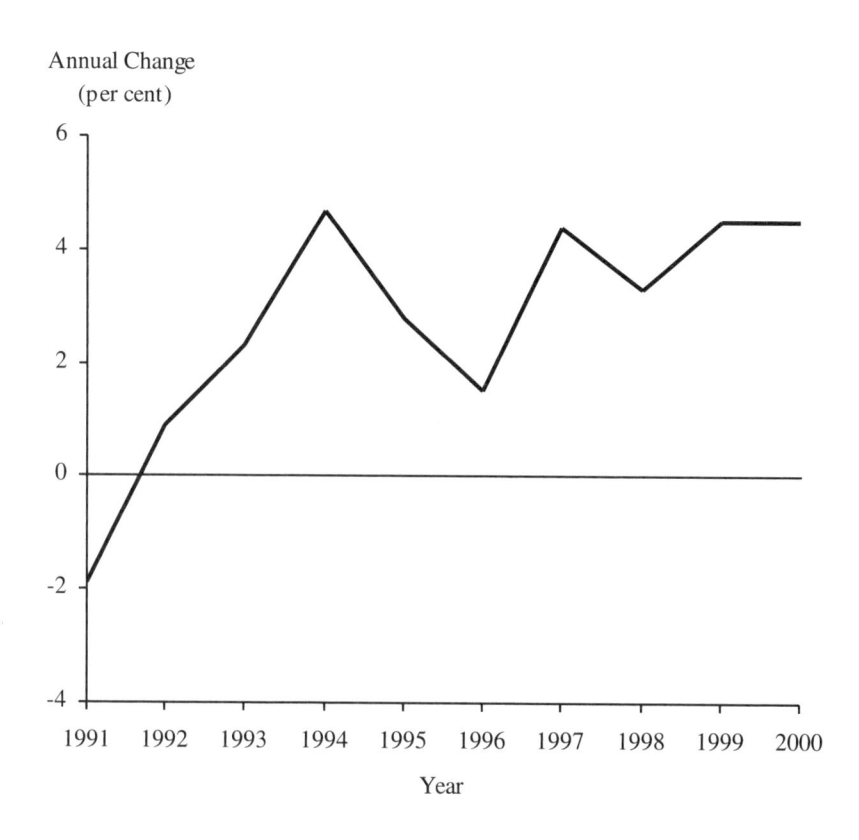

Source: Statistics Canada, *The Daily*, Cat #13-001, various years.

Figure B.7
Rates of Unemployment and Employment Growth
1991-2000

Note:
Employment growth rates and the unemployment rate apply to both sexes, 15 years and older, and are seasonally adjusted.

Source: Statistics Canada, *Historical Labour Force Statistics* (71-201), various years.

FISCAL FACTS AND TRENDS 323

Figure B.8
Interest Rates and the Consumer Price Index (CPI) 1991-2000

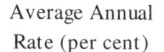

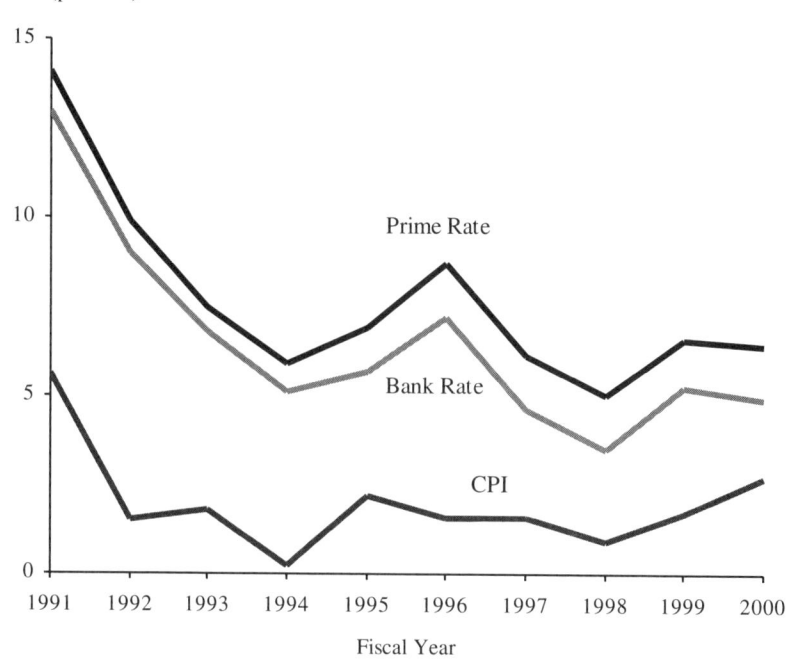

Average Annual Rate (per cent)

[Line chart showing Prime Rate, Bank Rate, and CPI from 1991 to 2000. Prime Rate starts near 14% in 1991, declines to about 6% in 1994, peaks at about 8.5% in 1996, drops to about 5% in 1998, and ends near 6% in 2000. Bank Rate follows a similar pattern slightly below Prime Rate. CPI starts at about 5.5% in 1991, drops to near 0% in 1994, and stays between 1-2.5% through 2000.]

Fiscal Year

Note:
The Consumer Price Index (CPI) is not seasonally adjusted. The Prime Rate refers to the prime business interest rate charged by the chartered banks, and the Bank Rate refers to the rate charged by the Bank of Canada on any loans to commercial banks.

Source: *Bank of Canada Review*, Table F1, various years; Statistics Canada, *The Consumer Price Index*, Cat. #62-001, various years.

Figure B.9
Productivity and Costs
1990-9

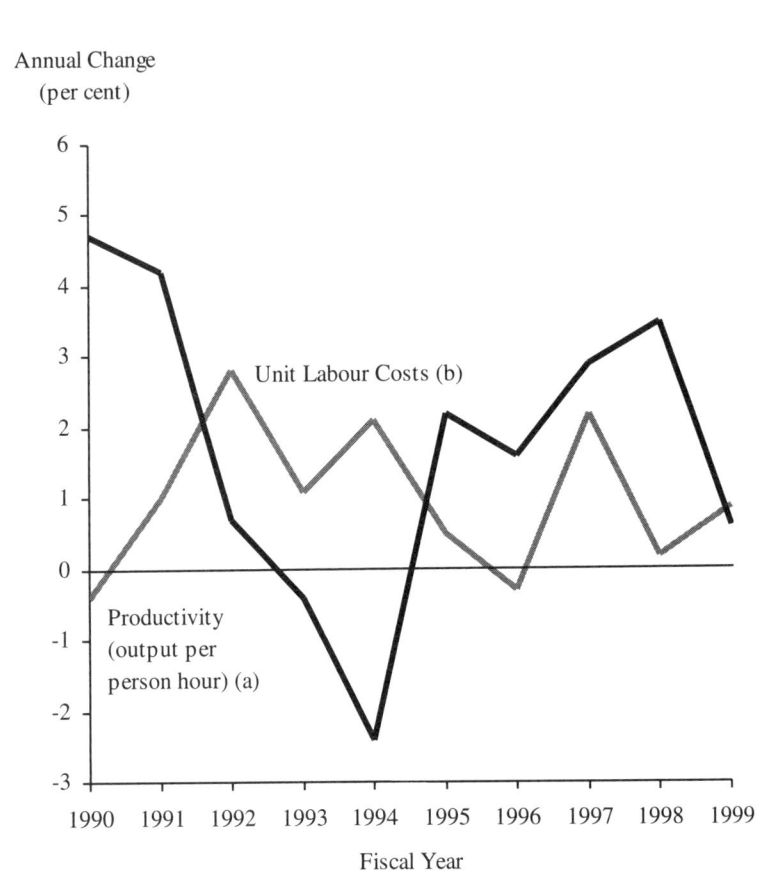

Annual Change (per cent)

Unit Labour Costs (b)

Productivity (output per person hour) (a)

Fiscal Year

(a) Output per person hour is the real GDP per person hour worked in the business sector, and is a measure of productivity. This trend shows the annual percentage change of this indicator. Real GDP is based on constant (1986) prices.

(b) Unit labour cost in the business sector is based on the real GDP, in constant 1986 prices. This trend shows the annual percentage change in this indicator.

Source: Statistics Canada, Cat. #15-204, various years.

FISCAL FACTS AND TRENDS 325

Figure B.10
**Balance of Payments
1990-9**

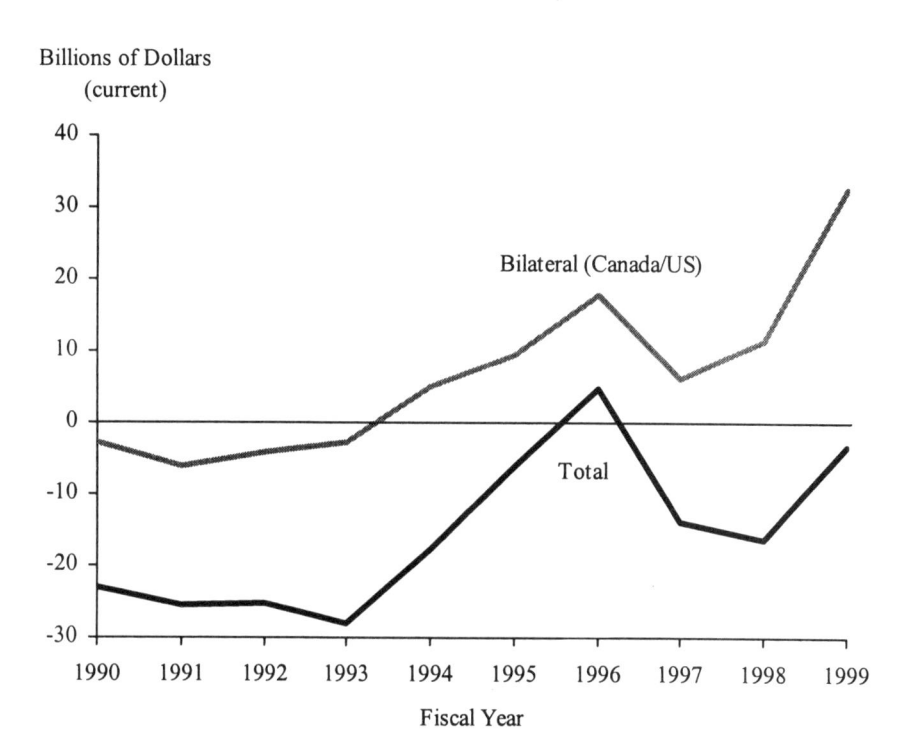

Billions of Dollars (current)

Source: Statistics Canada, Cat. #67-001, various years.

326 HOW OTTAWA SPENDS

Figure B.11
**Growth in Real GDP
Canada and Selected Countries
1990-9**

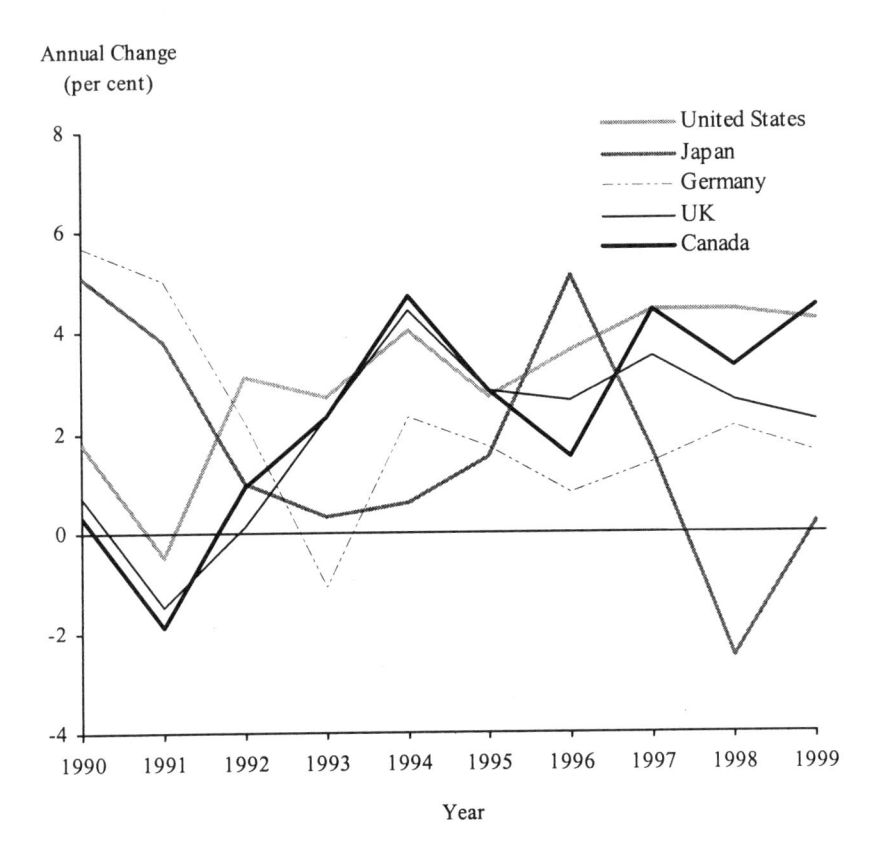

Source: Organization for Economic Cooperation and Development (OECD), *Economic Outlook*, December 2000, Annex Table 1.

Figure B.12
Unemployment Rates
Canada and Selected Countries
1990-9

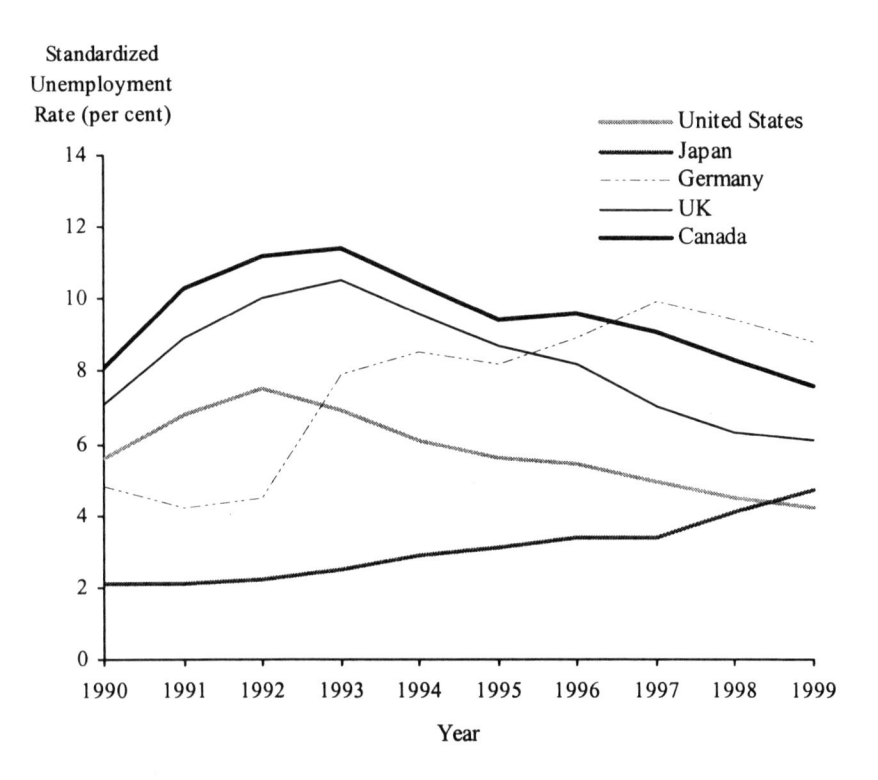

Source: *OECD Economic Outlook*, No. 68, December 2000, Annex Table 22.

328 HOW OTTAWA SPENDS

Figure B.13
**Annual Inflation Rates
Canada and Selected Countries
1990-9**

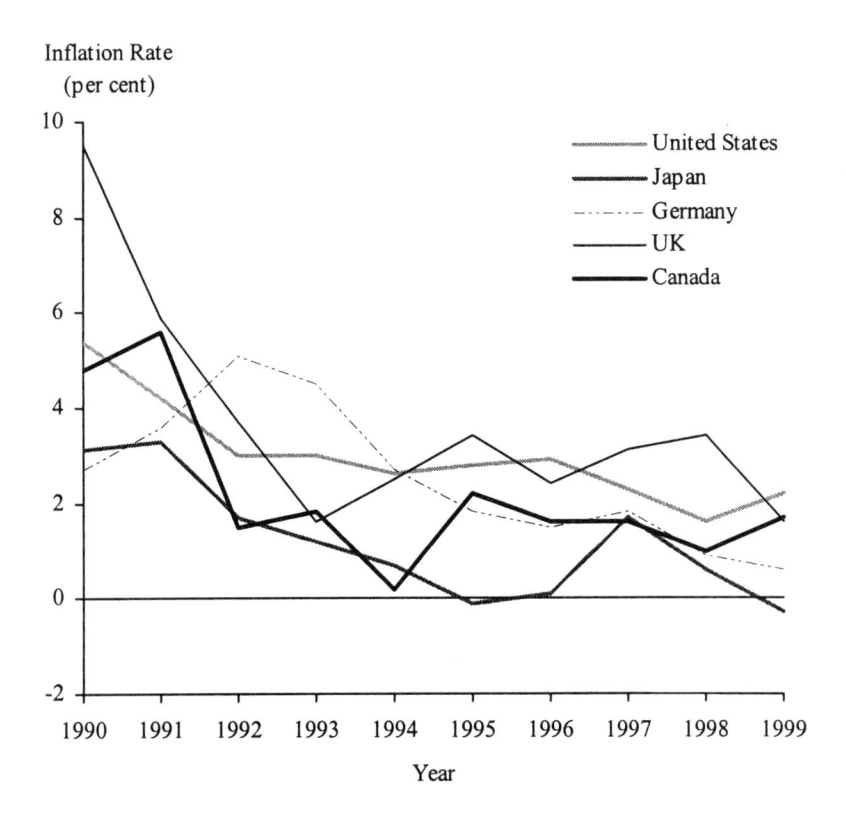

Source: *OECD Economic Outlook*, No. 68, December 2000, Annex Table 16.

FISCAL FACTS AND TRENDS 329

Figure B.14
**Unit Labour Costs
Canada and Selected Countries
1990-9**

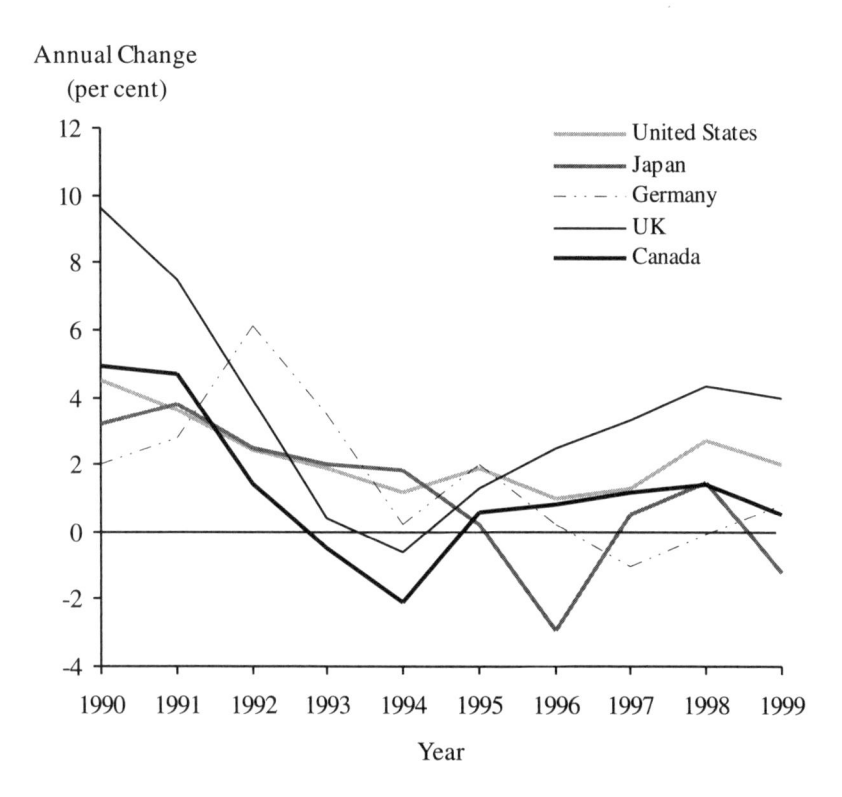

Source: *OECD Economic Outlook*, No. 68, December 2000, Annex Table 13.

Table B.3
International Comparisons
1990-9

Percentage Change from Previous Year

Growth in Real GDP

	1990	1991	1992	1993	1994	1995	1996	1997	1998	1999
Canada	0.3	-1.9	0.9	2.3	4.7	2.8	1.5	4.4	3.3	4.5
US	1.8	-0.5	3.1	2.7	4.0	2.7	3.6	4.4	4.4	4.2
Japan	5.1	3.8	1.0	0.3	0.6	1.5	5.1	1.4	-2.5	0.2
Germany	5.7	5.0	2.2	-1.1	2.3	1.7	0.8	1.4	2.1	1.6
UK	0.7	-1.5	0.1	2.3	4.4	2.8	2.6	3.5	2.6	2.2

Unemployment Rates

	1990	1991	1992	1993	1994	1995	1996	1997	1998	1999
Canada	8.1	10.4	11.2	11.4	10.4	9.4	9.6	9.1	8.3	7.6
US	5.6	6.8	7.5	6.9	6.1	5.6	5.4	4.9	4.5	4.2
Japan	2.1	2.1	2.2	2.5	2.9	3.1	3.4	3.4	4.1	4.7
Germany	4.8	4.2	4.5	7.9	8.5	8.2	8.9	9.9	9.4	8.8
UK	7.1	8.9	10.0	10.5	9.6	8.7	8.2	7.0	6.3	6.1

Increase in Unit Labour Costs

	1990	1991	1992	1993	1994	1995	1996	1997	1998	1999
Canada	4.9	4.7	1.4	-0.5	-2.1	0.6	0.8	1.2	1.4	0.5
US	4.5	3.6	2.4	1.9	1.2	1.9	1.0	1.3	2.7	2.0
Japan	3.2	3.8	2.5	2.0	1.8	0.2	-2.9	0.5	1.5	-1.2
Germany	2.0	2.8	6.1	3.5	0.2	2.0	0.2	-1.0	-0.1	0.8
UK	9.6	7.5	3.9	0.4	-0.6	1.3	2.5	3.3	4.3	4.0

Source: *OECD Economic Outlook*, No. 68, December 2000, Annex Tables 1, 13, 22.

ABSTRACTS/RÉSUMÉS

Gerard W. Boychuk
Aiming for the Middle: Challenges to Federal Income Maintenance Policy
The thrust of federal income maintenance policy over the Liberals' second mandate was to reorient federal policy both rhetorically and substantively toward the middle class. This change to Canadian income maintenance programs has been shaped by the nature of federal-provincial relations, by the shifting politics of budgetary restraint and surplus, and by electoral imperatives. The chapter provides a brief review of governance in this policy area over the past five years, a consideration of the role of income maintenance in the 2000 federal election as well as directions policy might take under the new Liberal mandate, and, finally, an overview of the impacts of this shift and the outstanding policy challenges that the government will continue to face. While federal income maintenance programs are now on more solid political footing, social protection for low-income Canadians, and particularly for women, has been weakened.

La politique fédérale en matière de maintien du revenu des particuliers au cours du deuxième mandat des libéraux a réorienté la politique fédérale, au niveau de la rhétorique et des effets réels, vers la classe moyenne. Ce changement dans les programmes de maintien du revenu a été influencé par la nature des relations fédérales–provinciales, par l'évolution de la politique relative aux restrictions et aux excédents budgétaires et par les impératifs électoraux. Ce chapitre fournit un bref examen de la gouvernance au cours des cinq dernières années dans ce domaine politique, une discussion du rôle joué par la question du maintien du revenu dans les élections fédérales de 2000 ainsi que des directions que pourrait prendre la politique sous le nouveau mandat libéral, et finalement, une vue d'ensemble des impacts de cette réorientation ainsi que des défis relatifs à cette politique que le gouvernement a encore à relever. Si les programmes fédéraux de maintien du revenu occupent maintenant une position politique plus solide, la protection sociale offerte aux Canadiens à faible revenu, et en particulier aux femmes, a été affaiblie.

Sandra Burt and Sonya Lynn Hardman
The Case of the Disappearing Targets: The Liberals and Gender Equality
In 1995, the Liberal government introduced its Federal Plan for Gender Equality. With this Plan, the federal government served notice that it was finally turning away from the targeted programs developed by the Trudeau Liberals in the early 1970s, and toward a policy of integration on status-of-women issues. As part of this process, the government adopted a policy of gender-based analysis, which would be implemented by Status of Women Canada and the Women's Bureau, within Human Resources Development Canada. In this chapter, we review the earlier approach of developing specific programs to improve the status of women in Canada, and assess this newer practice of applying a gender lens to all public policy. We conclude that there are significant structural barriers to the effective application of this gender lens.

En 1995, le gouvernement libéral a introduit son Plan fédéral pour l'Égalité des sexes. Le gouvernement annonçait ainsi son intention d'abandonner enfin les programmes ciblés élaborés par les libéraux sous Trudeau au début des années 1970 et de privilégier une politique d'intégration relative aux questions de la situation de la femme. Dans le cadre de ce processus, le gouvernement adoptait une politique d'analyse basée sur les sexes, qui serait appliquée par Condition féminine Canada ainsi que le Bureau de la main-d'oeuvre féminine à l'intérieur du ministère du Développement des ressources humaines Canada. Ce chapitre examine l'approche antérieure qui consistait à élaborer des programmes spécifiques pour améliorer la condition féminine, évalue la nouvelle pratique d'appliquer globalement l'optique de l'égalité des sexes à la politique gouvernementale, et en conclut que des barrières structurelles importantes empêchent l'application efficace de cette optique.

G. Bruce Doern and Monica Gattinger
New Economy/Old Economy?: Transforming Natural Resources Canada
This chapter examines the origins and evolution of Natural Resources Canada (NRCan) in the Chrétien era. NRCan's recent history has been

marked by the department's efforts to reposition itself as well as the natural resource industries, often perceived to be the quintessential *old economy*, as a *new economy* sector. In the first section, we examine how the innovation policy paradigm and the sustainable development policy paradigm have together propelled this repositioning by influencing both ministerial and departmental learning at NRCan. We also describe how government-wide institutional politics are driving NRCan's repositioning efforts. The second section sketches out the department's current mandate, linking it back to the organizational restructuring from which NRCan emerged. In the final section, we briefly highlight two contemporary issues in which old-economy versus new-economy tensions and trade-offs are evident: developments in mining and metals policy and the Sustainable Development Technology Fund.

Ce chapitre examine les origines et l'évolution de Ressources naturelles Canada à l'ère Chrétien. L'histoire récente du ministère a été marquée par les efforts de celui-ci pour se repositionner et repositionner les industries des ressources naturelles, que l'on perçoit souvent comme relevant de l'ancienne économie, comme secteur de la nouvelle économie. Dans la première partie, nous examinons la façon dont le paradigme de l'innovation en matière de politiques et celui de la politique de développement durable ont animé ces efforts en influençant l'apprentissage chez les ministres et au sein du ministère des Ressources naturelles. Nous décrivons également la façon dont la politique institutionnelle du gouvernement tout entier détermine ces efforts. La deuxième section donne un aperçu du mandat actuel du ministère, reliant ce mandat à la restructuration organisationnelle d'où est sorti le ministère. Dans la section finale, nous soulignons deux questions d'actualité qui montrent les tensions et les compromis entre l'ancienne et la nouvelle économie: l'évolution de la politique des mines et des métaux et le Fonds d'appui technologique au développement durable.

Rodney Haddow
Regional Development Policy: A Nexus of Policy and Politics
Federal government efforts to stimulate economic growth in Canada's less advantaged regions started in the late 1950s. They have been a

significant expenditure item ever since, fostered by the political objective of securing support in the affected regions and by policy arguments in favour of this type of spending. These political and policy parameters have, however, changed significantly during the past decade. There is no longer a consensus in favour of regional development spending among all of the major parties in the House of Commons: the merits of this instrument have also been called into question on public policy grounds. Nevertheless, the Liberal government renewed its commitment to regional development in the middle of its last term of office. It was motivated both by a desire to restore electoral support that it had lost in the 1997 election and by 'new economy' arguments about the potential value of strategic interventions by government for the long-term prosperity of regions. In view of the challenges that these policies now face, however, it may be that the fundamental dynamics in this policy area have changed radically and enduringly from those that prevailed between the 1950s and the 1980s.

Les efforts du gouvernement fédéral pour stimuler la croissance économique des régions désavantagées du Canada ont commencé à la fin des années 1950, et représentent depuis des dépenses importantes, favorisées par l'objectif politique d'assurer un appui électoral dans les régions affectées et par des arguments relevant de la politique gouvernementale en faveur de ce type de dépense. Ces paramètres politiques ont, cependant, sensiblement changé au cours de la dernière décennie. Il n'y a plus de consensus en faveur de dépenses en développement régional parmi les principaux partis de la Chambre des communes : les mérites de cet instrument ont également été remis en question pour des raisons de politique gouvernementale. Neanmoins, au milieu de son dernier mandat, le gouvernement libéral a renouvelé son engagement en faveur du développement régional. Cette décision a été motivée par un désir de regagner l'appui électoral perdu dans les élections de 1997 et par des arguments touchant à la valeur potentielle d'interventions stratégiques de la part du gouvernement, dans le cadre de la nouvelle économie, pour la prospérité à long terme des régions. Vu les mises en question actuelles, la dynamique fondamentale de ce domaine politique a peut-être changé radicalement, et de façon durable, par rapport à celle qui a prévalu entre les années 1950 et les années 1980.

Geoffrey E. Hale
Priming the Electoral Pump: Framing Budgets for a Renewed Mandate
This chapter examines the fiscal policies of the Chrétien government during its second term, which culminated in the tax-cutting pre-election budgets of February and October 2000. It analyses the changes to the budgetary processes introduced by Finance Minister Paul Martin to balance the expectations and demands of competing factions of the Liberal government while maintaining firm Finance Department control over the federal agenda. The budget surpluses arising from these tactics, combined with a fast-growing economy, enabled Martin to cover the government's political flanks as it approached the November 2000 election by simultaneously promising increases to health transfers, restoration of previous cuts to Employment Insurance, record reductions of personal and corporate tax, and substantial debt reduction. These policies, retro-fitted into Mr. Chrétien's '50-50' framework for the allocation of budget surpluses, reflect the Liberals' continued ability to balance competing political demands, while maintaining control of the broader policy agenda.

Ce chapitre examine les politiques fiscales du gouvernement Chrétien au cours de son deuxième mandat, qui aboutissent aux budgets de février et d'octobre 2000, juste avant les élections, où les impôts sont réduits. Nous analysons les changements aux processus budgétaires introduits par le ministre des Finances Paul Martin afin d'équilibrer les attentes et les revendications des factions au sein du gouvernement libéral tout en maintenant le contrôle qu'exerce son ministère sur le programme fédéral. Les excédents budgétaires résultant de cette tactique, de concert avec une économie en pleine croissance, ont permis à Martin de protéger le flanc politique du gouvernement à l'approche des élections de novembre 2000 en promettant simultanément des augmentations des transferts en matière de santé, une restitution des réductions antérieures apportées à l'assurance-emploi, des réductions record de l'impôt sur le revenu des particuliers et des sociétés eainsi qu'une réduction considérable de la dette. Ces politiques, ajustées au cadre « 50-50 » de M. Chrétien pour l'attribution des excédents budgétaires, reflètent la capacité continue des libéraux de tenir en équilibre des revendications politiques concurrentes, tout en gardant le contrôle du programme politique dans son ensemble.

Rainer Knopff
A Delicate Dance: The Courts and the Chrétien Government
Judges and political executives dance a regular *pas de deux* at the centre of Canada's political stage. The dance is subtle and complex, with both sides acting in highly strategic ways. Governments act strategically to acquire and spend legal 'resources', always attempting to strengthen their hand against other governments or partisan foes. Courts are just as strategic, in pursuit of their own interests and agendas. It is a dance that sometimes finds its partners drawn into a warm and approving embrace, and at other times sees them stepping more gingerly, at arm's length. Always, the two dance partners play not only to each other, but also to an audience composed of legislatures, parties, and public opinion. This chapter analyses the delicate dance between the courts and the federal government during Prime Minister Chrétien's first two mandates (1993-2000).

Les juges et les dirigeants politiques font constamment un pas de deux au centre de la scène politique au Canada. Il s'agit d'une danse subtile et complexe où les deux camps jouent un rôle hautement stratégique. Les gouvernements agissent de façon stratégique pour acquérir et dépenser des « ressources » en matière juridique, tout en essayant constamment de se prémunir davantage contre les visées d'autres gouvernements et d'adversaires partisans. Les tribunaux usent de tout autant de stratégie en poursuivant leurs propres intérêts et objectifs. Dans cette danse, les partenaires sont tantôt tendrement enlacés, tantôt à une distance prudente, La danse n'implique pas seulement les partenaires, mais également une assistance composée de corps législatifs, de partis politiques et de l'opinion publique. Ce chapitre analyse la danse délicate exécutée par le pouvoir judiciaire et le gouvernement fédéral au cours des deux premiers mandats du premier ministre Chrétien (1993-2000).

Evert A. Lindquist
How Ottawa Plans: The Evolution of Strategic Planning
At the beginning of each session of Parliament, the Speech from the

Throne (SFT) provides a statement of government intentions for the next legislative cycle. This event usually attracts only fleeting interest outside government, but is now understood to be an important part of a broader process of strategic planning within the government of Canada. Many of the traditional highwater marks of the budgeting and legislative cycle persist—SFTs, cabinet committee meetings and retreats, transition management, and the budget. For public service leaders, a critical question is how to adapt planning for a fundamentally different political environment, which is faster-paced, more complicated, and arguably more transparent than when the principles of strategic planning were first embraced in Ottawa.

This chapter begins with a review of the literature on strategic planning in the federal government and more general theories of planning, and then provides an overview of the key institutions involved in the planning cycle. The last two rounds of the planning cycle under the Liberal government are examined more closely. Although prominent features of the traditional planning process may have not changed very much, the integration of the planning cycle, combined with several subtle changes in the planning process, allowed the government to manage the transition from a singular focus on the deficit to maintaining discipline and identifying new priorities in a post-deficit environment. The chapter concludes by considering the prospects and challenges for strategic planning during the third mandate of the Chrétien government.

Au début de chaque session du Parlement, le discours du Trône énumère les intentions du gouvernement pour le prochain cycle législatif. Cet événement attire d'habitude peu d'intérêt en dehors du gouvernement, mais on le considère maintenant comme une partie importante d'un vaste processus de planification stratégique à l'intérieur du gouvernement du Canada. Plusieurs des points saillants traditionnels du cycle d'élaboration des budgets et de la législation persistent – les discours du Trône, les réunions et les journées de réflexion des comités du Cabinet, la gestion de la transition, ainsi que le budget. Pour les dirigeants de la Fonction publique, une question critique est la façon d'adapter la planification à un environnement politique foncièrement différent, au rythme plus rapide, plus compliqué et sans doute plus transparent que ce n'était le cas au moment où les principes de planification stratégique ont été premièrement épousés à Ottawa.

Ce chapitre commence par un examen des études sur la planification stratégique au gouvernement fédéral et sur les théories générales de la planification, et fournit ensuite une vue d'ensemble sur les institutions clés participant au cycle de planification. Nous examinons de près les deux dernières phases du cycle de planification sous le gouvernement libéral. Si les points saillants du processus traditionnel de planification ont pu changer très peu, l'intégration de ce cycle, de concert avec plusieurs changements subtils dans le processus, a permis au gouvernement de gérer le passage d'une concentration unique sur le déficit vers le maintien de la discipline et l'identification de nouvelles priorités dans un environnement post-déficitaire. Ce chapitre finit par discuter les perspectives d'avenir de la planification stratégique au cours du troisième mandat du gouvernement Chrétien, ainsi que les défis que celle-ci aura à relever.

Anne Perkins and Robert P. Shepherd
Managing in the New Public Service: Some Implications for How We Are Governed

Several important trends have been observed in the way in which contemporary government works, especially in the way in which programs and services are provided to citizens and clients. The Chrétien government has embraced these trends and is beginning to incorporate them into routine management practice. This chapter examines four such trends in Canadian public administration: partnering, service to the public, key mechanisms for allocating responsibilities, and increased dependency on technology. It further explores some of the implications of these trends on how the executive, Parliament, and the public service operate. The chapter concludes that these trends may have a significant impact on the representative and representing roles of national institutions, as well as on how policy is developed. In particular, there may be implications for interest-group representation, for the watchdog role of Parliament, for the role of individual public servants and the accountability of the public service as a whole, and for how the public sector delivers programs and services within new organizational forms.

On a observé plusieurs tendances importantes dans le fonctionnement des gouvernements contemporains, notamment dans la prestation des programmes et services aux citoyens et clients. Le gouvernement Chrétien a épousé ces tendances et a commencé à les incorporer dans les pratiques quotidiennes de gestion. Ce chapitre examine quatre de ces tendances dans l'administration publique canadienne : les partenariats, le service au public, les mécanismes clés de l'allocation des responsabilités, et la dépendance accrue à l'égard de la technologie. Nous explorons également certaines implications de ces tendances pour l'opération de l'exécutif, du Parlement et de la Fonction publique. Ce chapitre en conclut que ces tendances peuvent bien avoir un effet significatif sur les rôles de représentativité et de représentation que jouent les institutions nationales, ainsi que sur l'élaboration des politiques. Il peut y avoir, en particulier, des implications pour la représentation des groupes d'intérêt, pour le rôle de surveillance joué par le Parlement, pour le rôle des fonctionnaires individuels et la responsabilité de la Fonction publique dans son ensemble ainsi que pour la prestation des programmes et services du secteur public dans le cadre de nouvelles formes organisationnelles.

Susan D. Phillips
From Charity to Clarity: Reinventing Federal Government–Voluntary Sector Relationships
The Voluntary Sector Initiative (VSI) announced by the Chrétien government in June 2000 is a bold and novel experiment in building stronger relationships between the federal government and the voluntary sector. The VSI is a multifaceted strategy that includes support for an 'accord' that will clarify and guide the establishment of a stronger relationship, research and information-gathering on the sector, capacity building through skills and technology development, regulatory reform, and promotion of volunteerism during the International Year of Volunteers in 2001 and beyond. The success of the VSI will depend not only on its actual strategy, but on the process and structure through which it is implemented and on the ability of this process to bridge the

two distinctively different cultures of government and the voluntary sector. The chapter assesses each of these aspects—strategy, process and machinery, and culture—and concludes by speculating on the lessons learned from the VSI for collaborative governance more generally.

L'Initiative du secteur bénévole, annoncée par le gouvernement Chrétien en juin 2000, constitue une expérience hardie et originale destinée à renforcer les relations entre le gouvernement fédéral et le secteur bénévole. L'Initiative comporte une stratégie à multiples facettes: appui à un accord qui doit clarifier et guider l'établissement de liens plus resserrés, collectes de recherches et d'informations sur ce secteur, accroissement de capacités par le développement de compétences et de technologie, réforme de la réglementation, promotion du bénévolat pendant l'Année internationale des volontaires en 2001 et au delà. Le succès de l'Initiative dépendra non seulement de sa stratégie effective, mais aussi du processus et de la structure qui servent à l'appliquer et de la capacité de ce processus de combler le fossé entre les deux cultures nettement différentes du gouvernement, d'une part, et du secteur bénévole de l'autre. Ce chapitre évalue chacun de ces aspects – stratégie, processus et machinerie, et culture – et finit par spéculer sur les leçons générales que nous donne l'Initiative pour la gouvernance collective.

Michael J. Prince
Citizenship by Instalments: Federal Policies for Canadians with Disabilities
Citizenship has become the central organizing principle in disability-related advocacy, policy analysis, and intergovernmental agreements in Canada. Five fundamental elements of citizenship are examined in this chapter: discursive practices; legal and equality rights; democratic and political rights; fiscal and social entitlements; and economic integration. The chapter assesses the federal government's recent record on disability issues against these five elements, noting both achievements and those issues that remain to be addressed. For people with disabilities, the process of achieving full citizenship has been partial,

slow, and often disconnected from other policy domains. The promise of inclusion within Canadian society has in practice meant gaining full citizenship by instalments. For the Liberals' third mandate, the pace and scope of reform should quicken and deepen. Priorities in disability policy must include addressing the acute needs of Aboriginal peoples and children with disabilities and their families, and improving access to a wider range of supports and services.

La citoyenneté est devenue le principe organisateur central pour les groupes de pression, les analystes politiques et les accords intergouvernementaux au Canada relatifs aux personnes handicapées. Ce chapitre examine cinq éléments fondamentaux de la citoyenneté : pratiques discursives; droits d'égalité et droits légaux; droits démocratiques et politiques; droits fiscaux et sociaux; intégration économique. Ce chapitre évalue la fiche récente du gouvernement fédéral en ce qui concerne les questions relatives aux personnes handicapées en fonction de ces cinq éléments, en notant les réussites et les problèmes qui sont encore à aborder. Pour les personnes handicapées, le processus menant à la citoyenneté à part entière a été partiel, lent et souvent isolé d'autres domaines politiques. La promesse de l'inclusion dans la société canadienne a signifié, en pratique, une citoyenneté à part entière gagnée par étapes. Pendant le troisième mandat libéral, la réforme devrait prendre de la vitesse et de l'ampleur. Parmi les questions prioritaires de la politique sur les handicapés doivent figurer les besoins criants des peuples autochtones ainsi que ceux des enfants handicapés et de leurs familles, et un accès accru à une vaste gamme de soutiens et services.

CONTRIBUTORS

Gerard W. Boychuk is an Assistant Professor of Political Science at the University of Waterloo.

Sandra Burt is an Associate Professor of Political Science at the University of Waterloo.

G. Bruce Doern is a Professor of Public Policy and Administration at Carleton University, and holds a joint Research Chair in Public Policy at the University of Exeter.

Monica Gattinger is a Ph.D. candidate in Public Policy in the School of Public Policy and Administration at Carleton University.

Rodney Haddow is an Associate Professor of Political Science at St. Francis Xavier University

Geoffrey E. Hale is an Assistant Professor of Political Science at the University of Lethbridge.

Sonya Lynn Hardman is a Project Worker with the Brighton YMCA in Sussex, England.

Rainer Knopff is a Professor of Political Science and Associate Dean (Research and Development) in the Faculty of Social Sciences at the University of Calgary.

Evert A. Lindquist is Director of the School of Public Administration at the University of Victoria.

Leslie A. Pal is a Professor of Public Policy and Administration at Carleton University.

Anne Perkins is a consultant in public policy and management in Ottawa.

Susan D. Phillips is an Associate Professor of Public Policy at Carleton University.

Michael J. Prince is the Lansdowne Professor of Social Policy and an Associate Dean in Social Development at the University of Victoria.

Robert P. Shepherd is a Lecturer with the Faculty of Administration at the University of Ottawa, and a Senior Associate of the Regulatory Consulting Group Inc. in Ottawa.

THE SCHOOL OF PUBLIC POLICY AND ADMINISTRATION at Carleton University is a national centre for the study of public policy and public management.

The School's Centre for Policy and Program Assessment provides research services and courses to interest groups, businesses, unions, and governments in the evaluation of public policies, programs, and activities.

The *How Ottawa Spends* Series

How Ottawa Spends 2000-2001: Past Imperfect, Future Tense
edited by Leslie A. Pal

How Ottawa Spends 1999-2000: Shape Shifting: Canadian Governance Toward the 21st Century
edited by Leslie A. Pal

How Ottawa Spends 1998-99: Balancing Act: The Post-Deficit Mandate
edited by Leslie A. Pal

How Ottawa Spends 1997-98: Seeing Red: A Liberal Report Card
edited by Gene Swimmer

How Ottawa Spends 1996-97: Life Under the Knife
edited by Gene Swimmer

How Ottawa Spends 1995-96: Mid-Life Crises
edited by Susan D. Phillips

How Ottawa Spends 1994-95: Making Change
edited by Susan D. Phillips

How Ottawa Spends 1993-94: A More Democratic Canada…?
edited by Susan D. Phillips

How Ottawa Spends 1992-93: The Politics of Competitiveness
edited by Frances Abele

How Ottawa Spends 1991-92: The Politics of Fragmentation
edited by Frances Abele

How Ottawa Spends 1990-91: Tracking the Second Agenda
edited by Katherine A. Graham

How Ottawa Spends 1989-90: The Buck Stops Where?
edited by Katherine A. Graham

How Ottawa Spends 1988-89: The Conservatives Heading into the Stretch
edited by Katherine A. Graham

How Ottawa Spends 1987-88: Restraining the State
edited by Michael J. Prince

How Ottawa Spends 1986-87: Tracking the Tories
edited by Michael J. Prince

How Ottawa Spends 1985: Sharing the Pie
edited by Allan M. Maslove

How Ottawa Spends 1984: The New Agenda
edited by Allan M. Maslove

How Ottawa Spends 1983: The Liberals, The Opposition & Federal Priorities
edited by G. Bruce Doern

How Ottawa Spends Your Tax Dollars: National Policy and Economic Development 1982
edited by G. Bruce Doern

How Ottawa Spends Your Tax Dollars: Federal Priorities 1981
edited by G. Bruce Doern

Spending Tax Dollars: Federal Expenditures, 1980-81
edited by G. Bruce Doern